CLASSICAL PRES[ENCES]

General Edito[rs]
Lorna Hardwick   Jam[es]

CLASSICAL PRESENCES

The texts, ideas, images, and material culture of ancient Greece and Rome have always been crucial to attempts to appropriate the past in order to authenticate the present. They underlie the mapping of change and the assertion and challenging of values and identities, old and new. Classical Presences brings the latest scholarship to bear on the contexts, theory, and practice of such use, and abuse, of the classical past.

Classical Traditions in Science Fiction

EDITED BY
BRETT M. ROGERS
AND
BENJAMIN ELDON STEVENS

OXFORD
UNIVERSITY PRESS

OXFORD
UNIVERSITY PRESS

Oxford University Press is a department of the University of
Oxford. It furthers the University's objective of excellence in research,
scholarship, and education by publishing worldwide.

Oxford   New York
Auckland   Cape Town   Dar es Salaam   Hong Kong   Karachi
Kuala Lumpur   Madrid   Melbourne   Mexico City   Nairobi
New Delhi   Shanghai   Taipei   Toronto

With offices in
Argentina   Austria   Brazil   Chile   Czech Republic   France   Greece
Guatemala   Hungary   Italy   Japan   Poland   Portugal   Singapore
South Korea   Switzerland   Thailand   Turkey   Ukraine   Vietnam

Oxford is a registered trademark of Oxford University Press
in the UK and certain other countries.

Published in the United States of America by
Oxford University Press
198 Madison Avenue, New York, NY 10016

© Oxford University Press 2015

Library of Congress Cataloging-in-Publication Data
Classical traditions in science fiction / Brett M. Rogers and Benjamin
Eldon Stevens [editors].
pages cm. — (Classical presences)
ISBN 978-0-19-998841-9 (hardback); 978-0-19-022833-0 (paperback)
1. Science fiction, American—History and criticism.   2. Science fiction,
English—History and criticism.   3. Science fiction films—History and criticism.
4. Science fiction television programs—History and criticism.   5. Civilization, Ancient,
in literature.   6. Classical literature—Influence.   7. Civilization, Ancient—Influences.
I. Rogers, Brett M., editor of compilation.   II. Stevens, Benjamin Eldon,
editor of compilation.
PS374.S35C585 2014
813'.0876209—dc23
2013036304

1 3 5 7 9 8 6 4 2
Printed in the United States of America
on acid-free paper

Contents

Part III: Classics in Space

Part IV: Ancient Classics for a Future Generation?

Preface

Classical Traditions in Science Fiction was an after-hours topic of conversation for us long before it led to conference papers and panels, a scholarly review essay, invitations to write for more popular forums and to speak at symposiums, and the present edited volume. The physical fact of the book seems to offer some confirmation of Douglas Adams's idea for an "infinite improbability drive," in which faster-than-light travel is made possible by virtue of being not *completely* impossible, only very, *very* unlikely. Truly "unlikely" would this volume have seemed even a few years ago, much less two decades ago when we first started to talk about the topic while studying Classics at Reed College.

Historians of the future may be interested to know that together we founded and ran that college's first Classics Dorm in the academic year 1997–1998. As a special event, we screened, via a hard-to-acquire VHS copy, the 1986 animated science fiction feature film *Transformers: The Movie*. Fans will recall that the film pits Latinate "Autobots" (e.g., Optimus Prime) against Hellenic "Decepticons" (e.g., Megatron) in a plot that, to one editor's mind, seemed faintly to echo stories about the shifting tectonics of Hellenistic-era political states. To the *other* editor's mind, any such echo was very, *very* faint indeed . . .

. . . and so, for us, it began, with questions ramifying like parallel worlds:

- How might a comparative study of ancient classics and modern science fiction proceed?
- Could there be more at the intersection of those two seemingly disparate fields than a few signal texts? Beyond individual stars, were there whole galaxies awaiting discovery?
- Above all, could such a comparative study be put on a firm conceptual or theoretical basis, so that research could move beyond mere "scopophilia," Freud's term for a love of looking that is pleasing but ultimately pointless ?

It is with a science-fictional "sense of wonder" indeed that we are able to say that, at this point, an increasing number of scholars has been working internationally to suggest answers to such questions with energy and rigor. Classicists have, of course, been writing about science fiction, or SF, for decades—notably S. C. Fredericks and Nick Lowe—sometimes bridging the gap between SF and Classics. More recently, theoretical questions have been raised expressly by authors such as contributor Tony Keen (especially on his blog, *Memorabilia Antoniana*), Sarah Annes Brown (2008, "Plato's Stepchildren: SF and the Classics"), and the editors of a volume of essays in French, Mélanie Bost-Fiévet and Sandra Provini (2014, especially their introductions to the volume and to each of its four parts). Our own overview of the state of the art, which forms the basis for the introduction to this volume, was previously published in the *Classical Receptions Journal* (Rogers and Stevens 2012a) and is indebted to such pioneers.

That same desired level of sophistication and clarity is also reached for—in our view, it is indeed grasped—by the contributors to this volume. We are extremely grateful to have been able to consider a wide range of current research—some for a panel at the 2011 annual meeting of the American Philological Association (as of 2014, the Society for Classical Studies) in San Antonio, others via a subsequent call for papers—and we are pleased and honored to be able to present some of that work for publication here. Perhaps the most exciting aspect of all of this burgeoning area of interest is that there is still so much more to be done.

There is ancient history, and then there is the modern world, including the happy means to achieve even the most unlikely ends. We are grateful above all to the contributors for sharing their work so generously and for responding to questions and comments with rigor, energy, and aplomb. Special thanks are due to the production team at Oxford University Press, including Classics acquisitions editor Stefan Vranka, assistant editor Sarah Pirovitz, *Classical Presences* series editors Lorna Hardwick and James I. Porter, and the copyeditors, compositors, and others without whose remarkable work this volume simply would not exist.

Rogers would like to thank his wife, family, and colleagues for their all-too-patient encouragement, and in particular his brother, Scott Rogers, for nurturing his kid brother on a steady diet of SF, fantasy, and comics for over three decades; and would like to thank the students in his courses on Theories of Myth (Gettysburg College, Spring 2010) and

Classical Traditions (University of Puget Sound, Spring 2013) for their enthusiasm and insights as various ideas started to come together in his head.

Stevens would like to thank his parents for telling a school board that yes, it is okay that their son has asked for a SF novel as his spelling-bee prize; and would like to thank the students in a tutorial on SF (Bard College, Spring 2006) and in courses on traditions centering around Virgil (Bryn Mawr College, Fall 2014), Ovid (Bard College at Eastern Correctional Facility as well as Annandale, Spring 2013; Hollins University, Spring 2014), and Milton (Bard College, Fall 2012) for their inspiring visions of life on other (literary) worlds.

Special thanks go to Christina Salowey and Fred Franko of Hollins University for setting "Classics and Science Fiction" as the theme of the 2013 Classics Symposium there.

List of Contributors

Gregory S. Bucher is Associate Professor of Classical and Near Eastern Studies at Creighton University. In addition to classic science fiction, he has also published on Roman portraiture, Roman Imperial historiography, and epigraphical topics.

Robert W. Cape, Jr. is Professor of Classics at Austin College. He has published on Ciceronian oratory, Roman women, and Latin pedagogy. He is currently working on a survey of classical themes in the history of science fiction.

Joel P. Christensen is Associate Professor in the Department of Philosophy and Classics at the University of Texas at San Antonio. He works on Homer and early Greek poetry, as well as myth from linguistic and literary perspectives. In the classroom, he often combines his interest in ancient storytelling traditions with a lifelong love for fantastic literature, teaching Homer's *Iliad* and *Odyssey* alongside Frank Herbert's *Dune*.

Erik Grayson is Assistant Professor of English at Wartburg College in Waverly, Iowa, where he teaches courses in American literature. He has published criticism on Poe, Kincaid, Coetzee, Gaddis, Vonnegut, Mailer, and DeLillo; essays on topics ranging from Norwegian popular culture to academia; and works of prose fiction, poetry, and drama. In his spare time, he hosts a weekly punk rock radio show.

Gaël Grobéty received his Ph.D. from the University of Lausanne (Switzerland). His doctoral work was on receptions of the *Iliad* in contemporary American culture, focusing on popular culture during the last two decades. He is now a member of a research project on receptions of antiquity in Switzerland.

Antony Keen is a Research Affiliate and Associate Lecturer for the Open University and has taught classical studies, myth, film history, and science fiction and fantasy literature. He writes on classics and SF, and was chair of the 2013 conference *The Fantastika and the Classical World*. His book *Martial's Martians and Other Stories: Studies in Greece and Rome and Science Fiction and Fantasy* is forthcoming.

George Kovacs is Assistant Professor of Ancient History and Classics at Trent University in Ontario, Canada, where he researches and teaches Greek theater and stagecraft, as well as the reception of Greek myth in popular culture. With C. W. Marshall, he is co-editor of *Classics and Comics* (OUP 2011), *No Laughing Matter: New Studies in Athenian Comedy* (Bloomsbury 2012), and *Son of Classics and Comics* (forthcoming).

Marian Makins holds a Ph.D. in Classical Studies from the University of Pennsylvania and currently teaches in Penn's Critical Writing Program. Her current book project explores the representation of battlefield aftermath in Roman Imperial literature. Her research also includes classical receptions in Edward Lear's nonsense and the interaction between classical landscapes and classically educated soldiers during the First World War.

C. W. Marshall is Professor of Greek at the University of British Columbia in Vancouver, Canada. He has written widely on ancient theater and modern popular culture, and is the co-editor with George Kovacs of *Classics and Comics* (OUP 2011). His research has been generously supported by the Social Sciences and Humanities Research Council of Canada.

Rebecca Raphael is a National Endowment for the Humanities Distinguished Teaching Professor in Humanities and Associate Professor of Religious Studies and Philosophy at Texas State University. She is the author of *Biblical Corpora: Representations of Disability in Hebrew Biblical Literature* (Bloomsbury T & T Clark 2008). Her scholarly interests include disability studies, biblical studies, classics, and monsters.

Brett M. Rogers is Assistant Professor of Classics at the University of Puget Sound. His research focuses on poetics and performance in Greek poetry and drama, as well as classical receptions in contemporary media. He has published on a wide range of subjects, from Homer and classical drama to superhero narratives and *Buffy the Vampire Slayer.*

Benjamin Eldon Stevens, Visiting Assistant Professor of Classics at Bryn Mawr College, has taught at Hollins University, the University of Colorado at Boulder, and Bard College, including the Bard Prison Initiative. The author of *Silence in Catullus* (University of Wisconsin Press 2013), he has published on Latin poetry, linguistics, and the senses in culture, in addition to classical receptions.

Dean Swinford is Associate Professor of English at Fayetteville State University. In *Through the Daemon's Gate* (Routledge 2006), he offers an extended consideration of Kepler's *Somnium* and its debt to medieval dream narratives. His essays appear in various journals, including *Modern Philology, Journal of Medieval Religious Cultures, LIT: Literature Interpretation Theory,* and *The Mediæval Journal.*

Vincent Tomasso is Visiting Assistant Professor of Classics in the Romance and Classical Languages Department at Ripon College. He has written book chapters on receptions of the poet Homer by Greeks writing under the Roman Empire, and on the relationships that modern media articulate with classical antiquity, including in film (*300*'s Gorgo) and comics (*Sin City*).

Jesse Weiner teaches classics as a Visiting Assistant Professor at Hamilton College. He publishes broadly in Latin literature and classical reception studies. His work outside of academia includes service as a program scholar for Ancient Greeks/Modern Lives and work as a Latin consultant for Hollywood films.

CLASSICAL TRADITIONS IN
SCIENCE FICTION

Introduction: The Past Is an Undiscovered Country

Brett M. Rogers
and
Benjamin Eldon Stevens

If what we call "science fiction" begins with Mary Shelley's *Frankenstein* (published in 1818, revised in 1831), then we cannot help but wonder at Shelley's allusion, before the story even begins, to a decidedly ancient figure: the novel is subtitled "The Modern Prometheus" (see Figure 1).[1] This recalls the ancient Greek myth of Prometheus, the Titan who stole fire from the gods and gave it to humankind (e.g., Hesiod's *Theogony*, Aeschylus' *Prometheus Bound*); in one version of the myth (Plato's *Protagoras*), fire was our unique "gift," analogous to other animals' claws, thick hides, or ferocious speeds. Since the myth of Prometheus may be read as an explanatory account and as a symbol for the ongoing human relationship to technology, Shelley's subtitle further implies that *Frankenstein* will share with Greco-Roman literature and with mythology more generally an interest in the question of how "technology" of different types helps define human

---

[1] On *Frankenstein*'s receptions of earlier literature and mythology, see Pollin (1965) and Lecercle (1988). Mellor (2003) makes no reference to *Frankenstein*'s classical receptions. Pascoe (2006) discusses Shelley's *Midas* and *Proserpine* "as stage adaptations of Ovid's tales" (182), but otherwise refers only to "Latin plays" (183, citing Sunstein 1989: 138). The list of "Further Readings" in Schor (2003) makes no obvious reference to Greco-Roman classics.

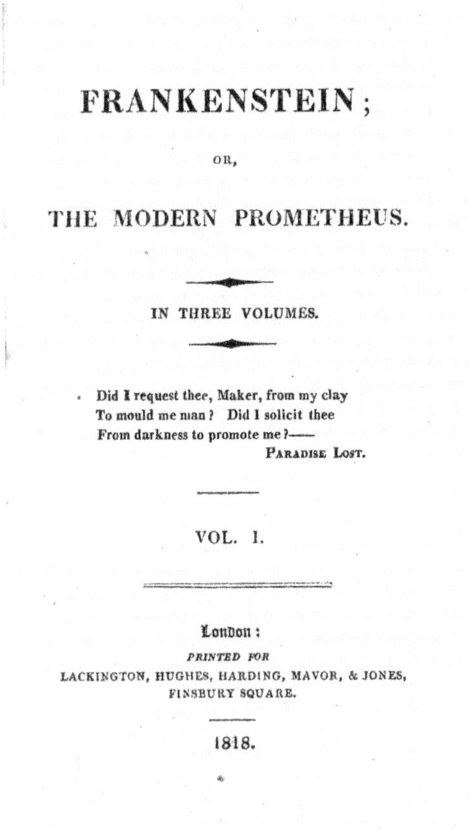

FRANKENSTEIN ;

OR,

THE MODERN PROMETHEUS.

IN THREE VOLUMES.

. Did I request thee, Maker, from my clay
To mould me man ? Did I solicit thee
From darkness to promote me ?——
                PARADISE LOST.

VOL. I.

London :

PRINTED FOR
LACKINGTON, HUGHES, HARDING, MAVOR, & JONES,
FINSBURY SQUARE.

1818.

Figure 1 The frontispiece to Mary Shelley's *Frankenstein; or, the Modern Prometheus* (1818), with quotation of Milton's *Paradise Lost.*

culture and, through it, our relationships to the natural world.[2] That question, among the most crucial that are facing modern life, is of course of central importance to the novel. It is worth emphasizing that already, from this perspective, *Frankenstein* raises that question about *modern* life, life in

---

[2] On "technology" in antiquity, see Cuomo (2007), esp. 7–40 ("The definition of *techne* in classical Athens"); Humphrey, Oleson, and Sherwood (1998). Prometheus is to be considered alongside Hephaestus (with references in Cuomo 2007, 38–39 nn.); cf. Calame (2005). For studies of this question in *Frankenstein*, see, e.g., Rauch (1995), and Mellor (1987).

a post-industrial and technoscientific world, first of all by invoking a story from an *ancient* culture, from a time that was pre-industrial and that would seem not to have been "technoscientific" in anything like a modern sense.

This first example of a classical presence in *Frankenstein* becomes even more interesting when we dig a little deeper. In its historical context, Shelley's subtitle recalls Greco-Roman antiquity through at least one *modern* intermediary. The phrase "The Prometheus of modern times" had been made famous by the German philosopher Immanuel Kant in a 1756 reference to the American experimentalist Benjamin Franklin (*Fortgesetzte Betrachtung der seit einiger Zeit wahrgenommenen Erderschütterungen*, vol. 1, p. 472). From this perspective, Shelley's engagement with ancient literature (and subsequently *Frankenstein*'s raising of that ancient question) is neither simple nor straightforward, as if Shelley had reached back to the ancient myth directly. Instead, *Frankenstein*'s use of Prometheus is complicated by its dependence on other modern uses of ancient materials. As Kant's phrase suggests, no longer in ancient myth alone, but now in living memory, too, has a man stolen lightning from the sky.[3]

Already in its subtitle, then, Shelley's *Frankenstein* draws attention to its status as a part of a *classical tradition*, enabling Shelley to locate a pressing concern within a longstanding stream of thought extending from Hesiod through Kant.[4] We may rather (or also) view Shelley's subtitle as an example of *classical reception*, emphasizing how Shelley "receives" and brings together several threads in a complex and meaningful manner.[5] We see that, at the same point in Shelley's book, the frontispiece (as seen in Figure 1), there is also an epigraph: "Did I request

---

[3] Electricity seems to be the novel's "Promethean fire," although the details are obscure: Frankenstein famously refuses to divulge the secret to his interlocutor, Walton.

[4] Mary Shelley is thus to be found in Grafton, Most, and Settis (2010) under the lemma "Prometheus," where she is introduced, in our view somewhat unfortunately, as "[Percy] Shelley's wife" and where her novel is likewise implicitly less "notable" than her husband's play *Prometheus Unbound* (1820); her allusion to Prometheus is considered an "embellish[ment]" (2010: 785; the author is Gordon Braden). (She is also referred to under the lemmata "Demeter and Persephone" (a play, *Persephone*, 1820) and "Midas" (a play of that name, also 1820). Although the two Shelleys' work interacts complexly, the chronology of publication (her *Frankenstein* in 1818, his *Prometheus Unbound* in 1820) would seem to suggest that in fact her work in this connection influenced his. In the case of *Frankenstein*, "the greatest number of Percy Shelley's revisions attempt to elevate his wife's prose style into a more Latinate idiom" (Mellor 2003: 14, after Robinson 1996).

[5] On "classical traditions" and "classical receptions," see recently, e.g., Grafton, Most, and Settis (2010); Hardwick and Stray (2008); Kallendorf (2007); Martindale and Thomas

thee, Maker, from my clay/to mould me man? Did I solicit thee/From darkness to promote me?" This epigraph comes from Milton's *Paradise Lost* (10.743–745). It places the novel in a Christian tradition: from our perspective, a second tradition that in its own right depends in part on the classical tradition, but is of course not identical to it. Insofar as Milton's epic had, by Shelley's time, achieved the status of a Christian "classic" in English on par with "pagan" Greek and Latin classics, we see that, again, *Frankenstein*'s manner of classical reception is indeed complicated: not a "direct" contact with classical antiquity, nor a passive acceptance of a simple classical tradition, but an active reception that is mediated by more recent authors, including, just in this brief overview, Kant and Milton.

Frankenstein's engagement with classical antiquity may thus be understood not only in terms of Shelley's own aims, but also (and crucially) in light of how Greco-Roman antiquity had been variously transformed *already*, prior to Shelley. In this particular case, that process of reception included centuries of Christian literature, mythology, and thought, taking forms seemingly as different from each other as Kant's analytical philosophy and Milton's epic poetry. This brief analysis of *Frankenstein*'s opening could be developed much further, resulting in an even more complex image of this moment in modern classical reception.

More important for our purposes in this introduction, however, is a different kind of complication, represented by the tendentious "if" in our opening sentence: namely, the fact that Shelley's novel has long been identified by scholars and other readers as the starting point of modern science fiction.[6] That identification is of course not a given, but a matter of energetic debate. But thinking of *Frankenstein* as a starting point helps us keep somewhat open the definition of "modern science fiction," an openness we believe is useful as we seek to explore modern science fiction for complex points of contact with classical traditions.

(2006); Hardwick (2003); and seminally Highet (1949). The phrasing used here to discuss the "classical tradition" is influenced in particular by Budelmann and Haubold (2008).

[6] See esp. Aldiss and Wingrove (2001); the proposal is variously repeated and debated in handbooks and companions. Carl Freedman (2000: 4) observes (with bibliography) that *Frankenstein* has "been listed in many genealogies of the genre as the first science-fiction novel" and "probably counts as the first important work of fiction to engage with modern science seriously and to feature a scientist as its protagonist."

This leads us to the more general question of what, precisely, science fiction is. Is it a "genre," a "discourse," a "conversation," or something altogether different? For our purposes, it is more important that any definition of modern science fiction be able to include *Frankenstein*, even if—or especially if—the novel challenges aspects of the definition, or *vice versa*. We therefore prefer to leave the question of science fiction's precise definition open, although we anticipate that the sort of study proposed herein will help answer it. In part to signal the openness of the question, we henceforth refer to modern science fiction as "SF." In this we follow many scholars; in particular we aim to be in the spirit of that abbreviation's acknowledged originator, Judith Merril, editor of twelve "Year's Best" anthologies (1955–1967). In the introduction to the 1967 anthology, Merril writes (ix):

> *Science fiction* as a descriptive label has long since lost whatever validity it might once have had. By now it means so many things to so many people that . . . I prefer not to use it at all, when I am talking about stories. *SF* (or generally, s-f) allows you to think *science fiction* if you like, while I think *science fable* or *scientific fantasy* or *speculative fiction*, or (once in a rare while, because there's little of it being written, by any rigorous definition) *science fiction*.

In this way we are able to accept the proposal that *Frankenstein* inaugurates modern SF. With *Frankenstein*'s status as the starting point at least provisionally in mind, then, and in light of the reading sketched above, we may say that modern SF has, from its very beginning, as it were, looked forward to the future and around at the present in part by looking farther back: to Greco-Roman mythology, to the literature of classical antiquity, to images of ancient history. As a locus of classical receptions, modern SF has engaged in historically and formally complex negotiations, not to say contestations, between pre-modern ways of knowing and being human, on one hand, and on the other hand, then-emergent and now-ascendant technoscientific thinking and practice. The complexities of *Frankenstein*'s reception of antiquity are, in our view, suggestive of how modern SF engages with "antiquities" in the plural, that is, with antiquity as it has been received and transformed already into various forms, objects, and products, and is being so transformed even now. In other words, to borrow from Ovid's

Metamorphoses, we are interested in the ways modern SF speaks of antiquity's many "changed forms" (*mutatas formas*) and participates in the production of new (and previously unimaginable) bodies (*in nova . . . corpora*; 1.1–2).

Our main purpose for both this introduction and the volume as a whole, then, is to suggest some of the ways in which serious discussion of the Janus-like character of modern SF might proceed.[7] From examples like *Frankenstein*—as well as from examples *unlike* it—we think that a wide range of modern SF should be of great interest to anyone already interested in the ancient world and its classics. Moreover, we hope that this volume's chapters demonstrate the relevance of a wide range of Greek and Roman classics for modern SF. Both as an area in which the meanings of classics are actively transformed, and as an open-ended set of texts whose own "classic" status is a matter of ongoing discussion and debate, SF stands to reveal much about the roles played by ancient classics as well as new "classics" in the modern world.[8] In short, we aim to justify the joint study of classics and SF, as well as to indicate certain areas that seem to our authors and ourselves to be especially open for immediate exploration. If modern SF is viewed, as we believe it must be, as a crucial and popular mode, even *the* mainstream mode,

[7] We refer of course to the divine figure in Roman mythology (e.g., Ovid, *Fasti* 1.1–294). In SF, *Janus/Aurora* was the name of an important feminist "fanzine" (1975–1990).

[8] Readers of SF already recognize on some level the importance of the classics in debates about the SF canon, as there are debates in the SF studies community about whether certain ancient texts—e.g., Homer's *Odyssey* (*Od.*), Lucian's *True History* (*VH*)—constitute significant precursors to SF or are themselves SF or "knowledge fiction." For example, Liveley (2006: 275–278) has argued that we find classical analogues to SF in such figures as the bronze giant Talos, the goddess Athena, Hephaestus' golden robotic slave-girls (Homer, *Iliad* 18.373–379), and the gold and silver watchdogs of Alcinous (Homer, *Od.* 7.91–94). We argue that the goal of such discussions should not be to determine in any conclusive manner whether priority ought to be accorded to particular classical moments in the study of SF. Instead there is, and there will remain, a need to develop clear and meaningful criteria for what we define as the differences between "classical antiquity" and "SF." For example, as in the examples cited from Homer, should we offer a product-oriented account and claim that "ancient knowledge fiction," or, as it were, "classical SF," is identifiable by the presence of certain kinds of advanced objects or technologies? Or might we take a process-oriented approach and argue that the critical point of contact between classical antiquity and SF lies instead in certain deeper epistemological structures; for example, an interest in technique, mechanics, or experimentalism? How these questions are answered, case by case and over time, clearly will have a profound effect on how we think about classics and SF interacting.

of thinking about life in a modern, technoscientific world, then the fact that it is also a site of significant classical receptions should be of real interest.[9] With that aim in mind, in this introduction we have three main goals.

First, we argue that the discipline of Classics has a stake in the study of SF because of the urgent ethical and epistemological questions SF raises about the humanities *vis-à-vis* science and technology. The possibility of an interdisciplinary field of study is important especially in light of the potential impact SF may have on popular perceptions of the classics. Second, as a step towards developing that argument, we offer a reading of two influential texts in SF studies: one primarily historical, the other primarily theoretical. Our main point here is that ancient classics and modern science fiction have in common a deep epistemological similarity; that is, a similarity in how each imagines the basic functioning of human knowledge. We conclude that if "the past is a foreign country" (in the words of Hartley) while the future is an "undiscovered country" (in the words of Gorkon), then the joint study of Classics and modern SF may permit us to contemplate simultaneously the (science fictional) future in all of its familiar foreignness and the (classical) past as an undiscovered country.[10]

Third and finally, we conclude this introduction by summarizing the 14 chapters composed for this volume, as each contributes meaningfully to the development of serious, systematic scholarship on the reception of classical antiquities in SF. So far, work in the field of Classics and SF has consisted mainly of studies of individual texts, often published in disparate places.[11] To our knowledge, to date there have been only two surveys, each partial in its own way: Brown (2008) and Fredericks (1980). The first book-length collection of essays, *L'Antiquité dans*

[9] Westfahl (2009: 2) similarly asserts that SF has become the dominant mode of mainstream popular culture.

[10] "The past is a foreign country: they do things differently there" is the opening sentence to L. P. Hartley's novel *The Go-Between* (1953); cf. Lowenthal (1999). The toast to "The undiscovered country—the future" is offered by the Klingon Chancellor Gorkon in *Star Trek VI: The Undiscovered Country* (dir. Nicholas Meyer, 1991); as Spock observes in the scene, the quotation comes from Shakespeare's *Hamlet* (Act III, Scene I), but Hamlet refers, not to the future, but to "the something after death,/The undiscovered country, from whose bourn/No traveller returns."

[11] McClellan (2010) (Lucan in *Frankenstein* and *Day of the Dead*), Caeners (2008) ("Humanity's Scarred Children: The Cylons' Oedipal Dilemma in *Battlestar Galactica*"), Käkelä (2008) ("Asimov's Foundation Trilogy: From the Fall of Rome to the Rise of Cowboy Heroes"), DiTommaso (2007) ("The Articulation of Imperial Decadence and Decline in Epic SF"), Lively (2006) ("Science Fictions and Cyber Myths: or, Do Cyborgs

8 *Introduction*

l'imaginaire contemporain: Fantasy, science-fiction, fantastique, edited by Bost-Fiévet and Provini (2014) was released just as this present volume was going to press. It remains the case then, as Brown herself notes, that "the relationship between SF and the Classics is still relatively uncharted territory" (2008: 427).[12] It is thus our hope that these chapters, ranging widely over texts and other works from antiquity and in modern SF, will work together to chart this territory further, to stimulate discussion and encourage debate about this burgeoning field, and to point to areas for future exploration.

THE ORIGINS OF THE FUTURE? EPISTEMOLOGICAL AND ETHICAL DILEMMAS FOR CLASSICS AND SF

The past few decades have seen an explosion of interest, both popular and academic, in modern SF. This is likely to continue. As we draw

---

Dream of Dolly the Sheep?"), Janney (2000) ("Oedipus E-Mails his Mom: Computer-Mediated Romance Develops as a Science Fiction Sub-Genre"), Clay (1999) (Plato's Atlantis), Cifuentes (1998) (Theseus and the Minotaur in *Blade Runner*), Georgiadou and Larmour (1998) (Lucian's *VH*), Palumbo (1998) (monomyth in *Dune*), McGiveron (1997) (Bradbury's reference to Hercules and Antaeus in *Fahrenheit 451*), Clayton (1996) (on Cixous's Medusa, Shelley's Frankenstein, and *Blade Runner*), Lundquist (1996) (myth in *Bill and Ted's Excellent Adventure*), Seed (1996) ("Recycling the Texts of the Culture: Walter M. Miller's *A Canticle for Leibowitz*"), Dutta (1995) ("'Very Bad Poetry, Captain': Shakespeare in *Star Trek*"), Holt (1992) ("H.G. Wells and the Ring of Gyges"), Desser (1991) (on *Paradise Lost* in *Blade Runner*), Holtsmark (1991) (*katabasis* in film, including the SF film *Cherry 2000*), Edgeworth (1990) ("The Poverty of Invention; or, Mining the Classics with Janet Morris and Harry Turtledove"), Tavormina (1988) ("A Gate of Horn and Ivory: Dreaming True and False in *Earthsea*"), Jolly (1986) ("The Bellerophon Myth and *Forbidden Planet*"), Desser (1985) (on *Blade Runner*), Cirasa (1984) (suspense in classical epic and *Dune*), Scafella (1981) (Sphinx in *The Time Machine*), Fredericks (1980) ("Greek Mythology in Modern Science Fiction: Vision and Cognition"), Ower (1979) (Aesop), Berman (1976) ("Forster's Other Cave: The Platonic Structure of 'The Machine Stops'"), Christianson (1976) (Kepler's *Somnium*), Fredericks (1976) (Lucian's *True History*), Swanson (1976), and Canary (1974) ("Science Fiction as Fictive History"). Additional such studies of particular works are undoubtedly forthcoming.

[12] Brown does not so much chart territory as sight some potential landmarks in both SF and classics (under three headings: "The Fall of Rome," "Myths of Greece," and "Alternative History"); her "Further Reading" lists only Roberts (2006a: 21–31) as on Lucian, Fredericks (1980) as "a comparatively early overview," and Bondanella (1987: 229–30) as discussing "Rome's relationship with SF." (Roberts is unfortunately missing from the bibliography of Hardwick and Stray [2008].) Fredericks limits himself to "Greek mythology in modern science fiction."

nearer to the bicentennial of *Frankenstein*'s first publication (2018), for example, we may anticipate not only a range of popular treatments, including new adaptations of the novel to film and video as well as treatments in news media, but also an increase in the number, popularity, and importance of scholarly treatments, including conferences and panels, journal articles, and edited volumes and monographs.

For our purposes, more important than the differences between such popular and scholarly treatments are their similarities; above all, an interest in two urgent questions raised by *Frankenstein*. These questions are encapsulated in the ambiguity that has attached to the novel's title and its *Nachleben*, as "Frankenstein" is used to refer both to the scientist (as properly in the novel) and the creature (as the term has come to be used in pop-cultural shorthand).[13] First, how does technoscience affect our understanding of the world? (In other words, how may our attempts to see and to manipulate the world be regarded as similar to Victor Frankenstein's?) Second, what is the relationship between such a technoscientific understanding of the world and human being or human action? (In other words, in what ways are both we and our actions the products of technoscientific knowledge and practice, like Frankenstein's *monstrum*?)

The first question is epistemological: What does it mean, for example, that our knowledge of the world is mediated so completely by technologies resulting from modern scientific research, especially as it has been industrialized and consumerized following the Second World War? The second question is ethical: Should a scientific understanding of the world guide our social, political, and moral decision-making? Should a technoscientific ideology be allowed to shape, or even to replace, philosophy as "the steersman of the soul"?

These questions are essential to asking what it means, and what we would like it to mean, to be human today. Taking them seriously is now a crucial part of studying or working in "the humanities." Putting it more strongly, we believe that no academic discipline that does not address those questions,

---

[13] The term "Frankenstein" has become generally available as a sort of shorthand expression for feared results of the misuse of science and technology, especially biology and genetics. See esp. Clayton (2006); cf. "Frankenstein monster" in Clute and Nicholls: "in common parlance . . . a monster that ultimately turns and rends its irresponsible creator" (1993: 449; the author is Peter Nicholls).

10 *Introduction*

and thus think through its own relationship to science, technology, and a prevailing technoscientific ideology, is today truly "humanistic."

We therefore believe it is important for classicists in particular to acknowledge that in more recent SF (as well as other genres) "the classics" have been transformed into something like "reliably esoteric, public-domain material for popular cultural ironization." In this way "the classics" are being made into vivid signifiers *neither* of the ancient past, *nor* even of professional knowledge of antiquity, *but* of a present moment: an advanced post-modern moment marked by a recomposition of past cultural products that is omnivorous and, from a scholarly perspective, generally uncritical.[14] These "classics," as it were, cobbled and stitched together into a new *monstrum*, constitute an imagistically vivid but ontologically indistinct entry in an advanced post-modern encyclopedism that is, in its own view, not hierarchical but associative and, so, willfully apolitical about its cultural recompositions.

In other words, there would seem to be the possibility that SF's reception and transformation of classical antiquity mean that the discipline of Classics is no longer necessary. For the ancient classics attend to modes of being that do not straightforwardly anticipate, and so do not seem to resonate with, the concept of the modern "human being" as it becomes increasingly technoscientific.[15] As a result, as the limits of that human being, including its potential change or even loss, increasingly are explored by SF, there is a way in which the classics—and with them Classics as a discipline—may seem, from a popular or mainstream perspective at least, at risk of being left behind.

[14] Cf. Paul (2010: 142) on classics and cinema: "the movies' settings are not so much Greek or Roman as simply, and vaguely, ancient." An example from film would be *Bill and Ted's Excellent Adventure* (dir. Stephen Herek, 1989), an SF film whose principal SF trope—a time-traveling telephone booth (perhaps interpretable as an allusion to the TARDIS in *Doctor Who*)—allows Socrates and his Athens to be included, indiscriminately, alongside many other historical personages and their contexts, including Genghis Khan, Joan of Arc, Napoleon, Billy the Kid, Sigmund Freud, and Abraham Lincoln. See, e.g., Lundquist (1996).

[15] An influential theorist of such technoscientific human being is Haraway (e.g., 1991), who sees in the figure of the "technobastard" cyborg in SF the potential to express a significant discontinuity with the classical/Western past. Whereas classical monsters (e.g., centaurs and Amazons) define and enforce limits so as to "map the conditions and the identity of the ancient Greek male—and, by default, female" (Lively 2006: 292), in Haraway's view, the cyborg monsters of SF instead "define quite different political possibilities and limits from those proposed by the mundane fiction of Man and Woman" (180) or, more to our point, the mundane fiction of Human.

It would seem, then, that modern SF poses an urgent and fascinating challenge to Classics. What may be done or even said in response to the modern, technoscientific world by a classicist—someone who, by professional definition, is a humanistic student of pre-industrial and pre-modern cultures? What, if anything, may be said about SF by students of the classics, and what, if anything, do they stand to gain from this discussion? Finally, what perils, if any, will SF itself as well as SF studies face if they proceed without any recognition or understanding of their many longstanding entanglements with the classics and classical traditions? Our conviction is that both Classics and SF have much to say to each other, and that both fields will benefit from the contributions of a large critical community composed of "fans of classics" as well as "fans of SF," fans who are willing to continue crossing the boundaries of academic canons and disciplines in order to engage in shared and meaningful dialogue about each other's most urgent questions.

A THEORETICAL JUSTIFICATION: ROBERTS, SUVIN, AND "KNOWLEDGE FICTION"

It is possible to develop a theoretical justification for the study of classics and SF by drawing, perhaps contrary to expectation, on SF studies, and on two important contributions to SF studies in particular. First is a critical history by Adam Roberts (2006a); second is a seminal theoretical study by Darko Suvin (1979). Both authors have significantly influenced SF studies. Considered together, Roberts and Suvin help us articulate ways in which classics and SF (the materials), as well as Classics and SF studies (the disciplines), may be brought together productively to address the urgent epistemological and ethical questions posed above.

In particular, we combine Roberts's emphasis on the recurrence of "non-theological thinking" with two concepts from Suvin, the notion of "cognitive estrangement" and the related notion of the "*novum*," to suggest that the rubric of SF is applicable to certain works whether or not they share the same historical contexts as modern SF or its engagement with a specially technoscientific ideology. In this way, not only may modern SF be considered a site of classical receptions, but certain ancient Greco-Roman works may also be read as "SF" in their own right. From this perspective, a work is meaningfully SF, and so open to being read according to SF studies heuristics, not in terms of its historical or cultural provenance, but in terms of how it engages with contemporary epistemologies; of particular interest is whether and how a work innovates with respect to such epistemologies.[16] The study of classics and SF would thus be interested not only in how modern SF receives antiquity, but also, and more consequentially, in how certain ancient works depart from something like a prevailing ancient epistemology: in how ancient works are "SF" or "knowledge fictions" in their own rights.[17]

Roberts and Suvin together help us to articulate this position. Roberts's main historical claim is that "the re-emergence of science fiction is correlative to the Protestant Reformation" (2006a: ix). This historical specificity underwrites Roberts's definitional claim that, in general, "SF

[16] In this connection, we find rather limiting the classification of certain ancient works as "proto-SF." As the article of that name in Clute and Nicholls (1993: 965) argues,
It seems inappropriate to describe as "science fiction" anything published in the early 18th century or before. Indeed, so intimately connected is our sense of the word "fiction" with the growth of the novel that it would seem most sensible to begin our reckoning of what might be labelled "science fiction" with the first speculative work which is both a novel and manifests a clear awareness of what is and is not "science" in the modern sense of the word (entry on 964–967, author Brian Stableford).
By apparent contrast, on the same page co-editor Peter Nicholls is mentioned as arguing
that sf is merely a continuation, without any true hiatus, of a much more ancient tradition of imaginative fiction whose origins are lost in the mythical mists and folkloric fogs of oral tradition. If this were accepted there would be no proto sf at all, and sf's history would begin with, say, Homer's *Odyssey* and continue with Lucian's *True History*.
Despite the differences between Stableford's and Nicholls's positions, implicit here is a common notion that "SF" is applicable only under strict literary-historical constraints: a work may be SF only if the historical context is totally "appropriate" (as Stableford argues) or totally irrelevant (as Nicholls is represented as arguing). In our view, such a constraint risks excluding *a priori* the possibility of discovering other, deeper commonalities among SF texts and certain classics. As we argue in this section, the latter may be more and other than "proto-SF."
[17] In this respect, we take a different tack than that taken by Liveley (2006), who seeks to construct a "genealogy of the cyborgs [and, it seems, SF?] of the second Christian Millennium [that] may be traced back to the mythical monsters of classical Greece" (278). In light of Liveley's focus on the particular figure of the cyborg, we might say that her criteria for the determination of SF in classical texts are "product-oriented." We are more interested here in developing criteria that are "process-oriented." (See also Section III.3 of Rogers and Stevens [2012a].) On ancient "knowledge fictions," see note 22, below.

develops as an imaginatively expansive and (crucially) *materialist* mode of literature, as opposed to the magical-fantastic, fundamentally religious mode that comes to be known as Fantasy" (x). In particular, Roberts sees modern SF as, in origin, a *re-emergence* of an *ancient* mode; that is, of

a nascent form of SF in Ancient Greece that disappears, or becomes suppressed, with the rise to cultural dominance of the Catholic Church; and which *re-emerges* when the new cosmology of the sixteenth century inflects the theology of Protestant thinkers in the seventeenth. (xiii; emphasis added)[18]

To summarize the complex historical argument, we may say that that "nascent form of SF" is a particular kind of "extraordinary voyage": "voyages into the sky, and especially voyages to other planets" (vii).[19] As Roberts puts it there:

The *ur*-form of the SF text is "a story about interplanetary travel" . . . Travels "upwards" through space, or sometimes "downwards" into hollow-earth marvels . . . are the trunk, as it were, from which the various other modes of SF branch off.

As examples of SF "branches," Roberts lists "stories of travel through space (to other worlds, planets, stars), stories of travel through time (into the past

---

[18] Roberts (2006a) is careful to stress that he is not claiming that "SF is Protestant while Fantasy is Catholic." In his view, materialist or scientific thinking was prohibited, in the imagination or at least in imaginative literature in Western Europe, by the world-view or metaphysics of medieval Catholicism, inimical to "scientific" thinking about the possibility of other worlds in the heavens. As a result "the balance of scientific inquiry shifted to Protestant countries, where the sort of speculation that could be perceived as contrary to biblical revelation could be undertaken with more (although not total) freedom" (2006a: ix).

[19] The historical argument as developed over the course of Roberts (2006a: especially 21–87) covers the ancient novel, AD 400–1600, the seventeenth century, and the eighteenth century, and draws special attention to how a growing insistence on materialist cosmology made possible a larger space, rather literally, for SF thinking. Walter Miller, Jr.'s *A Canticle for Leibowitz* (1960) offers a fictionalized account of such a historical process: in the aftermath of nuclear holocaust and an anti-technological revolt, "classical" (i.e., twentieth-century) technoscientific knowledge reemerges in the midst of monastic and pontifical politics, resulting in a renewed emphasis on materialism and even the somewhat reluctant acceptance of a materialist cosmology and interplanetary travel by one monastic order; see Grayson (this volume).

or into the future) and stories of imaginary technology (machinery, robots, computers, cyborgs and cyber-culture)" (viii).[20] As Roberts sees it, the roots of this genre-tree, "the roots of what we now call science fiction are found in the fantastic voyages of the Ancient Greek novel" (vii).

In this connection, our point is not that Roberts is necessarily right, nor even that such a link between, in this case, the *origins* of modern SF and the *return* of ancient Greek, Roman, or Greco-Roman modes must be made. Our point is rather that, since a claim like Roberts's *may* be right, we must take seriously the possibility of deep and, perhaps, surprising links between modern SF and the classics or the ancient world. The link could thus be made in other ways than by focusing on "extraordinary voyages" especially to other planets.

For example, one might consider the historical coincidence of the emergence of modern SF and the field of study, later the discipline, of Classics. If, per Roberts, modern SF is correlated to the Reformation, then it may be correlated in turn to the more general cultural context for that particularly religious movement. This context would be the reemergence into the Western European imagination, perhaps especially its literary imagination, of classical antiquity. In other words, the rise of modern SF seems correlative to the re-creation of classical antiquity as a field of inquiry: perhaps surprisingly, SF and the discipline of Classics seem to have developed simultaneously.

Going further, we may say that the links that are possible between Classics and SF need not be historical or literary-historical but could be, and perhaps should be, more generally epistemological. Roberts offers a formulation that, in our view, points to an important possibility for justifying the combined study of Classics and SF in epistemological terms:

I no longer see why a distinctively modern conception of "science" need underlie "science fiction," given that "science" more broadly conceived as *a non-theological mode of understanding the natural world goes back a great deal further than the nineteenth century*. (2006a: 4; emphasis added)[21]

---

[20] Roberts suggests that a "fourth form, utopian fiction," "must be discussed as a parallel development to SF . . . because utopian writing is fundamentally a satiric mode of literature" (2006a: viii).

[21] Cf. Roberts (2006a: 24): "It is taken as axiomatic in the present study that science fiction is distinct from theology, being natural and material where the latter is supernatural and spiritual."

It seems to us that one indeed stands to find, in certain ancient works, examples of just such a "non-theological mode of understanding the natural world." These works would rightly be called "fictions of understanding." In fact, we believe it would not be too much to call them, and to approach them as, "science fictions." Anticipating, however, some surprise at the suggestion that the rubric of SF, seemingly only modern, is applicable to certain ancient works, we propose an umbrella term: on the model of "science fiction," "knowledge fiction."[22]

Roberts thus provides one way of thinking through how, as it has been said, "the past is a foreign country": by considering deep "similarities" or even continuities—in his historical argument, "re-emergences"—between ancient and modern imaginaries. Another perspective on the same possibility may be reached by following the rest of that quotation about the past: "They do things differently there." To help emphasize "difference" in a theoretical justification of Classics and SF, we now consider the basic ideas of Darko Suvin. In a way that relates productively to how students of the classics approach the ancient past, Suvin defines SF as a mode of "cognitive estrangement" whose effects depend on a fictional work's most significant conceptual difference from the present, its "*novum*."[23]

In Suvin's view, SF is "a literary genre whose necessary and sufficient conditions are the presence and interaction of estrangement and cognition,

[22] The term "knowledge fiction" has been attributed to Theodore Sturgeon. A relatively obvious ancient example might be Lucretius, while his influence on later authors would seem to suggest that they also be examined from the same perspective (e.g., Ovid); for readings related to this suggestion, see Johnson (2000), Bloom (2011: 133–208) and Greenblatt (2011). Cf. Roberts (2006a: 7–8), where he describes SF as "a space where the sort of 'science' Feyerabend is proposing already takes place" (8), referring to Paul Feyerabend's famous dictum that, in science, "the only principle that does not inhibit progress is: *anything goes*" (2010: 7). Just prior to that point, Roberts suggests that "[o]ne of the most appealing consequences of Popper's position [sc. "science as 'imaginative creation'"] is its unstated implication that SF is a mode of doing science (or 'philosophy' more generally conceived) as well as a mode of doing fiction." In this mode "a scientific discourse and a speculative-fantastic discourse [may] come together" (2006a: 25, referring to early novels in ancient Greece). Roberts thus argues that SF is not limited to "technology fiction"; his section on "the technological" (9–15) therefore discusses Heidegger (esp. "The Question of Technology" and "What Calls for Thinking?") alongside Bernard Stiegler, Donna Haraway, and Michel Serres.
[23] These terms are first articulated in Suvin (1979), perhaps the single most influential work in modern SF studies. Cf. Hollinger (1999: 233): "More than any other study, Suvin's *Metamorphoses* is *the* significant forerunner of all the major examinations" of SF between 1980 and 1999 (at least).

and whose main formal device is an imaginative framework alternative to the author's empirical environment" (1979: 7–8). We may wish to allow for a more capacious definition of SF by replacing Suvin's "empirical" with "epistemological." This replacement would seem to allow for "SF" or, as we have proposed, "knowledge fiction" in response to environments other than those of (technoscientific) empiricism. That change notwithstanding, we also wish to emphasize the utility of thinking of SF as Suvin suggests: as "distinguished by the narrative dominance or hegemony of a fictional 'novum' (novelty, innovation) validated by cognitive logic" (63).

In this way the future, too, is made into—fictionalized as—a foreign country. From this perspective, we may consider (classical) past and (modern SF) future as analogous in their (admittedly different) differences and distances from the present environment of the reader. Suvin's ideas are then interesting for our purposes for two main reasons. First, as the term *"novum"* may already imply, Suvin refers to classical Latin authors to develop his ideas.[24] Suvin himself makes it clear that this is not a superficial connection but a deep one, albeit initially perhaps unconscious (xv):

the pleasing blend of protean formal-*cum*-substantial process identified by the (Lucretian rather than Ovidian) metaphor of metamorphosis kept recurring in my typewriter so often that I finally, as a materialist should, surrendered to my matter, *hominum deorumque genitrix.*

Here Suvin links his own innovation in SF studies, not to Latin literature in general or in the abstract, but to what he sees as a concrete difference of opinion between particular authors within it: between Lucretius' thoroughly materialist frame for changes in shape, and Ovid's allegedly more traditionally theological or, as it were, magical metamorphoses of bodies. It would be interesting to pursue Suvin's vision of the two classical authors further. For example, one might examine how, insofar as Suvin's work is influential, modern SF studies has proceeded under the aegis of a materialism that is explicitly "Lucretian."[25] Another, equally

---

[24] Suvin had borrowed the idea from Ernst Bloch (1968) and (1976).

[25] Suvin's work has received some criticism for privileging "literary" SF over "genre fiction" as well as other media. Other criticisms of it have focused on how not all SF seems to aim at "estrangement." (But, as Brian Stableford puts it, "[m]any voyages which pretend to be [offering a pleasant distraction] actually present worlds whose bizarre aspects reflect the real world ironically and subversively"; Clute and Nicholls [1993: 407], entry "Fantastic

interesting open question is what it would mean, by contrast, to study SF in an "Ovidian" mode, and indeed, which if any SF is "Ovidian."[26]

More important for our purposes is the methodological implication that a physical or metaphysical fact of "the author's empirical environment"—namely, "materialism," has epistemological consequences. What kinds of bodies there are in a literary imagination, and what kinds of changes they are imagined as susceptible to, must affect literary-historical classification.[27] Already we have suggested a natural link between modern SF and the classics in that both represent worlds that are, from our perspective, somehow not real (i.e., not yet; no longer). In the present connection, that link is strengthened in that both fields may, now, be seen to represent *possible worlds*: SF as a matter of that mode's self-definition, the classics in ways that stand to be discovered and explored in detail.[28]

Voyages.") It is worth noting that a great deal of the most influential SF criticism of the last 40 years has been "historical materialist" or even explicitly "Marxist" in orientation.

[26] We are grateful to an anonymous reader for this question and for the related question of whether an "Ovidian" approach might correspond to what Roberts calls the "magical-fantastic, fundamentally religious mode that comes to be known as Fantasy" (2006a: x); this would of course not be simply to attribute such a world-view to Ovid himself. This line of questioning would help in determining which classics are, properly, "knowledge fictions," or whether indeed all classics may in some way be placed under that rubric because of their distance, and difference, from our present "empirical environment."

[27] This line of thinking about the consequences of materialism is anticipated in Karl Marx's reflections on the dependence of art on material conditions. For our purposes here, Marx offers, in the unpublished version (from 1857) of his introduction to "Contribution to the Critique of Political Economy" (1859), a poignant meditation on the material effects of technoscience on classical myth:

> We know that Greek mythology is not only the arsenal of Greek art, but also its basis. Is the conception of nature and of social relations which underlies Greek imagination and therefore Greek [art] possible when there are self-acting mules, railways, locomotives and electric telegraphs? What is a Vulcan compared with Roberts and Co., Jupiter compared with the lightning conductor, and Hermes with the Crédit mobilier? All mythology subdues, controls and fashions the forces of nature in the imagination and through imagination; it disappears therefore when real control over these forces is established. What becomes of Fama side by side with Printing House Square?

See also von Staden (1975), who provides the quotation from Marx (on p. 125).

[28] On "possible worlds" in fiction see, e.g., Eco (1978; "Can we postulate a universe and then study with empirical instruments this postulate as if it were an object?"), Dolezel (1998: 1–36, 199–226), and, with special reference to certain classical receptions in SF and fantasy, Bost-Fiévet and Provini (2014: 271–278). This natural alignment may partly account for SF writers' affinity for images of classical antiquity, since the classics as syntagms are always liable to—indeed, require—reconstruction using another invented paradigm. The special remoteness of and paucity of evidence for classical antiquity, as

Second, then, we may link Suvin's ideas to Roberts's claims more directly in ways that are, we think, productive for thinking about how Classics and SF studies may begin to move forward holistically and seriously. From this combined perspective, both fields comprise texts that are enticingly incomplete: the texts are self-contained, syntagmatic structures of narrative for which the reader must always supply a missing paradigm, since the "world" the text points to does not (yet; any longer) exist outside of the text.[29] As we read the classics, the "world" is either past or may never have existed; as we read SF, the "world" is yet to come in a complex way, either as a thought-experiment or in relation to a "scientific past" that is, relative to our readerly present, also already gone.

Both fields therefore constitute "knowledge fictions" that place demands upon the reader to supply additional knowledge, as it were cracking a code with which to make meaning that connects the sentence to the world.[30] If, on the one hand, "the past is a foreign country," and on the other hand "[e]ven the *near* future may be very strange," then there is in our view a clear theoretical justification for the natural alignment between ancient classics and modern SF.[31] The strangeness of images of the ancient past is matched by the "cognitive estrangement" of futures imagined in modern SF. The same point may be made in slightly different terms: the past-*cum*-foreign country could be "mapped" in the manner of Fredric Jameson's "cognitive mapping," with interesting implications for how both antiquity and the future are reimagined by a post-modern present.[32] Although the precise terminology must remain open to refinement and debate, the classics and modern SF may productively be approached together: both of them as "knowledge fictions"

---

well as its privileged status in the Western imaginary, would seem to make it particularly susceptible to such affinity.

[29] Cf. Mathieson (1985: 23), citing Angenot (1979).

[30] Cf. Delany et al. (1987: 136). Acknowledgment of such code-breaking demands on the reader is something of a trope in introductions to SF studies: see, e.g., Mendlesohn (2003a: 5): "'He gave her his hand' or 'he turned on his side' raise numerous possibilities in the mind of the sf reader."

[31] The phrase "Even the *near* future may be very strange" comes from Russell Blackford in Aldiss et al. (2006: 391).

[32] See esp. Jameson (1990), whose thinking, of course, includes both Classics and SF studies as disciplines. Lacking the space to explore this point in detail, here we only suggest that this postmodernist justification would have the effect, in our view very positive, of emphasizing further the deep epistemological links between the fields and, so, the potential epistemological and ethical or political import of the enterprise.

and, therefore, certain ancient classics as they are, in ways to be exemplified in the chapters below, readable as examples of SF.

This may be, again, surprising. Beyond surprise, we anticipate—and hope—that any such link proposed between modern SF and the ancient classics will be the subject of vigorous debate, especially as the two fields are themselves subject, more or less continuously, to debate about their own self-definitions.[33] But we also hope that, although theoretical justifications for the link should indeed be debated and multiplied (or metamorphosed?), we have made it clear that there are reasons for wanting to make the link. One is to make sure that both the "traditional" humanities and their more—most—"modern" counterparts continue to address urgent and fundamental questions about humanity in the world: at this point, in a technoscientific world.

Another reason, no less valuable, is so that those who love both fields may enjoy their surprising and productive coming together in dialogue. In context of theoretical justifications like that provided by our reading of Roberts and Suvin, such a dialogue is not merely a matter of desire—as it were, a sort of "fan fiction" for lovers of academic disciplines. Instead, it is a matter of real possibility, even necessity. The overlaps of the classics and SF are a matter of real importance for the world of today and tomorrow. As that world is, it seems, increasingly technoscientific, we must work to understand how it may yet remain receptive to humanistic interests, beginning as ever with the ancient past.

OUTLINE OF THE VOLUME

We hope that these attempts at theoretical justifications suggest how the link between the classics and SF is rather more natural, and therefore much richer, than superficial differences—or even superficial similarities—might seem at first to imply. If we agree that the study of classical traditions and receptions in SF is therefore both justifiable and important, then it is imperative to articulate how best we may move forward with this work. The chapters collected in this volume offer

---

[33] The definition of SF is a matter of great debate in SF studies; see, e.g., the entry "Definitions of SF" in Clute and Nicholls (1993: 311–314; the authors are John Clute, Peter Nicholls, and Brian Stableford).

distinctive visions of how that future might look; taken together, they may be considered as conducting a sort of scholarly thought experiment, or even as constituting a sort of "speculative nonfiction," about points of contact between some of our most modern materials and some of the most ancient ones.

One significant theme common to the following chapters is that articulated above—namely, the possible deep epistemological similarities between (studying) the ancient past and (speculating about) the future. These chapters range widely in subject matter, treating some relatively lesser-known classics as well as works of longstanding "canonical" status, and likewise covering SF both well-known and less mainstream. Nevertheless, all of these chapters offer rich discussion of topics relevant to the possibility outlined above of treating ancient classics and modern SF as similarly "knowledge fictional."

Chapters are roughly organized in chronological order of primary SF sources. The chapters in Part I, "SF's Rosy-Fingered Dawn," explore some of the strong, surprising links between even the earliest SF and ancient classics. In general, the essays in this section suggest that similarities at literary levels of structure, language, and image are suggestive of deeper, philosophical connections, raising questions about epistemology and systems of belief.

Dean Swinford ("The Lunar Setting of Johannes Kepler's *Somnium*, Science Fiction's Missing Link") argues that Kepler's *Somnium* (ca. 1620–1630), in its close relationship to ancient sources such as Plutarch's *De Facie* and Lucian's *True History*, represents a development of medieval allegory: a step in the process by which Renaissance philosophers responded to ancient texts in order to distinguish "science" from "religion." Similarly, Jesse Weiner ("Lucretius, Lucan, and Mary Shelley's *Frankenstein*") deploys close literary analysis and documentary evidence to show that Lucretius' and Lucan's epic poems not only provide models for certain key moments in Shelley's novel, but also help us account for its interest in questions that are "ethical" as well as "scientific." A close relationship between Latin poetry and "canonical" SF is also treated by Benjamin Eldon Stevens ("Virgil in Jules Verne's *Journey to the Center of the Earth*"), who argues that Verne's rewriting of Virgil exemplifies how modern SF juxtaposes (classical) traditions to master narratives of modern science: "the classics" are effectively transformed into "mere tradition," while "knowledge" is reserved for the results of scientific practice. Antony Keen ("Mr. Lucian in Suburbia: Links Between the *True History* and *The First Men in the Moon*") focuses on two other "canonical" figures in SF to argue that Wells's direct engagement with the satirical tradition transmitted by Lucian may help explain differences in tone between Wells's novel and more commonly cited precursors such as Francis Godwin's *The Man in the Moone* (1638) and Kepler's *Somnium*.

All together, the first four chapters suggest that there is high value in considering modern SF not only in context of relatively recent precursors, but also in context of quite ancient works. While Part I explores how classical traditions influence the early stages of SF in the nineteenth and early twentieth centuries, Part II ("SF Classics") considers the varying kinds of classical influence in SF after the emergence of SF into popular consciousness during the early to mid–twentieth century.

Gregory S. Bucher ("A Complex Oedipus: The Tragedy of Edward Morbius") explores the production history of the movie *Forbidden Planet* (1956) in order to demonstrate how the film develops in close synchrony with Sophocles' fifth-century B.C.E. tragic drama *Oedipus Rex* and follows guidelines for tragedy set out by Aristotle in his fourth-century B.C.E. *Poetics*. Next, Erik Grayson ("Walter M. Miller, Jr.'s *A Canticle for Leibowitz*, the Great Year, and the Ages of Man") considers the cyclical nature of history in Miller's novel (1960), arguing that Miller's depiction of future ambivalence towards the "Ancients" figures contemporary ambivalence towards the classical tradition as a source of profound inspiration and as a cautionary tale about humanity's penchant for self-destructive surfeits. Joel P. Christensen ("Time and Self-Referentiality in the *Iliad* and Frank Herbert's *Dune*") discusses narrative and thematic characteristics shared by Homer's epic and Herbert's novel (1965), examining how those two "epics" raise questions about the relationship between "history" and the narrated tale, as well as self-reflexive knowledge of the power of myth and the dangers of storytelling. In a similar vein, Rebecca Raphael ("Disability as Rhetorical Trope in Classical Myth and *Blade Runner*") explores disability and hyper-ability in classical myths about artificial life forms, then sets them in dialogue with Philip K. Dick's novel *Do Androids Dream of Electric Sheep?* (1968) and its influential film adaptation (1982).

Parts I and II operate in dialogue. In Part II we see fewer moments of source criticism *per se*—fewer self-conscious classical quotations, allusions, and verbal echoes—than we did in the chapters of Swinford, Weiner, Stevens, and Keen. As SF emerges as a recognizable genre, the direct evocation of the classical past seems to fall away in many "SF classics." Nevertheless, Bucher and Grayson uncover compelling cultural histories and the surprising persistence in SF of particular classical epistemologies: how Aristotle shapes our ideas about how to produce drama; how Hesiod and Ovid shape our thinking about time. In contrast, the studies of Christensen and Raphael do not claim that particular classical texts or epistemologies have "influenced" the SF texts they examine. Instead, these latter chapters, in identifying generic features or tropes appearing in both ancient and SF texts, gesture towards the identification of a kind of transcultural poetics and demonstrate the revelatory potential for readers that can come from setting these texts in dialogue. That such a pattern emerges in the first half of this volume should not be taken to mean that certain methodologies apply neatly to particular eras in the history of SF. Indeed, the chapters in Parts III and IV emphasize a productive interplay of methodologies: source criticism, cultural history, transhistorical poetics, and more.

Part III ("Classics in Space") opens with a chapter by George Kovacs ("Moral and Mortal in *Star Trek: The Original Series*" [*TOS*]) that boldly explores Greek myth in several episodes of *Star Trek* (1966–1969), examining in particular a repeated link between longevity/immortality and emotional or moral immaturity. Kovacs argues that this establishes a continuity between the viewer's past and present and *TOS*'s humanist, utopic future, authorizing allegorical and didactic readings of the show. Next, Brett M. Rogers ("Hybrids and Homecomings in the *Odyssey* and *Alien Resurrection*") glosses the notion of an "odyssey" as a thought experiment about the nature of the human in the context of "homecoming." Reading Homer's *Odyssey* alongside the film *Alien Resurrection* (1997), Rogers suggests that the film's dramatization of the ethical implications of its protagonist's hybrid nature sheds valuable light on Odysseus' actions and indeed his "humanity." Finally, Vincent Tomasso ("Classical Antiquity and Western Identity in *Battlestar Galactica*") considers evocations of ancient Greek religion in the television series *Battlestar Galactica* (2003–2009 [BSG]), arguing that they raise unanswered questions about "tradition" and "progress." In Tomasso's view, *BSG* proposes a hybridity that resists dichotomization; the classical tradition is not so much irrational as non-rational, a central part of humanity's past, present, and future, and an important alternative to the destructive potential embodied by science.

Together, the chapters in Part III suggest that such topics as the breakdown of boundaries, utopias and dystopias in society, and hybridities in the human body and indeed in "humanity" are not only "science fictional" but are equally of interest in certain ancient classics. The chapters in Part IV ("Ancient Classics for a Future Generation?") round out the volume's emphasis on links between those seemingly disparate worlds by suggesting that a theme of great importance in modern SF is the capacity of other worlds, whether future, past, or simply alternative, to serve as thought experiments about important or contentious aspects of this world.

Gaël Grobéty ("Revised Iliadic Epiphanies in Dan Simmons's *Ilium*") thus explores the politics of "epiphany" by considering how Simmons's novel (2003) retells Athena's appearance to Achilles in Homer's *Iliad*. With an ancient supernatural sort of epiphany replaced by a modern (SF) technological type, modern SF like Simmons's emphasizes the epistemological uncertainties of the human mind and the related desire to be rid of tyrannical powers. A similar politics of tyranny and liberation informs Marian Makins's chapter ("Refiguring the Roman Empire in *The Hunger Games* Trilogy"). Makins locates Suzanne Collins's vision (2008–2010) of a tyrannical future America in a tradition of negative depictions of Imperial Rome, arguing that Collins, by recalling satires by writers like Petronius, Tacitus, and Juvenal, hints at the darkness surrounding such seemingly innocent entertainment as "reality television." Finally, C. W. Marshall ("Jonathan Hickman's *Pax Romana* and the End of Antiquity") treats a different modern vision of Imperial Rome in the form of a comic in which the Catholic Church sends soldiers back in time to help Emperor Constantine and Christianity "win" a perceived centuries-long war against paganism. Marshall argues that, once the relevant history is changed, the reader is presented with a world that never left antiquity. It may thus be argued that much of what we think we know about antiquity depends less on "fact" than on an overwhelming cultural continuity, an epistemology or *episteme*.

Marshall's particular epistemological point usefully serves to raise questions generally applicable to the volume's collected work. In concert, the chapters in this part and in the volume as a whole thus position us to ask: What is "antiquity," truly, and how does its definition depend on the intervention of the Middle Ages and subsequent history? Without those particular receptions, how would "antiquity" seem to be shaped? In particular, the question raised by this volume is: How do classical receptions in SF work to reconstitute antiquity, or to do away with it? Do classical receptions in SF function like matter transporters, reconstituting materials from antiquity in a new place and time? Or are they rather like disintegrators, scattering the "atoms" of ancient materials irrevocably? Each chapter presented herein represents a particular approach to answering those urgent questions, and it is our hope that all of them together prove as inspiring to the volume's readers as they have to us. *Ad astra per antiqua!*

Part I

SF's Rosy-Fingered Dawn

translation of the *De Facie* and his intention that the translation be included with the *Somnium* in its final printed form. As far as the content of *De Facie* is concerned, Kepler seems most influenced by Plutarch's treatment of the moon as a material object, even as he, like Plutarch, maintains a belief that the moon holds significant spiritual properties.

As one of the chief proponents of Copernicanism, Kepler has done much to transform thought regarding the position of humanity in an essentially material universe. His *Somnium*, however, reveals that the astronomer himself was never fully able to replace the mythical moon with the scientific moon. The degree to which these two moons coexist in the *Somnium* demonstrates the work's importance in the process by which SF came into being in the seventeenth century. (Here, "SF" indicates a genre that uses narrative in the service of scientific speculation.) That a story written about the moon by an astronomer with mystical tendencies should be regarded as the first work of SF is no surprise, given the imaginative pull of the moon for writers of all eras. As SF author and critic Brian W. Aldiss writes, "The Moon has been the most powerful of symbols over the ages: as it has drawn the ocean's tides about the Earth, so it has attracted the ambition to travel upwards towards the closest astronomical body."[3]

To make the argument for the scientific and literary ramifications of Plutarch's influence on Kepler and, by extension, SF, this chapter begins with an overview of the *Somnium* that contextualizes its composition in relation to the development of Kepler's career. This section is followed by an examination of the *Somnium*'s position in the history of SF. Kepler's representation of a populated moon establishes a significant legacy for SF; his appropriation of classical sources, in turn, helps position the *Somnium* as a missing link between classical and modern modes of speculative fiction. The final two sections of the chapter turn to Plutarch's *De Facie*. The first of these presents Plutarch's advocacy for the materiality of the moon. The final section assesses the impact of Plutarch's idea that the moon is an object on Kepler's choice of the moon as a narrative setting.

The main point made here regarding classical influence is that Kepler appropriates not just a narrative motif but also a scientific idea. In fact, the motif of cosmic ascent comes from the corresponding principle that

---

[3] Aldiss (1995: 150).

a material body serves as the endpoint of such an ascent. The importance of this claim for the study of the history of SF is that the development of the genre is not a linear progression from uninformed fantasy to factually informed speculation. Instead, the influence of literary precursors can be conceptual as well as structural. Kepler recognizes in Plutarch a writer who matters for his ideas as well as for the way he presents these ideas.

THE FORM OF THE *SOMNIUM*

The *Somnium* encompasses the breadth of Kepler's development in its content and constituent components. It is a relatively minor piece, especially when compared to the achievements of the *Astronomia Nova* (1609) and *Harmonice Mundi* (1619). Unlike these works, the *Somnium* has the distinction of resting in some form on Kepler's desk, or at least in his thoughts, for much of his life. He started it in 1593 and added material to it over the course of his life; he corrected the proofs of a printed version a month before his death in 1630. As for the initial idea of a moon-centered universe, Kepler wrote a disputation—what we might call an argumentative or expository essay—on the topic in 1593 as a student in Tübingen, Germany.[4] In the introduction to his translation of the *Somnium*, science historian Edward Rosen formulates the prompt on which this early essay was based, as follows: "How would the phenomena occurring in the heavens appear to an observer stationed on the moon?"[5] While no known draft of this essay exists, we do know that Kepler wrote the essay to stimulate argument on Copernicanism and, specifically, "Copernicus's idea that the earth moves very rapidly, rotating and revolving around the sun, but the people living on the earth cannot see or feel this."[6] Despite his enthusiasm for the subject, Kepler

---

[4] Rosen (1967: xx). In this early version, Kepler intended to demonstrate the validity of Copernicus's theory of heliocentrism. Kepler became intrigued by the Copernican theory through the tutelage of Michael Mästlin, a well-known astronomer of the time. Kepler knew of the theory through Mästlin's lectures, but had not actually read Copernicus at that point. See Westman (1975) for a discussion of Mästlin's intellectual background and approach.

[5] Rosen (1967: xvii).

[6] Connor (2005: 67).

ultimately refrained from presenting the piece, due to the hostile reaction of his teacher, Veit Müller.[7]

The central question driving the disputation led to the next development in Kepler's composition, an enhanced description of the habits and characteristics of the moon's inhabitants. He completed this feature of the work in 1609 during his time in Prague as the royal astronomer to Emperor Rudolph II. Instead of merely explaining the viewpoint of a lunar observer from a purely expository standpoint, Kepler added a narrative frame of himself dreaming, as a clever way to incite discussion among his colleagues. He composed an extensive series of 223 explanatory footnotes between 1622 and 1630, primarily as a way to counter personal issues, including the imprisonment for witchcraft of his mother, Katherine Kepler, by accusers who used a version of the *Somnium* as support for their contentions of her necromantic proclivities.[8]

The overall structure of the *Somnium* reflects its various stages of composition. The narrative consists of at least four interlocking frames: in the first, the narrator, presumably Kepler, falls into a deep sleep after watching the stars and the moon. Next, the sleeping Kepler finds, and begins reading, a book written by an astronomer named Duracotus. Within the book, Duracotus provides the speech of a daemon capable of traveling between earth and the moon. Over a hundred pages of explanatory footnotes constitute the outermost frame, and, as they account for the majority of the work, they "spare no explanation— physical, geometrical, optical, geographical, mythographical, psychological, philological, literary—concerning the life of Duracotus and the Daemon's marvelous sermon."[9] The footnotes permeate the text to such

---

[7] As Connor (2005) explains, "Müller hated Copernicus's ideas and would not listen, nor would he let the thesis be heard" (67).

[8] The ramifications of the early distribution of a version of the *Somnium* have both positive and negative components; the most negative is clearly Katherine Kepler's imprisonment. As Aaron Parrett points out, the distribution of a pirated version of Kepler's working copy had the additional positive effect of "influencing and inspiring . . . Bishop Godwin, John Donne, and other writers of lunar travels." See Parrett (2004: 39).

[9] Paxson (2001: 140). Paxson's essay deals with the difficulty of counting or distinguishing frames in this heavily embedded narrative. The obsessive length of these notes invariably captures the attention of critics, who seem to sense that, in Kepler's use, Anthony Grafton's assertion that the footnote is always defensive has been taken to an unprecedented extreme. Aldiss (1995), for example, writes that "Kepler's notes . . . are much longer than his story [which] occupies eighteen pages [while] the Notes occupy almost one hundred and twenty pages" (151), while Parrett (2004) says that the "add[ed]

an extent that they cannot be excised from the narrative itself. In addition, Kepler's use of the first person throughout the notes as well as in the beginning section of the narrative serves to connect these frames. As William Poole observes, the narrating voices "are all bound together by the voice of the *notator*, who speaks as the biographical Kepler."[10] This intermingling of voices joins the various levels of the text so that they operate in a recursive, rather than hierarchical, fashion.

As the *Somnium* opens, Kepler provides some background on events surrounding the act of dreaming. The first sentence locates the night of the dream in 1608, a time significant because of "a heated quarrel between the Emperor Rudolph and his brother, the Archduke Mathias" (11). Kepler's time in Prague was relatively peaceful when compared to his residence in other cities; he was not, for example, persecuted because of his religious faith (Lutheran, as distinct from prevailing Catholicism and Utraquism). The patronage of Emperor Rudolph II explains Kepler's religious and intellectual freedom while in Prague, since the emperor fostered the arts and sciences during his reign. The political threats faced by the emperor, then, had a direct bearing on the conditions under which Kepler completed his work. That Kepler and fellow astronomer Tycho Brahe valued this patronage is most directly evidenced by Kepler's publication of data collected by the two during their time in Prague, as the "Rudolphine Tables."[11] Despite the emperor's support of scientific research, however, "the imperial throne did not radiate bright resplendence." The emperor's interest in science can be attributed, according to authoritative Kepler biographer Max Caspar, to "a sick soul's capricious zeal for compiling."[12] While the emperor contributed to the development of the new astronomy by housing Kepler and Brahe in Prague, "it is obvious that [. . .] state affairs must have suffered" as a result of Rudolph's excessive interest not only in astronomy, but in the related work of

---

notes [are] so copious that in the end the commentary [is] almost ten times longer than the narrative proper" (39).

[10] Poole (2010: 66).

[11] Connor (2005: 124). As Parrett (2004) observes, Kepler's partnership with Brahe and use of data contributed significantly to Kepler's successes: "It was access to Brahe's previously unmatched and immense collection of precise data about the paths of the planets through the sky that enabled Kepler to make his own great contributions to the new astronomy" (39).

[12] Caspar (1993: 149).

"wizards, alkymists, Kabbalists, and the like."[13] Matthias seized control of the state at least partly as a result of the emperor's steady retreat to "the labyrinth of his *Kunstkammer*, his personal imperial museum."[14]

The narrator takes a great interest in the political controversy surrounding this escalating conflict and, in seeking solace from the instability he sees in the future, turns to the past by "reading about Bohemia" (*Somnium* 11). In his reading, he comes upon "the story of the heroine Libussa, renowned for her skill in magic," a subject that sets the stage for the mystical character of the prophetic dream that follows and testifies to the correspondences between the work's narrative layers; the powers of the legendary Libussa in this exterior frame find expression in the magical prowess of characters encountered in the next (11).

After falling asleep, the narrator dreams that he is walking through a market in Frankfurt. There he purchases a book detailing the life of Duracotus, the fictional Icelandic astronomer who serves as a kind of narrative double for Kepler. Indeed, as Parrett points out, motifs such as narrative doubling and the oneiric reading of an imagined book "plunge . . . us into an almost Borgesian reading adventure."[15] The story of Duracotus and his path towards becoming an astronomer parallels Kepler's own and is replete with persecution, mysticism, and, of course, the pursuit of truth through astronomy. Like Kepler, Duracotus works with Tycho Brahe, the real astronomer who maintains such a pull on historians because he sounds so much like a fictional character.[16] Duracotus studies on Hven, the Danish island where Brahe maintained an observatory and headed an energetic and, at times, tumultuous household made up of family, servants, and students of astronomy. After his years of study under Brahe, Duracotus returns to Iceland. Upon returning home, he is reunited with his mother, Fiolxhilde, a wise woman equal to Brahe in her knowledge of the cosmos. A witch, Fiolxhilde has learned about astronomy through her ability to

---

[13] Ibid. (150).

[14] Connor (2005: 159).

[15] Parrett (2004: 40). (Fictional) Icelandic scholarship and a dreamlike experience of scientific discovery figure prominently in Jules Verne's *Journey to the Center of the Earth*; see Stevens (this volume, chapter three).

[16] By the time of Kepler's association with Brahe in Prague, Brahe "had fallen out with his Danish royal patrons, [and] left Hven": Lear (1965: 24). For a fascinating recent study of his larger-than-life qualities, presented as part of a case to prove that Kepler actually murdered Brahe in order to steal his data, see Gilder and Gilder (2004).

communicate with the daemons of the moon, or "Levania," through magical ritual. Eager to expose her newly returned son to the secrets of the moon, Fiolxhilde guides Duracotus through a ritual that summons a lunar daemon. Once invoked, this daemon lectures on a variety of subjects that range from the geography and biology of the moon, through the processes necessary to travel between earth and the moon, to the contrasting perspectives of the universe provided by Levania and earth, which the inhabitants of the moon call "Volva." The daemon's speech ends abruptly as a severe storm breaks through Kepler's bedroom window and rouses him from his dream.

SIGNIFICANCE FOR SF

That the *Somnium* is "the first work of science fiction in the modern sense," as Arthur Koestler contends in *The Sleepwalkers: A History of Man's Changing Vision of the Universe*, has become a commonplace in studies of the historical roots of the genre.[17] Critics point to several of its components to explain exactly why it occupies this position. Darko Suvin suggests that the events surrounding its composition and eventual publication—Veit Müller's unwillingness even to entertain the idea behind the 1593 disputation, the troubles that befell Kepler's mother, the fact that it was not officially published until after Kepler's death—are symptomatic of its status as SF, which he describes as an "often materially and most always ideologically persecuted tradition."[18] The elements within the text that draw the greatest attention have to do with its scientific content and its description of lunar inhabitants. First, it uses a fictional frame to make a point about the specifics of astronomy. In the most general sense, some critics value the work because it is fiction used to explain science: "Kepler's text is formally fictional, but it also participates in contemporary astronomical speculation. Science-fiction, then, if heavy on the science."[19] In response to its scientific focus, Parrett goes as far as to term it "a techno-novel."[20]

---

[17] Koestler (1959: 421).
[18] Suvin (1979: 87).
[19] Poole (2010: 65).
[20] Parrett (2004: 40).

Of greater importance is Kepler's representation of an inhabited moon. Everett Franklin Bleiler contends that, of its elements, the daemons' depiction of lunar geography is central to the work's position in the history of SF.[21] Brake and Hook see the representation of inhabited worlds beyond earth as central to any classification of the *Somnium* as SF: "Kepler was a pioneer of the new vision of deep space as the home of a plurality of inhabited worlds. There is no greater testament to the power and imaginative sway of science fiction than this."[22] Wyn Wachhorst argues that this device animates the lunar narratives that followed, to the extent that "Kepler's notion of a world in the moon prompted fables of escape to simpler but superior peoples on other planets."[23] Brian W. Aldiss concurs that Kepler's descriptions of lunar inhabitants established a legacy for the genre that continues into the present: "And from Kepler's way of populating his planet with plausible aliens—at least plausible in their day—we hardly deviate to this day."[24] Brian Stableford goes as far as to present this feature of the *Somnium*, not just as a crucial starting point for SF in general, but also for a significant subgenre, evolutionary fantasy.[25]

Such estimations of the work's importance are not intended to indicate that the *Somnium* is the first work to ever deal with such themes, however. While the *Somnium* may be said to inaugurate SF as a modern genre, it is clearly indebted to a classical tradition that employs many of the same tropes that Kepler bends to his scientific thesis, including fictional travel to the fantastic islands of the Western seas and that one "island" floating above the sea, the moon. Kepler makes no secret of the fact that two classical texts in particular, Plutarch's *De Facie* and Lucian's *True History*, contributed to the literary devices and tropes he employs.[26]

---

[21] Bleiler (1990: 404).

[22] Brake and Hook (2008: 11).

[23] Wachhorst (1996: 116). From a generic standpoint, then, the *Somnium* is more than SF. It is also, for Patrick Parrinder (2001), an example of a literary utopia: "Kepler's and Campanella's inhabited moons are utopias by [Ernst Bloch's] definition" that a utopia is a thought experiment that "is always elsewhere and which functions as a critique of what is present" (8).

[24] Aldiss (1995: 151).

[25] Stableford (2005: 106).

[26] Of these, Christianson recognizes Plutarch as the "more important source of inspiration" of the two: Christianson (1976: par. 20); Chen-Morris (2005) attributes this added relevance of Plutarch to Kepler's attraction to "speculative myths that point beyond rational scientific procedures" (225).

To this end, critics such as Roger Bozzetto concur that the *Somnium* occupies an important position in the history of SF, but add that it should be regarded more as a missing link between the classical and modern, and less as a proto-SF text that emerged *ex nihilo*. Thus, while Bozzetto contends that the lunar dream "seems to me the first representative of that which is a 'primitive' science fiction and also 'hard science fiction,'" he adds the important caveat that because of Kepler's clear influence by the classical tradition, the *Somnium* "constitutes a 'missing link'" in a continuum stretching from the second century c.e. to the present.[27] Marjorie Hope Nicolson draws a similar conclusion in *Voyages to the Moon*, which plays a significant role in the modern reception of the *Somnium* as a result of Nicolson's argument that this obscure work exerted a considerable influence on canonical British writers such as John Donne, Thomas More, and John Milton. Importantly, Nicolson contends that the multimodal and multigeneric qualities of Kepler's writing produce a fusion of the supernatural and the scientific that reveals the lunar dream to be "a chief source of cosmic voyages for three centuries" as well as the descendant of a long and established tradition of speculative writing in classical and medieval literature.[28]

Kepler's use of elements taken from classical sources contributes to the *Somnium*'s scientific utility and imaginative evocation of life beyond earth. Scientifically and imaginatively, Kepler's treatment of the moon as a setting reveals a clear classical influence, as well as a figurative flight beyond the bounds of these classical precursors. The lunar voyage marks a shift in the imaginable features of a possible world inhabited by the characters of speculative fiction and the language used in descriptions both scientific and imaginative. Remarking on the significance of the new astronomy for the development of SF, Darko Suvin points out that these scientific developments influenced fantastic narratives and precipitated their subversiveness: "Expelled once again from official culture, significant SF shifted from utopian seas to the planets, which were the forefront of attention after Copernicus and Galileo."[29] The sociopolitical context of the *Somnium*'s publication, then, has a direct bearing on Kepler's appropriation of the narrative elements of his classical precursors. Kepler's

[27] Bozzetto (2000); translations mine. See also Bozzetto (1992).
[28] Nicolson (1948: 41).
[29] Suvin (1979: 103).

indirect defense of heliocentrism through a narrative rooted deeply in the classical philosophical tradition, paired with his desire to join the *De Facie* and *Somnium* in a single book, operates on one level as a defense mechanism designed to insulate him from an indictment of his ideas.[30] While this may have been the most practical purpose for his use of Plutarch, it had the added result of creating an example of a quintessentially modern genre from materials found in that least modern of genres, the classical philosophical dialogue.[31]

THE MOON IS AN OBJECT

Critics who identify the *Somnium* as a missing link between a classical tradition of speculative writing informed by myth and a nascent modern genre that uses narrative to explain and explore scientific concepts are supported by Kepler's stated influences and objectives for the work. Kepler clearly reveals that his reading of Plutarch's *De Facie* and Lucian's *True History* have contributed to the literary devices and tropes he employs. The pull of Plutarch's work is especially powerful, as Kepler observes in one of the *Somnium*'s explanatory footnotes that he is "exceedingly amazed and keep[s] wondering by what chance it happened that our dreams or fables coincided so closely" (32). The device of the dream voyage in the final version of the *Somnium* derives from Kepler's reading of these two writers; in addition, Kepler believes that the initial idea to describe the viewpoint of observers on the moon, which he imagined before reading Plutarch, connects him in some mystical or spiritual way to his classical forebear. Significantly, his use of the moon as a setting and his recognition that the moon is a physical object, like the earth, come from the influence of Plutarch. Thus, Kepler's appropriation of Plutarch is particularly important for the development of SF, in that a key scientific premise of the work, as well as a central narrative motif, come from a classical source.

[30] Parrett (2004: 37–38).
[31] So, while Kepler did the most to encourage acceptance of Copernicanism, as Thomas Kuhn argues, he did so at a time of increasing political and religious resistance to the idea—hence the need for the indirect approach offered by narrative. See Kuhn (1996: 111–136).

His intention to include a translation of Plutarch's *De Facie* in the completed, published version of the *Somnium* was a deliberate move to position his work as a continuation and refinement of the scientifically minded ideas and concerns expressed in the *De Facie*. The weight of Plutarch's *De Facie* on the new astronomy is, however, not specific to Kepler. Copernicus, too, was influenced by Plutarch and was aware that his "revolutionary" idea was, in fact, a rediscovery: "Copernicus indicated his awareness of the source of his idea when he stated in the introduction to *De Revolutionibus* that he had found initially in Cicero that Nicetas thought the earth moved, and later he had discovered through Plutarch that there were others who held the same opinion."[32] It could be said that the *De Facie* provides a bridge between the classical and early modern periods through its role as a repository, or time capsule, of the many ideas regarding the moon that were held by classical thinkers.

In response to any suggestion that Plutarch is speaking in the language of myth and not science, Kepler remarks in his Latin translation of the *De Facie* that Plutarch "could hardly have written in this way merely from an unfettered imagination" (*Somnium* 31n.). This sentiment differs from the reaction any reader could reasonably have to Lucian's *True History* (*VH*), which states quite directly that "nothing I say is true. Moreover, I am writing about things which I have neither seen nor felt nor heard from others" (4), though Kepler claims that this "highly daring tale" also "offered some intimations concerning the nature of the entire universe" (*Somnium* 32–33n.). This enthusiasm may have resulted from Kepler's rationale for reading these works in the first place. Kepler used a German translation of Lucian's *True History* when he was at Tübingen to help him master Greek; as Lear suggests, this may have been part of a deliberate course of action, after Müller's rejection of Kepler's initial thesis, "to discover precedents for his thinking in classic Greek literature that were acceptable to Aristotelians."[33] While Lucian "didn't make the slightest bit of sense scientifically," Kepler's reading of the work gave him the "linguistic confidence to tackle the original Greek text of Plutarch's *The Face on the Moon*."[34]

[32] Eurich (1967: 104).
[33] Lear (1965: 42); *Somnium* 32n.
[34] Lear (1965: 43).

The *De Facie* takes the form of a philosophical dialogue among a number of different characters. These characters introduce and discuss the possibility of various opinions about the moon, ranging from the possibility that the moon's surface is a face, to the idea that the moon is a mirror that reflects the sea. Moreover, Plutarch connects individual characters to schools of thought. The narrator, Lamprias, affirms the claim that the moon is, like the earth, a body composed of a physical substance. The third speaker, Apollonides, is an expert in geometry, while another speaker, Pharnaces, represents Stoic ideas. After the formal dialogue ends, the speakers listen to Sulla recount a myth of the island of Cronus in the Western seas. The topics of the conversation are clearly rooted in the particulars of competing philosophical schools contemporaneous with Plutarch, allowing the text to serve as a kind of summa of classical astronomical theory. That the work exerted such a strong pull on Copernicus and Kepler should come as no surprise. Summing up its significance for the new astronomy, James Attlee sees the conversation among Plutarch's characters—that "the moon is composed of glass or ice and that the light of heaven shines through it, making the moon a lens and moonlight the projected illumination of another world"—as particularly prescient in that it seems to prefigure the science of optics and the revolution in astronomy precipitated by an important concrete application of this science, the telescope.[35] Attlee's point about the move from the conceptual to the practical inspired in Kepler by Plutarch is equally applicable to the dialogue's representation of the physicality of the moon as an object that can be understood through observation.

The overall importance of this idea in relation to the many thoughts about the moon expressed by the dialogue's participants corresponds to the key role held by Lamprias, its greatest champion, as the narrator who steers the course of the conversation. Though Attlee's claim is an intriguing one for its evocation of the long-lasting poetic power of the *De Facie*, the dialogue has as its primary purpose the representation of the moon as something quite mundane. Throughout, Lamprias defends those "who declare that the moon is not a tenuous or smooth body as water is but a heavy and earthy one" against arguments that the moon must exist as a kind of cosmic mirror (Plutarch, *Moralia* [*Mor.*] 936E).[36] Rather

---

[35] Attlee (2011: 14–15).
[36] Translations of *De Facie* come from Cherniss and Helmbold (1957).

than a star or celestial mirror, the moon is an object like the earth, and "this which appears to be her face, just as our earth has certain great gulfs, so that earth yawns with great depths and clefts" (935C).

Like Lamprias, another speaker, Lucius, objects to classification of the moon as anything other than a planetoid or planet like the earth: "regarded as earth the moon has the aspect of a very beautiful, august, and elegant object; but as a star or luminary or a divine and heavenly object she is, I am afraid, misshapen, ugly, and a disgrace to the noble title" (*Mor.* 929A). Lamprias praises Lucius for his logical defense of the moon's materiality, saying "congratulations upon having added to an elegant account an elegant proportion" (931D) after Lucius explains that the moon must be like the earth because the light from the sun affects them in similar ways: "the things upon which the same agent produces the same effects must be of a similar nature" (931C). When Pharnaces disputes Lucius' claims for the moon's materiality, and says, rather, "that this very point above all proves the moon to be a star or fire" (933F) Lamprias quickly intervenes: "This . . . is the objection of one who speaks . . . to the name rather than like a natural scientist and mathematician to the fact" (934A).

The connection of a scientific idea to the narrative trope of lunar inhabitants that Kepler uses to such great effect in the *Somnium* is presaged most directly by this point in the *De Facie*. Lamprias offers a clear and authoritative defense of the physical features of the moon as the constitutive components of the moon's face. The primary issue of the dialogue solved, Lamprias then proposes a formal end to the dialogue and a transition to Sulla's narrative, which he describes as a pleasurable reward for the intellectual labor just undertaken and "the agreed condition upon which he was admitted as a listener" (*Mor.* 937C). After the "official" end of the dialogue and before Sulla's narrative begins, the speakers broach one last subject, the inhabitability of the moon, at the urging of Theon, who announces that "I should like . . . to hear about the beings that are said to dwell on the moon—not whether any really do inhabit it but whether habitation there is possible" (937D).

This subject follows naturally from the dialogue's conclusion that the moon is like the earth. As Theon explains, "if it is not possible, the assertion that the moon is an earth is itself absurd" based on the premise that all created things must have some discernible purpose (*Mor.* 937D). But, as Lamprias points out after Theon rehearses possible objections to the idea that the moon is inhabited, "nothing that has been said proves impossible the alleged inhabitation of the moon" (938F). Instead, Lamprias emphasizes the fundamental distinctions between actual life on earth and possible life on the moon. While the moon is made of a substance like the earth, it is also a very different place. To that end, what counts as life on the moon may not look familiar to earthbound observers. Summing up this line of reasoning, Lamprias clarifies:

[T]hose who demand that living beings there be equipped just as those here are for generation, nourishment, and livelihood seem blind to the diversities of nature, among which one can discover more and greater differences and dissimilarities between living beings than between them and inanimate objects. (940B)

To bring the speculation back to earth, Lamprias adds that the "multifarious shapes" of an ocean "full of beasts" exist, but can just as easily be construed by those unfamiliar with the sea as the things "of myths and marvels" (940E).

While the insistence that the moon is a body does not seem particularly revolutionary to modern readers, the importance of this claim in its historical context cannot be overstated. Kepler emphasizes the moon's materiality elsewhere in his writing, and full acceptance of its truth can be seen as a precondition for acceptance of the revolutionary decentering of the earth necessitated by Copernicanism. In the *Cosmic Mystery*, "Kepler . . . repeated Mästlin's teaching that the earth and the moon were made of similar stuff."[37] In his *Optics* as well, Kepler speaks to the importance of this point: "Therefore, the peripatetics should stop being angry at Plutarch because he dragged the earth up into the heavens, that is, gave it out that the moon's body is earthlike."[38] He disparages the "peripatetics," or Aristotelian thinkers in antiquity who opposed Plutarch, in order to align himself with Plutarch against the Aristotelian thinkers of his own day. He translated Plutarch as a way to secure rhetorical ammunition against his Aristotelian opponents. Kepler views his work as an extension of Plutarch's in that he, like Plutarch, seeks to counter those who, in accordance with Aristotle's teaching, view the universe as "a nature pure and undefiled and free from qualitative change" (*Mor.* 928F).

[37] Lear (1965: 6).
[38] Donahue (2000: 267).

The doctrine of the immutability of the heavens that Plutarch disputes in the *De Facie* is the same idea that inhibited acceptance of Copernicanism.

THE MOON IS A SETTING

Kepler's appropriation of Plutarch's logic has a direct bearing on the narrative features of the *Somnium*. To the extent that the moon is a physical body, it is also a place that can be inhabited. If the moon can be inhabited, it can serve as a setting. Moreover, it can serve as a setting for those who watch the earth, a SF motif that persists in a number of forms, including the character Uatu the Watcher in the Marvel universe. The lunar world of the *Somnium*, while clearly a product of Kepler's imagination, follows from his physical observations. In describing the moon, he notes that it "consists of two hemispheres. One of these, the Subvolva, always enjoys its Volva, which among them takes the place of our moon. The other one, the Privolva, is deprived forever of the sight of Volva" (*Somnium* 17). In this statement, Kepler describes and names the two sides of the moon based on their position in relation to the earth. The dark side of the moon, the Privolva, never faces the earth, while the true face of the moon (Subvolva) always looks at the earth. The moon that is renamed and described in this speech within a book within a dream maintains the physical characteristics and motion of the actual moon, though it is encountered at several removes from external reality. The dream moon, then, follows the same orbit as the actual moon, and this orbit is described in accordance with the moon as it appears to earth-dwellers.

Like Lamprias and Lucius in the *De Facie*, Kepler emphasizes the mountains and other natural land formations visible on the Subvolvar hemisphere. The "serpentine" creatures of the moon use the caves, valleys, and shadows produced by the high mountains as protection from the elements (*Somnium* 28). In the "Geographical or, if you prefer, Selenographical Appendix" to the *Somnium*, Kepler elaborates on his suggestion in the *Somnium* itself that "the Subvolvan hemisphere is comparable to our cantons, towns, and gardens," and presents the moon's clearly observable features as cities: "Those lunar hollows, first noticed by Galileo, chiefly mark the moonspots. . . . And in them the moon-dwellers usually measure out the areas of their towns" (28, 151). He ends this appendix by reminding readers "these are playful remarks"

(152). The credit he gives to Galileo for first observing and describing these lunar features shows that his fantastical depiction of lunar cities takes empirical observation as its starting point.

In some ways, Kepler simply affirms and playfully embellishes a point that Plutarch arrives at through logic and that Galileo's championing of the telescope made provable through direct observation. Kepler initially turned his disputation of 1593 into a narrative between 1609 and 1610, a time when he also composed and published *Dissertatio cum Nuncio Sidereo*, his response to Galileo's revolutionary *Sidereus Nuncius*. In the history of science, Galileo's sketches of the moon and publication of *Sidereus Nuncius* served as harbingers of an emergent modernity. Galileo's work enabled a transformation in consciousness regarding the moon that was so powerful that it constituted, in the words of Mark Brake and Neil Hook, "the first time the Moon becomes a real object for us."[39] Modern-day fabulist Italo Calvino, who lauds Galileo's prowess as a writer as well as a scientist, says something similar about Galileo's account of the moon, and uses equally universal language to evoke its transformative impact: "When I read Galileo I like to seek out the passages in which he speaks of the moon. It is the first time that the moon becomes a real object for mankind, and it is minutely described as a tangible thing."[40] For Kepler, Galileo's emphasis on physical observation as enabled by the telescope afforded the opportunity to overlook the "*mundo chartaceo*," by which he means the limited perspective offered by an Aristotelian "world of paper" that inhibited acceptance of Copernicanism.[41]

While he gives credit to Galileo for providing observations that affirmed the existence of mountains on the moon, Kepler also clearly points out that his belief in these features of the lunar landscape "is older than the Dutch telescope" and, in fact, should be "ascribe[d] . . . entirely to Mästlin, my teacher in astronomy," who first introduced him to Plutarch's *De Facie* (both quotations from *Somnium* 125).[42] In his treatment of this subject in the *Optics* (1604), Kepler attributes his understanding of the moon's landscape directly to Plutarch, who

---

[39] Brake and Hook (2008: 13).

[40] Calvino (1997: 31).

[41] Hofstadter (2009: 53).

[42] In his conversation with Galileo, though, he says that "In order to prove th[e] proposition [that the mountains on the moon are taller than those on earth], your telescope was needed and your observational skill"; Lear (1965: 31).

"correctly said [that the moon is] a body as the earth is, uneven and mountainous."[43]

Kepler's willingness to credit Plutarch wholeheartedly and Galileo only with reservations should come as no surprise, given the very real differences separating these two proponents of the *nova astronomia*. Galileo took umbrage with Kepler's observations regarding the moon, particularly his theory that it influenced the tides on earth.[44] In his *Dialogue*, Galileo only recognizes Kepler in order to ridicule the astronomer's suggestion that the moon affects the tides. Galileo derides Kepler's endorsement of the idea of "the moon's domination over the water" as a wrong-minded attribution of "occult properties" to the moon that should be avoided by anyone "whose mind [is] free and acute."[45]

Kepler's obsession with the moon struck Galileo as overly mystical, leading him to discount Kepler even though Kepler's mysticism led him to empirical truth. In explaining the lunar influence of tides, Kepler notes that "The moon is a body akin to the earth," a conclusion that enables him in his *Commentaries on the Motions of the Planet Mars* to postulate the attractive power exerted by the moon on the water in the seas. This formulation seems to come directly from Plutarch. In the *Somnium*, Kepler also explains this process, but, in keeping with the conceit of the allegory, refers to the "daemons" as agents that facilitate the influence of the moon on the water. Thus, "if the daemons . . . undertake their work when the moon is favorable, its presence in the shadow will aid their efforts with the magnetic pull of a kindred body" (*Somnium* 70).[46] His explanation of this concept suggests both the gravity (which he defines as "a force of mutual attraction, similar to magnetic attraction") of the moon and an alternate, but equally significant, mystical force aligned with the moon (71). This explanation likewise affirms Neoplatonist theories stressing the existence of planetary souls, while also pointing to the proliferation of meanings enabled by the allegorical

[43] Donahue (2000: 262).

[44] As Rosen points out, "Kepler's discovery of the process by which the moon's attraction helps to cause the tides was not accepted by Galileo" (1967: 69n).

[45] Finocchiaro (1997: 304).

[46] Kepler also believed that the earth "breathes," and that this, in addition to the pull of the moon, causes the tides: "the earth adjusts its breathing, as it were, to the motion of the sun and moon, just as the times when the animals are asleep and awake by turns coincide with night and day" (*Somnium* 70n).

form of the text—the form of Kepler's explanations allows him to suggest the complex and harmonic interplay of physical phenomena and spiritual forces at work in a single eclipse or wave.

For Kepler, then, the moon is a planet with an atmosphere, as James Gunn explains, but it is also something more, a spiritual body that exerts its influence as part of an essentially mystical universe.[47] This dual nature of Kepler's thinking leads Nell Ulrich to remark that "Kepler could report scientifically on the elliptical motion of the planets and, at the same moment, worship fervently and mystically the powers of the sun, and hold onto an essentially Platonic and Pythagorean idea of the universe."[48] In this as well, he shows the influence of Plutarch. While Plutarch presents the moon as a body like earth, he also, through Sulla's myth of the island of Cronus, presents the moon as a repository of souls: in Sulla's description of astral ascent, "the route followed by voyagers to the moon had been heavy with traffic of the souls of the unborn and the dead, wailing back and forth between the earth and the moon in the shadow of the earth."[49] The pull of souls that pass through space on planetary shadows comes from Plutarch's representation of Neoplatonist eschatology and becomes, in Kepler's formulation, an allegorized image of a physical force that exerts its power because of, and not in spite of, its mystical origin.

The difference between Kepler and Galileo on this point of the moon's materiality takes us back to the two main areas that critics discuss when they consider what makes the *Somnium* SF. First, the *Somnium* is fiction that explains and speculates. Second, it uses the crucial, perhaps foundational, SF trope of extraterrestrial life in the service of speculative explanation. In order to inhabit that world, Kepler first had to recognize it as such—as a world. While the telescope certainly helped him identify the moon as a world like earth, much of his imaginative representation of the moon as a place from which to observe the earth can be traced to his reading of Lucian and, foremost for the purposes of this discussion, Plutarch.

---

[47] Gunn (2006: 184).

[48] Eurich (1967: 119).

[49] Lear (1965: 45). Aldiss (1995) makes the observation that Plutarch "concludes that demons inhabit our sister world; the violent ones are sometimes exiled from the Moon to Earth" (150).

2

Lucretius, Lucan, and Mary Shelley's *Frankenstein*

Jesse Weiner

Through pervasive allusion to such texts as *Faust* and *Paradise Lost*, *Frankenstein* situates itself within a literary tradition of myths of sinful knowledge. As the novel's subtitle, *The Modern Prometheus*, suggests, we may read *Frankenstein* (*F*) as signaling the genre's classical origins.[1] Science fiction (SF) is, after all, a genre concerned, not only with the speculative possibilities of science, but also with the ethical boundaries of human knowledge, and it is therefore fitting that what is widely considered the first SF novel should look back to the Western tradition's

[1] As a number of scholars point out, the genealogy of Shelley's monster can also be traced to the myths and literature of ancient Greece. See Liveley (2006: 277–278). On the many philosophical, mythological, and literary sources for *Frankenstein*, see especially Lecercle (1988) and Pollin (1965). I do not suggest that classical literature is, for Shelley, sinful in itself. Rather, certain classical myths, such as Prometheus' theft of fire and Pandora's box, feature forbidden knowledge as prominent motifs. In such myths, the pursuit of certain knowledge, science, and/or technology is frequently portrayed as a crime against God or nature. I am grateful to the editors of this volume for the analogous point that Western traditions have frequently described "deviant" sexual behaviors as "crimes against nature" (*crimina contra naturam*). Kant's writing on "unnatural" sex provides one particularly prominent example; on *crimina contra naturam* in Kant, see especially Denis (1999).

earliest explorations of these motifs.[2] It is perhaps less obvious that Mary Shelley's engagement with classical literature extends beyond the comparison of Frankenstein with Prometheus. For instance, Frankenstein's monster educates himself with a copy of Plutarch's *Lives*, while the novel's narrator, Captain Walton, resolves to face death with "the lessons learned from Seneca" (*F* 1818: 236).[3] These two particularly explicit allusions indicate not only Shelley's interest in the classics, but also that works of Greek and Latin literature serve as sources of ethical orientation in *Frankenstein*.[4] In this essay, I focus on two sources: two Latin epic poems whose influence on *Frankenstein* has gone largely unexplored. Victor Frankenstein's quest to animate a sentient being through the recombination of pillaged body parts finds a scientific and poetic model in the material physics and atomism of Lucretius' *De Rerum Natura* (*DRN*). A second classical archetype for Shelley's monster is found in the Erichtho episode of Lucan's *Bellum Civile* (*BC*). Allusion to these two epic poems colors both the science and the ethics of *Frankenstein's* necromancy.

MODELS OF RECEPTION: THE CULTURAL MATRIX, MARY SHELLEY'S JOURNALS, AND THE MANUSCRIPT EVIDENCE

Over the course of this essay, I argue somewhat intermittently for two very different modes of intertextuality. The first mode supposes an intertextual

---

[2] Carl Freedman (2000) observes (with bibliography) that *Frankenstein* has "been listed in many genealogies of the genre as the first science-fiction novel" and "probably counts as the first important work of fiction to engage with modern science seriously and to feature a scientist as its protagonist" (4); see also Aldiss (1976: 20–31). Brantlinger (1980: 31–32) points out in response to Aldiss that, while it is not difficult to push the origins of SF both backwards and forwards, *Frankenstein* at the very least constitutes a clear, early example from which to trace the history of the genre. While *Frankenstein* clearly could not anticipate its later canonization as a foundation text for the genre of SF, its intertextual strategies do situate the novel within a tradition of literature that explores the ethical consequences of epistemological pursuit.

[3] Unless otherwise noted (as here), references to the pagination of *Frankenstein* apply to the 1831 Standard Edition as printed in Shelley (2007). This particular line, present in the first published edition of *Frankenstein* (Shelley 1818), was removed from the text and is not found in the 1831 edition. It should be noted that Victor Frankenstein's artificial man is never named: over the course of the novel, he is variously referred to with words such as "monster," "daemon," "wretch," "devil," and "fiend."

[4] Seneca was a prominent Stoic philosopher, while Plutarch's *Lives* are biographies written to teach moral values.

strategy that is not necessarily, though very likely may be, through the conscious intention of the author. In this formulation, intertextuality is a stylistic device, employed in the hope of engendering a particular response from an astute and (specifically to the conjured text) well-read audience. In this formulation, intertextuality might well be called "allusion," as I have done only few sentences ago. I also argue for a second, radically different mode of intertextuality. This mode, particularly employed at the close of the section "Lucan and Monstrosity," supposes that every reader brings his or her own experience and interpretive strategies to a text; that texts therefore exist as fragments in a web of textuality; and that intertextuality is an activity of audiences rather than of authors.[5] I suggest that, in either formulation, texts can reflect back upon those to which they allude, thereby investing old texts with new meanings. By this logic, I ask not only what Lucan might do for *Frankenstein*, but also what *Frankenstein* might do for Lucan.

Let us now consider historical reasons why the poetics of Lucretius and Lucan came to be present in a novel written by a teenaged Englishwoman in the nineteenth century. To issue an introductory caveat, I do not wish to overstate the importance of Shelley's biography to the intertextual relationships I have sketched below; as I have just suggested, texts can engage in dialogue across space and time, coloring each other with meanings independent of authorial intent and historical particulars. Nevertheless, the copious biographical details left behind by Shelley herself do warrant mention and discussion.

We know, for instance, that Mary Shelley began her study of Latin as an adolescent, and this interest in Latin literature is transposed onto Victor Frankenstein and his sister Elizabeth, who in their youth "learned Latin and English, that we might read the writings in those languages."[6] In her journals, Mary Shelley explicitly professes to have read both Lucretius and Lucan; yet these remarks complicate the model of reception every bit as much as they support the systems of allusion for which I will argue. The problems are temporal. Mary Shelley began her work on *Frankenstein* in the summer of 1816; completed her draft on May 14, 1817; published the

---

[5] For an introduction to theories of intertextuality over the past decades (including those outlined here), see Ott and Walter (2000). Useful to classicists is Hinds (1998); with special reference to Roman poetry, Edmunds (2003).

[6] Sunstein (1989: 49, 118); Morrison and Stone (2003: 242). The quote is from the 1818 first edition of *Frankenstein* and is omitted from the 1831 text. Victor Frankenstein remains an avid reader of Latin in the standard 1831 version.

novel's first edition anonymously in 1818; and released the third and final edition of the book in 1831.[7] According to her journal, Mary Shelley began her reading of Lucan sometime in June or July of 1819 and finished *Bellum Civile* towards the end of September.[8] It was not until 1820 that Shelley purported to have read Lucretius, beginning *De Rerum Natura* on June 28th of that year and completing the poem on August 29th.[9] This is despite that fact that, in an entry dated April 18, 1815, Shelley noted that she had purchased an edition of John Mason Good's 1805 translation of the epic. Thus, Shelley appears to have read both poems in question, yet only *after* she had already published *Frankenstein*'s first edition, the text of which contains all of the passages discussed below.

What then do we make of this chronological inconsistency, and how did Lucan and Lucretius make it into Shelley's novel *before* she claims to have read them? Shelley herself offers little help in solving this, as the relevant journals tend only to state facts in the shortest and simplest possible terms. Consider the following excerpt from 1819, which is representative of the journals' style:

Monday, SEPT. 13. – Read Lucan; finish the 8th book. Read Beaumont and Fletcher. Visit Mrs. Gisborne. [Percy] Shelley reads Boccaccio aloud, and Calderon with Charles Claremont.
Tuesday, SEPT. 14. – Read Lucan. Visit Mrs. Gisborne. [Percy] Shelley reads Calderon, and Boccaccio aloud in the evening. Read 23rd and 24th cantos of Dante with him.
Wednesday, SEPT. 15. – Read Lucan. . . . [10]

Entirely absent are subjective evaluations of what the Shelleys read. What did Mary think of Lucan when she read him? We cannot even be sure that when Mary Shelley read *Bellum Civile* and *De Rerum Natura* over the course of 1819–1820, she was reading them for the first time. Perhaps Shelley had in fact read her Good translation of Lucretius back in 1815, but, like all classicists of good conscience, waited to add it to her list of completed books (also included in the journals) until she had read

[7] Morrison and Stone (2003: 157–158).
[8] Jones (1947: 122–124).
[9] Ibid. (135–137).
[10] Ibid. (124).

the entire poem in Latin. This certainly would reflect the attitude and influence of Percy Shelley, who believed that "the spirit of the literature of ancient Greece . . . could only be found in its original language."[11] The possibilities are all speculative, but it is plausible that Shelley had already read both Lucan and Lucretius in translation—perhaps even some passages in Latin—prior to the composition of *Frankenstein*.

Irrespective of her own reading history, Shelley lived and wrote in what Martin Priestman has dubbed the "second Lucretian moment in Britain."[12] Mary Shelley attributes the novel's inspiration to the experiments of Erasmus Darwin, who had himself written a didactic poem, *The Temple of Nature* (1803), which was very much indebted to Lucretius. The scientific and anatomical literature of Enlightenment and Romantic Britain was deeply influenced by Lucretius, and Shelley would almost surely have absorbed some Epicurean scientific principles and Lucretian rhetoric from these sources. Lucan was an important author of the French Revolution, and Shelley would also have read of the witch Erichtho through Dante.[13] It hardly seems a coincidence that the witch makes an appearance in Goethe's *Faust II* (1832) in addition to *Frankenstein*, given that the two roughly contemporaneous works address nearly identical themes and are themselves intertextually intertwined.[14]

Mary Shelley inevitably would have benefited from her coterie, being privy to and participating in the discussions among Percy Shelley, Lord Byron, and the like. In her preface to the 1831 edition of

[11] Ingpen (1909: 880).

[12] 1790–1820. Priestman (2007: 289) sets the first British Lucretian moment at the close of the seventeenth century.

[13] On Lucan and the French Revolution, see especially Tucker (1971). The French Revolution clearly made a number of impressions on Mary Shelley, and Julia Douthwaite has recently shown that François-Félix Nogaret's 1790 novella *Le Miroir des événemens actuels, ou La Belle au plus offrant: Histoire à deux visages* imagined "an inventor named Frankenstein who builds an artificial human" a generation before Shelley began work on *Frankenstein*; see Douthwaite (2012). At *Inferno* 9.22–27, Dante's Virgil claims to have been summoned once before to the lower circles of hell by "cruel Erichtho, who recalled shades to their bodies" (*Eritón cruda / che richiamava l'ombre a' corpi sui*). Virgil says that he was at the time "newly separated from his flesh" (*di poco era di me la carne nuda*) when his shade was summoned. Thus, Dante's reanimation of Virgil via Erichtho bears several similarities to the Erichtho episode in Book 6 of *Bellum Civile*. In Book 6, Erichtho conscientiously chooses to reanimate a fresh corpse.

[14] Levine (1979). On Shelley's familiarity with Goethe, see also Morrison and Stone (2003: 175–176).

the novel, Shelley writes that "many and long were the conversations between Lord Byron and [Percy] Shelley, to which I was a devout but nearly silent listener . . . various philosophical doctrines were discussed . . . " (*F* 2007: 8). Percy Shelley's very Lucretian poem, "Mutability" (1816), is quoted verbatim by Frankenstein, who declares that "Man's yesterday may ne'er be like his morrow; / Nought may endure but mutability!" Percy's ever-growing obsession with Greek and Latin literature is well documented,[15] and both Lucretius and Lucan figure prominently in his poetic influences. According to Mary's journals, Percy Shelley completed his reading of Lucretius in 1816, and *De Rerum Natura* provided a natural poetic model for the poet's atheism.[16] Likewise, Byron considered *De Rerum Natura* "the first of Latin poems."[17] As for Lucan, Percy Shelley observed in an 1815 letter that *Bellum Civile* is "a poem, as it appears to me, of wonderful genius and transcending 'Virgil.'"[18]

It is therefore tempting to posit that many of the Lucretian and Lucanian elements in *Frankenstein* reveal the editorial or even co-authorial hand of Percy Shelley. Percy did, after all, edit Mary's draft in 1817, and the anonymous preface to the 1818 first edition (itself infused with the language of atomism) was written by Percy, not Mary. Whether Mary Shelley was simply the beneficiary of the discussions of the company she kept, or whether Percy assumed a more active role in the writing of *Frankenstein*, remains a controversial question. However, with respect to the specific intertextual relationships outlined below, the manuscript evidence appears to preclude assigning the novel's engagement with Lucretius and Lucan to the intervention of Percy.

---

[15] For a survey of the classicizing tendencies of Percy Shelley, see Burriss (1926).

[16] Shelley had previously published a pamphlet entitled *The Necessity of Atheism* (1812). On Percy's engagement with Lucretian physics and cosmological vocabulary, particularly in *Prometheus Unbound*, see Miller (2005: 595–596).

[17] Lord Byron, with whom the Shelleys were close friends, was also a Lucan enthusiast. On allusion to Lucan in Byron, see Dover (2001: 569) and MacDonald (1986: 62). Byron's comments are from his 1821 letter to **** ****** [John Murray] on Bowles. As Priestman (2007: 297) observes, Byron appreciated the poetry of Lucretius while questioning aspects of its ethics. Byron's principal reservation about Epicureanism seems to have been its advocacy of "apolitical disengagement." Byron, of course, famously traveled to Greece to fight in the Greek Revolution.

[18] Ingpen (1909: 445).

In his recent critical edition of two early drafts of *Frankenstein*, Charles Robinson elevates Percy Shelley to the status of co-author, suggesting on the basis of handwriting analysis of marginalia that Percy penned some 5,000 of the novel's 72,000 words.[19] Despite the obvious methodological complications of adding two drafts to three published versions of *Frankenstein* (which texts present the "real" *Frankenstein*?), Robinson's study offers a valuable glimpse into the novel's composition. I have earlier observed that the Lucretian and Lucanian elements are already present in the 1818 edition of *Frankenstein*. Provided that we accept Robinson's manuscript work, we can firmly push these intertextual relationships back to Mary Shelley's original 1816–1817 draft—that is to say, *before* Percy laid his editorial hands on the text—as the passages cited over the course of this essay are all more or less present and intact in the earliest version.[20] Despite the fluidity of the *Frankenstein* text, engagement with Lucretius and Lucan appears consistent throughout its variants. This, of course, does not preclude Percy's influence in developing Mary's exposure to and interest in the classics, but the manuscript evidence suggests that Mary Shelley's engagement with Lucretian atomism and Lucanian black magic may be her own.

LUCRETIUS AND ATOMISM

Studies of *Frankenstein* have eagerly pointed out that the novel "is not a story about alchemy and magic but about science . . . natural philosophy, chemistry, and galvanism."[21] Frankenstein's monster is a patchwork man, a collage of ill-assorted preexisting parts, grotesque in the artificiality of their combinations.[22] This is how Lucretius approaches monstrosity, as at several points in *De Rerum Natura*, Lucretius defines "monsters" as discordant assemblages of limbs (*discordia membra*, DRN 5.894) and argues against the existence of mythological monsters on the grounds that such

---

[19] Robinson (2009). The manuscripts of Mary's drafts are housed in the Bodleian Library at Oxford University.

[20] This is true, with the exception of the introductory letters of the narrator, Walton, which are absent both from the 1816–1817 draft and the second draft, edited by Percy.

[21] Reichart (1994: 136–137).

[22] Ibid. (155); Baldick (1987: 13).

atomistic combinations are prohibited by the laws of nature.[23] For instance, at *De Rerum Natura* 5.916–924, Lucretius writes that:

For while there were many seeds of things in the ground at the time when the earth first poured forth animals, there is no evidence that it was possible for mixed creatures to be made and the limbs of various animals joined together. This is because the things which even now spring forth in abundance from the earth—the various kinds of plants, grain, and luxuriant trees—cannot be joined together, but each thing proceeds by its own rite, and all things preserve their distinctions by the fixed law of Nature.[24]

Nam quod multa fuere in terris semina rerum
tempore quo primum tellus animalia fudit,
nil tamen est signi mixtas potuisse creari
inter se pecudes compactaque membra animantum,
propterea quia quae de terris nunc quoque abundant –   920
herbarum genera ac fruges arbustaque laeta –
non tamen inter se possunt complexa creari,
sed res quaeque suo ritu procedit, et omnes
foedere naturae certo discrimina servant.[25]

Likewise, the *semina rerum* of Frankenstein's artificial man—the scientist frequently refers to them as "lifeless matter," "materials," and "minute parts"—are *discordia*; the monster is hideous in his patchwork assemblage despite the fact that Frankenstein has meticulously chosen each individual component with "such infinite pains and care" and with an eye towards beauty and proportion (*F* 2007: 58).

This is not to say that the Lucretian model of monstrosity maps onto *Frankenstein* with absolute precision; Frankenstein's artificial man is

[23] Though Lucretius denies their existence, the conception of monsters as discordant assemblages may be drawn in part from Empedocles, whose influence on Lucretius was profound. On monsters in Empedocles, see Wright (1981: 212–215).

[24] Unless otherwise noted, translations are my own. Lucretius offers a similar definition of monsters at *De Rerum Natura* 2.700–729. Lucretius emphatically denies the possibility that such monsters can be produced or were ever produced by nature. In a point of clarification that presciently points towards biotechnology ("Frankenfruit" has made its way into modern parlance; and see Nelkin [1996] for brief discussion of a brilliant example in contemporary art), Lucretius states that this impossibility of mixed beings in nature applies not only to *animalia* but also to "all things" (*omnia*) (2.718–719). On the nonexistence of mythological monsters, see also 3.1011 and 4.732–743. Lucretius does not reckon with the possibility that such creatures *contra naturam* might be created artificially.

[25] I use the text of Bailey (1947).

assembled from the parts of other humans, not from an assortment of species. Nevertheless, despite this "eye towards beauty and proportion," the monster's assemblage of parts is entirely unnatural, atomistic, and perhaps less proportional than it might appear. There is a tacitly ghoulish element to Frankenstein's corporeal rearrangements, which elucidates the unnatural atomism of his monster. The monster stands eight feet tall and is well proportioned. As it is difficult to imagine a plethora of eight-foot corpses at the scientist's disposal, the reader is left to assume that each of Frankenstein's *membra* are themselves atomistic assemblages of any number of smaller *corpora*.

Frankenstein may merely be a bad artist, but the Modern Prometheus' aesthetic revulsion at his creation reveals his far greater, very much Lucretian, corruption of Nature.[26] Throughout Shelly's narrative, Frankenstein's creative "transcendence is equivalent to transgression" and "invested with the aura of a primal sin against nature."[27]

Lucretius' atheism and materialist science provide an obvious secular paradigm for Shelley's "tale of a *modern Prometheus*," as it is "a secular myth, with no metaphysical machinery, no gods: the creation is from mortal bodies with the assistance of electricity, not spirit; and the deaths are not pursued beyond the grave."[28] The novel works entirely "within the limits of the visible, physical world."[29] Whatever details we are given about Victor Frankenstein's exploration of "the deepest secrets of creation" are described through the language and imagery of Lucretian physics. Shelley conspicuously personifies *natura*, and the frequent repetition of "material" throughout the episode invokes the fleshly materialism of Epicurean philosophy, which had recently experienced a revival of sorts in Romantic Britain.[30] The monster's amalgamation of limbs evokes the <u>atom</u>istic recombination of

---

[26] As Chris Baldick (1987: 13–14) points out, at the beginning of the *Ars Poetica*, Horace defines *bad art* as the "ridiculous and unnatural combination" of mismatched parts. In her preface to the 1831 edition of *Frankenstein*, Shelley recalls her initial idea for the novel and describes Victor as a bad artist terrified by his success, with an emphasis on moral transgression: ". . . supremely frightful would be the effect of any human endeavour to mock the stupendous mechanism of the Creator of the world. His success would terrify the artist. . . ."

[27] Sherwin (1981: 83).

[28] Levine (1979: 4).

[29] Ibid. (7).

[30] Priestman (2007) and (1999). On British receptions of Lucretius in the seventeenth and eighteenth centuries, see Hopkins (2010: 88–112). On Lucretius' influence on the science and art of Britain in the later nineteenth century, see Dawson (2003). Percy

Lucretian anatomy and monstrosity, and numerous verbal echoes over the novel's course confirm Lucretius as a source for Shelley. Most significantly, Dr. Frankenstein's project of bringing forth a living creature from dead and decaying material appears to draw its inspiration from Lucretius' favorite example of spontaneous generation.[31] At five points in *De Rerum Natura*, Lucretius explains spontaneous generation via the rise of worms from putrid matter and rancid corpses—the bodies are described as *putrifactum, putor,* and *rancens* (*DRN* 2.871–873, 898–901, 928–929; 3.719–736; 5.797–798). Moreover, he posits that this is due to the rearrangement of matter:

> But these [substances of the earth], when they have been putrefied, as it were, by the rains, bring forth little worms, because the bodies of matter, having been moved from their ancient order by a new condition, are combined such that animated beings must be born.

> Et tamen haec, cum sunt quasi putrefacta per imbres,
> vermiculos pariunt, quia corpora materiai
> antiquis ex ordinibus pernata nova re   900
> conciliantur ita ut debent animalia gigni. (*DRN* 2.898–901)

> How do corpses exhale worms through flesh now rotten, and how does such a great abundance of animated creatures, boneless and bloodless, flow out from the swollen limbs?

> Unde cadavera rancenti iam visere vermes
> expirant, atque unde animantum copia tanta   720
> exos et exanguis tumidos perfluctuat artus? (*DRN* 3.719–721)

Shelley's interest in Lucretius has been well documented, and Lucretius must certainly be included among "his reading (with Mary Shelley) of philosophical works associated with radicalism"; see Tiffany (2009: 194). See especially Turner (1959). For a recent treatment of Lucretius' rediscovery in the Renaissance and his impact on early modern Europe, see Greenblatt (2011).

[31] *Frankenstein*'s engagement with Lucretius may here be mediated through Erasmus Darwin. Famously, in her authorial introduction to the 1831 standard edition of *Frankenstein*, Mary Shelley says she drew her inspiration from a reported science experiment of Erasmus Darwin, "who perceived a piece of vermicelli . . . til by some extraordinary means it began to move with voluntary motion" (*F* 2007: 8). Erasmus Darwin himself wrote a didactic poem profoundly influenced by Lucretius. On Darwin and Lucretius, see Priestman (2007: 291–292), and Johnson and Wilson (2007: 143). Priestman observes that Shelley's dream of vermicelli points more directly to Lucretius than Darwin.

Frankenstein, meanwhile, observes the "natural decay and corruption of the human body," describing a churchyard as "the receptacle of human bodies deprived of life, which . . . had become food for the worm" (*F* 2007: 52).

The imagery of worms seemingly arising from death and decay is not at all haphazard, as it is repeated again in the very same paragraph. There Frankenstein declares that

I saw the corruption of death succeed to the blooming cheek of life; I saw how the worm inherited the wonders of the eye and brain. I paused, examining and analysing all the minutiae of causation, as exemplified in the change from life to death, and death to life, until from the midst of this darkness a sudden light broke in upon me—a light so brilliant and wondrous, yet so simple, that while I became dizzy with the immensity of the prospect which it illustrated, I was surprised, that among so many men of genius who had directed their enquiries towards the same science, that I alone should be reserved to discover so astonishing a secret.

Shelley thereby appears to borrow Lucretius' *vermiculos*; she also attributes the origin of her story to "a dream of vermicelli" (*F* 2007: 8). The allusion is hence employed as creative inspiration both internally and externally to the text.

In addition to incorporating Lucretius' imagery of spontaneous animation, the passage is full of Lucretian language. Frankenstein's command over the "minutiae of causation" mirrors that of Lucretius,[32] and its context reduces mankind and the phenomena of life and death to the combinations of inert matter. The natural scientist describes his epiphany as "a sudden light, a light so brilliant and wondrous" breaking through "the midst of this darkness" (*F* 2007: 53). This recalls Lucretius' address to Epicurus at the opening of *De Rerum Natura*'s Book 3, which begins, "O you who first amid so great a darkness were able to raise aloft a light so clear, illuminating the blessings of life" (*E tenebris tantis tam clarum extollere lumen / qui primus potuisti illustrans commoda vitae*; 3.1–2).

The poetics of *De Rerum Natura* continue to make their presences felt throughout the novel.[33] Lucretius frequently illustrates his

---

[32] See Miller (1989: 66).

[33] One example not discussed here in detail is suggested by Rand Miller (1989: 70–71), who observes that Shelley seems to appropriate Lucretius' imagery of storms and

atomistic principles though wordplay. Strikingly, while recounting his early days of existence, Frankenstein's monster appears to recall the *De Rerum Natura*'s most famous pun. As a didactic demonstration of atoms and their combinations, Lucretius employs paranomasia, a play on words, to show that, just as many of the same *elementa* slightly amended and reshuffled create both *ignis* (fire) and *lignum* (wood), there are atomic elements embedded in wood that could produce fire:[34]

Therefore, do you not see, as I said a little before, that it is often of great import with what and in what position these same first-beginnings are contained, and what motions they give and receive among themselves, and that the same elements changed a bit in their combinations create both fire and wood? Just as the words themselves are made from elements a little changed in their relations to each other, we signify fire and wood with different vocal sounds.

Iamne vides igitur, paulo quod diximus ante,
permagni referre eadem primordia saepe
cum quibus et quali positura contineantur
et quos inter se dent motus accipiantque,   910
atque eadem paulo inter se mutata creare
ignes et lignum? Quo pacto verba quoque ipsa
inter se paulo mutatis sunt elementis,
cum ligna atque ignes distincta voce notemus. (*DRN* 1.907–914)

The didactic context of the pun—explicating atomic combination through a comparison to language—is echoed in *Frankenstein*. As the monster, himself an atomistic combination of corporal elements, describes his early attempts to make sense of the world (including language), he declares, "I examined the materials of the fire, and to my joy found it to be made of wood" (*F* 2007: 107). The monster thus attributes his cosmological education to the material relationship between fire and wood, and his "joy" reflects a reader's response to Lucretius' clever wordplay.

---

whirlwinds to depict the natures of both Frankenstein and his monster. By "poetics," I refer to both the formal and the stylistic features of poetry. In modern parlance, the term has acquired sufficiently broad scope as to apply also to the literary features of prose.
    [34] Lucretius employs the same word (*elementa*) for both fires and letters, appropriating a Greek trope reaching back at least to Aristotle. On this pun, see especially Snyder (1980) and Friedländer (2007).

This ludic engagement with Lucretian poetics underlies a more serious (and, as we will see, sinister) relationship between bodies and their constitutive parts. Lucretius held that objects reflect their atomistic makeups, displaying the very qualities inherent in the atoms themselves. For instance, harsh or bitter-tasting substances are composed of sharp or hooked atoms, while sweet-tasting honey is formed from the unions of smooth, round atoms (*DRN* 2.398–407).

The qualities of individual atomic building blocks manifest themselves in the larger bodies they compose: we might refer to this proposition of Lucretius' as *atomistic essentialism*. This brand of atomistic essentialism is visible in Frankenstein's monster, especially when one considers the legal culture of late eighteenth and early nineteenth-century England. In 1752, Parliament passed the Murder Act, for "better Preventing the horrid Crime of Murder." This law, which remained in place throughout the writing and editing of *Frankenstein*, dictated that the bodies of all those convicted of murder be subject to public dissection. In addition to providing a supply of corpses for anatomical research, the effect of the Murder Act was to create a "popular association between dissection and murder."[35] Although Shelley's novel is silent as to whether Victor Frankenstein actually garners his materials from the bodies of murderers, this connection between murder and corporeal dissection in British consciousness invites a Lucretian reading of the monster's relationship to his atomistic makeup. Frankenstein's monster was composed of dissected *membra*. There is therefore a tacit suggestion that, at the atomic level, violence was embedded in the very fibers of the monster's being.[36] The monster proceeds to commit numerous murders over the course of the novel, thereby displaying the innate qualities of what were his likely building blocks, which in turn smuggles Lucretian cycles of growth and decay, union and dissolution, into Shelley's text. Once the monster became a murderer, British law mandated that upon his death, he, too, should undergo corporeal dissection. Thus, according to the British sensibilities of Shelley's day, the monster was legally

---

[35] Marshall (1995: 21).

[36] This *topos* of grafting continues to have traction in speculative fiction, especially in the horror genre. *The Hands of Orlac* (1924—remade in 1935 as *Mad Love* and again as *The Hands of Orlac* in 1960) provides one example, as does much of David Cronenberg's film *oeuvre*.

destined to return to the disconnected and discordant *semina rerum* from which he was made.[37]

Lucretius provides another image of importance to *Frankenstein* in his description of natural philosophy as an intoxicating draught. At the opening of *De Rerum Natura*'s Book 4 (Percy Shelley's personal favorite),[38] Lucretius explains his choice of epic poetry as a didactic medium:

For just as, when physicians try to give children bitter wormwood, they first coat the rims of the cups with sweet honey, so that the rash youth of the children might be deceived as far as the lips, and so that meanwhile youth will drink the bitter juice of wormwood and, though beguiled, will not be betrayed, but rather, restored by such means, will become well, so now do I: since this doctrine often seems harsh to those who have not tried it, and most people shrink back from it, I have chosen to set forth my doctrine to you in sweet-speaking Pierian song and, as it were, to touch it with the sweet honey of the Muses, if by chance I can hold your mind in my verses this way, while you take in the entire nature of things and perceive its utility.

Nam veluti pueris absinthia taetra medentes
cum dare conantur, prius oras pocula circum
contingunt mellis dulci flavoque liquore,
ut puerorum aetas inprovida ludificetur
labrorum tenus, interea perpotet amarum   15
absinthi laticem deceptaque non capiatur,
sed potius tali pacto recreata valescat,
sic ego nunc, quoniam haec ratio plerumque videtur
tristior esse quibus non est tractata, retroque
volgus abhorret ab hac, volui tibi suaviloquenti   20
carmine Pierio rationem exponere nostram

---

[37] While it may be objected that neither Frankenstein nor, presumably, the corpses that lend their body parts to the monster's construction are British, we should not forget that the entire novel is framed with an Englishman (Captain Walton) as the primary narrator. Walton's sister, the addressee of his letters, has the initials *M.W.S.*, which are conspicuously the initials of *Frankenstein*'s British author, who wrote the novel for a primarily British audience.

[38] In a letter written in 1817 (the year of *Frankenstein*'s completion), Percy Shelley declared: "I am well acquainted with Lucretius . . . The 4th book is perhaps the finest"; quoted in Turner (1959: 269). *DRN* Book 4 is devoted to the explication of sensory perception, especially visual images.

et quasi musaeo dulci contingere melle,
si tibi forte animum tali ratione tenere
versibus in nostris possem, dum percipis omnem
naturam rerum ac persentis utilitatem. (*DRN* 4.11–25)   25

Materialist philosophy is bitter, like absinthe,[39] yet important enough to warrant the sweetening touch of the poet in order that, with the senses beguiled, it might be more easily swallowed.

The intoxicating honey of poetry and creative inspiration, spread around the rim of the already intoxicating cup of scientific knowledge, is problematized in *Frankenstein*, as Shelley prominently employs the metaphor to introduce Frankenstein's tale. Shelley's narrator, Captain Walton, is himself on a naturalist voyage of discovery. Upon his declaration of commitment to the "acquirement of the knowledge which I sought for the dominion I should acquire and transmit over the elemental foes of our race," Frankenstein rebuffs him, exclaiming, "Have you drunk also of the intoxicating drought [*sic*]? Hear me—let me reveal my tale, and you will dash the cup from your lips!" (*F* 2007: 29).

Shelley thereby employs the allusion for a contextually meaningful purpose, while inverting the ethical agenda of Lucretius; whereas the bitter taste of materialist philosophy is something to be sweetened by versification in *De Rerum Natura*, its asperity betrays its status as a source of moral corruption and misfortune in *Frankenstein*. For Lucretius, this knowledge is a healing medicine; for Frankenstein, it is his undoing, which is materially reflected by his continually declining health and mental stability. Lucretius thus serves as both a positive and a negative exemplum.

Shelley's moral rejection of Lucretian science in *Frankenstein* has been described as "a reaction against the Promethean radicalism of her husband, and of her father and mother—William Godwin and Mary Wollstonecraft."[40] Be that as it may, Shelley's ethical antipathy to Lucretius and the promises of modern science need not refute their epistemological legitimacy. As Carl Freedman argues, *Frankenstein*'s hostility to material science in no way cancels the novel's

[39] In the Greek and Roman world, *absinthe* referred to wormwood itself, often used as medicine, rather than to the alcoholic beverage. However, there is evidence that *absinthium* was used in combination with alcohol (Pliny, *Natural History* 27.45–52). For an overview of absinthe's Greco-Roman history, see Lanier (1995: 1–8) and Welsh (2006).
[40] Brantlinger (1980: 32).

sense that the most fundamental of material and intellectual categories—condensed into the problem of life itself—can no longer be taken for granted but are now up for grabs and can be challenged and rethought. Victor Frankenstein's experiment is monstrous, to be sure, but its viability amounts to intellectual revolution, to an awareness that what the text itself might designate a moment of 'Promethean' critical thought is at hand."[41]

Frankenstein's creation of man may be Promethean, but its scientific grounding in atomistic physics and secular cosmology constitutes a Lucretian moment of intellectual revolution.

Shelley's ambivalent handling of Lucretian material in her novel extends to a motif of gigantomachy, or war among giants.[42] Lucretius famously celebrates the gigantomachy, likening the attempts of various mythological giants to overthrow the Olympian pantheon through force to his own attempt to liberate mankind from superstition through reason and science (*DRN* 5.110–125).[43] Frankenstein has, of course, attempted to usurp the power of God and Nature through science, and the rebellion of Frankenstein's monster (who is, quite literally, a chthonic giant) forms the novel's conflict. Rebelling against their creators, Frankenstein and his monster are not merely latter-day Prometheis; they are modern giants. The dialogue of their conflict frames the strife in terms of hierarchical inversion and martial imagery of the thunderbolt, the weapon used by Zeus to defeat Typhon, a giant monster who rose against Olympus. The Frankenstein myth as a gigantomachy is tantalizingly suggested by Percy Shelley, who describes the experience of reading *Frankenstein* with imagery drawn from the Greek myth of the giants Otos and Ephialtes: "Pelion is heaped on Ossa, Ossa upon Olympus."[44]

[41] Freedman (2000: 4).

[42] *Gigantomachy* refers to a number of myths in which various gigantic monsters rebelled against the regime of Zeus. In addition to her exposure to classical sources, which include but are not limited to Hesiod, Lucretius, Virgil, and Lucan, Shelley would have been familiar with gigantomachy through Dante. In *Inferno* 31, the giants Ephialtes, Briareus, and Typhon are each mentioned or encountered (as are Antaeus and Tityus). A good bit of this material appears to have been drawn from Lucan; see Singleton (1970: 574–579). The motif of gigantomachy is likely employed by Dante as a standard by which to compare the towering Lucifer; see Kay (2002: 17). If this is the case, we might perhaps read an added layer of meaning when Shelley uses "devil" to refer to Frankenstein's monster.

[43] See Hardie (2009) and (2007).

[44] Shelley (1880). This short essay was originally published posthumously in *The Athenaeum* in November of 1832. According to Dante Gabriel Rossetti, these remarks of

The monster tells Frankenstein, "Slave . . . You are my creator, but I am your master—obey!" and "soon the bolt will fall which must ravish from you your happiness forever . . . you can blast my other passions . . .!" (*F* 2007: 172–173). Frankenstein accordingly responds like Zeus to Typhon, imprisoned beneath Mount Etna, exclaiming, "Devil, cease; and do not poison the air with these sounds of malice."[45] Famously in Greek mythology, Typhon had attempted to overthrow Zeus in order to avenge the god's coup against his own creators, the Titans.[46] While Shelley does not share Lucretius' enthusiasm for such a gigantomachy of reason, *De Rerum Natura* nevertheless provides the model for Victor Frankenstein's own subversion of god/nature through scientific exploration.

Frankenstein is as much a novel about ethics as it is about science, and this ethical dimension has led some scholars to locate the "origin of modern science fiction" in the "moral ambiguity created in the face of speculative science."[47] For the Epicureans, of course, science and ethics are inextricably intertwined, as *ataraxia*—a conscious state of mental tranquillity pivotal to the Epicurean conception of happiness—is arrived at through contemplation and understanding of atomism. The value of Lucretius for Shelley is ethical as well as scientific, for the novel ultimately rejects Romantic passions in favor of what Lucretius calls a *pectus tranquillum* ("tranquil heart"; *DRN* 3.293). Frankenstein interrupts his

---

Shelley were probably penned in 1817, the year in which Percy edited Mary's original manuscript.

[45] Compare to *DRN* 1.722–725, in which Etna is credited with "menacing rumblings" and the ability to "cast flaming lightning bolts to the sky." The association of Frankenstein's monster with Etna/Typhon is developed by H. M. Milner in his 1826 *Frankenstein: or, The Man and the Monster*, which climaxed with the monster meeting his doom by leaping into Mount Etna; see James (1994). Milner's connection of the monster with Etna becomes all the more powerful if we read the influence of Empedocles on the monster (be it direct or via Lucretius), especially given that Shelley frequently refers to the monster as a "daemon." Empedocles (fragment 107.115 in Wright [1981]) writes of long-living *daimones* who wander from air, to sea, to land, to fire (not unlike the wanderings of Frankenstein's monster, who traverses mountains and seas en route to his pyre or, in Milner's version, the fires of Etna). On the connections between *daimones* and Etna, see Wright (1981: 270–275).

[46] One early source for this myth, Hesiod's *Theogony*, describes Typhon in terms that resonate powerfully in *Frankenstein*. In addition to providing an extended epic simile on the terrible sounds emitted by Typhon, Hesiod ghoulishly relates that Typhon is a child of Earth and Tartarus—like Frankenstein's monster, Typhon is a chthonic monster born from the home of the dead. Hesiod's Typhon is also an atomistic mash-up of discordant body parts (*Theogony* 820–870).

[47] Fredericks (1980: 95), who cites Scholes and Rabkin (1977: 191–196).

creation narrative with an excursus on the virtues of Epicurean philosophy and the pursuit of *ataraxia*. On the verge of his breakthrough, Frankenstein exclaims: "A human being in perfection ought always to preserve a calm and peaceful mind, and never allow passion or a transitory desire to disturb his tranquillity." (*F* 2007: 56) "Tranquillity" recalls *tranquillitas*, a Latin word for *ataraxia*, and Shelley's "calm and peaceful mind" invokes the poetics of Lucretius, who praises tranquillity of mind on a dozen or so occasions over the course of his epic.[48]

As the passage continues, Frankenstein retrospectively rebukes himself, arguing that unbridled scientific exploration corrupts this tranquillity, which is again described using the language of Epicurean atomism:

I do not think that the pursuit of knowledge is an exception to this rule. If the study to which you apply yourself has a tendency to weaken your affections, and to destroy your taste for those simple pleasures in which no alloy can possibly mix, then that study is certainly unlawful, that is to say, not befitting the human mind. (*F* 2007: 56)

This ethical digression concludes with a brief enumeration of *exempla* employed to illustrate the disastrous consequences of deviation from *ataraxia*. Included in this list is a reprimand of Caesar that plays with the dictator's historical leanings towards Epicureanism.[49] Frankenstein declares that, "If this rule were always observed; if no man allowed any pursuit whatsoever to interfere with the tranquillity of his domestic affections . . . Caesar would have spared his country . . . " (56). Had Caesar followed his own philosophical doctrines, decades of civil war might have been avoided.

The pursuit of *ataraxia* over ambition is structurally employed to introduce not only the birth of the monster, but also the death of Frankenstein. Frankenstein's last words revive the theme as he leaves Walton with one last bit of parting advice: "Farewell, Walton! Seek happiness in tranquillity, and avoid ambition, even if it be only the apparently innocent one of distinguishing yourself in science and discoveries" (*F* 2007: 220). Recalling that Frankenstein's tale is provoked by Walton's

[48] *DRN* 1.42, 44–49; 2.16–19, 646–651, 1093–1094; 3.292–293, 939, 962; 5.10–12, 1117–1119, 1154, 1203; 6.73–78.
[49] Sallust, *Bellum Catilinae* 51.20, 27, 33. See especially Bourne (1977).

claim that he sought scientific knowledge "for the dominion I should acquire and transmit over the elemental foes of our race," the scientist's last words provide a ring-composition to his story. As the passage continues, Frankenstein concludes: "Why do I say this? I have myself been blasted in these hopes, yet another may succeed" (220).

Frankenstein's final words emphasize once again Shelley's ambivalence towards Lucretius and the Epicurean tradition. Frankenstein has, of course, *not* failed in distinguishing himself as a scientist; scientifically speaking, his experiment succeeded fabulously. Frankenstein's faith in reason and the capacity of materialist science to explain the underpinnings of the universe are confirmed by his success, and *ataraxia* is put forth prominently as a virtue. His failure, rather, is ethical. Whereas science provides for Lucretius a path towards *ataraxia*, the pursuit of knowledge leads Frankenstein astray from this ethical course, and it is difficult to read any confidence in his afterthought that "another may succeed." At the opening of the novel, Walton, like Lucretius, celebrates gigantomachy in his passionate quest to master Nature. *Frankenstein's* denouement censures just such a pursuit in ethical terms. Victor Frankenstein's last words, that "I have been blasted" in these hopes, resurrect once more the motif of gigantomachy. Having been ruined by his attempt to usurp the power of Nature, he likens his demise to the fate suffered by Otos, Ephialtes, and especially Typhon, mythological figures of classical antiquity who challenged the natural order of the universe and were destroyed by Zeus' thunderbolt.

LUCAN AND MONSTROSITY

Shelley's censures of both Caesar and gigantomachy suggest an affinity with the anti-Caesarian *Bellum Civile*. Allusion to Lucan (whose poetics are no less materialist than those of Lucretius) augments the novel's construction of monstrosity and its ethical condemnation of necromancy as an act against nature. That Shelley might appeal to Lucan is not surprising, given Percy Shelley's admiration of Lucan and Lucan's influence upon revolutionary France.[50] Lucan also provides a poetic

---

[50] Percy Shelley viewed Lucan as a kindred spirit; see Walde (2006: 56).

model for the atomistic deconstruction of the body, especially through the Erichtho episode of Book 6, classical literature's most famous scene of corporeal reanimation.[51]

The relationship is suggested in a passage quoted above, wherein Frankenstein's monster is accused by his creator of polluting the air by means of his voice: "Devil, cease; and do not poison the air with these sounds of malice." This recalls a charge that had been levied by Lucan against Erichtho: " . . . and she [Erichtho] has lain waste to the air, which did not previously bear pestilence, by breathing" (*et non letiferas spirando perdidit auras*; BC 6.522).[52]

We have earlier observed of this line of *Frankenstein* that Shelley weaves the motif of gigantomachy into her tale, and that gigantomachy as a metaphor for scientific progress is borrowed from Lucretius. Simultaneously, however, Shelley remains uncomfortable with the ethical consequences of such an overthrow of nature, and thereby diverges from her Epicurean model. In this, Shelley follows Lucan. Lucan's treatment of gigantomachy is contextually relevant to *Frankenstein*, as it reinforces the Lucretian use of the myth as a model for scientific exploration, while simultaneously buttressing Shelley's ethical condemnation of necromancy and the manipulation of life and death. Lucan's use of gigantomachy is doubly symbolic. As the Caesarean and Pompeian forces arrive in Thessaly, the site of the battle of Pharsalus, Lucan introduces the ill-fated place (*damnata tellure*; BC 6.413) by locating it as the arena of the gigantomachy: "Now impious Aloeus sent his offspring against the gods, when Pelion raised himself nearly to the stars, and Ossa, rushing against the planets, stopped their courses" (*inpius hinc prolem superis inmisit Aloeus / inseruit celsis prope se cum Pelion astris / sideribusque vias incurrens abstulit Ossa*; 6.410–412).

Lucan's ethical condemnation—Aloeus is *inpius*, or "impious"—of the gigantomachy serves a dual purpose. First, and most obviously, the mythical battle is used to introduce the land of Thessaly, site of Pharsalia. In this epic battle, two Romans of colossal stature—Caesar and Pompey—each attempted to overthrow the dominant civic structure of

---

[51] On Lucan's debt to Lucretius and atomism, with an extended discussion of the Erichtho scene, see Weiner (2011) and Esposito (1996). On the general motif of bodily dissection and dismemberment in Lucan, see also Most (1992a).

[52] I use the text of Housman (1927).

the Roman Republic.[53] More importantly for this argument, however, these lines introduce the Erichtho episode. By virtue of their structural location within Lucan's text, especially considering the epic's disavowal of the divine apparatus, we are invited to read the witch's necromancy in terms of the gigantomachy. Like Frankenstein, Erichtho usurps the power of Nature to reanimate a corpse that has been reduced to the sum of its constituent parts, and Thessalian witchcraft is explicitly conceived as an act of martial rebellion against the gods (*ibi plurima surgunt / vim factura deis*; *BC* 6.440–441). Whereas gigantomachy had for Lucretius represented the triumph of science and reason over religious superstition, gigantomachy was for Lucan a site of scientific *hubris* that is *inpius* and *nefas*, prohibited for religious reasons.

Erichtho's corpse provides a natural archetype for the radical corporeality of Frankenstein's monster. While reanimated talking corpses would become commonplace in later Latin and Greek prose genres, the corporeality of Lucan's dead prophet was without precedent in Greek and Roman epic.[54] In Virgil's *Aeneid* 6, for instance, the figure of Anchises is an incorporeal shade through whom Aeneas passes his arms three times in a futile attempt to embrace it. Erichtho's corpse, however, is material and vitally so; Erichtho chooses him for his intact lungs and reanimates the entire body. Frankenstein's monster recalls the corpse reanimated by Erichtho, both in aspect and behavior, at his naissance and again when he vows to ascend his own funeral pyre in the novel's final lines. Allusion to this macabre scene in *Bellum Civile* stains the Lucretian atomism of the monster with the grotesque.[55] Through this intertextual strategy, Shelley's narrator denounces his scientific breakthrough as *nefas*.

---

[53] Though Pompey has at times been read as Lucan's hero, since he is the head of the Republican forces, one must recall that Lucan introduces the general as a would-be king, no different from Caesar: "for Caesar was no longer to bear anyone above him, nor Pompey an equal" (*nec quemquam iam ferre potest Caesarve priorem / Pompeius parem*; *BC* 1.125–126). Thus, the two may easily be likened to the *Gigantes* in Lucan's poem. While Pompey and Caesar are clearly adversaries rather than allies, Lucan suggests that each is equally hungry for a kingship (at 1.109, Lucan refers to Rome under Pompey as a *regnum*). Lucan aligns them with both Hannibal and Juba, Africans who attacked the Roman Republic. See Ahl (1976: 102–104).

[54] On talking corpses in later Greek and Latin prose, see Gleason (1999).

[55] Lucan himself was indebted to Lucretius to a far greater extent than has generally been acknowledged. On allusion to Lucretius in the *Bellum Civile* and its significance, see especially Esposito (1996) and Weiner (2011). Though they do not argue for a detailed allusive engagement between *Frankenstein* and Lucan, Braund and Raschke (2002) were

Like Frankenstein's monster, Erichtho's corpse is described as an atomistic combination of its anatomical parts, and, upon animation, the two bear a striking resemblance to each other. As Erichtho's *vates,* chosen for his physically intact lungs, awakens, Lucan writes: "Now all the limbs tremble . . . the eyes open with the mouth gaping wide" (*nunc omnis palpitat artus . . . distento lumina rictu / nudantur*; *BC* 6.754–758). Likewise, Frankenstein's one-sentence description of his monster's awakening reads, "I saw the dull yellow eye of the creature open; it breathed hard, and a convulsive motion agitated its limbs" (*F* 2007: 58). Both creatures are initially silent and spend their first moments weeping: "But the mouth, having been bound, issues forth no sound" (*sed murmure nullo / ora astricta sonant*; *BC* 6.760–761). Prior to uttering his first words, Erichtho's "wretched corpse" merely stands there "with tears flowing" (*maestum fletu manante cadaver*; 6.776). For its part, Frankenstein's daemon is silent upon his animation, and the monster later concedes while describing his first moments that he was a "miserable wretch," and that, not yet knowing how to speak, he wept (*F* 2007: 106–107).[56] Each of the reanimated corpses is "dazed by his restoration to this world," and each is remarkably quick, yet stiff-limbed.[57]

The two monsters are therefore similarly constructed in life, and they appear even more alike at their ends. Erichtho's corpse cannot die naturally, as "death, having exerted all its power already, could not claim the life again" (*BC* 6.823–824). After the requisite spells and potions are administered, the undead man (6.822–823), "standing in sorrow" and "demanding to die" (6.821), willingly climbs his own pyre (6.825). The scene is recreated at the close of Shelley's novel, as the unnamed monster exclaims, "I should have wept to die; now it is my only consolation . . . where can I find rest but in death?" (*F* 2007: 225). Frankenstein's

---

the first to suggest such a connection, briefly noting the thematic similarity between the atomistic construction of Frankenstein's monster and Lucan's *discors machina*.

[56] This bit of information is provided by the monster, not the narrator, and not until much later in the narrative. Nevertheless, the revelation that the monster spent its first moments weeping helps form a composite picture of its animation that is eerily similar to that of Erichtho's corpse.

[57] Frankenstein's monster is depicted as remarkably fast-moving throughout the novel. In describing himself in a fit of monstrous rage, the monster remarks that he possessed a "staglike swiftness" (*F* 2007: 138). Though the monster is indeed dextrous, it is twice compared to a mummy as it stands with its limbs outstretched (59 and 221). Erichtho's corpse, meanwhile, rises from the earth swiftly and stiff as a board (*BC* 6.755–757).

creation likewise requires extreme circumstances in order to die; he is impervious to hunger and the elements, nor is there any suggestion that he physically ages over the course of the novel. Both book and monster find their denouement as the daemon leaves Walton's ship, vowing to "ascend my own funeral pyre" (225). Shelley thereby bases the life cycle of the corpse reanimated by Frankenstein on Lucan's infamous necromantic episode.

Reading such a parallel between the two monsters places Victor Frankenstein on par with Lucan's Erichtho as creators who transgress *natura* through their midnight labors.[58] Both witch and scientist are depicted as extremely pale (*BC* 6.517 and *F* 2007: 55, respectively); wild and haggard (*BC* 6.515–518; *F* 2007: 26–7 and 151); gnashing their teeth (*BC* 5.549 and 5.565–566; *F* 2007: 27); and speaking in inarticulate utterances (*BC* 6.686–687). Each participates in grave-robbing, practices corporeal dissections, and professes interest in chains of causation.[59] When Erichtho prepares to animate the corpse, she does so in part through materials pillaged from animals: the froth of dogs (*spuma canum*), the viscera of a lynx (*viscera lyncis*), the hump of a hyena (*nodus hyaenae*), the marrow of a stag that had eaten snakes (*cervi pastae serpente medullae*), the mythical *echenais*, eyes of dragons (*oculi draconum*), an Arabian flying snake (*Arabum volucer serpens*), a viper (*vipera*), and the ashes of the phoenix (*cinis phoenicis*; 6.671–680). Frankenstein does not elaborate in quite so much detail—Lucan's epic catalogue has no generic place in the Romantic novel—but his narration pairs "the horrors of my secret toil as I dabbled among the unhallowed damps of the grave" with the confession that he "tortured the living animal to animate the lifeless clay" (*F* 2007: 55). Frankenstein thereby recalls *Bellum Civile* 6.726–727, which depicts Erichtho reanimating her corpse by lashing it with a *living* serpent: "Enraged with death, she lashes the motionless corpse with a live serpent" (*irataque morti / verberat inmotum vivo serpente cadaver*).

---

[58] Andrew McClellan (2010) has compared Shelley's Frankenstein to Erichtho, observing that the two are each "students of the occult." While he stops short of arguing for an intertextual relationship between Shelley's novel and Lucan's poem, McClellan provocatively suggests that Frankenstein and Erichtho are very similar figures whose creative processes overlap extensively.

[59] Frankenstein says that "to examine the causes of life, we must first have recourse to death" (*F* 2007: 52). Likewise, Erichtho tells Pompey of the *series causarum* (*BC* 6.612).

Moreover, Frankenstein's repeated discussion of "the corruption of death" echoes the use of *sanies* and *tabes* to describe the activities of Erichtho. This subtly supports *Frankenstein*'s atomistic and anatomical approach to the body, and, more important, further paints artificial creation as *nefas*. Erichtho's ethical baggage includes impious spells (*inpia carmina*; *BC* 6.443–444), criminal rites (*ritus scelerum*; 6.507), and a horrific and polluted mouth (*os nefandum polutumque*; 6.706–707).

Erichtho begins the verbal component of her spell with an invocation of infernal powers: "Hear you my prayers, Furies and the horror of Styx and the punishments of criminals . . ." (*Eumenides Stygiumque nefas Poenaeque nocentum . . . exaudite preces*; *BC* 6.695–706). Erichtho adds Hecate, Pluto, and numerous other chthonic powers to her catalogue. Her unholy prayer is echoed in Frankenstein's own vow of revenge, spoken in rage with quivering lips:

By the sacred earth on which I kneel, by the shades that wander near me . . . I swear; and by thee, O Night, and the spirits that preside over thee . . . And I call on you, spirits of the dead; and on you, wandering ministers of vengeance, to aid and conduct me in my work. (*F* 2007: 206)

Frankenstein's transformation and moral descent into an Erichtho figure is now complete. The construction of Frankenstein via Erichtho helps establish the monstrosity of the scientist as well as his "hideous progeny."

Shelley thus constructs Frankenstein's monster via Lucan's reanimated corpse and provocatively invites us to read Frankenstein as an Erichtho figure, thereby casting additional aspersions upon her protagonist and his creative act. Moreover, Frankenstein's monster looks just like his maker.[60] Frankenstein's uncanny resemblance to his monster has prompted one scholar to describe the monster as "an opposing, distorted reflection of Victor"—the "Monster in the Mirror."[61] The two resemble each other in aspect and behavior. Over the course of the novel, both Frankenstein and his monster are depicted as wild and

[60] See also González and Calvo (1997: 17).
[61] Thornburg (1987: 9). Thornburg goes on to argue that "Victor Frankenstein, creating a being in *his* own image, necessarily acted out of what he himself saw as evil and ugly; thus the Monster is precisely what his maker despised and feared within himself" (ibid. 98–99).

haggard (the monster's unkempt hair obscures his face; *F* 2007: 221), speaking in inarticulate utterances (Frankenstein's speech is often impaired, and at 206, "rage choked my utterance"), gnashing their teeth, trembling with rage and horror, exhibiting "boundless rage" (102), and laughing maniacally (62; 206). The reciprocal nature of the relationship between scientist and monster is suggested by the novel's very first description of Victor Frankenstein, as Robert Walton, the primary narrator, declares that he "restored him [Frankenstein] to animation" (26), foreshadowing the climactic act of necromancy, and rendering Frankenstein himself both a practitioner and a victim of reanimation.[62]

The traits shared by Frankenstein and his creation invite a Foucauldian reading of monstrosity in Shelley's novel, which may easily be transposed onto Lucan's Erichtho. Michel Foucault invokes the Latin *monstrare* as the etymological origin of "monstrosity," arguing that a "monster" is someone or something to be *shown*.[63] Foucault thereby adapts the etymology offered by Cicero, who states that:

Again, predictions and presentiments of things to come declare nothing else to men except those things which may be shown, demonstrated, portended, and predicted—from which they are called signs, *monstra*, portents, and prodigies."

Praedictiones vero et praesensiones rerum futurarum quid aliud declarant nisi hominibus ea quae sint ostendi monstrari portendi praedici, ex quo illa ostenta monstra portenta prodigia dicuntur. (*De Natura Deorum* 2.7)

Cicero offers a similar formulation of monstrosity, though significantly rephrased, in his *De Divinatione*: "For because they show, portend, demonstrate, and predict, they are called signs, portents, *monstra*, and prodigies" (*quia enim ostendunt, portendunt, monstrant, praedicunt, ostenta, portenta, monstra, prodigia dicuntur*; 1.93). Here, Cicero has switched to the active voice. Monsters are not only things to *be shown*, but also things that *show*. In the case of *Frankenstein*, the daemon is a monster in the active voice, exhibiting

---

[62] Later in the scene, the narrator also says of Frankenstein that "a new spirit of life animated the decaying frame" (*F* 2007: 28).

[63] Foucault (1967: 68–70).

the transgressions and previously internalized ugliness of his creator. Ultimately, the monstrous qualities of Victor, which include disproportionate rage, violence, delusions of grandeur, and the inability to control emotion,[64] are what the monster must make public and show.

Provided that we accept an intertextual strategy by which Frankenstein and his monster are written in part via Erichtho and her reanimated corpse, I suggest that as active readers we might revisit Lucan's text and take note of the way these monsters, too, fit the Foucauldian paradigm. The reanimated corpse is largely a reflection of the witch who raises him, and his lone purpose is quite literally to speak for her.[65] Lucan employs the same vocabulary to describe both monstrous figures, as Erichtho and the corpse are each dubbed *vates* (*BC* 6.651 and 6.628, respectively) whose primary activity is *canere* (6.708; 6.717). Each in turn responds to Sextus Pompey's inquiry by naming another *vates* to prophecy for them.[66] Lucan suggests that each has gone down to the underworld and communicated with the dead, and the poet uses *pallor* to describe the physical appearance of both (Erichtho at 6.517; the corpse at 6.758). The corpse thereby *shows* (in addition to his prophecy) the attributes of its animator and master. Thus, the traits and mannerisms shared by Erichtho, the corpse, Frankenstein, and his monster offer a retrospective reading of Erichtho as a Frankenstein figure—the abominable creator of her own monstrous reflection.

CONCLUSION

As I hope I have shown, intertextual engagement with Lucretius and Lucan helps construct the science and stain the ethics of necromancy in *Frankenstein*. Nevertheless, despite the numerous connections and points of confluence among them, *De Rerum Natura*, *Bellum Civile*, and *Frankenstein* inevitably remain three very different texts, most obviously along generic lines. Neither Latin poem can rightly be called

---

[64] For an introduction to Victor Frankenstein's numerous character flaws, with particular emphasis on feminist criticism, see Mellor (2003).

[65] See O'Higgins (1988).

[66] The corpse ends his speech by deferring to Pompey Magnus (called a *vates certior*; *BC* 6.812), though this ghost does not appear in the (probably) unfinished text as we have it.

SF. *De Rerum Natura* is a didactic poem expounding atomistic physics and Epicurean ethics, while *Bellum Civile* is an historical epic that laments a particularly dark period of Rome's past more than it anticipates any future. How, then, might we draw these disparate texts together? Why do Lucretius and Lucan lend themselves as source texts to what is arguably the first SF novel? And how might these commonalities look forward to the generic development of SF?

Perhaps the characteristic that binds all three of these works, as well as the SF genre at large, is that each of these texts displays tensions between old traditions and a new rationalism. Even while writing within established generic conventions about a philosophical tradition that had persisted for centuries, Lucretius proposed a radical materiality that changed the poetics of Latin literature and challenged the foundations of Roman political and religious thought, values, and culture. Although Lucretius wrote epic poetry versifying philosophical treatises that were by no means new, the poem was nevertheless so far ahead of its time that it has recently been argued that *De Rerum Natura*'s rediscovery fifteen hundred years after its publication changed the course of Western civilization and helped give birth to modernity.[67]

Lucan, for his part, was every bit as revolutionary. The tensions between old and new surface in his chosen subject matter: the violent transition from an older, traditional form of government (the Roman Republic) to a new political order (the Augustan principate). As mired in the past as he was, writing epic poetry about martial themes from the perspective of history's losers, Lucan simultaneously deconstructed the literary conventions of epic through his very participation in the genre. Out is fate (*fatum*); in are chaos and a world governed by chance (*fortuna*) and human actions. Out is the heroic code of piety; in are uncomfortably human protagonists ruled by cruelty and ambition. While perhaps not to the same ends and certainly not with the same celebratory gusto as Lucretius, Lucan dispenses with the divine apparatus as the guiding mechanism of the universe. Left in its wake is a new material realism, which seeks to explain cosmological phenomena and historical accidents alike through a rational chain of causality (*causarum*

---

[67] Greenblatt (2011).

series; *BC* 6.612).[68] In their respective iconoclasms, both Lucan and Lucretius break with generic convention to such an extent that the status of each as epic continues to be challenged.[69]

And so we may return to *Frankenstein*. Shelley's novel accepts the scientific promises of rationalism, materialism, and atheism, but not without deep apprehensions that some primordial and ancient laws of nature stand to be transgressed. Nowhere are these tensions between old and new, tradition and invention, more evident than in the ever-conflicted figure of Frankenstein himself. Despite his cutting-edge scientific experiments and discoveries, Victor's influences hark back to past traditions. He is an avid reader of Latin, and his obsession with Cornelius Agrippa and the alchemists marks him as archaic in comparison with his teachers and peers. The monster, for its part, is an entirely new and artificial life form, yet he educates himself with a copy of Plutarch's *Lives*, drawn from the classical origins of Western literature. In the end, Mary Shelley's intertextual strategies look backwards, acknowledging several millennia of literary tradition, while the novel she wrote has been credited with establishing a new and distinctly futuristic genre.

Just as SF concerns itself with the moral ambiguities created in the wake of speculative science, it also explores the tensions between new developments and established traditions, and between modern rationalism and old superstitions. These tensions are literary as well as ethical. In order to comment on our present, as inevitably it must, SF is compelled to contend with the literary past even as it explores the future. Numerous works of SF later than *Frankenstein*—Frank Herbert's *Dune*, Kurt

---

[68] Very significantly for the comparison I have sketched above between Frankenstein and Erichtho, it is Erichtho herself who espouses this interest in cosmological chains of causality. In his introduction to the poem, Lucan's narrator defines his task as "setting forth the causes of such great things" (*causas tantarum expromere rerum*; *BC* 1.67).

[69] Conte (1994); Hainsworth (1991). Also on the absence of on-stage "divine machinery" in Lucan, despite the pervasive sense of supernatural influence haunting the poem, see Feeney (1991). Hainsworth argues that "Lucan's experiment stripped the epic of so many of its formal features that in the common view . . . it ceased to be recognizable as an epic" (132). Earlier, Hainsworth levied a similar charge against Lucretius: "We may wish to say that Lucretius' didactic poem *De Rerum Natura* shows the influence of the epic tradition, but it would be misleading to call it an epic" (4). Quint (1993: 134) observes that "Tasso, epic's greatest theorist," argues "that Lucan is not a poet at all." On ancient critics of Lucan, especially Quintilian, see Sanford (1931).

Vonnegut's *Cat's Cradle*, Dan Simmons's *Ilium* and *Olympos*, and *Battlestar Galactica*, to name but a few—blend their futuristic visions with ruminations on the classical tradition. The myriad ways in which the classical past mediates the future in the literary present, and likewise the ways in which contemporary works of speculative fiction might reflect their classical sources, are indeed fertile grounds for further inquiry.

3

Virgil in Jules Verne's *Journey to the Center of the Earth*

Benjamin Eldon Stevens

Jules Verne's novel *Journey to the Center of the Earth* (1864a [*Journey*]) makes frequent and meaningful references to Greek and Roman classics, paying special attention to the Latin language and its literature.[1] In this chapter I argue that *Journey*'s engagement with the Roman poet Virgil—via quotations, allusions, and a deep structural parallel to Virgil's epic poem, the *Aeneid* (ca. 19 B.C.E. [*Aen.*])—exemplifies how modern science fiction (SF) may be read as drawing on classical traditions in order to articulate master narratives of modern science. In general, the ancient classics are displaced from their previously privileged position of "knowledge," becoming instead "mere tradition," while "knowledge" is limited to the results of modern scientific practice (or, as

[1] An early version of this material was presented at the 2010 Annual Meeting of the Classical Association of the Atlantic States. It could not have reached its present form without the assistance of various readers, including the Press's anonymous reviewers and the team acknowledged in this volume's introduction. Special thanks are owed to my father for weekly visits to comicbook shops; *à ma mère d'avoir étudié le français lorsque j'étais enfant*; and to Brett M. Rogers, co-editor, colleague, and indefatigable friend on many fantastic journeys.

in Verne's case, science writing).[2] In *Journey* in particular, Verne—described by his publisher J.-G. Hetzel as "the man of perpendiculars"—replaces Virgil's unsystematic cyclical cosmology (as described to Aeneas by the ghost of his father, Anchises) with the nascent science of geology and its consequences for a linear model of human history, including prehistory. Whereas Virgil's hero encounters figures from his own past from whom he may acquire knowledge about an ideal future for his people, Verne's hero experiences a vision, even a sort of "epiphany," of a far more distant, depersonalized past—a prehistory—that is said by the new scientific narrative to be shared by reader, author, and characters alike.[3] In this way, following a sort of perpendicular deviation from ancient epic, *Journey* offers an image of the "hero" redefined as modern scientific man.

At the same time, as it replaces and displaces the classics, Verne's narrative may also be read as offering a critique of modern science, in part by showing appreciation for what science does not seem to capture adequately. In this connection, Latin in general and Virgil above all are represented as natural means of expressing personal feeling, especially the "romantic" feelings of wonder, affection, and love. In the world envisioned by the novel, Latin is simultaneously the language of scholarly

[2] Cf. publisher J.-G. Hetzel's description of the project of Verne's *Extraordinary Journeys*: to "outline all the geographical, geological, physical, and astronomical knowledge amassed by modern science and to recount, in an entertaining and picturesque format . . . the history of the universe" (in the prologue to Verne [1866]); on this project, see further Evans (1988: 7–31). Work of such scope admits contradictory readings: e.g., Verne's writing has been said to emerge directly from bourgeois ideology as it pertains to science (Barthes 1957) but also to articulate fractures in that ideology (Butour 1949, Macherey 1966). Some other interpretations of *Journey* are noted below. Raymond and Compère (1976) is a useful introduction to Verne studies, while Compère (1977) is good on *Journey*. A special issue of *Science Fiction Studies* (32.1 [2005]) is devoted to essays on Verne's work. On the man himself, see Butcher (2006).

[3] Ancient epic heroes like Aeneas are set in motion against their wishes, struggling to get home or, as in Aeneas' case, to reach a new place that must substitute for a home that has been lost. By contrast, modern heroes like Verne's leave home in order to explore unknown places *and then return*, finding that little if anything has changed; on Verne's circular cartographies, see Harpold (2005), generally Butcher (1991, paying special attention to *Journey* on 60–74), and Martin (1985: 144–150). Such modern travelers may have more in common with ancient explorers like the Greek historian Herodotus (fifth century B.C.E.), possessed of a certain rationalizing impulse, than with heroes like Aeneas, driven by powers beyond their comprehension and control. On "epiphanies" ancient and modern, see Grobéty (this volume, chapter twelve).

communication and the language of personal expression. Relatedly, the novel's narrator understands Latin in terms that would distinguish "science" from "poetry." This evaluative distinction interacts with the novel's general engagement with the classics in complex and interesting ways.

In what follows, I attempt to justify this reading of *Journey*'s classical receptions by focusing on the novel's three full quotations from Virgil. (Some other references to ancient material are discussed in the notes, and all are gathered in an appendix to this chapter.) Although the third quotation is perhaps the most important for the novel's reception of classical material overall, since it occurs at an especially climactic moment in the story, all three together suggest ways of understanding Vernes's engagement with Virgil, Latin, and the classics, and so may serve to organize my argument. Above all, I hope to show how productive it can be to read modern SF as a kind of classical reception that draws on classical tradition to articulate and to complicate its own master narratives.

ET QUACUMQUE VIAM DEDERIT FORTUNA SEQUAMUR: LATIN FOR "SCIENTIFIC" COMMUNICATION AND "ROMANTIC" EXPRESSION

Journey's first quotation from Virgil occurs when the narrator, the journeyman scientist Axel, and his uncle, Professor Lidenbrock, are leaving Reykjavik (where they have stopped overnight) for their overland journey to the entrance into the earth's depths (ch. 11).[4] As they leave, they are bidden goodbye by one of their hosts, Mr. Fridriksson, with, as Axel puts it, "that line from Virgil that seemed ready-made for us, voyagers uncertain of the way: *Et quacumque viam dederit fortuna sequamur*" (*Aen.* 11.128).[5] In English, the Virgil is: "And let us follow whatever road fortune has

[4] Uniquely among his novels, *Journey* was revised by Verne between editions. In this chapter I use the shorthand *Journey* to refer to the 1867 edition—the seventh—which includes the climactic encounter in the "underworld" (chs. 37–39) discussed below (in the sections "'Scientific' Epiphany and 'Romantic' Elegy" and "'Scientific' Epiphany and an Un-epic Epistemology"). For the reader's convenience, all translations of Verne into English are from Butcher (2008), with some modifications. All translations from Latin are my own.

[5] Butcher (2008: 60). *Journey* ch. 11: "M. Fridriksson me lança avec son dernier adieu ce vers que Virgile semblait avoir fait pour nous, voyageurs incertains de la route." "Voyagers uncertain of the way" is my replacement for Butcher's "uncertain travellers on

given!" The quotation is apt, and its placement at the end of the chapter produces some dramatic effect, somewhat in the manner of a serialized novel. Likewise, it may give an insight into Axel's feeling, melodramatic (even if it is accurate as a prediction) in combining the personal with the grandiose. The fact that such a "romantic" feeling is somehow best expressed in Latin is emphasized both at this moment and by the extended scene in Reykjavik. At the moment of goodbye, whereas Professor Lidenbrock could express his warm thanks to their host "in Icelandic," Axel himself "strung together a cordial farewell in [his] best Latin."[6] Previously in the Reykjavik scene, Mr. Fridriksson is introduced as a "humble scholar [who] spoke only Icelandic and Latin: he came and offered his services in the language of Horace." Therefore Axel "felt that [they] were bound to understand each other." Axel's feeling that Latin allows for solidarity is emphasized: "He was in fact the only person I could converse with during my entire stay in Iceland"; as a result, Axel declares Mr. Fridriksson is "charming" and his conversation "quite precious."[7] It seems then that, by the end of their brief stay in the capital, not only is Latin Axel's only means of communication with anyone, but the language is also positively charged with warm feeling.

Readers familiar with the Latin classics may not be surprised that Axel's standard of comparison is poetry; most often—and at the most important moments—Virgil. A crucial aspect of *Journey*'s engagement with the classics as they are implied in (Virgil's) Latin is thus a sort of tension between Latin as a language of communication among scholars, focusing on accurate and enduring description in scientific terms, and Latin as a vehicle for personal expression, which by contrast conveys a vivid impression in a particular moment. For convenience, we may call these two modes "scientific" and "romantic."[8]

---

the road": the phrase should capture the connection between Axel's uncertainty and his feeling that the quotation from Virgil is *therefore* perfectly apt. This should also make it clear to readers without French that "voyageurs" is, of course, an echo of the novel's title.

[6] Butcher (2008: 60). On Lidenbrock's mastery of many languages, see note 20.

[7] Immediately preceding quotations from Verne in English are from Butcher (2008: 48). *Journey* ch. 9: "Mais un charmant homme, et dont le concours nous devint fort précieux, ce fut M. Fridriksson, professeur de sciences naturelles à l'école de Reyjkawik. Ce savant modeste ne parlait que l'islandais et le latin; il vint m'offrir ses services dans la langue d'Horace, et je sentis que nous étions faits pour nous comprendre. Ce fut, en effet, le seul personnage avec lequel je pus m'entretenir pendant mon séjour en Islande."

[8] Cf. Evans (1988: 33–102) on how the "Ideological Subtexts in the *Voyages Extraordinaires*" comprise a "positivist perspective" (37–57) and a "romantic vision" (58–102).

Although during the Reykjavik scene Axel refers to the Roman poet Horace, a contemporary of Virgil's, two other moments help make clear Axel's feelings that Virgil is the high point of Latin and, as a result, that Latin is especially well suited to personal, "romantic" expression. We will see that Lidenbrock's understanding of Latin is the more "scientific," although the two are not completely opposed to each other.

At the first of the two moments in question, Axel offers his appraisal of the technical terms of his uncle's primary area of scientific interest, mineralogy.

> Now, in mineralogy, there are many learned words, half-Greek, half-Latin, and always difficult to pronounce, many unpolished terms that would scorch a poet's lips. I do not wish to criticize this science. Far from it. But when one is in the presence of rhombohedral crystallizations, retinasphalt resins, ghelenites, fangasites, lead molybdates, manganese tungstates, zircon titanites, the most agile tongue is allowed to get tied in knots.[9]

The context for this appraisal is Axel's extended first description of his uncle, focused here on his "slight pronunciation problem."[10] For our purposes, however, the most interesting feature of this paragraph is Axel's insistence that his dislike of the "learned words," what we could call "scientific terminology," is distinct from his positive feelings towards the learning or science itself. Axel is concerned, not with scientific precision, which he grants, but with these terms' aesthetic effect—what he refers to as their "poetry." We may therefore say that his dislike of the terms is not scientific but linguistic and aesthetic: there is something regrettable about "half-Greek, half-Latin" forms, the problem being,

---

[9] Butcher (2008: 4). *Journey* ch. 1: "Or, il y a en minéralogie bien des dénominations semi-grecques, semi-latines, difficiles à prononcer, de ces rudes appellations qui écorcheraient les lèvres d'un poète. Je ne veux pas dire du mal de cette science. Loin de moi. Mais lorsqu'on se trouve en présence des cristallisations rhomboédriques, des résines rétinashpaltes, des ghélénites, des fangasites, des molybdates de plomb, de tungstates de manganèse et des tianiates de zircone, il est permis à la langue la plus adroite de fourcher."

[10] This "pronunciation problem" appears later, when Lidenbrock, while giving an extemporaneous "lecture" on the human skeleton they have discovered underground, stumbles over the title "Gigantosteology" (ch. 38; *Gigantosteology* is an actual work, Habicot [1613]).

again, that such forms do not seem "poetic."[11] Since Axel makes this clear in *Journey*'s first section, and since the novel is entirely his narration, the whole novel may be taken as proceeding with this distinction in mind.

The distinction between "scientific" and "poetic" language is emphasized in the second of the two moments currently in question. Axel and Lidenbrock have just succeeded in decoding a cryptogram in runic writing discovered between the pages of Snorri Sturluson's *Heims-Kringla*.[12] This decoding process is what precipitates the journey: as Axel puts it, "these bizarre forms . . . led Professor Lidenbrock and his nephew to undertake the strangest expedition [of] the nineteenth century" (*Journey* 9). Once the message has been transliterated from runic letters to Roman letters and then read in the right order, in Lidenbrock's view "nothing is easier" than identifying it as Latin.[13] As Lidenbrock reasons it, the writer of the cryptogram, one Arne Saknussemm,

was an educated man. Now, when he was not writing in his mother tongue, he must naturally have chosen the language customarily used amongst educated people of the sixteenth century—I refer to Latin. If I am proved wrong, I can try Spanish, French, Italian, Greek, or Hebrew. But the scholars of the sixteenth century generally wrote in Latin. I have therefore the right to say, *a priori*, that this *is* Latin.[14]

[11] Cf. the complaint voiced by the classicist A. E. Housman as depicted in Tom Stoppard's *The Invention of Love*: "Homosexuals? Who is responsible for this barbarity? . . . It's half Greek and half Latin!" (1997: 91).

[12] Verne seems to have borrowed the idea of such a cryptogram from Poe's "The Gold Bug" (1843); Verne analyzed Poe, including that short story, in "Edgar Poe et ses oeuvres" (1864b). It may be that the cryptogram marks its knowledge as forbidden: Butcher notes (2008: 221 n. 13) that "Galileo's letter of 30 July 1610 used an anagram to hide the revelation that Saturn's ring was composed of two satellites."

[13] Butcher reports (2008: xxxii) that in a recently discovered manuscript of *Journey*, made known to scholarship only recently, and as of this writing not completely available, "a large number of details in the cryptic message are not the same" as in the published novel; he does not say which, but presumably would have mentioned if, as seems unlikely, the language were not Latin. Sturluson's *Heims-Kringla*, or "The History of the Kings of Norway," is of course an additional indication of *Journey*'s engagement with Icelandic themes.

[14] Butcher (2008: 13–14). *Journey* ch. 3: "Ce Saknussemm . . . était un homme instruit; or, dès qu'il n'écrivait pas dans sa langue maternelle, il devait choisir de préférence la langue courante entre les esprits cultivés du XVIe siècle, je veux dire le latin. Si je me trompe, je pourrai essayer de l'espagnol, du français, de l'italien, du grec, de l'hebreu. Mais les savants du XVIe siècle écrivaient généralement en latin. J'ai donc le droit de dire

There is, then, a very real way in which the journey is inspired by knowledge of Latin, particularly as Latin is regarded as having been the language of scholarly communication.[15]

Also important for our purposes is how the Latin is evaluated. Axel is surprised, even dismayed, by his uncle's deduction about the language of the inscription: "for [his] recollections of Latinity revolted against the pretension of this assemblage of uncouth words to belong to the soft tongue of Virgil."[16] In Axel's mind, in contrast to Virgil's poetry, the cryptogram is "bad Latin" (*mauvais latin*). This negative evaluation helps emphasize how Axel's image of Latin is "classical" indeed or, more precisely, "classicizing": in Axel's view, Latin is a language of poetry and thus a cultivated vehicle for heartfelt self-expression. In this way the novel links the "soft tongue" of Virgil with a narrator whose interest in modern science is in certain ways secondary to his sentimentalism. Again, this distinction between "scientific" and "romantic" or "personal" plays out in language. Axel thus comments on his feelings for Lidenbrock's godchild, the object of Axel's affections: "I adored her—if, that is, the word exists in the Teutonic language."[17] Likewise, when Axel is made to test out his uncle's theory about the arrangement of letters in the cryptogram, he writes, "I love you so much, my darling Graüben!" He writes this "immediately" and "like a love-sick fool," as if without complete control over his action.[18] In part this is a gleeful depiction by

<hr>

a priori: ceci est du latin." Saknussemm is "loosely based on Professor Árni Magnússon (1663–1730), an Icelandic scholar . . . who always wrote in Latin" (2008: 221 n. 13).

[15] On Latin as a language of international communication, especially among scholars, see, e.g., Waquet and Howe (2001); Farrell (2001).

[16] Butcher (2008: 14). *Journey* ch. 3: "Mes souvenirs de latiniste se révoltaient contre la prétention que cette suite de mots baroques pût appartenir à la douce langue de Virgile." The phrase "soft tongue of Virgil" may recall Byron's *Beppo*, stanza 44: "I love the language, that soft bastard Latin, / Which melts like kisses from a female mouth. . . ." Although by "bastard Latin" Byron means Italian, the poem nonetheless seems to evoke something like Axel's feelings about Latin. Byron's sensuality seems to go farther than Verne's, but Verne himself may be read as having a "volcanic" sensuality; for the term, Butcher (2008: xx), and for some thoughts on symbolized sexuality, idem (2008: xxv–xxvi).

[17] Butcher (2008: 15). *Journey* ch. 3: "je l'adorer, si toutefois ce verbe existe dans la langue tudesque!"

[18] Butcher (2008: 15 and 16). *Journey* ch. 3: "Je t'aime bien, ma petite Graüben!" and "Oui, sans m'en douter, en amoureux maladroit, j'avais tracé cette phrase compromettante!" In the manuscript referred to above, note 13, Axel's feeling for Graüben is evidently given additional emphasis; see Butcher (2008: xxxii).

the very French Verne of a quite un-German and un-scientific immod-
esty. From such a character we might well expect spontaneous expression of emotion, and a "soft tongue" like that embodied in Latin poetry
serves as the appropriate vehicle.

Evaluation of the language and of its appropriate use is also evident in
Professor Lidenbrock. In contrast to Axel's "romantic" view, Lidenbrock
represents an image of Latin as mainly "scientific," the *lingua franca* of
scholars. Since Lidenbrock is something of a comic figure, his image of
Latin's importance may be mocked as out of date: Latin as a means of
learning is ascribed to the sixteenth century, whereas modern scientists
of the nineteenth century, including Lidenbrock himself, communicate
in modern languages. There would seem to be no question in the novel of
Latin's return to international importance.[19] We may also note that
Lidenbrock nowhere seems concerned, as Axel is, with questions of
style: for him the Latin of the cryptogram is, like the *lingua franca* of an
earlier age, a means to an end. In a similar vein, although Axel may
expect his uncle to be able to "produce pompously from his mouth a sentence of Latin majesty," this would seem to be a matter of his general
admiration for his uncle's knowledge of all things ("my uncle was an
authentic scholar—I cannot emphasize this too much"; Butcher 2008: 5),
including a great many languages, rather than specific to "Latinity" as
such.[20] For Lidenbrock, then, Latin is not so much necessarily "classical,"
much less the property of Virgil in particular, as it is "historical," merely
one language among many and thus to be understood like any other.

In the several moments we have considered so far, *Journey* figures Latin
complexly, as both a language of precise, professional, "scientific" description and as a vehicle for evocative, personal, "romantic" expression. With

[19] Whether this is complicated by Verne's Catholicism is beyond the scope of this
chapter.
[20] Butcher (2008: 17). *Journey* ch. 3: "j'attendais donc que le professeur laissât se
dérouler pompeusement entre ses lèvres une phrase d'une magnifique latinité."
Parenthetical quotation, ch. 1: "mon oncle, je ne saurais trop le dire, était un véritable
savant." Lidenbrock is described by Axel as "a genuine polyglot: not that he spoke fluently
the 2,000 languages and 4,000 dialects employed on the surface of the globe, but he did
know his fair share" (Butcher 2008: 10). *Journey* ch. 2: "Lidenbrock . . . passait pour être
un véritable polyglotte. Non pas qu'il parlât couramment les deux mille langues et les
quatre mille idiomes employés à la surface du globe, mais enfin il en savait sa bonne
part." In context of a journey "to the center of the earth," the phrase "on the surface of the
globe" could foreshadow certain confusion in the world below.

Latin and Virgil standing in for the classics more generally, the classical tradition is likewise a matter of complex presentation: the classics are a matter of significant common knowledge, even as "tradition" is yielding to scientific "knowledge." Conversely, the tradition is also a matter of personal expression, even as that expression—and the genre of the novel—is gently mocked. Complexity of tone aside, the general implication is that Latin and the classics have changed in status from "classic" to "(merely) traditional."

FACILIS DESCENSUS AVERNO: THE DESCENT OF THE EPIC HERO AND THE ASCENT OF THE SCIENCE-HERO

Having developed a first impression of *Journey*'s complex image of Latin, Virgil, and the classics, we may turn to the novel's second and third quotations from Virgil. The second quotation shows that Verne's appreciation of Virgil is combined with serious departures from him, while the third represents a dramatic and consequential departure indeed, at precisely the moment we might expect: the deepest and most climactic part of the journey. The second quotation occurs when Axel, Lidenbrock, and their Icelandic porter Hans, who have all spent the night at the bottom of the chimney of the dormant volcano Snaeffels, begin the descent proper, moving into what would be utter darkness if not for their "electric torches." Axel is disturbed by losing sight of the sky. But soon he is able to say to himself *facilis descensus Averno* (quoting *Aen.* 6.126): "easy [is the] descent into the Underworld."[21] This quotation serves to express Axel's renewed

[21] Translating Virgil's *Averno* as "Underworld" depends on a sort of metonym, since Avernus is not the Underworld as such but an entrance into it. As Butcher puts it (2008: 224 n. 92), Avernus is "a lake in a crater near Naples, believed to be the source of the river Styx." Translating it as "Underworld" also unfortunately obliterates a wordplay that was of evident interest to Verne and that, in a plot set in motion by a cryptogram, should interest us: that linking the name of the entrance, "aVERNus," and the name of the author, "VERNe." Butcher suggests (2008: xxvii) that "[t]he novel is generated by the personal anagram, not once but repeatedly," pointing to crucial terms like "à l'ENVERs" ("backwards"), "RENVErsé" ("reversed"), "caVERNE" ("cavern"), "gouVERNail" ("helm"), and "ViRlaNdaisE" (Graüben's toponym). Going further, "the word *Averni . . .* may indicate a source of inspiration in medieval ideas of an underground Hell" (Butcher 2008: xvii). Verne thus draws on Virgil complexly, both directly and via intermediaries (e.g., Dante). Certain significant departures from Virgil's underworld are discussed below. Virgil himself of course draws on and deviates from earlier authors, including Homer (*Odyssey* Book 11 [*Od.*]).

good humor and even delight, emotions he feels "in spite of" himself, at two things. Most immediately, he responds to the physical ease of the descent: "we were able to simply let ourselves go on these inclined slopes, without taxing ourselves. It was Virgil's *facilis descensus Averni*," or "easy way down into the Underworld."[22] More generally, he is taken by the spectacle provided by this first truly underground experience.[23] As in the novel's complex image of Latin, Axel's response at this moment combines the scientific and the romantic, blending the mineralogical, the domestic, and the supernatural:

> The lava, porous in places, was covered with little round bulbs; crystals of opaque quartz, decorated with clear drops of glass, hung from the vaulted ceiling like chandeliers, and seemed to light up as we passed. It was as if the spirits of the underground were lighting up their palace to welcome their guests from the Earth.[24]

The last sentence especially gives a sense of the ancient underworld, as it was populated with "spirits." In this connection, it matters that the quotation from Virgil occurs in the *Aeneid* just prior to the entrance into the underworld.[25] For our purposes, it is also important that Axel does not complete the quotation. In Virgil, *facilis descensus Averno* is only the beginning of what is said by the Sibyl, a prophetic figure, to Aeneas once

[22] Butcher (2008: 92). *Journey* ch. 18: "nous nous laissions aller sans fatigue sur des pentes inclinées. C'était le *facilis descensus Averni* de Virgile."

[23] Cf. Aeneas' "amazement" (root *mir*-) at aspects of the Underworld: the souls gathering on the near side of the river Styx (*Aen.* 6.317), the Elysian Fields (6.651), and Anchises' naming of Romans-to-be, leading to his famous injunction to "spare the defeated and battle down the proud in war" (*parcere subiectis et debellare superbos*; 6.853; at 6.854 the Sibyl shares Aeneas' amazement). Aeneas' experience, like Axel's in this passage and elsewhere, is intensely visual; verbs for "seeing" occur frequently in *Aeneid* Book 6, and already in Book 2 the veil has been stripped from Aeneas' eyes by Venus (2.604ff.).

[24] Butcher (2008: 92). *Journey* ch. 18: "La lave, poreuse en de certains endroits, présentait de petites ampoules arrondies: des cristaux de quartz opaque, ornés de limpides gouttes de verre et suspendus à la voûte comme des lustres, semblaient s'allumer à notre passage. On eût dit que les génies du gouffre illuminaient leur palais pour recevoir les hôtes de la terre." This may recall Psyche's first sight of the palace of Cupid as described by Apuleius (*Metamorphoses* 5.1).

[25] For introductions to scholarship on the *Aeneid*, see, e.g., Kennedy (1997) and the chapters in Farrell and Putnam (2010), esp. chapters 1–7. Several recent translations have included thought-provoking introductions: see esp. Bernard Knox's introduction to Robert Fagles's translation (1998) and Elaine Fantham's introduction to Frederik Ahl's translation (2007).

he has made clear his intention to journey below (*Aen.* 6.126–131).[26] "The way down into the Underworld is easy," says the Sibyl, for "night and day the doorway of black Dis stands open." But then she continues: "But to call your step back, and to fly out to the air above, this is the work, this is the labor." Moreover, successful return has depended on truly exceptional circumstances, including outstanding virtue or, better, divine ancestry: "A few, whom Jupiter loved well or whose own ardent virtue carried them up to the upper atmosphere, those few born to the gods could do it." Certain of these factors apply to Aeneas: he is protected by Jupiter from the worst of Juno's anger, and he is a son of Venus.

In contrast, it would seem that none of these factors could apply to Verne's voyagers. A prior question is whether they should: whether it is useful to read Axel's quotation somehow in the light of its original context and, therefore, to think of what follows *facilis descensus Averno* as somehow "missing" or "suppressed."[27] I think that *Journey*'s deep engagement with Virgil requires us to do so: not so as to impose Aeneas' experience on the voyagers, but as a way of describing the effect of the relationship between the two works more precisely. Given Virgil's place in education at the time, Verne himself would certainly have known the original context, and it is likely that his intended readers, too, could be expected to recognize the famous passage. Axel's quotation thus has the effect of introducing a certain ironic suspense or foreboding. Will Verne's modern heroes, like their ancient predecessor, face a difficult ascent? If so, will the difficulty be of a similar sort?

With these questions we touch on an aspect of the *Aeneid* that has long puzzled readers: Aeneas' ascent does not seem to be "difficult" at all; in fact, he seems to leave the underworld with ease. His return to the surface is, however, not therefore straightforward, and the complexity may help us understand Verne's appropriation more deeply. In Virgil,

---

[26] *Facilis descensus Averno: / noctes atque dies patet atri ianua Ditis; / sed revocare gradum superasque evadere auras, / hoc opus, hic labor est. pauci, quos aequus amavit / Iuppiter aut ardens evexit ad aethera virtus, / dis geniti potuere.*

[27] In this chapter I do not adopt a particular theory of reception; see, e.g., Hardwick and Stray (2008), Martindale and Thomas (2006), and Hardwick (2003). On the value of considering the fullest available "backstory" to a quotation or allusion, granting that the full story might not have been "live" in the minds of all intended readers, see, e.g., Mastronarde (2002: 44–45).

there are two gates by which Aeneas could return to the surface, each with a different implication:

> There are twin gates of sleep, of which the one is said to be
> horn, through which easy exit is given to true shades,
> while the other has been made to shine with gleaming ivory,   895
> but [through it] the shades send false dreams to the heavens.
> To these, then, Anchises followed his son and the Sibyl
> with words and sends them out through the ivory gate.[28]

As noted, Aeneas simply exits, and once out he seems, also simply, to "return to his ships and companions";[29] in the six books of the *Aeneid* that follow this moment, there is no reference to the matter of the gates or to any particular "difficulty." We may nonetheless ask whether anything is implied by Aeneas' exit being through the gate of ivory, reserved as that is for "false dreams."[30] It could be that Aeneas, being no kind of shade (i.e., spirit of the dead), simply must use that gate.[31] In contrast, it would seem unsatisfying were the gates merely a way for Virgil to suggest "the time of night."[32] While insisting, then, on *some* meaning, we may need to conclude, as Austin puts it, not only that "no one knows the full implication" of this exit, but also that "[t]here is no means of knowing what deeper significance [Aeneas' exit] held in Virgil's mind for Aeneas' experience in the Underworld."[33]

---

[28] *Aen.* 6.893–898: *Sunt geminae Somni portae, quarum altera fertur / cornea, qua veris facilis datur exitus umbris, / altera candenti perfecta nitens elephanto, / sed falsa ad caelum mittunt insomnia Manes. / his ibi tum natum Anchises unaque Sibyllam / prosequitur dictis portaque emittit eburna.* These lines are modeled on Homer *Od.* 19.562–557.

[29] Strictly speaking, Aeneas "follows a path to the ships and sees his companions again" (*ille viam secat ad navis sociosque revisit; Aen.* 6.900). In choice of verb (*revisere*), Virgil may subtly emphasize how remarkable it is for anyone to escape the underworld and "see again"—that is, to return to "life," which is conventionally equated, in ancient literature, with "light."

[30] The question has excited scholarship; for some general remarks see Austin (1986: 274–278) and West (1990).

[31] Aeneas' unshadelike physicality is emphasized, e.g., when he boards Charon's ferry to cross the river Styx, and the weight of his living body causes the ferry to take on water (*Aen.* 6.413–414). In *Journey* (ch. 39), Verne's heroes cast no shadows: although this may recall Dante's shades, which likewise do not cast shadows (unlike the pilgrim Dante, who does), it is given a pseudoscientific explanation that further distinguishes *Journey*'s world from that of the epic; see below.

[32] This view is discussed and dismissed by Austin (1986: 276).

[33] Ibid. (275).

For our purposes, it is enough to be able to think of Aeneas' exit as suggesting something profound about ascent and the underworld, something that may affect our understanding of how the Sibyl's prophetic utterance to Aeneas (*facilis descensus Averno. . .*) is appropriated by Verne. If the Sibyl is not to have been wrong in her confident description of "difficulty," then we may wish to understand her as having spoken metaphorically, focusing on how the underworld affects the hero. In particular, Aeneas cannot easily "leave" the underworld in emotional terms. He spoke there with his father, whose death he calls "the most grievous" and surprising event on his voyage to Italy (*Aen.* 3.708–713), and he sought in vain to speak with his beloved Dido, whose death half-surprised him and must be laid in part at his feet (6.450–476). Emotionally, Aeneas is consigned to a kind of hell; he carries it with him.[34] The hero is changed by his journey.

We may now ask whether Verne's explorers are affected by their ascent in a way that makes them comparable to Virgil's deeply troubled hero. What is implied by the journey's proceeding under the sign of Aeneas' "easy descent and difficult return"? By contrast, what is meant by Axel, Lidenbrock, and Hans returning to the world above as they do? Echoing Virgil's "true dreams" and "false shades," it has seemed to Verne's readers that parts of Axel's experience under the earth are framed in ways reminiscent of dream-narratives or altered consciousness. For example, Axel falls asleep just before the descent proper (*Journey* ch. 17). Is the journey under the earth therefore a kind of "dream"? Similarly, just before the final moment of the ascent, Axel loses consciousness (ch. 43). Is his return to the surface world a sort of "waking dream"? In the terms provided by Virgil, would such a dream be "true" or "false"? Whatever the answer, there is thus a way in which the voyage is under the sign of "dream," and so may be linked to Virgil's dream-gates.

---

[34] Arguably, this crucial component of Aeneas' character precedes his experience in the Underworld: he has already had to leave behind his wife, Creusa, in the conflagration of his home city of Troy (*Aen.* 2.768–794). That loss may be marked as especially isolating; Aeneas has been faced with her shade in the world above but does not encounter her in the Underworld. By contrast, Dido, whom Aeneas does encounter in the Underworld, is paired there with her loving spouse, Sychaeus. Cf. Satan's famous self-description in Milton, in terms that recall Aeneas' harassment by divine anger and his inability to escape himself: "Which way shall I fly / Infinite wrath and infinite despair? / Which way I fly is Hell; myself am Hell" (*Paradise Lost* 4.73–75).

By some contrast, although in Verne the ascent itself is rather longer and a matter of great physical difficulty indeed, the result would seem to be wholly positive. The voyagers ascend on a "raft" raised by a column of water caused by eruption of an active volcano, Stromboli.[35] The violent activity of Stromboli stands in implicit contrast with the dead chimney of Snaeffels on the initial descent, forming a ring-structure that gives vivid closure to the journey into the earth.[36] Verne describes Stromboli in evocative terms: it belongs to "the Aeolian archipelago of mythological memory, [and is] the ancient Strongyle, where Aeolus held the wind and storms in fetters" (*Journey* 213). While the journey's exit- and end-points therefore differ markedly from Virgil's, their explicit

---

[35] Cf. the younger Pliny's description of the eruption of Vesuvius in 70 C.E. (*Epistulae* 6.16).

[36] That closure is one example of Verne's preference for circularity; see above, note 3. A similar inversion, with its own evocation of an earlier underworld, may be detected in Axel's having seen, through "the 3,000-foot long tube" formed by the chimney of the initial descent, "a brilliant object": a star that Axel identifies as "Beta of the Little Bear" (Butcher 2008: 89–90); *Journey* ch. 17: "j'aperçus un point brillant à l'extrémité de ce tube long de trois mille pieds, qui se transformait en une gigantesque lunette. C'était une étoile dépouillée de toute scintillation, et qui, d'après mes calculs, devait être B de la Petite Ourse"). When the time comes to descend further, Axel similarly "raised [his] head and looked through the long tube at the sky of Iceland, 'that I would never see again'" (Butcher 2008: 92); *Journey* ch. 18: "je relevai la tête, et j'aperçus une dernière fois, par le champ de l'immense tube, ce ciel de l'Islande 'que je ne devais plus revoir'." I have not discovered why the phrase "that I would never see again" is marked as a quotation; it is repeated in Verne's later *The Floating Island* (1871), but I do not know an earlier appearance. These two moments together may recall the end of Dante's *Inferno*, when the pilgrim Dante and Virgil, having traveled together through Hell, see at last the open sky and the stars (34.139). When Verne's travelers emerge, it is daytime, and the sun, evocatively called "the radiant star" ("l'astre radieux"), is "pouring on to [them] waves of splendid irradiation" (Butcher 2008: 210; *Journey* ch. 44: "nous versait à flots une splendide irradiation"). There is much to be said about how Verne's "underworld" draws on Dante's in its own right and as it transmutes Virgil's. Here I can only note that, in a profound and mysterious way, when European literature, especially after Dante, goes into the earth, it seems to go there with Virgil; see, e.g., Hardie (1993: 57–87) and generally the chapters in Farrell and Putnam (2010), esp. Jacoff (2010). For discussion of Virgil's more general influence on premodern authors including Dante, see Ziolkowski and Putnam (2008). As far as SF and the linked genre of fantasy go, perhaps the most important modern example of underworlds being Virgilian is provided by J. R. R. Tolkien's *The Lord of the Rings* (1954–1955); see, e.g., Obertino (1993) and Simonis (2014). I intend to explore classical receptions in Tolkien's underworlds further in future work. One rich contemporary example, among many others, is provided by A. S. Byatt's *The Children's Book* (2011), which makes powerful use of Virgil's *facilis descensus* (e.g., 250–254), via a story-within-the-story called "Tom Underground" (esp. chapters 16ff.); I have discussed Byatt in Stevens (2013), after Cox (2011: 135–152).

association with Aeolus forms a link to Aeneas' *first* experience in the *Aeneid*, a catastrophic storm rained down by none other than Aeolus and his winds (1.81–156). By linking his voyagers' exit from the underworld to Aeneas' very first experience, Verne effects a precise sort of reversal, in which the ancient epic, storehouse of "mythological memory," is rewritten to reflect a new, modern, scientific understanding of the world and "underworld." In particular, the latter seems now to be only literally "the world below," not primarily a symbol of something figuratively deeper.[37] It would seem, then, that the very concept of a "journey" as well as its consequences have been transformed.

We may therefore conclude this reading of themes suggested by *Journey*'s second quotation from Virgil by saying that what is for Aeneas a real source of danger is for Axel and his companions a matter of immaterial "mythological memory" alone. Attributed as it is to Axel, the reference to Aeolus adds a note of romance—and that may be all. In strong contrast to Aeneas, then, Verne's characters are, at this point, *not* heroes of the sort populating ancient epics: they are *not* subject to laborious wandering caused by capricious gods. Although they are surprised at their destination, they accept their "fate" as being the result of rational causes; and importantly, that destination is not final, for they are able to return home. Whereas the narrator of the *Aeneid* asks, rhetorically, "Is there such great anger in the hearts of the gods?" (*tantaene animis caelestibus irae*; 1.11), the narrator of *Journey*, Axel himself, is in the very different position of reporting on causes he has already discovered or

[37] We could develop this image further by contrasting Verne's scientific understanding of the volcano's activity with ancient mythologies in which monsters like Typhoeus or the Cyclops, having been trapped under the earth, cause eruptions and earthquakes; thus did ancient mythology account for, e.g., Sicily's Mount Aetna. (A connection to the Cyclops would be strengthened by how Axel's encounter with the monstrous guardian, discussed below, echoes Odysseus' reported encounter with the Cyclops in *Od.* Book 9.) Recalling such monsters only to dismiss them allows Verne to emphasize modern science over mythography. Likewise, the fact that Verne's heroes escape on a "raft," as if by means of a "sea" but one powered by a sort of fire, is suggestive of how the traditional domain of Vulcan has been appropriated and de-mythologized by modern technoscience. On Vulcan de-mythologized, cf. Marx's unpublished version (from 1857) of the introduction to his "Contribution to the Critique of Political Economy" (1859), quoted above, in the introduction to this volume. Cf. Milton's famous "correction" of Vulcan's fall as described by Homer (*Iliad* 1.591–593 [*Il.*]): "Men called him Mulciber, and how he fell / From Heav'n they fabled .... Thus they relate, / Erring" (*Paradise Lost* 1.740–747); Milton's "correction" is of course theological, not technoscientific. For additional examples of this sort of appropriation in *Journey*, see the chapter appendix.

experienced. For that matter, he reports on them from home, indeed from a bourgeois sort of domestic bliss, accepted as a member of an international scientific community and with his beloved Graüben by his side. Again, then, Verne's voyagers may have more in common with an ancient explorer like Herodotus, interested in firsthand experience (*autopsy*) and rational explanation (*logos*), than with the sorts of "heroes" whose mythological misadventures Verne actively rewrites.

From this perspective, Axel could be the sort of man called "blessed" by Virgil in an earlier poem, the *Georgics* (c. 29 B.C.E. [*G.*]): the sort "who was able to understand the reasons for things" (*qui potuit rerum cognoscere causas; G.* 2.490). This sort of rational understanding means conquering the (irrational) fear of death: as Virgil puts it, such a person has "ground the groan of greedy Acheron," a river in the underworld, "beneath his feet" (*subiecit pedibus strepitumque Acherontis avari;* 2.492). Although the river Acheron is in a way metaphorical, the image here also has a certain material force: lying behind Virgil's lines in the *Georgics* is Lucretius' poem *De Rerum Natura* (from the second quarter of the first century B.C.E.), which argues that death should not be feared, since it cannot be a new state of being (much less the literal underworld of the epic tradition) but is the end of all conscious experience. From this perspective, there would be, then, something about Axel, and about the world of his novel, that is less Virgilian and spiritual—certainly less "Aeneidic," as we may call the quality of having one's question about causes, precisely, go unanswered (*Musa, mihi causas memora; Aen.* 1.8)—than Lucretian and material, befitting a rational modern scientist.[38]

None of this means that everything Axel reports is credible. He himself expects that his report will meet with disbelief: it is "a tale which many people, however determined to be surprised at nothing, will refuse to believe. But I am armed in advance against human scepticism."[39] As we have been seeing, that skepticism may be read as

---

[38] For Virgil and Lucretius, see Braund (1997); Farrell (1997); and chs. 7, 9, and 12–19 in Gillespie and Hardie (2007). Lucretius has played an important role in "scientific" thinking in Europe; see Johnson and Wilson (2007) and Greenblatt (2011). For discussion of Lucretius in connection with SF, see Rogers and Stevens (this volume, introduction) and Weiner (this volume, chapter two).

[39] Butcher (2008: 214). *Journey* ch. 45: "Voici la conclusion d'un récit auquel refuseront d'ajouter foi les gens les plus habitués à ne s'étonner de rien. Mais je suis cuirassé d'avance contre l'incrédulité humaine."

arising in part from the way that *Journey* figures "traditional" ways of knowing, including the ways represented by the Greco-Roman classics, as newly subordinate to scientific practice, which alone is able to produce "knowledge" as such. If Axel and his fellows went under the earth in a manner reminiscent of ancient epic heroes, after their return—and as a result of Axel's own narration—they are something decidedly new: science-heroes.

IMMANIS PECORIS CUSTOS, IMMANIOR IPSE: "SCIENTIFIC" EPIPHANY AND "ROMANTIC" ELEGY

Journey may thus be read as a sort of *Bildungsroman*, a "coming-of-age novel," in which the young scientist discovers, among other things, his own maturing capacity for "science." As we have seen, however, that capacity is not completely separate from Axel's "romantic" or "poetic" inclinations, which are expressed partly in terms drawn from his beloved Virgil, among other Latin authors. Axel thus figures the scientist as a sort of rewritten epic hero, following in ancient footsteps even as he seeks to offer modern scientific explanations for what he sees. This combination of structural similarity and profound epistemological difference is perhaps clearest in the moment surrounding the third quotation from Virgil. In particular we will see how Verne replaces Virgil's cyclical cosmology and image of divine "prophecy" with the nascent science of geology and its implications for linear history, including human prehistory. In a related way, the ancient epic's sense of emotionally unfulfilling duty and death is replaced by a modern, "romantic" novel's sense of life and love as comedy. Finally, the third quotation also serves to emphasize further the complex literary history that lies behind Verne's reception of Virgil.

At the journey's deepest point, Axel reports that he followed his uncle's excited gaze:

I looked, shrugging my shoulders, determined to push incredulity to its furthest limits. But struggle as I might, I had to give in to the evidence. There, less than a quarter of a mile away, leaning against the trunk of an enormous kauri pine, was a human being, a Proteus of these underground realms, a new son of Neptune, shepherding that uncountable drove of mastodons! *Immanis pecoris custos, immanior ipse! "Immanior ipse"* indeed![40]

Before considering the Latin, it is worth noting that the passage insists on the sort of spatial limits characteristic of Verne, as well as on the significance of numbers, as if to emphasize "scientific" observation. In the French there is, however, also a pun between Axel's "looking," *regardai,* and the monster's "guarding," *gardai*: the pun serves as a first indication of how Axel and the guardian constitute each other, the one observing and the other observed. However disparate, the two are thus made to "double" each other: in that connection, Axel's reaction is caused in part by the shock of recognizing something in the guardian that—unthinkably, uncannily—resembles something in himself;[41] see Figure 3-1 for an evocative illustration by Édouard Riou from the 1867 (seventh) edition of *Journey.* This doubling is discussed somewhat further below (in the section " 'Scientific' Epiphany and an Un-epic Epistemology").

In the meantime, we may focus first on the scene's classical reception. The Latin means "A tremendous herd's guardian, more tremendous himself! Yes, more tremendous himself!" By this point in the novel, we are not surprised to see Axel turn to Virgil for an expression of emotion. But if we are right to consider Verne's quotations of Virgil in their original contexts, and therefore to ask what effect if any is had on the novel, in this case, too, it matters that the quotation is not direct. The original

<hr/>

[40] Butcher (2008: 186). *Journey* ch. 39: "Je regardai, haussant les épaules, et décidé à pousser l'incrédulité jusqu'à ses dernières limites. Mais, quoque j'en eus, il fallut bien me rendre à l'évidence. En effet, à moins d'un quart de mille, appuyé au tronc d'un kauris énorme, un être humain, un Protée de ces contrées souterraines, un nouveau fils de Neptune, gardait cet innombrable troupeau de Mastodontes! *Immanis pecoris custos, immanior ipse!* Oui! *immanor ipse!*" These lines, and portions of surrounding sections (the end of chapter 37, part of 38, and all of 39), were added by Verne to *Journey*'s seventh edition (1867). Scholarly consensus is that the additions were made to take advantage of public interest in prehistory spurred by the recent publication of Charles Darwin's work. This does not mean that Verne replicates Darwin: his characters seem to express instead "a divine plan progressivism" (Standish 2004: 126).

[41] On doubles and the uncanny, see seminally Freud (1919), including discussion of Otto Rank's concept of "the double," and Jentsch (1906), with discussion of E. T. A. Hoffman's "Der Sandmann" (1816). In Freud's terminology, the encounter in *Journey* is "uncanny" (*Unheimlich*); see note 53. As a result, the "science" is, at least at first, called into question; cf., e.g., Harris (2000), Unwin (2000), and Martin (1985: 122–179), portions of which are quoted below, in note 51.

Figure 3-1 Axel and Lidenbrock flee from the sight of the shepherd and his herd of mastodons: *"Immanis pecoris custos, immanior ipse!"* Édouard Riou, public domain.

is slightly different: *formosi pecoris custos, formosior ipse*, such that flock and guardian are originally "shapely" (or "well-kempt," since the context is animal husbandry) rather than "tremendous." Axel's expression may therefore gain some of its force from an implicit difference from that ancient precedent: if we recall *formosior*, we may be more prepared to be struck by *immanior* and so feel greater sympathy with Axel's own stricken speech.[42] In a further complication to the quotation's literary history, this difference from Virgil is not Verne's: Verne borrowed the line, already so changed, from Victor Hugo's *The Hunchback of Notre-Dame*.[43] In this way Virgil had already been refurbished for modern use.

As with *facilis descensus Averno*, so here does the quotation's original context complicate matters further. Unlike the first two quotations, both from the epic *Aeneid*, this one comes from Virgil's earliest collection of poems, the pastoral *Eclogues* (ca. 39 B.C.E. [*Ecl.*]).[44] In the fifth *Eclogue*, Mopsus reports an epitaph demanded of shepherds for their fellow Daphnis, who has just now died (5.40–44):

> sprinkle the ground with leaves, draw shadows over the fountains,   40
> shepherds (the command that such things be done is Daphnis' himself),
> and make a funeral mound, and over the funeral mound add this poem:
> "I, Daphnis, was—in these woods, from here to the stars—well-known,
> a shapely flock's guardian, shapelier on my own."[45]

Since this lies behind *Journey*'s climactic classical reception, some discussion of the original context is in order. Briefly, *Eclogue* 5 focuses on the interaction of mortal and immortal[izing] forces at a moment, and therefore on the relationship between poetry and time or eternity. This in turn suggests an interest in the relationship between lived experience and the larger forces that affect human life. The poem thus develops an image of responses to death that are reassuring in their conventionality or in their symbolic correspondence to nature, the natural world, as such. To take the concluding example, the shepherds are asked to construct a monument whose commemorative power derives in part from

---

[42] In a pun-loving author like Verne, it is possible that *immanior* not only means "tremendous" but also, via a pun with Latin *manes*, "shades," suggests an "unshadelike" or "unghostly" aspect to the guardian. This would serve to emphasize further the difference between Virgil's land of insubstantial, spiritual shades and Verne's material "underworld."

[43] *Notre-Dame de Paris*, 1831; ch. 4, sect. 3, title.

[44] For overviews of the *Eclogues*, see Martindale (1997) and Clausen (1995).

[45] *Spargite humum foliis, inducite fontibus umbras, / pastores (mandat fieri sibi talia Daphnis), / et tumulum facite, et tumulo superaddite carmen: / "Daphnis ego in silvis, hinc usque ad sidera notus, / formosi pecoris custos, formosior ipse."*

its raw materials' being natural, insofar as they are *both* constants of (pastoral) experience *and* themselves changing or fleeting: leaves, water, and shade.[46] Although the poem demanded of the shepherds is expressly intended to be written atop the burial mound, the interconnections among the lines suggest a close relationship between epitaph and falling leaves or rushing water, both of which were traditional symbols for change. All is thus strongly suggestive of passing time. We may imagine the leaves decaying, the water continually passing and so washing them away, and the mound itself succumbing to erosion by the water and weather.[47] In these ways the commemorative monument becomes less memorable; it thus serves, not only to recall a past person, but also, per-haps more powerfully, to symbolize his passing moment or era.

All of this is in implicit contrast to the ideal endurance or desired immortality of the song, which takes on two forms: the epitaph in the meter of epic, dactylic hexameter, which seems intended to preserve memory forever, as are the epics; and the *Eclogue* itself, which as poetry may last in ways that leaves, streams, and a mound of earth may not. The feeling of distance, of desire unfulfilled, is intensified by the fact that Virgil's lines are modeled on a similar speech put into the mouth of the bucolic character Thyrsis by the Greek poet Theocritus (*Idyll* 1, esp. 119ff.; ca. third century B.C.E.). In this context, Virgil's self-conscious allusion draws attention to the historical contingence, the accident, of any such literary relationship. As a rewriting, the *Eclogue* thus expresses the same elegiac feeling about passing time as in its image of death and evanescent memorial.[48] Concretely, Daphnis—as Mopsus suggests—represents a

---

[46] The presence of shadows or ghosts (both *umbrae*; the ambiguity in the Latin may be deliberately emphasized) is Virgil's innovation in pastoral poetry; for some differences between Virgil's landscape and that of his chief model, Theocritus, see Clausen (1995: xxvi–xxx).

[47] In a context informed by the epic, this image recalls the famous simile—in Homer, Virgil, Dante, and others—comparing human lives or souls to autumn leaves; see also note 55. Cf. Thomas Hardy's "few leaves lay on the starving sod; / —They had fallen from an ash, and were gray"; and his "pond edged with grayish leaves" ("Neutral Tones" 3–4 and 16). If Virgil's flowing water is in one sense revivifying, in another it is a source of some despair, for traditionally water symbolized how human meaning cannot be made permanent: e.g., Catullus writes of how a seductive lover's words "ought to be written on the wind and running water" (*in vento et rapida scribere oportet aqua*; 70.4); cf. Heraclitus' famous dictum that one cannot step into the same river twice.

[48] To refer again to Hardy, in parallel to the gray and decaying leaves, Virgil's poem would be the "gray-brown" thrush singing its song coincidental to the poet's mourning;

time before agricultural labor: the "Golden" or Saturnian Age, when the earth gave freely of her bounty. Likewise, Daphnis' death symbolizes the transition to the harder "Iron" or Jovian Age in which we toil still and which presented Virgil's idealized shepherds with actual difficulties.

Verne's quotation of Virgil thus evokes an exemplary shepherd whose death serves to symbolize the passing of an age. Verne's own monstrous shepherd, as well as the world he represents, may likewise be understood as limited in time; in the metafiction of the novel, that world is in fact present to us only within the frame of the narrator's recollection. But whereas the *Eclogues* mourns the past age by mourning Daphnis, *Journey* seems to approach the past neutrally or even comically: awe at discovery, including the shock of recognition, gives way in the end to relieved laughter. In part this difference in tone may be attributed to differences between the narrators. Virgil's Mopsus is a shepherd himself, and so identifies in a way with Daphnis: Daphnis's death prefigures the end of Mopsus' similar way of life. When Mopsus sings of Daphnis' death to help himself and his interlocutor Menalcas pass the time, it is partly in response to how a time—an era—seems to be passing despite them. The entirety of Daphnis' story thus echoes back, in anticipation, the shepherd-poets' own mortality; nor may they expect lasting commemoration, their compliments on each other's performance notwithstanding. This is complicated further by Menalcas' response to Mopsus, which develops the theme of Daphnis' death by focusing on his afterlife: we may follow Daphnis as he "wonders at the threshold of unfamiliar Olympus, / and sees the clouds and stars beneath his feet" (*insuetum miratur limen Olympi / sub pedibusque videt nubes et sidera*; *Ecl.* 5.56–57). The extraordinary continuity of Daphnis' story, his "life" of sorts after death, serves to emphasize, in its explicit status as a fiction, the discontinuity of ordinary life. From this perspective, life is in fact severely time-limited, so the knowledge of the world one may gain in life seems limited as well.[49]

---

although the "Darkling Thrush" is not expressly "gray-brown," the poem bearing its name shares Virgil's elegiac feeling. The poet also directs some of his regard to himself, resulting in a feeling similar to Coleridge's description of the man, the "poor wretch," who "filled all things with himself, / and made all gentle sounds tell back the tale / of his own sorrow" ("The Nightingale" 19–21).

[49] A reading of the Daphnis episode as having to do in part with the limits imposed on knowledge by mortality may be strengthened by the similarity between Virgil's description of Daphnis' projected literal or physical ascent, with the heavens "beneath his feet"

IMMANIS PECORIS CUSTOS, CONT'D.: "SCIENTIFIC" EPIPHANY AND AN UN-EPIC EPISTEMOLOGY

In sharp contrast to the worlds depicted by Virgil, lives in Verne's fiction would seem to be in no such danger. As noted, by the end of the novel, again, his voyagers are safely back amidst the bourgeois comforts of home. But in light of Verne's engagement with Virgil and the classical tradition, there may be a different kind of danger faced during the journey itself. In the passage surrounding Verne's third quotation from Virgil (*immanis pecoris custos. . .*), Axel sees two things that cause him to exclaim in astonishment and fear. First is a "herd" of woolly mammoths, otherwise extinct, each the imposing height of a tree.[50] Second is the herd's "more tremendous guardian," a towering super-primitive man. In his size and "impossibility"—his survival is, if anything, unlikelier than the mastodons'—he is immediately suggestive of how material discovery may outstrip human comprehension. In other words, then, any danger facing Verne's heroes would have to do with the limits of knowledge: it is epistemological.[51] To reiterate the general situation, "human knowledge" was formerly classical but must now be scientific; as both result and prerequisite, the classics are redefined as mere "tradition."

(*sub pedibus*; *Ecl.* 5.57) and the more figurative or mental ascent by the man who has divined the reasons for things and can therefore position death likewise "beneath his feet" (*sub pedibus*; *G.* 2.492); see above, note 38.

[50] The mastodons' "trunks swarming about below the trees like a host of serpents" (Butcher (2008: 186); *Journey* ch. 39: "les trompes grouillaient sous les arbres comme une légion de serpents") recall the dangers of the Garden of Eden, perhaps as transmuted by Milton, who imagines the fallen angels transformed into snakes (*Paradise Lost* 10.504ff). Verne's engagement with Biblical literature would repay close study; see Chelebourg (1988).

[51] For Verne's interest in epistemological problems, cf. Martin (1985: 122–179), arguing that the "*Voyages* seek to construct an encyclopedism and an academy. . . . But the *Academy* and the *Encyclopédie* were no longer, in the age of Verne, stable institutions" (172). As a result, "[e]pistemologically, the ultimate particles of Vernian matter elude quantification and designation. Aesthetically, the realist enterprise of definitive description is indefinitely postponed" (178). Martin refers to this tendency as "anepistemophilia," something like "love of ignorance." Cf. Butcher's appraisal (2008: xxvi–xxvii): "*Journey* cannot be excluded from the general orbit of late Romanticism. But Verne is simultaneously a Realist. . . . The paradox, though, is that so much Realism in the externals leads to the opposite of realism in the mood: Verne's positivistic aspects culminate in the wildest longings and imaginings. . . . The *Journey* proves that the most down-to-earth Realism can . . . lead to the most high-blown Romanticism."

In particular here, as Verne's "underworld" replaces Virgil's, the guardian serves to represent the limits of traditional, "spiritual" or supernatural understandings when confronted with merely "material" nature that is unexpectedly rich and strange. The guardian is astonishing in his materiality, his physical reality, in a way that emphasizes just how Verne's underworld is unlike those found in ancient authors: pointedly, it lacks shades, the bodiless ghosts that confronted ancient epic heroes; this is emphasized by how it also lacks simple shadows, as discussed below. In place of those immaterial spirits, Verne's underworld is flush with grosser matter. This includes not only the mastodons and their massive guardian, but also stupendous mushrooms, sea-monsters or living dinosaurs, and finally a human skeleton (*Journey* ch. 38). That last find serves to symbolize how, in this material underworld, death is not metaphorical, as if serving mainly to illuminate human life in mirror-image, but literal and physical—its actual end.

All of this is profoundly defamiliarizing: for such a guardian to be living is astonishing indeed. In *Journey* that fact is not cause for an ironic poetic lament as in *Eclogue* 5, much less for the sort of knowledge about the future that comes to the epic hero in *Aeneid* Book 6. Instead, the encounter causes dismay: it is precisely uncanny, as the scientist wonders whether to believe his own senses. Importantly, however, that feeling passes: although Axel expects his report to be met with readers' skepticism, the fact of the novel makes it clear that he has recovered his certainty. In contrast, at the same time the classical tradition is made to show its limits. Whereas Virgil suffices for Axel's emotional expression at the moment, any explanation of the guardian, as of everything else in this strange material world, must now be discovered and presented by new, modern means.

The possibility of such explanation is complicated here by how Axel's encounter with the guardian is a kind of self-discovery: although he may wish to reject any similarity between himself and the guardian, the latter is of course somehow "human." Axel and the guardian are thus mutually constitutive, doubling each other asymmetrically. In the context of *Journey*'s deep engagement with Virgil, if Axel is a sort of inverted Aeneas (the narration requires that, unlike Aeneas, he has already returned home to safety and love), then the guardian at this moment replaces the ghost of Aeneas' father, Anchises. Whereas Anchises was emphatically immaterial (Aeneas tried and failed to embrace him three times; *Aen.*

6.700–702, lines that are identical to 2.792–794, where the immaterial being is Aeneas's dead wife, Creusa), the guardian is astonishingly physical and real. Moreover, although the guardian is, in a way like Anchises, an "old man" of sorts—he is compared to Proteus, the "old man of the sea" who prophesizes when captured, while the shade of Anchises relates the future—this similarity is superficial, and he can be assumed to offer nothing like Proteus' or Anchises' knowledge of the future.[52]

As a remnant of the past, an offshoot of human prehistory, the guardian has no connection to history as such, much less to what Verne's modern science might imagine as its rational continuation. Evoking and distorting Daphnis from the quoted *Eclogue*, and displacing Aeneas' father Anchises from the *Aeneid*, the guardian is *Journey*'s most vivid representation of how classical "traditions" must now yield to "knowledge" as such.[53] The guardian thus serves as a powerful symbol, not of physical danger, but of how a new materialism comes with changed epistemological possibilities and limits. In his very monstrosity and silence, he embodies a kind of the "sublime," for which a classical tradition including Virgil's poetry may provide analogies, but one that only a modern scientific practice can explain.

At this moment, the modern scientist is, of course, Axel, observing from an actual and notional distance. He sees the giant "at a quarter of a mile away, leaning against the trunk of an enormous kauri pine." The forest is "[b]athed in waves of electric light." This light, associated with the modern technology *par excellence*, electricity, dispels all shadows: "By a phenomenon I cannot explain, the light was uniformly diffused, so that it lit up all the sides of objects equally. It no longer came from any definite

---

[52] For Proteus, see Homer *Od.* 4.412ff.; Virgil *G.* 4.387ff.

[53] Limitations of space prevent me from discussing more fully the complex literary history of the scene's other classical references, including to Proteus and Neptune. I regret in particular not having the space to consider how Verne's revision of Virgil's underworld looks back to Homer's, in which Odysseus encounters a giant shepherd (*Od.* Book 11). The epistemological situation described here—a tenuous "scientification" of the uncanny encounter with the double, now material—is an important trope in modern SF; see note 41. To be traced back at least to *Frankenstein* (1818), this trope appears in many later works, e.g., Stephenson's *The Strange Case of Dr Jekyll and Mr Hyde* (1886), Tolkien's *The Hobbit* (1937), *Solaris* (Andrei Tarkovsky 1972), and *The Thing* (John Carpenter 1982). Interestingly for the early history of modern SF, it appears in connection with Percy Shelley: his *Prometheus Unbound* includes an encounter with a *Doppelgänger* (1.191–199), while Percy himself is reported, by Mary, to have once encountered his own double (Bennett 1980: 245).

point in space, and consequently there was not the slightest shadow."[54] Although this underground forest may call to mind the ancient epic image of the dead gathering on the near bank of the river Styx, thick as autumn leaves, the absence of shadows is also of a piece with the absence, in this material world, of spiritual beings including "shades."[55] The fact that the tree is pine, with its everlasting green, may strengthen this reading, for its lack of any leaves to fall precisely rewrites those earlier epics so as to exclude even symbols of migratory souls: there is no autumn here. At the same time, the "kauri" pine in particular implies a certain kind of survival: this is a type of pine that was widespread during the Jurassic period and so betokens the material survival of a past that is so prehistorical as to be, by definition, pre-classical. In this way, any classics are present only in recollection or feeling, not in material fact: in Virgil's underworld as rewritten by Verne, the classics are no longer, quite, real.

CONCLUSION

In this chapter, I have tried to show how Jules Verne's *Journey to the Center of the Earth* engages with Virgil quite complexly, both respecting and replacing him. Ultimately Virgil is surpassed, as pieces of his influential works are, as it were, left behind in the underworld, even buried. Quotations from Virgil stud the enlarged—if rapidly contracting—"scientific" earth like precious stones: they are beautiful and expressive, even "romantic," but are not intrinsically more interesting or meaningful, to mineralogists like Axel and his uncle, than other "minerals," the various material and real, physical objects and phenomena that surround them. Virgil himself has become a sort of "primitive" in comparison to Verne's modern science-heroes . . . and yet, if he has therefore become somehow "unacceptable," to borrow from Susan Sontag, he "cannot be discarded" (1966: 6). At the time of Verne's writing and revision of *Journey* (1863–1867), Virgil's

---

[54] Butcher (2008: 184). *Journey* ch. 39: "Par un phénomène que je ne puis expliquer, et grâce à sa diffusion, complète alors, la lumière éclairait uniformément les diverses faces des objets. Son foyer n'existait plus en un point déterminé de l'espace et elle ne produisait aucun effet d'ombre."

[55] The image of people, especially the dead, gathering thick as falling leaves may be found in, e.g., Homer (*Il.* 6.146), Virgil (*Aen.* 6.309–310), and Milton (*Paradise Lost* 1.301–303). Cf. Dante's wood of ghostly trees (*Inferno* 13).

identification by T. S. Eliot as "the classic of all Europe" (1945: 31) may have been a distant eighty years in the future but it was not therefore less certain. For there is hardly an underworld in the last two thousand years of Western literary tradition that does not look back to Virgil, seeing, as did Dante's pilgrim, that he is—as Anchises and Creusa were for Aeneas, or as Eurydice for Orpheus—already "immaterial," already gone.

Verne's engagement with Virgil in *Journey* thus reveals much about the peculiar status accorded to the ancient classic in more recent Western literary culture, especially in context of emergent and ongoing master narratives of modern science. Read with special attention to its classical receptions, *Journey* exemplifies a modern kind of scientific-romantic "epic," in which the hero's hard-won knowledge is about the distant past and the present rather than the future. Where do ancient classics fit into this experience? The novel suggests how "knowledge" is limited with regard to the hero's affective experience, his inner life and his emotions. Somewhat paradoxically, personal, emotional experience in the present, as well as hopes for the future, would seem best expressed in the language of the past—pre-scientific or even non-scientific and therefore poetic or romantic. This might be related to Verne's feeling that, as the modern, material world is more thoroughly explored—as each unknown area becomes known—the only "place" truly open for exploration is the past. For the romantic feeling that accompanies and inspires exploration, the more distant the past, the better. This may mean that a new, materialist definition of "knowledge" excludes the classics entirely, classifying them as mere "tradition."

In an important article, "Literary Intertexts in Jules Verne's *Voyages Extraordinaires*," Arthur B. Evans, having surveyed Verne's extremely wide range of quotations from and allusions to other authors, writes that, while "a limited number of these intertextual phenomena have been identified and discussed in the critical scholarship . . . most have yet to be fully explored, and the potential for detailed comparative exegesis remains very rich indeed."[56] Evans refers here in particular to Verne's frequent and meaningful engagement with Edgar Allen Poe, but his point may be taken more generally. In this chapter I have sought to show one way in which that "rich potential" may be actualized: by studying Verne, exponent of modern SF, in relation to the classics and

[56] Evans (1996: 180–181).

the classical tradition. I have not attempted to offer a complete account of *Journey*'s reception even of Virgil, much less to explore at any depth the novel's other classical references. Together with post-classical material, these form the strata of Verne's geologically learned writing and "volcanic" feeling.[57] And of course no single modern work, even one as influential in the SF tradition as *Journey*, may on its own justify the claim that there is a fundamental difference in epistemology between ancient literature and modern SF.

But I do hope to have shown that the argument is plausible. In particular I hope it has been clear that the journey undertaken by Verne's science-heroes, inspired in the narrative by Arne Saknussem, in literary-historical terms is modeled on, and modifies, an ancient epic-heroic journey under the earth as depicted, vividly and influentially, by Virgil. Perhaps the most crucial and consequential difference between Verne's modern, "romantic" novel and Virgil's ancient epic is the novel's insistence on the materiality of the world below, as against the epic's tradition of an underworld that is rather more spiritual or metaphysical. In Virgil, as in much of the tradition after him, it is the hero himself who is thus *strangely* material in a world otherwise inhabited, if that is the word, by insubstantial shades.[58] In contrast, in *Journey* the salient difference between the explorers and the living inhabitant of the world within the earth is not material or metaphysical, for they are all of them similarly material and real. Instead, the deepest difference is epistemological: the voyagers observe him, they are able to categorize him, they can "understand him," while he does not seem to notice them and, unlike the shades encountered by the ancient epic hero, can offer no knowledge of the historical past, much less prophesy the future. That monstrous guardian may well be compared to figures from classical mythology but he stands for a time that is far more ancient still, glimpses

---

[57] One example of *Journey*'s classical sources aside from Virgil is Xenophon's *Anabasis*; see L'Allier (2014: 286–287). For a sketch of some of *Journey*'s most important post-classical sources, see Butcher (2008: xvii–xx, and x). Many of these are premodern and share what may be described, in Butcher's words, as a "medieval belief, not entirely dismissed in the nineteenth century, that the centre of the Earth could be reached via huge openings at the poles" (xix–xx); on "hollow earth" stories, see Standish (2004). Verne's beloved Poe was a "clearing-house for many" of these ideas (Butcher 2008: 221 note 25).

[58] Cf. the discussion by Weiner (this volume, chapter two) about the unprecedented corporeality of the corpse reanimated by the witch Erichtho in Lucan's *Bellum Civile*.

of which are made possible by sciences, like geology, unanticipated in antiquity. In the light—or in the shadow?—cast by such a figure, a figure of the modern scientific imagination, ancient classics can become something like "mere tradition." Read in this way, *Journey* stands as one example of how modern SF remains profoundly fascinated with, and yet also profoundly challenges, the classical tradition.

APPENDIX OF EXPLICIT CLASSICAL REFERENCES IN *JOURNEY TO THE CENTER OF THE EARTH*

I hope that this list will help make possible further study of *Journey*'s, and Verne's, classical receptions. As throughout this chapter, here the French is drawn from the 1867 edition, translations from the French are drawn from Butcher (2008) (with page numbers), and translations from the Latin are my own (see note 4).

Journey ch. 1: "Il était professeur au Johannaeum." Butcher (2008: 219): "a famous classical grammar school"

Journey ch. 4: "ce travail logogryphique, qu'on eût vainement proposé au vieil Oedipe!" Butcher (2008: 18): "that word-puzzle . . . solved": Oedipus and the Sphinx.

Journey ch. 4: "Enfin, dans le corps du document, et à la troisième ligne, je remarquai aussi les mots latins 'rota,' 'mutabile,' 'ira,' 'nec,' 'atra.' 'Diable, pensai-je, ces derniers mots sembleraient donner raison à mon oncle sur la langue du document! Et même, à la quatrième ligne, j'aperçois encore le mot 'luco' qui se traduit par 'bois sacré.' Il est vrai qu'à la troisième ligne, on lit le mot 'tabiled' de tournure parfaitement hébraïque, et à la dernière les vocables 'mer,' 'arc,' 'mère,' qui sont purement français. . . . Quel rapport pouvait-il exister entre les mots 'glace, monsieur, colère, cruel, bois sacré, changeant, mère, arc ou mer'?" Butcher (2008: 19): "I spotted the Latin words *rota, mutabile, ira, nec*, and *atra*. . . . 'These last few words seem to confirm my uncle's view about the language in the document! In the fourth line I can even see *luco*, which means "sacred wood." It's true that the third line also includes *tabiled*, that sounds completely Hebrew to me, and the last one, *mer, arc*, and *mère*, pure and unadulterated French.'" "What possible connection could there be between *ice, sir, anger, cruel, sacred wood, changeable, mother, bow*, and *sea*?"

Journey ch. 4: "des mots latins, entre autres 'craterem' et 'terrestre'!" Butcher (2008: 20): "Latin words like *craterem* and *terrestre*!"

Journey ch. 5: "Ce qui, de ce mauvais latin, peut être traduit ainsi: Descends dans le cratère du Yocul de Sneffels que l'ombre du Scartaris vient caresser avant les calendes de Juillet, voyageur audacieux, et tu parviendras au centre de la Terre. Ce que j'ai fait. Arne Saknussemm." Butcher (2008: 25): ""In Snaefells

Yoculis craterem kem delibat umbra Scartaris Julii intra calendas descende, audas viator, et terrestre centrum attinges. Kod feci. Arne Saknussemm." Which, when translated from the dog-Latin, reads as follows: Go down into the crater of Snaefells Yocul which the shadow of Scartaris caresses before the calends of July, O audacious traveller, and you will reach the center of the Earth. I did it. Arne Saknussemm."

Journey ch. 16: Pluto. Butcher (2008: 83).

Journey ch. 30: Proserpina. Butcher (2008: 139).

Journey ch. 37: Wild Ajax. Butcher (2008: 175).

Journey ch. 38: Orestes' body, Pausanias, Polyphemus (giants), Cimbrians. Butcher (2008: 181).

4

Mr. Lucian in Suburbia: Links Between the *True History* and *The First Men in the Moon*

Antony Keen

Science fiction (SF) is often said to originate in classical literature.[1] This chapter aims to take a particular case study of a classical work and a "classic" SF novel, and discuss possible connections between Lucian of Samosata's *True History* (second century C.E. [*VH*]) and H. G. Wells's *The First Men in the Moon* (1901 [*First Men*]). Lucian is often seen as the first "SF novel," mostly because of the lunar voyage contained in its first book, while Wells's novel is both in a tradition of lunar voyages that follows works of Johannes Kepler (*Somnium*, 1634) and Cyrano de Bergerac (*L'autre monde: où les États et Empires de la Lune*, 1657), and can

[1] The material in this chapter was originally delivered at *Trips to the Moon and Beyond: Lucian to NASA*, a conference that took place in December of 2008 at Royal Holloway, University of London. It was subsequently re-presented at the H. G. Wells Society conference, *H. G. Wells: From Kent to Cosmopolis*, at the University of Kent, Canterbury, England, in July 2010. I would like to thank Professor Edith Hall of Royal Holloway for the original invitation, the H. G. Wells Society for the opportunity to present the arguments to a different audience, and the audiences at both conferences for their comments.

ultimately be traced back to Lucian; *First Men* is also an important part of Wells's body of work, pivotal in the creation of modern SF. However, there is little detailed discussion of direct influences of Lucian on Wells. This chapter aims to correct that. After a brief introduction to Lucian's tale, there is a discussion of whether his work can be considered "SF." This is followed by detailed examination of potential links between the two works and the two authors, including drawing attention to the overt reference to Lucian in the epigraph of *First Men*.

THE TRUE HISTORY

The *True History*,[2] by Lucian of Samosata, a Greek writer of the Roman period (second century C.E.), is seen as an early example of what has been described as "proto-SF."[3] H. G. Wells (1866–1946) is rightly recognized as one of the key figures in the origin of the genre of SF as it is now known. Yet little has been written about the relationship between the two authors, and in particular on any relationship between Wells's *First Men* (1901) and the lunar voyages of Lucian, found in his works *True History* and *Icaromenippus*. As will be seen, this overlooks the epigraph that opens Wells's novel, which was taken from Lucian (this epigraph is omitted from most modern editions; though not, as we shall see, from the 2005 Penguin Classics version). I argue that there is in this novel a close relationship between Wells and Lucian, and that the Lucianic influence is perhaps more immediate and significant in Wells than is the influence of commonly cited precursors to Wells such as Francis Godwin's *The Man in the Moone* (1638) or Kepler's *Somnium*.[4] A number of passages in the Wells novel may be seen as echoing similar passages in Lucian's works. But more important, the influence of Lucian may be also felt in the *tone* of the novel. A more direct engagement with the Lucianic satirical tradition may explain the differences in tone, as

---

[2] I use the singular translation of the Greek title, *Alēthē Diēgēmata* (in Latin, *Verae Historiae*) rather than the more pedantically correct plural, because I believe it is in slightly more common usage, at least outside the world of classical scholarship. For a translation, see Sidwell (2004: 309–346). For studies of the work, see Rütten (1997); Georgiadou and Larmour (1998); and von Möllendorff (2000).

[3] On "proto–science fiction," see Stableford (2012b).

[4] For the usually cited influences on Wells, see Nicolson (1948: 247–250).

noted by critics such as Patrick Parrinder and Frank McConnell, between this novel and earlier scientific romances.[5]

Lucian of Samosata was born on the banks of the River Euphrates and lived in the second century C.E.[6] He was described at the time as a "Sophist," that is, a teacher of display oratory, although the term was sometimes used as a catch-all term for any intellectual of the early Roman Empire who wrote or spoke primarily in Greek.[7] (In *Apology for "Salaried Posts in Great Houses"* 15, Lucian denies that he is a *sophos* or "wise man.") Lucian was extremely prolific, and a significant number of his writings survive.[8] Critics of SF often single out from this corpus *True History* because of its voyage to the moon and interplanetary war. It has often been identified as the first SF novel.[9] However, as Adam Roberts has argued,[10] there are dangers in taking the *True History* out of the context of the rest of Lucian's works. (This issue will be addressed later in this chapter.) H. G. Wells is, of course, identified as a key figure of the emergence of what is now recognized as SF,[11] though Wells himself referred to his works as "scientific romances."[12]

Yet the issue of direct links between the two authors is not often discussed. Indeed, some commentators have deliberately distanced Lucian from SF. The genesis of this chapter was a throwaway remark by Niall Harrison, then editor of the British Science Fiction Association's critical

[5] Parrinder (1996: 63); McConnell (1981: 154).

[6] For an introduction to Lucian and his works, see Edwards, Browning, and Anderson (2003); or for more detail, see Sidwell (2004: ix–xxvii).

[7] On Lucian as a marginal sophist, see Swain (1996: 70); Whitmarsh (2005: 21–22); and Emlyn-Jones (2008: 53). He is not mentioned by the main historian of the "Second Sophistic" of the second and third centuries C.E., Philostratus, in his *Lives of the Sophists*. On the slippery nature of the term "sophist," see Whitmarsh (2005: 17–19).

[8] The full Lucianic corpus includes 86 works (Sidwell 2004: 347–351), though some are certainly, and some others probably, spurious.

[9] See, for discussions, Suvin (1979: 5, 10, 54); and Seed (2011: 2), though Seed himself would not go so far as to call the work SF. Fredericks (1976) discusses the way in which Lucian anticipates many of the tropes of SF, though unfortunately without direct reference to Wells. Ashley (2011: 10) identifies *True History* as an early (parodic) example of the tradition of the imaginary voyage. Clute (2012) writes, "Lucian stands at the beginning of the somewhat problematic line of prose fictions that lead eventually to what we might legitimately think of as SF proper." This is only a small selection of references to the identification of Lucian as at the head of the SF tradition.

[10] Roberts (2006a: 28).

[11] As a single example of many texts expounding this view, see Crossley (2005).

[12] Wells (1933).

journal *Vector*, made in a comment on a post in *Torque Control*, the *Vector* editorial weblog. In the course of a discussion about whether the Bayeux tapestry counts as "comics" or not, he said:

Lucian of Samosata wrote about a trip to the moon in the second century, but I don't think it's particularly useful to call that book "science fiction," because it's clearly not part of a tradition that gives rise to modern sf. (It anticipates sf, sure.)[13]

In my response to Harrison, I said that I thought there might be more in common between *True History* and, as an example, Wells's *First Men* than Harrison would allow.[14] This chapter examines how closely linked *are* the two works, through an investigation of the issues originally sparked by Harrison's comment, though in the end I have moved away from the debate about categorization that Harrison was discussing to an examination of possible receptions of Lucian within Wells.

IS THE *TRUE HISTORY* SF?

True History is the fictional story of a voyage of exploration mounted by one "Lucian" who sets sail with fifty comrades to explore the Atlantic beyond the Pillars of Hercules (Gibraltar).[15] After "Lucian" and his crew visit an island where the rivers and trees are full of wine, their ship is caught up by a waterspout and then a burst of wind. It eventually reaches the Moon, where "Lucian" becomes involved in a war over colonization rights between the people of the Moon and those of the Sun. This war settled, "Lucian" and his comrades return to Earth, where they are swallowed by a giant whale and live inside the beast for a while, encounter giants who row islands instead of ships, and speak to various famous dead people on the Isles of the Blest.[16] The work ends with "Lucian"

---

[13] Harrison (2008).

[14] Keen (2008).

[15] The narrator names himself at *VH* 2.28. I refer to the narrator as "Lucian" in quotation marks, to distinguish him from the author of the work.

[16] This sequence, one may suspect, inspired the fate of Geppetto in Carlo Collodi's *The Adventures of Pinocchio* (1883), who similarly ends up living inside a whale. This is best known from the Walt Disney movie version (U.S.A., 1940).

promising to relate further adventures in future books—a promise that, as far as we can tell, was never fulfilled.

As noted, because of the lunar voyage and the space battle, *True History* is often called the first SF novel. This is possibly controversial; and it must not be forgotten, as it sometimes is, that Lucian's work is a parody of fantastic-voyage literature.[17] This is something that Lucian clearly states in the opening of the work.[18] As Adam Roberts states,[19] the *True History* needs to be understood in the context of Lucian's other works. By considering it in isolation, the reader risks missing some of the parodic intent and the extent to which Lucian is engaging in satire, especially at the expense of philosophers. This can result in taking the premise of the *True History* rather too seriously. This tendency is further encouraged by the fact that the accidents of textual survival mean that, while the *True History* survives, little of its contemporary "straight" fantastic-voyage literature survives. As a result, Lucian has come to shape the genre, as found in later authors such as François Rabelais's *Gargantua and Pantagruel* (1531–1564) and Jonathan Swift's *Gulliver's Travels* (1726).[20]

Harrison's point, of course, is that, just because *True History* features a lunar voyage, this does not mean that it is a work of SF in the same way (as I suspect Harrison would think) that *First Men* is. I think I am largely in accord with Harrison—*True History* is not SF. My reasons will lead us, very briefly, into the mire of definitions of SF, about which several books can be, and have been, written. Personally, I am attracted to the novelist and critic Damon Knight's 1956 definition: ". . . it will do us no harm if we remember that [SF] means what we point to when we say it."[21]

I believe that is both the biggest cop-out in SF criticism, and the only sensible thing it is actually possible to say about defining genre. It is extremely difficult to come up with watertight criteria for defining

[17] Note the reference in Baxter (2006: 268), which treats *True History* as a work firmly in the non-parodic fantastic-voyage tradition.

[18] Photius, *Bibliotheca* 166 (111a), states that it was specifically drawing on Antonius Diogenes' *Ta Hyper Thoulē Apista* (*The Incredible Wonders Beyond Thule*), and this is followed by Fredericks (1976: 58, n. 5); but Lucian is probably parodying the entire fantastic-voyage genre, from Homer onwards, but especially those written by his contemporaries, rather than one specific work.

[19] Roberts (2006a: 28).

[20] Clute (2012).

[21] Knight (1996: 11).

something as SF, yet most readers know what SF is when they see it.[22] It is not enough for me alone to point to something and say "that is SF"—a majority, or at least a significant minority, consensus has to agree with me.

But obviously, there must be something driving my feeling for whether a text is SF or not, and I cannot leave this unexamined. Inevitably, terms will get a little fuzzy here, and in my opinion, any attempt to produce a definition of SF that can always be applied without question to anything that I, or anybody else, will recognize as SF, other than the Knight definition, is doomed to failure; there will always be debatable regions at the definitional margins. But there is a formulation from Adam Roberts that I find very useful: "Fantasy is premised on magic, the supernatural, the spiritual. . . . Science fiction is premised on a material, instrumental version of the cosmos."[23]

Roberts leads on into his conception of SF as a "Protestant" mode, as opposed to "Catholic" fantasy, a notion developed more fully in his Palgrave *History of Science Fiction*,[24] and by which I am rather less convinced. But the basic idea, that SF is driven by the rational and fantasy by the irrational, is one I am happy to embrace. According to that criterion, *True History* is not SF. Certainly, it belongs to the literature of the fantastic, as does a large amount of Graeco-Roman literature, from Homer, through Euripides, to Apuleius. This is not exactly surprising. As critics such as John Clute, Farah Mendlesohn, and Edward James remind us, the separation of "realistic" or "mimetic" literature and the literature of the fantastic is a fairly recent phenomenon.[25] But for me, too much of the *True History* relies on the irrational, on gods and the afterlife, for it to be a work of SF as I understand SF.

Of course, there are other bases, more related to the forms than the content of SF, on which one could argue that the *True History* is SF. Fredericks feels that Lucian provides an example of what Darko Suvin calls "cognitive estrangement."[26] On the other hand, Sarah Annes Brown says that the

---

[22] Seeking to define who "most readers" are, or what it is they recognize as SF, merely leads recursively back to the problem of definition. The problem is that the more precise any definition of genre becomes, the more it will collapse in the face of exceptions.

[23] Roberts (2006b: 119).

[24] Idem (2006a).

[25] Mendlesohn and James (2009: 7); Clute (2011: 20–21).

[26] Fredericks (1976: 54), citing Suvin (1972), followed by Georgiadou and Larmour (1998: 46). Suvin's most extended discussion of the term is in his "Not Only But Also"

True History "lacks SF's hallmark verisimilitude."[27] Edith Hall comments that "one element missing . . . in comparison with SF is the science."[28] This is a debate that will run and run, and is possibly the wrong question to focus on—already in 1999 Russell Shone was asking whether there was any real distinction in ancient literature between works that might be conceived of (in modern terms) as SF and those that might be conceived of as fantasy, and there is a good case for saying that there is not.[29]

However, it is much more commonly agreed that *True History* stands at the beginning of a tradition that leads eventually to SF. It is described as "*ur*-SF" by David Seed.[30] The influence of Lucian on various texts that are often considered "proto–SF,"[31] such as Sir Thomas More's *Utopia* (1516), Cyrano de Bergerac's *L'autre monde: où les États et Empires de la Lune* ("The other world, or the states and empires of the Moon," 1657),[32] or Jonathan Swift's *Gulliver's Travels*, is well documented.[33] I can happily accept that position (and here I do disagree with Harrison's implications).

THE FIRST MEN IN THE MOON AND THE TRUE HISTORY

The First Men in the Moon was H. G. Wells's ninth novel, and the seventh of his "scientific romances," following in the wake of novels such as *The Time Machine* (1895), *The Island of Doctor Moreau* (1896), and *The War of the Worlds* (1898). Published in 1901, it tells the story of one Mr. Bedford, who takes a break from his creditors and goes to Kent to write a play. While there, he meets Professor Cavor, who is working on a material, "Cavorite," that reflects gravity. Together they build a space

---

(1979). Suvin himself thought Lucian fulfilled this criterion for SF, and was quite clear that Lucian was at the head of a tradition that led through Cyrano and Swift to Wells and beyond (1979: 5, 10, 54).

[27] Brown (2008: 415).

[28] Hall (2008: 82–83). I am not sure that I accept that narratives of science are necessarily a defining feature of SF. Though this forms the popular perception of the genre, much SF engages with social issues of future or alternate cultures, rather than scientific novelty.

[29] In an unpublished paper delivered at the 1999 Classical Association conference in Liverpool.

[30] Seed (2011: 3).

[31] The term goes back to Knight (1962: 78); see Prucher (2007: 157); Stableford (2012b).

[32] See Nicolson (1948: 163).

[33] See Ashley (1997: 598).

capsule and travel to the moon. There, under the satellite's surface (hence *The First Men* **in** *the Moon*) they discover an insectoid civilization. Bedford escapes back to Earth, while Cavor remains on the Moon. He manages to communicate with Earth, and provides a detailed description of the "Selenite" civilization before he is killed. Just as Wells had pioneered time travel and alien invasion stories, here he provided a template for science fictional lunar exploration.

There is not a great deal written about any relationship between the *True History* and *First Men*, or at least I have not been able to find much on the subject. Christopher Robinson's book on Lucian's influence wraps itself up in the eighteenth century, though he does write as if Lucianic influence on the fantastic-voyage genre[34] came to a close with Swift and Ludvig Holberg's *Nicolai Klimii iter subterraneum* ("Niels Klim's Journey Under Ground," 1741).[35] When *True History* and *First Men* are mentioned together, the approach usually employed is that found when Arthur C. Clarke or China Miéville[36] wrote introductions to editions of *First Men*, or Paul Turner, or Aristoula Georgiadou and David Larmour,[37] did the same for Lucian. This is to place *True History* as the fountainhead of the lunar voyage tradition, a tradition to which Wells eventually contributes, at least in the sense of being seen as the originary work from a post-classical perspective.[38]

Few critics remark upon direct, rather than indirect, influence of Lucian upon Wells. Suvin does say of Wells that he "approach[es] again the imaginative veracity of Lucian's and Swift's story-telling centered on strange creatures,"[39] but he is not necessarily suggesting direct influence here. When Marjorie Hope Nicolson discusses the works on which Wells has drawn,[40] she mentions Francis Godwin's *The Man in the Moone*

[34] For this genre, see Stableford (2012a).
[35] Robinson (1979: 129–144).
[36] Clarke (1993: xxx); Miéville (2005: xiv).
[37] Turner (1961: 17); Georgiadou and Larmour (1998: 46–47).
[38] There is one possible earlier lunar voyage narrative, Antonius Diogenes' *The Incredible Wonders Beyond Thule*, discussed in Roberts (2006a: 26–27). This work clearly antedates *True History*, although it is unclear by how much; however, it is only known in a brief summary (Photius, *Bibliotheca* 166 [109a–112a]) that gives little detail of the lunar visit. Indeed, it is not entirely clear that the characters do go to the Moon, rather than just near the Moon. For a translation, see Pearse (2002).
[39] Suvin (1979: 211).
[40] Nicolson (1948: 247–250).

(1638); Cyrano de Bergerac, Ludvig Holberg; Athanasius Kircher's *Mundus Subterraneus* (1664); Robert Paltock's *The Life and Adventures of Peter Wilkins* (1751); and most of all, Johannes Kepler's *Somnium* ("Dream," 1634), which Wells makes specific reference to (2005, ch. 13, 87);[41] as well as Swift and Milton. Nicolson does not mention Lucian.

Yet there is a definite idea in *First Men* that this is the work of an author firmly situated in the cultural tradition of Greece and Rome. Like any educated child of the nineteenth century, Wells had some degree of classical background. He had been educated in Latin and Greek at the Midhurst Grammar School, and had enjoyed the subjects.[42] References to classical antiquity can be found in his earliest SF; his first time-travel story was entitled "The Chronic Argonauts," alluding of course to Jason and his companions. There are also allusions to Homer, and sequences of schoolboy Latin, in Wells's third novel, *The Island of Doctor Moreau* (1896).[43]

It is established in the first sentence of *First Men* that the narrator is writing his account in southern Italy (*First Men* 5); the locale is later revealed in chapter 21 ("Mr. Bedford at Littlestone") to be Amalfi (160).[44] The opening chapter of *First Men* includes a description of the Kent (England) town of Lympne's history as a Roman port (7).[45] Other classical references include an allusion to Sybaris (6) and the description of the lunar crater that the characters land in as an amphitheater (49). Later on, there are overt references to William Cowper's 1782 poem "Boadicea: An Ode" and its allusions to Caesar (78),[46] and to the Capitoline

[41] All page and chapter references are to the 2005 Penguin edition, which has different chapter numberings than some editions; see Parrinder (2005: xxxii) for an explanation. Steven McLean, in his note (Wells 2005: 209), thinks it unlikely that Wells's Latin was good enough to read Kepler, at that point not yet translated into English; there was no published translation until Lear (1965). Personally I see no reason why Wells's Latin could not have been up to the task, but in any case he clearly obtained information about the book's contents, possibly, as McLean suggests, from a friend. It is possible that there were summaries of the work published in the nineteenth century, though I have not been able to establish this.

[42] Wells (1934: 140). There is no evidence that he read Lucian at the time.

[43] See Keen (forthcoming).

[44] All citations here refer to Wells (2005).

[45] See Batchelor (1985: 57). Wells wrote the novel while living at Sandgate, six miles from Lympne.

[46] Despite McLean's note (Wells 2005: 209), the reference is not necessarily to *Julius Caesar*. The reference, incidentally, survives in the 1964 movie version of *First Men*. In 1902, the lines of Cowper to which Wells alludes were used on the base of the statue of Boadicea erected outside the Houses of Parliament. I do not know if Wells knew of this in advance.

Hill at Rome (191).[47] These should be read in the context of the criticism of British imperialism that is central to the novel.[48]

Moreover, Wells was clearly aware of Lucian's work. Wells makes no mention of Lucian in *Experiment in Autobiography*. But in the 1931 edition of Wells's historical non-fiction *magnum opus, Outline of History* (though not in the 1919 edition),[49] Wells names Lucian as an honorable predecessor: "a great and original imaginative writer . . . who still commands our interest and admiration."[50] In the introduction to his 1933 collection, *Scientific Romances*, Wells names a number of predecessors for the tradition in which he felt he was writing when he produced his scientific romances.[51] Two of these are classical texts. One is Apuleius' *Golden Ass* (or *Metamorphoses*): the picaresque adventures of Lucius, who is magically transformed into an ass.[52] The other is the *True History*. It is clear from this that Wells acknowledged Lucian as an influence.

And then there is a "smoking gun." *First Men* actually carries an epigraph from Lucian (though not, as will be discussed later, from the *True History*). This epigraph is little known, because most editions omit it (hence, perhaps, its absence from Nicolson's discussion). It is not in the 1926 "From the Bookshelf" edition, nor in my 1956 Collins hardback edition, nor the Everyman edition of 1993, nor the Gollancz SF Masterworks edition, nor The Modern Library Classics edition, nor the BiblioBazaar edition.[53] It is, however, in Patrick Parrinder's 2005 Penguin edition, and, of course, on the title page of the 1901 George Newnes first edition.[54] I shall return to this epigraph later.

[47] Though the reference to "Ara Cœli" is, as McLean sees (Wells 2005: 213), to the Church of Santa Maria in Ara Coeli in Rome, Wells has stripped the allusion of any Christian referents, leaving only the pagan "altar of heaven."

[48] On the criticism of colonialism and imperialism in *First Men*, see Miéville (2005: xx–xxiv).

[49] The 1919 first edition of *Outline of History* was castigated, at least as far as the Greek and Roman chapters were concerned, in an early publication by the great historian of Greece and commentator on Thucydides, A. W. Gomme (1921).

[50] Wells (1931: 491).

[51] Cited by Sawyer (2008). Cf. also Warner (2005: xvi).

[52] The *Golden Ass* is itself based on a work that is attributed to Lucian, though it may not actually be his. Bedford sees himself as an ass in chapter 20, "Mr. Bedford in Infinite Space" (Wells 2005: 146).

[53] Wells (1926; 1956; 1993; 2001; 2003; 2007).

[54] And in Leon Stover's annotated first edition (Wells, 1998). Stover discusses the epigraph at Stover (1998: 24).

Wells was clearly, therefore, familiar with the *True History*, and it seems reasonable to assume that this was the case when he wrote *First Men* in 1898–1901.[55] Francis Hickes' 1634 translation of *True History* had been republished in 1894, with illustrations by Aubrey Beardsley, and this may have brought the work back to Wells's attention. Wells did later claim that the first impetus for the novel was the idea of "Cavorite," and only later was the journey to the Moon added.[56]

Given that, it is worth asking whether there are any sequences in Wells's novel that might echo Lucian. I would advance four (with a fifth that is much more questionable):

1. In chapter 11, "The Mooncalf Pastures" (*First Men* 76–79), the two explorers, the narrator, Bedford, and Professor Cavor, eat vegetation on the moon. They rapidly become intoxicated. Something similar happens to "Lucian" and his companions when (before they have left the Earth) they eat fish from a river of wine in an island beyond the Pillars of Hercules (*VH* 1.7).[57]

2. "Lucian" is transported to the Moon through a whirlwind (*typhōn*) suddenly picking up his ship (*VH* 1.9). Bedford and Cavor, of course, travel by using the gravity-opaque material Cavorite. But when this is first created (*First Men* 20–26), it causes a near disaster, as the air above the Cavorite becomes weightless, exerts no pressure on the surrounding air (Wells's science becomes deliberately obscure here), and is pushed out by the surrounding air, which then itself becomes weightless, repeating the process. The rush of air, and the destruction it causes, is something that Cavor subsequently suspects will be explained as the product of a cyclone. The later external observation of the launch of the sphere in chapter 21 is less like Lucian's ship, but it does go straight up in the air, "[l]ike . . . a rocket" (155).

3. Lucian includes what would now be described as a xenobiological description of the inhabitants of the Moon at *True History* 1.22–26 (as well as a description of their armed forces earlier). Wells has a similar description, at least in approach, if not in detail, of the Selenites, in chapter 24, "The Natural History of the Selenites" (*First Men*

[55] For the date, see Parrinder (2005: xxxi).
[56] Miéville (2005: xxi). Miéville himself is not convinced.
[57] Though the Lotus Eater sequence from Homer *Odyssey* Book 9, is probably also an influence on Wells (and also upon Lucian).

173–187). Of course, here Wells is more closely influenced by Victorian scientific publication, especially that of Charles Darwin and Wells's mentor, T. H. Huxley.[58]

4. Wells did not invent the term "Selenite" for his lunar inhabitants. Stephen McLean, in the notes for the Penguin edition,[59] states that the first use of the word appears to be in a letter of James Howell, ca. 1645.[60] But this is only the first recorded use in English. The word is derived from the Greek,[61] and *hoi Selēnitai* (οἱ Σεληνῖται), derived, of course, from the Moon goddess Selene, is Lucian's term for the inhabitants of the Moon (*VH* 1.18).[62] In Hickes's translation, the term "Selenitans" is used. Other lunar narratives, such as Godwin's and Kepler's, do not use the term "Selenite."[63]

5. I also note a slight similarity between Claude Shepperson's illustration of the Selenites in the first publication of *First Men*, and at least one of the beings illustrated in *Lucian's Strange Creatures* by Aubrey Beardsley. This Beardsley illustration was created, with others, ca. 1893 or 1894, for the new edition of the Francis Hickes's translation of *True History*, but this one was rejected. However, Shepperson, or indeed Wells, may have seen it.[64]

I do not wish for a moment to suggest that Wells intended *First Men* to be a refiguring of *True History*. Wells is far too subtle for that. But I do think there are echoes of Lucian in Wells. Perhaps it is even more productive to search for these in the style and tone of Wells's novel rather than in the content. To do this, I would like to reposition *First Men* in the various traditions of fantastic lunar voyages.

---

[58] Wells had written a similar speculative nonfiction piece in "The Man of the Year Million" (1893). It was suggested to me at the Wells Society presentation of this paper that Huxley may have himself briefly discussed the notion of lunar people, but I have been unable to trace this reference.

[59] Wells (2005: 208).

[60] See also Prucher (2007: 179). The *Oxford English Dictionary* also cites T. Urquhart and T. W. Webb.

[61] Prucher (2007: 179).

[62] The term had already been used, in the feminine form, by Herodorus (fragment 28 Müller) in the fifth century B.C.E., but Lucian's work will have been the more familiar in the Victorian period.

[63] Kepler does use the term "Selenographical" to refer to lunar (Gk. *selen-*) geography; see Swinford (this volume, chapter one).

[64] It was suggested to me that the illustrations might have been republished in *The Yellow Book*, a literary journal of the 1890s that Beardsley was co-editor of, but this is not the case.

THE FIRST MEN IN THE MOON AND
FANTASTIC LUNAR VOYAGES

Brian Stableford, in his article "Moon" for the *Encyclopedia of Science Fiction*, identifies a number of different traditions about lunar voyages. One is "a standard framework for social satire,"[65] into which category he places the *True History*. Wells's novel is treated as being separate from that tradition, in a discussion about works that have a "serious interest in the Moon as a world in its own right." But, as Stableford notes, Wells's setting is "no more than a convenient literary device" for the exploration of the Selenite society that follows, which is a variation of the Darwinist speculations Wells first worked with in *The Time Machine*.

I believe Wells is writing much more in a Lucianic satirical tradition than is often acknowledged; even more so than Wells's other scientific romances, all of which Wells himself (as noted above) places in a tradition of the fantastic going back to *True History*. That *First Men* is satire is, I think, established.[66] But the influence of Wells's earlier scientific romances can cloud perceptions of *First Men*. It is not a straightforward SF novel. As some have recognized, it is rather different from the likes of *The Time Machine* or *The War of the Worlds*. Patrick Parrinder, in *Shadows of the Future*, notes that it has fewer scientific ideas than the author's earlier works, and Frank McConnell talks of the "dreamlike, comic quality" of the novel.[67] Writing this sort of novel about the Moon and life on (or in this case, under) the satellite's surface was, in the late Victorian period, becoming harder and harder as scientific knowledge of the Moon grew. Wells himself was well aware that, contrary to what he writes in the novel, there is no atmosphere on the Moon; he demonstrated this in a popular science article he wrote in 1895.[68] So *First Men* sits, if not necessarily consciously, at the end of a tradition that began with Lucian (or Antonius Diogenes), but was subsequently replaced by more scientifically accurate visits to a barren rock, of the sort exemplified by the movie *2001: A Space Odyssey* (U.S.A., directed by Stanley Kubrick, written by Stanley Kubrick and Arthur C. Clarke, 1968). When

---

[65] Stableford (1999: 820); Stableford and Langford (2013).
[66] Huntingdon (1982: 87–97); Miéville (2005: xx).
[67] Parrinder (1996: 63); McConnell (1981: 154).
[68] Wells (1895).

First Men was filmed in 1964 (U.S.A., directed by Nathan Juran, written by Nigel Kneale), a framing sequence involving modern astronauts had to be added to give the story more credibility to a contemporary audience, and references to the moon's surface atmosphere were removed. The influence of Lucian on the tone of Wells's novel can perhaps be seen, not so much in the obvious science fictional elements, such as the moon and other elements mentioned above, but in the characterization of the protagonists. Both "Lucian" and Wells's Bedford describe themselves as being at least partially motivated by curiosity (for "Lucian," see *VH* 1.5). But both tend to blunder from one misadventure to another, and both are ever-ready to turn to violence to solve problems. This can be seen in the readiness of "Lucian" to join Endymion's war against Sun, in which he has no real stake (1.12), and to start wars within the whale (1.36–39). Bedford's violent nature is best shown in *First Men*, chapter 16 ("The Giddy Bridge"), where he resorts to violence in order to avoid crossing a bridge that he thinks is too narrow. For Wells, of course, the implication he wants to make is that the British Empire was built by similarly bungling, violent imperialists. Such a criticism of empire is probably not so explicit in Lucian.

THE FIRST MEN IN THE MOON AND
THE *ICAROMENIPPUS*

I mentioned earlier that *First Men* has an epigraph from Lucian. But that epigraph is not from the *True History*; it is from a different work, the *Icaromenippus*.

Three thousand stadia from the earth to the moon. . . . Marvel not, my comrade, if I appear to be talking to you on super-terrestrial and aerial topics. The long and the short of the matter is that I am running over the order of a journey I have lately made.[69]

---

[69] The source is *Icaromenippus* 1.1–13 (abridged). Stover (1998: 24) says that the translation is that of Hickes (using the common misspelling "Hicks"); it is not, though there are some similarities. The translation is therefore presumably Wells's own. Steven McLean calls this a "loose translation" (Wells 2005: 205), but it is a perfectly fine rendition of the Greek. McLean's reasons for his comment appear to be based on an over-reliance upon the loose translation of Turner (1961). McLean's comment that "'order' should actually be 'total distance'," uses Turner's translation of ἀναλογίζομαι τῆς ἔναγχος ἀποδημίας ("I'm trying to calculate the total distance," 111).

Icaromenippus is Lucian's other Moon-voyage narrative.[70] In it, the third-century B.C.E. satirist and Cynic philosopher Menippus (a regular narrator in Lucian's works) relates a journey of his to the Moon. There he meets the philosopher Empedocles, and subsequently goes to Olympus on a mission for Selene, the Moon goddess. The *Icaromenippus* is less well-known than *True History* (as a measure of this, Sidwell omits it from the selection in his recent Penguin edition).[71] But it is also the work to which Aphra Behn referred when she cited Lucian in *The Emperor of the Moon* (1687).[72] This leads to the interesting possibility that *First Men* might actually have more in common with the *Icaromenippus* than with the *True History*.

In the *Icaromenippus*, Menippus travels to the Moon by attaching an eagle's wing and a vulture's wing. To a degree, this is a version of the Icarus legend—hence the title *IcaroMenippus*. But it is also a pseudo-scientific explanation with more in common with Cavorite than the whirlwind that transports "Lucian" into space in *True History*—here we find the interest in the means of travel that Edith Hall notes is lacking from *True History*. Menippus observes the Earth from the Moon, in the same way as Bedford and Cavor observe the Earth from their sphere in chapter 5, "The Journey to the Moon" (*First Men* 42–43),[73] though there is also a brief scene of viewing the Earth from the Moon in *True History* (1.10).

Menippus compares the people he observes on Earth to ants living in an ant-hill. Might we see in that the germ of Wells's ant-like Selenites?[74] And Lucian's narrator Menippus and the scientist he finds on the Moon, Empedocles, might be the models for Wells's Bedford and Cavor. I am wary about going too far down this road, as it risks becoming positivist. I could be on my own fantastic voyage here, sailing into the unknown seas of speculation.

---

[70] For a translation, see Costa (2005: 45–60).

[71] Sidwell (2004).

[72] This is not clear in Miéville's introduction to the Penguin edition of *First Men* (2005: xiv) when he cites Behn.

[73] Compare the elevated, and far less detailed, view of Earth from Mars at the end of Wells's 1897 story "The Star."

[74] There are ant-like creatures in *True History* as well (1.16), but they are in the service of the Sun rather than the Moon.

CONCLUSION

However the Lucianic influence actually manifests itself, it is clear that Wells did know Lucian, including both of the works that related to lunar voyages. It may not be easy to point clearly to specific moments in which Wells is receiving Lucian in *First Men*. But I feel sure that this is what he is doing.

The final question is what recognizing Lucian's influence means for a reading of Wells's novel. For many casual readers, it probably does not make much difference, any more than they particularly care about the influence of Godwin or Kepler. However, I do think it is possible to get a clearer idea of how both the *True History* and *The First Men in the Moon* can be read in the context of the history of SF. There is a continuity between the two works that is sometimes ignored. Lucian deserves to be restored to the list of Wells's influences.

Part II

SF "Classics"

5

A Complex Oedipus: The Tragedy of Edward Morbius

Gregory S. Bucher

Dis manibus Leslie Nielsen †11.28.2010
Dis manibus Anne Francis †1.2.2011

The superb and intelligent film *Forbidden Planet* (1956, directed by Fred
M. Wilcox) has long provoked critical interest.[1] It cleverly molds
Freudian ideas onto an armature constructed from Shakespeare's
Tempest, while its production values and compelling story still com-
mand respect. By 1960, Kingsley Amis had already perceived that

[1] In this paper, ED = an early draft of Hume's script dated from 8/26/54 to 9/3/54 (a
typo on the first page gives the date as 8/26/53), FD = the final draft, dated 3/17/55, and
PC = the postproduction continuity script, cited by reel and page numbers in the format
"PC 1.1–2." Unless otherwise noted, all quotations from the film are from the PC, which
reflects the film exactly as it was released. The more verbose ED valuably supplements the
shooting script.

For much valuable feedback, I thank Geoffrey Bakewell, Christopher Celenza,
Christina Clark, Tu-Uyen Nguyen, Seth Rosenzweig, and Scott Slemmens, as well as the
editors and anonymous referees of this volume. I also gratefully acknowledge many helpful comments on versions of this paper delivered at Creighton University and the
University of Texas, Austin.

Forbidden Planet adapted *The Tempest*,[2] and yet its debt to Greek tragedy,[3] and in particular the *Oedipus Rex*, has hardly been noticed. I am aware of only two studies linking *Forbidden Planet* to the *Oedipus*. Psychoanalyst Herbert Stein's groundbreaking essay, *"Forbidden Planet"* (2010), understandably comes at the problem from a Freudian viewpoint, through the Oedipal complex the film supposedly depicts;[4] David Sheppard's *Eternal Return* (2012) also perceives Sophoclean elements in *Forbidden Planet* but takes them to stem from constants in the underlying nature of the human psyche, again starting from Freud.[5] Both studies anticipate some of the thematic links between the two stories that are the focus of this essay, but I think it is time to jettison a distracting and illusory hermeneutic based on Freud's theory of sexuality, for reasons I will discuss below. Instead, I seek to demonstrate that *Forbidden Planet* is a morally serious story animated by a Sophoclean heart, a brilliant revival of the classical tradition, owing a direct debt to the *Oedipus Rex* and Aristotle's later discussion of Greek tragedy in the *Poetics*.

[2] Amis (1960: 30) and Morsberger (1961: 161) offer the earliest recognitions of Hume's adaptation of *The Tempest*; Campos (1998) and Caroti (2004) the most detailed; and Knighten (1994) perhaps the most sensitive. Willson (2000: 101–109) studies *Forbidden Planet* against the background of Shakespeare adaptations in American cinema. Buchanan (2001) reviews the film's reception and offers a skeptical analysis of Block's inferable claim to have been responsible for bringing elements of *The Tempest* into *Forbidden Planet; pace* Knighten (1994: 36).

[3] The story has been called a tragedy, and parts of it have been called tragic in a generic sense more than once: cf. Knighten (1994: 36) and Warren (2010: 297). Hume suggestively alludes to the tragic aspect of the story in Adams's final speech ("triumph and tragedy. . . ." PC 6.15).

[4] Stein (2010: 17): "The film may have been based on *The Tempest*, but I think we could make a closer comparison with *Oedipus Rex*. . . . this is the story of a powerful king ([Walter] Pidgeon) who is aware of a terrible hidden murderer in his kingdom only to find that the murderer is himself. In fact, it is a particularly interesting variation on *Oedipus Rex* because here we see Oedipus not as a son but as a father caught up in much the same tragic dynamics with his daughter." Stein (20): "Like Oedipus, Morbius is aware of a terrible crime committed on his planet twenty years earlier, the death of his fellow colonists. Like Oedipus, Morbius, with much outside interpretation from Captain Adams, comes to realize that he was the murderer."

[5] Sheppard (2012: ch. 4): "Dr. Morbius, of course, has his origin in both Oedipus and Prospero although he'll not control the action, as did both of them. In many ways, *Forbidden Planet* is closer to the Oedipus myth than *The Tempest*, which is strange considering that the storyline for the movie was consciously and deliberately taken from *The Tempest* with no mention of the Oedipus myth. This could well signify that the cosmic story has an unconscious organic unity in the human psyche that allows various aspects of it to resurface from time to time."

Thanks to recent painstaking research by Bill Warren, we know much more about the screenplay's genesis and evolution than we did just a few years ago. Warren has read the archival copy of "Fatal Planet," Allen Adler and Irving Block's original story proposal to Metro-Goldwyn-Mayer (MGM), reporting that it reads more like a typical 1950s monster story than the classic it would become thanks to the pen of Cyril Hume, the Yale-trained screenwriter. In fact, Hume appears to have been responsible for the screenplay's grand scope and the admixture of Freud, the Bard, and Greek tragedy.[6] A knowledge of the *Oedipus Rex* and Aristotle's discussion of it, staples of undergraduate general education courses then as now,[7] can reasonably be inferred in Hume, who revealed his interest in, and more than casual knowledge of, classics by going to the trouble of having a character (aptly) quote some Catullan verse in Latin.[8] Though Block deposed at a fairly late date that *The Tempest* was his favorite play and that he was "particularly fond of mythology and the classics,"[9] Judith Buchanan has argued convincingly against Block's influence on the final story, though she overstates her case by adopting too skeptical a view of *Forbidden Planet*'s debt to *The Tempest*.[10]

The literature on *Forbidden Planet* characteristically draws valuable parallels with contemporary culture or other works of literature. Here I seek to establish what I will call a strong claim; namely, that Hume consciously adapted the *Oedipus* as seen through an Aristotelian lens. An inquiry into Hume's authorial intent is not easy, since the screenplay mentions no sources, though the character "Doc" Ostrow's reference to the id does bring Freud unmistakably into the picture. Despite the

---

[6] Warren (2010: 297): "Cyril Hume was hired to flesh out the thin story; he apparently researched both science and science fiction, and almost everything that makes *Forbidden Planet* notable was present in his story outline (not in screenplay form) of November 11, 1952."

[7] See Tomcho et al. (1994: esp. 96).

[8] ED 30. Doc, looking at Altaira as she summons her tame bird "friends": *et tristis animi levare curas* (Catullus 2.10; *levare* is misspelled *lemaro* in the ED). Hume may well have had the erotic reading of Lesbia's *passer* in mind here: the ensuing discussion of Altaira's power to tame wild animals further sexualizes her with its frank discussion of the power of a virgin ("maiden") to tame a unicorn (ED 31–32). Later, however, although Doc claims still to prefer the "medieval explanation" for Altaira's power, he rationalizes it by ascribing this taming power to the electromagnetic emanations of "an exceptionally fine human brain in a totally unawakened female body" (38).

[9] Clarke and Rubin (1979: 6).

[10] Buchanan (2001: esp. 152–153).

difficulty, almost all scholars accept *Forbidden Planet's* conscious debt
to the *Tempest*, a debt established only by circumstantial evidence that
boils down to striking similarities in the situation (remote desert planet,
marooned father/daughter, etc.) and action (daughter falls for the young
captain, bibulous cook drinking with the father's servant, etc.). There is
enough of it, however, and it is complex enough to put the case effectively beyond dispute. This is the sort of case I want to make for the
Oedipus and the *Poetics*, as opposed to a weaker (if easier) claim that
Forbidden Planet is animated by many of the concerns raised by the
Oedipus. (That it is, but that weaker claim would also admit coincidental
similarities of a sort I will not pursue here.)

Nontrivial similarities in plot and action, then, will serve as controls,
their complexity and number effectively ruling out chance as the cause.
Then we will move on, as we should, to see whether the similarities
extend to individual characters.[11] Too many studies argue initially or
primarily from individual character traits that Edward Morbius owes a
debt to, for example, Marlowe's Faustus,[12] or Jewish émigré philolo-
gists,[13] or J. Robert Oppenheimer,[14] offering us a weaker form of evidence that at best supports a tenuous claim.

Lastly, Hume's mid-century, educated-layman's take on Freudian
theory, the *Oedipus*, and Aristotle's *Poetics* no longer prevails, at least in
specialist circles.[15] If we are wise, therefore, we will try to do justice to
the film by viewing it through the lens of contemporary, and not current, interpretations of the *Oedipus*, the *Poetics*, and concepts like the
tragic flaw and *hubris*.[16]

The *Oedipus* I take to be sufficiently familiar to the present audience, but a careful plot summary of *Forbidden Planet* is in order. In
the twenty-third century, the United Planets cruiser *C-57-D*, under

---

[11] Tarratt (1970: 334) sees, with Amis (1960: 30), the importance of structural and
thematic connections in analyzing the debt of *Forbidden Planet* to *The Tempest*.

[12] Knighten (1994: 37).

[13] Lerer (2000: *passim*). Harris (2001/2002: Part IV) sees Nietzsche in Morbius on the
basis of the philology connection.

[14] Roberts (2000). Trushell (1995: 85) already saw in *Forbidden Planet* the
McCarthy-era attack on egghead scientists like Oppenheimer.

[15] See, e.g., the overview in Halliwell (1998: 316–323), and the unsympathetic comments of Jones (1962: 159–166).

[16] We are helped here by E. R. Dodds's catalog of common mid-century misunder-
standings of the *Oedipus* (1966: *passim*).

the command of Captain J. J. Adams, arrives at the planet Altair IV to investigate the status of an expedition that had gone there twenty years before. They discover that only one member of the original expedition, the ship's philologist, Edward Morbius, has survived an encounter with what Morbius calls a "planetary force" that violently destroyed the rest of the expedition and its ship, the *Bellerophon*. Adams; his second in command, Jerry Farman; and ship's doctor, "Doc" Ostrow, discover that Morbius had a daughter, Altaira, by one of the other crew members whom he had married en route. His wife having died a natural death not long after the rest had been killed, Morbius and Altaira have been alone, *à la* Prospero and Miranda, for nearly twenty years.

Adams needs to consult Earth authorities about what to do with Morbius, but his efforts to communicate are frustrated by incidents of increasingly violent destruction of equipment and men. Morbius has no desire to return to Earth, but he—and his remarkable robot, Robby— seem to be excluded as suspects. In the course of their investigation, Adams and his men discover that Morbius's house sits atop an entrance to a machine, 8,000 cubic miles in size, left by a now-dead race called the Krell. The purpose of the machine, which has fantastic amounts of power at its disposal, is unclear to Morbius. He has, however, used a machine that he calls the "plastic educator" in a Krell laboratory near the surface. Though it killed the captain of the *Bellerophon* instantly, Morbius survived, and found (to his delight) that the experience permanently doubled his IQ. With this expanded intellect, Morbius has been working contentedly away deciphering the rudiments of the Krell knowledge, and he has no desire to share it or be taken away from it. One discovery Morbius has made is that the Krell seemed to have been devoting their entire racial energy to eliminating instrumentality just before they disappeared.[17]

Meanwhile, Adams and Farman have taken an interest in the intelligent and ingenuously sexy Altaira, and the issue is raised that she should return to Earth "for her natural development." Altaira in turn falls for Adams (losing her innocence in the process), and forms a connection with him that her father does not like. A frightful night attack on the now wary crew of the *C-57-D* reveals that the attacker is an

[17] The ambiguous term "instrumentality" camouflages the secret of the id monster.

invisible monster that can withstand the energies of the ship's massed batteries; we cut to Morbius, awakened by Altaira's cries. As he awakens, we see over his shoulder numerous power gauges in the Krell lab sink from registering high power use to zero; the attack on the ship ends abruptly.

Adams and Doc make their way to Morbius's house that night for some answers. While Adams is distracted, Doc sneaks down to the Krell lab for a brain boost. After it he is brought dying to Adams, and manages to gasp out the explanation for the attacks: "monsters from the id." Morbius, jealously enraged at the now-dead Ostrow's effrontery in taking the brain boost, is further provoked when Altaira, put off by his ungenerous attitude toward Doc's death, tells him she is leaving with Adams for Earth. At just that moment, while Adams is putting together the pieces of the puzzle about the id, Robby announces that the monster is coming through the woods toward the house.

A quick flight to the Krell laboratory, with its impenetrable Krell-metal doors, gives Adams time to explain to Morbius that, with his boosted intellect, Morbius has been unconsciously activating the Krell machine, which, we now see, was designed to translate the thoughts of the Krell into material substance—the elimination of instrumentality. Morbius's conscious mind lacks the power to control the machine, but his subconscious,[18] with its powerful yet ignoble (and normally suppressed) appetites for things like getting its own way, and possession of the only woman on the planet, does have the strength to activate the machine and has repeatedly, unbeknownst to Morbius, broken out into murderous rampages. The Krell, it transpires, wiped themselves out when the subconscious demons of the collected minds of an entire race were unleashed in a single night. Morbius confronts his guilt just as the monster, using almost all of the machine's power, burns through the Krell-metal doors, and he interposes himself between the monster from his mind and Adams and Altaira on the other side of the lab. The monster strikes him down, killing itself, and Morbius, in his dying breaths, blesses the couple and instructs them to destroy the Krell machine.

---

[18] The screenplay consistently uses "subconscious" for what I believe Freud would call the "unconscious mind." Morbius has no knowledge of, or control over, the id monster.

FORBIDDEN PLANET ON THE ARISTOTELIAN TEMPLATE

Because it involves a basic problem in the interpretation of *Forbidden Planet*, and because Aristotle was concerned with it, I begin with plot structure. Aristotle famously asserted (*Poetics* [*Poet.*] 1450b) that a tragedy has a beginning, middle, and end. *Forbidden Planet*, too, as Warren rightly notes, "is classically structured; it almost falls into acts."[19] It is problematic, therefore, that the film has seemed to many to end on an anticlimax.[20]

Far from being an anticlimax, however, Morbius's recognition of his guilt and suicidal interposition of his body between the monster and his daughter form an astonishing and powerful climax suited to a tragedy. The problem is that we do not see the monster. At the end of the film (PC 6.13–14), we see Morbius run toward the Krell-metal doors as the monster breaks through; Adams draws his blaster, but then lowers it; we see Morbius confront the monster in a monster's point-of-view shot from above.[21] Adams and Altaira react in horror as something unpleasant occurs offscreen, and then they run to a prostrate Morbius. Warren sums up critical confusion: Morbius "seems to die from strain."[22] The monster would thus seem to have departed because Morbius shooed it away or disavowed it.[23] This makes no sense: central to the story is the fact that Morbius *has no voluntary control* over the monster. Warren,

---

[19] Warren (2010: 303).

[20] Ibid. (303): "The climax is missing" because we do not see Morbius confront the id monster.

[21] Actually, not quite a true point-of-view shot, though it was intended to be (see note 48); *Forbidden Planet* tends to avoid them and use objective shots, as when, taking coffee with Farman, Altaira turns to glance at Adams and Ostrow, and we cut to them staring back at her: into the right foreground (PC 2.11). Within the limits of this convention, however, the final shot of Morbius's confrontation with the monster may be taken to be from the monster's point of view.

[22] The quotation is from Warren (2010: 302). For examples of the confusion, see Steinbrunner and Goldblatt (1972: 279–280); Brosnan (1978: 124); and Luciano (1987: 94). Willson (2000: 106) goes as far as to argue that the id monster "disappears" and does not see that Morbius has been fatally stricken. The otherwise clear-thinking Worland and Slayden (2000: 141–142) equivocate: "Realizing his terrible mistake, Morbius confronts and renounces the monster—a self-realization tantamount to self-annihilation, which nevertheless spares the life of his daughter." No: the self-realization (or "recognition," as Aristotle would say) leads to self-annihilation.

[23] Kawin (1995: 320) adopts a Freudian analysis: Morbius, in confronting the monster and accepting it as his, resolves a psychological crisis, and is accordingly cured, resolving the "Oedipal nightmare" of the monster's rampage. This view founders on the fact that Morbius dies at the end; as Biskind (1983: 110) makes clear, in this scenario, "therapy is useless."

moreover, produces evidence to show that the filmmakers intended to insert a special effect of the monster striking Morbius down.[24] It was deleted (if ever made), perhaps after they saw how inadequate the effect looked in the earlier scene when the animated monster "grabs" Farman during the night attack (5.13): it is painfully obvious that a stiff, stuffed dummy is being manipulated on wires. Nor is the climax as we have it just a counsel of desperation to sidestep a difficult special effect, for Hume and the filmmakers suggest an easier ending, had their wish merely been to get Adams and Altaira out of harm's way expediently. In the early draft, Hume has Adams draw a bead on Morbius's head with his blaster (ED 108), and even in the filmed version he points his blaster in the direction of Morbius and the monster. Now, the night attack on the ship (PC 5.11–13) had shown Adams clearly that the ship's massed batteries (not to mention one sidearm) had no effect on the monster: Adams can only be drawing his blaster to disintegrate Morbius's brain, which would instantly shut off the monster. It was a more sophisticated move to have Adams refuse to disintegrate Morbius's brain while permitting the latter to face the monster (offscreen). There was no more need to show it than there was to show Oedipus' offstage self-blinding at the climax of the *Oedipus*.[25] By having Morbius confront the monster instead of being taken out of the action by a blaster shot to the head, Hume preserves his agency to the end and the plot maintains a tight focus on him, as befits his role as the tragic figure.

Aristotle would refer to this tight focus on the tragic hero as a single unified action. More memorable to most readers of the *Poetics* are probably the concepts of recognition and reversal (*Poet.* 1452a). By *recognition* (*anagnōrisis*), Aristotle means a shocking realization such as Oedipus' sudden realization that he has not only killed his father but he has indeed fathered four children on his mother. A *reversal* (*peripeteia*) is "a change from one state of affairs to its exact opposite," an unexpected change for the worse in the tragic figure's circumstances—Aristotle points to the *Oedipus*' messenger who arrives eager to help, but merely ends up giving Oedipus the final piece of the puzzle that destroys him. Morbius

---

[24] ED (108) makes it clear that Morbius interposes his body, is seized by the monster, and is killed without being physically rent. Baxter (1970: 114) interprets the scene correctly. See the further evidence in Warren (2010: 301).

[25] Warren (2010: 302) sees the wisdom of leaving the monster offscreen in the climax.

Figure 5-1 Morbius confronts his guilt in the Krell laboratory at the climax of *Forbidden Planet* (PC 6.12). From *Forbidden Planet*, MGM studios, dir. Fred M. Wilcox, 1957.

undergoes a classic sudden recognition, signaled to us by Hume when, at bay in the Krell lab, the former cries out "Guilty! Guilty!" (PC 6.12); Morbius's recognition of his guilt is seen in Figure 5-1.

Thanks to an arrogant pride in his intellect (which I will return to below), Morbius suffers a precipitous fall from a sense of autonomy and control over the circumstances of his life to a self-loathing understanding that he has misunderstood everything and unwittingly caused many deaths. The recognition and reversal here, as shocking and as dramatically effective as anything Sophocles ever put on stage, occur together, precisely in the way Aristotle deemed best and thought best exemplified in the *Oedipus* (*Poet.* 1452a).

In addition to a recognition and reversal, *Forbidden Planet* also manifests two carefully interwoven features of Aristotelian plot development (*Poet.* 1455b): complication (*desis*) and unraveling (*lusis*). As the men of the *C-57-D* come closer to the facts about Morbius, and Adams comes closer to Altaira, these complications summon forth the id monster, which leads the action ever more swiftly toward the *dénouement*. Admittedly, Wilcox directs the film at a stately pace, but the *story* moves swiftly, over a pair of

days, to its climax. The comic scenes with the cook and Robby obtrude (PC
3.3–4; 5.1–2; 5.5–6), but they were forced into the plot by producer Nicholas
Nayfack, motivated by a desire to appeal to a juvenile audience, and justifiable, perhaps, as echoing the memorable Shakespearean scene with
Stephano, Trinculo, and Caliban and serving the useful purpose of establishing an alibi for Robby during Quinn's murder.[26]

Aristotle strongly recommended keeping the irrational offstage
(*Poet.* 1454b). Hume wisely took this advice and played to the more
materialistic expectations of technologically sophisticated mid-century
audiences, eschewing Shakespeare's fantastic sprite Ariel and substi-
tuting the science of psychology and the "magic" of advanced technology in its place.[27] Though I retain the term as a piece of shorthand,
there is in fact no "monster" at all in *Forbidden Planet*, merely the natural operation of a machine that reads the electromagnetic impulses of a
normal—all too normal, despite enhancement—human brain. Morbius
is set up for a fall by a sequence of events set in motion by his triumph
over the alien plastic educator.

As mentioned above, any discussion revolving around a mid-century
understanding of the *Poetics* and the *Oedipus* has to confront
now-outdated conceptions of the "tragic flaw" and *hubris*. The latter
does not figure in the *Poetics* but (to quote one recent scholarly treatment) has been commonly but wrongly interpreted as "pride, overcon-
fidence, or any behavior which may offend divine powers."[28] Likewise,
the concept of a tragic flaw as a systematic character defect arises from
a moralizing misreading of Aristotle's term *hamartia* (*Poet.* 1453a).
Hamartia is better understood as "mistake," but under an older understanding, scholars looked for ingrained character defects in tragic heroes,
and *hubris*, misread as a prideful moral flaw, met the requirements well.[29]
It is in the light of the older prevailing reading of *hamartia* and *hubris*
that we ought to consider Morbius.

---

[26] Booker (2006: 45) sees this.
[27] Warren (2010: 11–12); I paraphrase Arthur C. Clarke's "third law": any sufficiently
advanced technology will be indistinguishable from magic. Both Baxter (1970: 114) and
Harris (2001/2002: Part IV) have made this connection well; Harris most cleverly: "Morbius's
technology and his intelligence are in the realm of magic, a la [sic] Clarke's Law, and at the
end of the film, Morbius wears the wizard robes of Shakespeare's Prospero to illustrate this."
[28] This view has now been superseded: *hubris* is best interpreted as deliberately and
offensively belittling behavior, up to and including assault. See Fischer (2003: 732).
[29] On *hamartia*, see Dodds (1966: 220–221); Whalley (1997: 94–96).

When we meet him, Morbius is an eminently respectable philologist, and a highly prosperous one at that, for he, a scholar and intellectual, sits in sole possession of the greatest puzzle known to man, with a mind powerful enough to make inroads into it and no serious distractions (Adams, in anger, subsequently speaks of Morbius's "egomaniac empire"; PC 6.10). It is his nature to be focused on the acquisition of knowledge—in this case, the secrets of the Krell.[30] Yet this eminent and enviable position is tainted by an arrogant pride. In an important scene, Morbius confronts the possibility of dispatching the Krells' knowledge to Earth. Here is the dialogue as spoken (5.3–4), with Hume's stage directions and my italics (ED 76; FD 62):

MORBIUS: One moment, commander. For close on twenty years now I've been constantly, and, I hope, dispassionately, considering this very problem. And I have come to the unalterable conclusion that man is unfit, as yet, to receive such knowledge—such almost limitless power.

DOC *(gently):* Whereas Morbius, with his artificially expanded intellect, is now ideally suited to administer this power for the whole human race.

MORBIUS *(unruffled):* Precisely, Doctor. *(increasingly arbitrary)* Such portions of the Krell science as I may from time to time deem suitable and safe, I shall dispense to Earth. Other portions I shall withhold. And in this I shall be answerable exclusively to my own conscience and judgment.

Morbius sweeps past Ostrow's irony and appears to have proprietary feelings about the Krell knowledge. Compared with his famous speech about the high benevolence of the Krell (PC 4.3),[31] this speech suggests that Morbius, after his long years in the Krell laboratory, identifies with them, and sees his hard-won understanding of their science as his own: an attitude that gives away his prideful arrogance as well as anything could.

This piece of dialogue, however, is not only pregnant, as we have seen, with evidence of Morbius's arrogant pride, but is also an exquisite example of crushingly heavy dramatic irony. Morbius refuses to send the

---

[30] Cf. Prospero, *Tempest*, Act II, Scene 2: "I, thus neglecting worldly ends, all dedicated / To closeness and the bettering of my mind."

[31] Harris (2001/2002: Part I) explicitly recognizes the importance of this speech and notes (correctly) that it is in "almost blank verse." The highly polished speech survives with its cadenced wording largely unchanged from the ED (61–62), suggesting its importance to the plot in the minds of the filmmakers. Hume specifies that, as Morbius speaks, "there is now a special sort of dignity about him" (ED 61, FD 48), again signaling Morbius's emulous reverence toward the Krell.

Krell knowledge back to Earth because he clearly sees its danger. This is at once patronizingly arrogant (as Hume signals to us through Doc's gentle irony) but also benevolently high-minded, something we are apt to forget as Morbius's anger propels the story into increasingly violent action. And so we are left with a man who, thanks to his brain boost, considers himself to be the one person best suited to act as the protector of his species, while having no conscious control over, or even awareness of, the terrible, destructive outbreak of his impulses. We might fittingly compare the similarly high-minded Oedipus, at once the protector of Thebes and also the unwitting cause of Thebes' plague, the man least aware of the true nature of his life.

In fact, Hume gives us so many examples of Morbius's arrogant pride that it is clear he was stressing it as a fundamental characteristic (one might say a flaw) of the man.[32] He behaves by turns patronizingly and cruelly toward the men of the *C-57-D* from the moment he "washes his hands" of the consequences of their landing without bothering to give them a full explanation of the danger they might be in. When Morbius explains Robby to the officers of the *C-57-D*, he takes visible pleasure in trying to frighten them by provocatively showing them how Robby is unable to shoot Adams when ordered to do so (PC 2.2–4),[33] and affects a rather unconvincing regret for startling them with the "parlor magic" of his house's steel shutters (2.5).[34] His daughter casually reveals how she has been indoctrinated against Earth by telling Farman how lucky she is that the three Earth people she happens to have met are "such very fine exceptions" (2.11).[35] Morbius evidently has had a contempt for people from the beginning: he and his wife were the only ones who wanted to remain on Altair IV when the rest of the *Bellerophon* crew wanted to leave, and he suggests (rather feebly) that it was the Morbiuses' special love of the planet that made them immune to the "planetary force" (2.6).

---

[32] Hume overdetermines his characterization of the ingenuous Altaira: she has never seen men before, she does not understand Farman's innuendos, she thinks nothing of kissing Farman, thinks nothing of wearing what she wants, is able to tame tigers, etc., etc.

[33] ED 20: Morbius "plainly respects" Adams for staring down the barrel of his own blaster, but chuckles at the end of the "test."

[34] ED 21: Morbius is "ironically amused" at the officers' defensive reaction to the shutters.

[35] ED 29: Altaira speaks when Morbius opens the possibility that she might visit Earth: "But why should any sane person want to visit such a dreadful, nasty little planet as Earth!?"

Again, when Morbius says goodbye to Adams, Farman, and Ostrow after their first meeting, he insultingly turns solely to Ostrow and says "To tell the truth, Doctor, I sometimes still miss the conversation of such men as yourself" (PC 2.16).[36] He is later openly contemptuous of the military (4.9),[37] and bullies a hesitant Adams and Ostrow to look down the 7,800 levels of the Krell ventilator shaft (4.12). The most telling exhibition of Morbius's arrogant pride comes when Ostrow has died using the plastic educator and he explodes, "The fool! As if his ape's brain could hold the secrets of the Krell!" (6.4). Morbius has an ape's brain, too, but that he does not remember it shows how completely he now identifies himself with the Krell.[38] Ostrow's death propels the action to the final act; upon hearing Morbius's callous dismissal of Ostrow's death, Altaira makes it clear that her father's behavior has convinced her that she must depart with Adams for Earth. This provokes the final appearance of the id monster, with attendant revelations.

Hume, incidentally, left no doubt that he saw Morbius's pride as his great flaw, though he understandably used neither "hubris" nor "tragic flaw" in the screenplay. In a line cut from the final confrontation scene, Hume even had Morbius himself identify his flaw, which he terms a "crime" (cut lines in italics: ED 107):

Morbius: Guilty. Guilty. *My crime was pride, and that I failed to love my fellow men. And now my punishment is that I cannot even save my own child.* My evil self is at that door, and I have no power to keep it out.[39]

---

[36] According to Boss (1990: 63), Morbius here thus reproaches Adams for failing to thank him for lunch.

[37] ED 66: Morbius, "repressing a twinkle," suggests Ostrow be tested before Adams. Boss (1990: 63) misreads the scene, seeing a conspiracy of humor between Morbius and Ostrow over Adams's comparatively low IQ. There is no evidence in any version of the screenplay I have seen, nor in the film, that Ostrow is complicit in deriding Adams. Cf. Morbius's respect for Adams, cited in note 33.

[38] In his great speech giving the history of the Krell, he adumbrates this view when, after suggesting that the Krell brought back terrestrial biological specimens, he says "(gravely ironical) Though evidently our own bestial primitive ancestors were beneath the notice of the Krell." As George Bernard Shaw once said, "Beware of the pursuit of the superhuman—it leads to an indiscriminate contempt for the human" (*Man and Superman*, Act 3).

[39] Cf. Sheppard (2012: chapter 3): "This again is reminiscent of Oedipus' words, 'I am discovered to be evil,' and Prospero owning up to Caliban, '. . . this thing of darkness, I / Acknowledge mine.'" Biskind (1983: 110) interestingly sees the potential of (psychological) therapy in Morbius's recognition, but because Morbius dies, thinks it is not effected. (His thesis is that a category of SF films has a therapeutic view, which focuses on the perfectibility—or at any rate improvability—of man.) In Aristotelian terms, however,

MORBIUS AND OEDIPUS

We must not hope to see direct parallels in Morbius and Oedipus, only significant analogies. I would love to support my thesis by linking incestuous desires between Morbius and Altaira to Oedipus' incestuously siring four children on his mother, and I would have virtually every serious critic of *Forbidden Planet* on my side. All very well, except for one obvious fallacy: incest is merely a plot circumstance in the *Oedipus*, who had no incestuous desire for his mother; he coupled with her in ignorance and had abandoned what we must assume was for the most part a life of ease and prestige as the putative son of the King of Corinth to distance himself from the woman he thought was his mother, once he had heard Apollo's grim prophecy. Moreover, though the film has sophisticated sexual themes, there is not even a hint of any incestuous intent or relations between Morbius and Altaira in it; instead, the idea has been imported by critics wanting to press the film into a mold in the shape of Freud's theory of sexuality. What happens in Morbius's unconscious can only be guessed at by observing the actions of its proxy, the id monster, which never makes clear to us whether (for example) Morbius is sexually interested in Altaira or (more plausibly) angry over the disturbance of his "egomaniac empire."[40] All we can reasonably infer is that Morbius resents Adams's intrusion. The incest connection is illusory, and emerges, it seems, from critics' tacit and erroneous assumption that, if Hume cites Freud's theory of the unconscious mind, his theory of sexual development (which is a different thing) must also come along for the ride. If we resist the temptation to invoke it and content ourselves with simply calling both men's actions "flawed" (or "crimes," to use Morbius's term: ED 107), then, by blurring our focus to that extent, we can more clearly see the complicated array of plot, theme, and character traits that link the two stories.

Looking for complex analogies between Oedipus and Morbius, therefore, we can begin by noting that Oedipus is a capable man who has overcome a deadly test that proved the quality of his intellect and

---

where the therapy (or catharsis) is aimed at the audience and works through pity and fear, Morbius's death is not only explicable, but preferable.

[40] Here Warren (2010: 297) goes astray, though with some caution: "Arguably, a central theme of *Forbidden Planet* is repressed incest—Morbius desires Altaira, aware of this only in his dreams. But even if only a subtheme, the darker side of parental relations is certainly a major element."

achieved great things. Unfortunately, his greatest acts (abandoning his putative parents in Corinth so as to protect them, defeating the Sphinx, and rescuing Thebes) put him directly, if unwittingly, on the path to fulfilling an unpleasant destiny predicted by the gods. Thinking to outsmart fate, the gods, or both, he is subsequently blindsided by the sudden and terrifying revelation that his life, in retrospect, has not at all been what his human powers of knowing and perception told him it was. Edward Morbius, too, seemingly stands at a summit of achievement reached after passing the deadly test of the plastic educator which (im)proved the quality of *his* intellect.[41] Like Oedipus, Morbius learns that he is not what he thought he was, and that his great intellectual achievements are little beside being suddenly revealed as a murderer, even an unconscious one, as shown by his final self-loathing impulse to blow up Altair IV and with it his life's work (PC 6.14).

Like Oedipus, however, Morbius ignores some pretty obvious clues pointing to his culpability. Why has Morbius *not* thought hard about the machine he lives atop? As well ask why Oedipus evidently never asked Jocasta, in a marriage long enough to beget four children, about Laius' death and the fate of their children, if any. This is an illogicality that Aristotle worries about (*Poet.* 1460a) and recommends keeping out of the action.[42] Given Oedipus' intelligence, however, perhaps it is not irrelevant to forming an opinion about him. But however that may be in the specific case of the *Oedipus*, Hume more than once explicitly brings these sorts of questions concerning Morbius's situation to the fore, showing that he wants us to think about them.

Specifically, Morbius is twice asked direct questions about what we later learn (or can deduce) is the action of the great machine. This is hardly idle chit-chat. Hume raises ideas we are to consider and puts Morbius's answers at our disposal. To both questions Morbius offers weak, conjectural answers. In the first place, Adams asks Morbius about his and his wife's immunity to the "planetary force," and Morbius offers

---

[41] Sheppard (2012: chapter 3) missteps here: "Morbius gaining the knowledge of the Krell is reminiscent of Oedipus having the knowledge necessary to solve the Sphinx's riddle, which led to his doom."

[42] Dodds (1966: 221), defending the play on its own grounds, stresses the "critical principle that *what is not mentioned in the play does not exist*" (Dodds's emphasis). This advances his argument against certain critics of the play with whom he does not agree, but arbitrarily disallows certain strands of thoughtful inferential analysis by the audience.

that he and his wife differed from their murdered colleagues only in
their special love for the planet (PC 2.6). Then, when Adams asks
Morbius point-blank what the machine does (4.13), Morbius tells Adams
and Ostrow that sometimes the machine's power gauges register when
the buck deer fight in the autumn, and birds fly over in the spring.
Strikingly, he does not explain the logic behind this connection. These
scenes are valuable diagnostic indicators that Hume trusts us to perceive
it (even if only in hindsight) when characters make wrong inferences.[43]

Morbius also offers his answer to a third important question that we
must infer he asked himself in the past: why is there so much terrestrial
flora and fauna around his house? His hypothesis is that the Krell
brought them back from a visit to Earth (PC 4.3). But in fact, no type of
plant or animal native to Altair IV is ever mentioned in the screenplay
drafts (though there are some purple-tufted truffula trees on the
Morbius house set), whereas we see or are told that Morbius's house is
surrounded by terrestrial plants and animals, such as an *althea frutex* (a
type of hibiscus), tigers, deer, and a small monkey. In the early draft,
there were also birds like cockatoos and parakeets, as well as insects like
butterflies and bees.[44] But still, why so many *terrestrial* specimens? And
why does the Krell machine register a little power when the buck deer
fight, or when the birds fly overhead, as Morbius relates? It demands an
explanation that, to judge by his weak inferences and non-answers,
Morbius has not thought much about, or at any rate, not successfully. In

[43] Made clearer in ED (71–72):

ADAMS: But—what's it for?
MORBIUS glances at him, and looks away.
MORBIUS (oddly evasive): Sometimes the gauges register a little when the buck deer
  fight in the autumn, or when the birds pass over in the spring. And nearly a whole
  line became active when your ship first approached from space.
ADAMS: I asked you—<u>what's it for?</u>!
MORBIUS stands gripping the railing, staring down into the abyss.
MORBIUS (haggard and haunted): <u>I don't know</u>! In twenty years I have been able to
  form absolutely no conception at all.
Clarke and Rubin (1979: 12) thought it sufficiently important to quote this passage
from the ED (or another draft with identical wording), but only Worland and Slayden
(2000: 144) see the implication (from the filmed version, to their credit): "Morbius clearly
does not know, and quickly changes the subject."
[44] ED 22: Ostrow remarks on the lack of screens in Morbius's windows. There are bees
and butterflies, but no mosquitos or flies, despite the "sub-tropical climate." Ostrow also
notices "extraordinary hybrid flowers"—perhaps a mishmash of flower types analogous to
the impossible mixture of creatures making up the id monster. ED 30 mentions the birds.

retrospect, once we learn the secret of the Krell machine and how Morbius has been able to activate it, the answer is clear: Morbius created all of it out of an unconscious expectation that those things should be there, in the way they are, just as he is (unconsciously) able to generate the id monster he calls the "planetary force."[45]

In fact, Hume daringly shows us the Krell machine in action (on a small scale), in the device Morbius calls the "plastic educator." With its aid, Morbius is able to consciously create a three-dimensional "living" simulacrum of Altaira by the power of his mind alone, and when asked, he explains that the simulacrum lives because Altaira lives in his mind from microsecond to microsecond. This striking phrase sits in the back of our minds, perhaps, until Ostrow not long thereafter analyzes the monster's ability to keep coming at the *C-57-D* despite being hit by the ship's massed batteries: the monster must be reconstituting itself "from one microsecond to the next."[46] If Ostrow could rapidly deduce this, then Morbius, with his enhanced mind, has apparently been blind to it, for he had the pieces of the puzzle at his disposal; the dying Ostrow rapidly sizes up Morbius's inability to solve the problem presented by the machine and the "planetary force": "Morbius was too close to the problem" (PC 6.3). I take him to mean that Morbius's near-worship of the Krell robbed him of the ability to think that anything they made could be as dangerous and flawed as the great machine turned out to be. Given the evidence cited above of Morbius's identification with the Krell, we begin to see why Morbius may not have thought very long or very hard about his own role in the unpleasant events on Altair IV.

Hume has rather carefully crafted his story to perch Morbius in a castle of comforting illusions in a manner closely paralleling Oedipus' situation. It is fair to ask something of Oedipus: "You abandoned what you thought was your home in Corinth because the oracle told you that you would kill your father. Would you not therefore take a great interest in any older man you happen to kill?" Like Morbius, Oedipus gives himself the benefit of the doubt because he thinks that he is in control of his life, and he lets an obvious question lapse in silence, though Sophocles does not. When Tiresias refuses to openly denounce the murderer of Laius, Oedipus angrily mocks him for what he takes to be prophetic

---

[45] Booker (2006: 54–55) sees this.
[46] Seen by Wierzbicki (2005: ch. 5).

blindness, mistaking a voluntary silence for an inability to prophesy. Tiresias fires back, hinting at Oedipus' blindness to several very pertinent facts about his own life (and of course, the irony lies in Oedipus' ultimate self-blinding); that Tiresias raises these issues means Sophocles in fact wanted us to think about them, just as Hume has put Morbius's answers to three telling questions at our disposal.

With equally effective dramatic irony, Morbius inadvertently points to his terrible secret. When Morbius first explains the "planetary force," Adams notes that it has been silent the last twenty years, and Morbius pregnantly replies (PC 2.8: my italics):

Yet sometimes *in my mind* I feel the creature still lurking somewhere close at hand, sly and irresistible, and only waiting to be reinvoked for murder.

Again, when Ostrow analyzes the cast of the monster's foot, he concludes, more precisely than he knows, "anywhere in the galaxy this is a nightmare!" (5.5). At Quinn's funeral, Morbius foresees more attacks on the *C-57-D*, and Adams presses him, asking how he knows (5.7):

Know? I—I simply seem to visualize it somehow. I—If you wish, call it a premonition!

When Altaira decides to defy her father by leaving Altair IV with Adams, and though they do not know it, the id monster is already en route to Morbius's house to exact a terrible punishment, Morbius presciently exclaims to Adams, "Young man, my daughter is making a very foolish mistake and she will be terribly punished!" (6.5)

Because Aristotle lauded it in the *Oedipus* (*Poet.* 1452a), I discussed above the synchronism of Morbius's *anagnōrisis* and *peripeteia*. It is worth a second look. It cannot be a mere accident of circumstances that Morbius comes full circle and finally recognizes his guilt in the Krell laboratory, the very place where he passed the near-fatal test of *his* Sphinx, the plastic educator, and triumphantly discovered that he had won the keys to an intellectual kingdom (or egomaniac empire, if you prefer) in the form of a doubled mental capacity and possession of the Krell databank.[47] The collapse of Morbius's illusory sense of autonomy is given expressive visual form in the film: we last see Morbius, before he is

[47] As Telotte (1995: 123) sees.

struck down, from the monster's point of view. Morbius looks up, small and half-panicked, holding his hands up in a warding gesture, leaving the impression that his world is tumbling down around him (PC 6.13).[48]

Morbius also parallels Oedipus in his rationalism. When Adams compels Morbius to face the facts, he reminds Morbius that we all possess a monstrous side in our subconscious, and adds, in a beautifully cadenced line, "so we have laws, and religion" (PC 6.9). We should probably also recall another analogy in the action of both stories. Just as Oedipus thought to rescue his reputation at the last minute by noting an apparent contradiction in the story of the murder of Laius,[49] so, too, Morbius points out an "obvious fallacy" in Adams's argument that the machine gave vent to the "mindless beasts of the subconscious" of the Krell and is responsible for the more recent killings, too: "the last Krell died 2,000 centuries ago, but today, as we all know, there is still at large on this planet, a living monster" (6.6). Both men are grasping at straws and are doomed to disappointment. In Adams's remonstrance to Morbius that we have laws and religion to combat the monsters in our subconscious, we can see an echo of any number of similar warnings to Oedipus to respect the gods and their prophecies. Not only, therefore, did Hume carefully work out the logic of Morbius's *hubris* (though it is up to us to follow the traces), but he also even echoes Oedipus' difficulties in seeing his own guilt.

CONCLUSION

Morbius is a complex character, as all interesting ones are. Seeing in his story elements of Oedipus' helps us recognize that he is intentionally portrayed as a tragic figure, one in whom good and bad are mixed, and in whose experiences we see commentary on our own human limitations and indirect moral instruction. He is a victim not of

---

[48] Carefully visualized by Hume, ED 108: "HIGH ANGLE—CLOSE SHOT—MORBIUS arms still outspread, looking up into the monster's face, and recognizing himself there with loathing." Warren (2010: 301) provides evidence that at the end the monster was to become visible and take on Morbius's features. On such uncanny doubling in SF, see the chapters by Weiner and Stevens (this volume, chapters two and three, respectively).

[49] Oedipus knows he killed the old man at the crossroads by himself, whereas Jocasta's report (at second hand) seems to indicate that more than one person killed Laius.

technology run wild, but of himself.[50] *Forbidden Planet* is no more a
meditation on the dangers of powerful, mysterious technology than
the *Oedipus* is a warning not to kill your father and sire children on
your mother. Both stories are universal cautionary tales warning us
not to put too much faith in our ability to see the hidden workings of
the world even though we are armed with reason, and they both transcend the plotting particulars out of which they have been
constructed.

Forbidden Planet's story has stood the test of time, even as its acting,
editing conventions, and special effects have taken on a patina of age.
Perhaps, too, the notion of basing a film on "big ideas" (classical or
otherwise) is out of date, for criticism of the film has focused upon
contingencies of plotting (atomic power, supposed Oedipus conflict,
etc.) as being central to the film's theme. Sometimes films do have a
proximate target; 1967's *Guess Who's Coming to Dinner* had a timely
and obvious point to make. But in looking for what a film wants to tell
us, too often we start by looking around us and (again, starting from a
weak line of evidence) seek a film's point in what is most readily at
hand: current affairs. A good, fairly recent example in science fiction
(SF) is the recurrent idea that *The Revenge of the Sith* was written as
commentary on the Bush administration, despite George Lucas's strong
assertion that the plot was worked out long before Bush was president.[51]
Analogously, modern critics have, in my opinion, too often looked for
the point of 1950s SF films in contemporary events, and *Forbidden
Planet* is no exception.[52] This is not to argue that writers like Hume
developed ideas and wrote stories without being influenced by current
events, or indeed that (for example) nuclear power was not a concern to
them. I think, though, that especially for the age of film, we have such
extensive and easily accessible documentation of current events that
this knowledge acts as a sort of static, or fog, that can hinder us from
seeing older ideas that may be embedded in a film. A striking example
of what I mean is provided by Warren, who has noted that, for all the
inevitable critical discussion of atomic power, the atom, in its various

[50] Strick (1982: 34) sees that *Forbidden Planet* was a break from previous SF movies of
the fifties as "the first 'inner space' story"; that is, it is not about technology but is, rather,
animated by more universal humanist interests.
[51] Germain (2009).
[52] Cf. Sheppard (2012: conclusion).

manifestations, is many times just a convenient plot device, and not necessarily a reflection of crippling social anxieties of the 1950s.[53] It is apt to repeat the pseudepigraphic Freudian quote here: "sometimes a cigar is just a cigar." Certainly critics can legitimately connect *Forbidden Planet* with (for example) societal fears about atomic power, but not because of the 9,200 thermonuclear reactors that power the Krell machine and destroy Altair IV: it is human fallibility, the subject of *Forbidden Planet,* that makes atomic power (and any nontrivial technology) dangerous for us.[54]

Nor would I argue that other interpretations of Morbius and *Forbidden Planet* are impermissible or excluded: an author arguing for a third major source for the film would be foolish to preemptively deny that there could be a fourth or a fifth. The film is rich enough in ideas and intertexts[55] to repay further research, even leaving aside the question of its sources: see, for example, how the Barrons' utterly distinctive electronic score[56] is, with immense cleverness, implied to be Krell music by having it seamlessly cross the line into a diegetic performance of a Krell recording in Morbius's study.[57] We infer that *Forbidden Planet* has a Krell score (we might call it a "space opera").[58]

While we await further research on the sources and influences of *Forbidden Planet,* I think we can say the following about its genesis. Hume took Adler and Block's original idea about an invisible monster and built up a story on a rudimentary framework provided by the *Tempest,* adding the story of the Krell. The monster was rationalized by

[53] Warren (2010: 9). For an encapsulated discussion of the atomic connection, see Worland and Slayden (2000: 146–150, with bibliography).

[54] Harris (2001/2002: Part I and *passim*) intelligently analyzes the film chiefly as a meditation on uncontrolled or uncontrollable technology, and Worland and Slayden amply repay a close reading of their argument that the film "suggest[s] the panacea of consumption for easing [mid-century nuclear] fears."

[55] Booker (2006: 47).

[56] As discussed by Leydon (2004: 62–63).

[57] Leydon (2004: 70–73) notes the permeability of the boundaries between the score and the sound effects, as well as the sophisticated narrative links adumbrated by the former.

[58] That Leydon (2004) and Wierzbicki (2005) do not see this is perhaps due to their depth of analysis in isolating the distinctive features of the individual cues of the soundtrack. From contemporary audiences' point of view, the Barrons' score as a whole was unlike anything else in contemporary cinema, and that a characteristic (if, at a deep analytical level, admittedly unique) part of it is said to have been played by Krell musicians 2,000 centuries before clearly implies that the entire score is Krell.

using Freud as a bridge between it and the machine, and the underlying theme of the story, a cautionary tale about human fallibility, was adapted from the *Oedipus*. Though *Forbidden Planet* is hardly a version of the *Oedipus*, and is at best a loose adaptation, it nevertheless shows the extraordinary power and relevance possessed by the classical tradition. It even anticipated the first filmed version of the *Oedipus Rex* by a year.[59]

---

[59] *Oedipus Rex* (1957, dir. Tyrone Guthrie). See the Internet Movie Database (IMDB), http://www.imdb.com/title/tt0050792/.

6

Walter M. Miller, Jr.'s *A Canticle for Leibowitz*, the Great Year, and the Ages of Man

Erik Grayson

In his seminal study of apocalyptic fiction, W. Warren Wagar describes Walter M. Miller, Jr.'s *A Canticle for Leibowitz* (*Canticle*) as "a critic's dream-book, rich with symbol and metaphors, open to many conflicting interpretations."[1] Not surprisingly, in the five decades since Miller's novel won the Hugo Award in 1961, it has been the subject of numerous critical studies in disciplines ranging from theology to history and literature. Commentators such as Dominic Manganiello, Gary Herbert, and Patrick Parrinder,[2] among others, have produced insightful examinations of the novel's treatment of history, focusing primarily on Miller's considerable debt to medieval ecclesiastical and Renaissance history. Elsewhere, critics such as John A. Stoler and Russel M. Griffin have analyzed and discussed the influence of biblical and medieval names on names for characters in Miller's novel.[3] In this chapter, I would like to

---

[1] Wagar (1983: 84).
[2] See Parrinder (1980), Manganiello (1986), and Herbert (1990).
[3] See Griffin (1973) and Stoler (1984).

add to these conversations by examining an aspect that has been somewhat neglected in previous studies of Miller's novel—namely, the
author's relationship to the Greco-Roman cultural tradition. Thus,
while the aforementioned discussions of history in Miller's novel are
correct in identifying monastic records of the Middle Ages as the
author's primary source material for constructing events in the novel,
I argue that his vision of human history, given its decidedly cyclical
nature, is actually closer to visions conceived of by the Greek
Pythagoreans and Roman Stoics and articulated most eloquently by
Hesiod, Plato, and Ovid than to that of medieval Christians. Similarly,
while many of the surnames one finds in *Canticle* are clearly biblical in
origin, Miller also populates his novel with individuals bearing names
with Greek and Latin roots or drawn from Greek and Roman history
and mythology. Taken together, Miller's cyclical vision of history and
playfully allusive onomastics reveal another layer of meaning in the
novel. We are invited to read *Canticle* as a cautionary tale that likens
contemporary Western superpowers to their Greco-Roman predecessors and, in the process, warns us against repeating the mistakes that led
to the fall of Western antiquity's last great empire.

MILLER'S *MAGNUS ANNUS*: THE HISTORICAL
CYCLE OF *A CANTICLE FOR LEIBOWITZ*

A brief review of Miller's narrative will be useful in establishing both
the parallel between the author's vision of our post-apocalyptic future
and the fifteen hundred years leading up to the present, and the novel's
implicit equation of the technologically savvy "ancients" responsible for
the cataclysmic nuclear holocaust preceding the opening of *Canticle*
with the Greco-Roman cultural ancestors Western Europeans and
Americans regard as "ancients" today. Set in an isolated desert region we
soon understand to be the devastated remains of the American south-
west, "Fiat Homo," the first of the novel's three sections, opens with a
young novice monk named Francis Gerard exploring the "anomalous
heaps of stone . . . which tradition ascribed to the ruins of an earlier
period" of human civilization more advanced than that of the novice's
day (*Canticle* 14–15). A seemingly chance encounter with a "pilgrim
with girded loins" (3) results in the hapless young monk's uncovering a

cache of texts eventually determined to have belonged to the "ancient and rather obscure technician named Leibowitz" (106) after whom Francis's monastic order is named. As the story progresses, the reader learns how, following a cataclysmic exchange of nuclear warheads, the world of the twentieth century was reduced to smoldering heaps of irradiated rubble. In the aftermath of the global nuclear war, "a hate was born" as the "remnants of mankind [tore] other remnants limb from limb, killing rulers, scientists, leaders, technicians, teachers, and whatever persons the leaders of the maddened mobs said deserved death for having helped make the Earth what it had become" (62). The result of the Luddite mobs' wrath was the Simplification, a systematic destruction of virtually all the accumulated wisdom, culture, and scientific knowledge of mankind in an effort to "teach our children that the world is new, that they may know nothing of the deeds that went before . . . and then the world shall begin anew" (62). Doubly devastated by the death of his wife in the conflagrations and the Simplification's hostility towards learning, the technician, Isaac Edward Leibowitz, joined the Order of the Cistercians, became a Catholic priest, and founded a monastic order devoted to the preservation of knowledge through the "six centuries of darkness" (64) that followed the nuclear war. The fact that the maintenance and expansion of the monastery's collection of fragmentary texts, dubbed "the Memorabilia," becomes the order's *raison d'être* suggests that Miller models the Albertian Order of Leibowitz on the widespread "monastic preservation of memory" (177) by "memory specialists" (76) whom Patrick J. Geary (1994) identifies as central to monastic life in medieval Christian abbeys.

Similar to the ways in which "Fiat Homo" recalls the text-laden scriptoria of medieval Christian monasteries, "Fiat Lux" and "Fiat Voluntas Tua"—the second and third sections of *Canticle*—draw upon the cold rationalism of Renaissance-era academic secularism and the increasingly computerized Atomic Age hyper-industrialism of the twentieth century to render each segment of the book an eerily familiar vision of the distant future. Set both in the royal court of the illiterate but wealthy emperor Hannegan II and the centuries-old Leibowitz Abbey, "Fiat Lux" chronicles the efforts of Thon Taddeo Pfardentrott—a staggeringly brilliant scholar (and half-brother of the emperor) widely believed to stand at the vanguard of an "intellectual revolution" (*Canticle* 210) that will lead to a world in which "the mastery of Man over the Earth shall be renewed"

(211)—to wrest knowledge out of the Memorabilia.[4] At the center of "Fiat
Lux" is the conflict between the emphatically amoral Pfardentrott's
desire to usher in a utopian vision of a future in which a capital-T Truth
will conquer the "[i]gnorance [that] has long been our king" (210) and
establish a rationalistic "empire [that] shall encompass the Earth" (211),
fulfilling the Church's wish to preserve the bulk of human knowledge
until, as the scholar sardonically puts it, "Man is good and pure and holy
and wise" (221). Importantly, in his belief that "[i]f you try to save wisdom until the world is wise . . . the world will never have it" (221–222),
Thon Taddeo reflects the moral relativism many Christians feared would
be the result of the secularism so prominent among Renaissance-era
thinkers. Presciently, given the narrative's eventual transformation of the
world into irradiated slag heaps in the wake of yet another nuclear war,
Thon Taddeo even acknowledges the inevitable destruction that human
intellectual progress will bring with it (211):

Ignorance is king. Many would not profit by his abdication. Many enrich
themselves by means of his dark monarchy. They are his Court, and in his
name they defraud and govern, enrich themselves and perpetuate their
power. Even literacy they fear, for the word is another channel of communication that might cause their enemies to become united. Their weapons are
keen-honed and they use them with skill. They will press the battle upon
the world when their interests are threatened, and the violence which follows will last until the structure of society as it now exists is leveled to rubble, and a new society emerges.

Thus, regarding the political ambitions of Hannegan II—and rulers like
him—as "impersonal phenomena beyond his control like a flood, fam-
ine, or whirlwind," Thon Taddeo "accepted them as inevitable—to avoid
having to make a moral judgment" (211). In effect, the scholar's sentiments unite intellectual development with the cyclical downfall of mankind, setting the stage for the fulfillment of this very scenario in "Fiat
Voluntas Tua."

The cyclical nature of human development is at the forefront of the
novel's final chapter, which brings the Albertian Order of Leibowitz into

---

[4] Cf. Bucher (this volume, chapter five), who discusses the ruinous interest shown by
Forbidden Planet's Morbius in the knowledge of a long-dead civilization.

the thirty-eighth century, an era in which "[t]here were spaceships again" (*Canticle* 243) as well as automobiles, nuclear weapons, and the unrelenting anxiety of Cold War brinkmanship. Miller ensures that the leaden gloom of inevitable and imminent apocalypse permeates the final chapter by highlighting at its outset the inescapable cycle of human history (243):

It was inevitable, it was manifest destiny, they felt (and not for the first time) that such a race go forth to conquer stars. To conquer them several times, if need be, and certainly to make speeches about the conquest. But, too, it was inevitable that the race succumb again to the old maladies on new worlds, even as on Earth before, in the litany of life and in the special liturgy of Man: Versicles by Adam, Rejoinders by the Crucified.[5]

"Fiat Voluntas Tua," then, depicts a future society that has rediscovered and reapplied the knowledge of the ancients to create a vision of the future that is remarkably similar to the mid-to-late twentieth-century world in which Miller lived. The East–West tensions of the original Cold War have been rekindled—this time emerging out of the political conflicts between the governments operating in Asia and North America— and the Church, with its deep concern for discerning the right from the merely true, has been reduced to the role of moral gadfly, irritating men of science with pesky questions of conscience. The predictable result of mankind's slow ascent back to the light of secular knowledge is a second global nuclear war. At the conclusion of the novel, a small band of monks and pilgrims set out to colonize a distant planet as the world once again bears witness to mankind's self-destruction.

"DOOMED TO DO IT AGAIN AND AGAIN AND AGAIN": HISTORY AS OUROBOROS

In his examination of Western history's place in *Canticle*, Thomas P. Dunn echoes many previous scholars of the novel in claiming that Miller "brings humanity full circle from one major destruction to the

---

[5] For another conception of the plurality of worlds in a Christian context, see the discussion of Kepler's *Somnium* in Swinford (this volume, chapter one).

next and implies in many different ways that such cycles of destruction have occurred in the past and will recur in the future."[6] Dunn continues by noting that Miller structures *Canticle* around the "carefully patterned, three part format" outlined above in order to invite readers to draw parallels between each of the imagined future epochs and crucial transitional periods in actual human history. Thus, while "Fiat Homo," "Fiat Lux," and "Fiat Voluntas Tua" occur six hundred, twelve hundred, and eighteen hundred years in the future, each one presents a decidedly familiar world roughly analogous to those one might expect to find in historical accounts of the Dark Ages, the Renaissance, and the Atomic Age, respectively. The scope of Miller's cyclical historical vision becomes increasingly apparent as the reader progresses through the book.

However, it is significant to note that the implication of Miller's cyclic view of history is not merely that mankind is doomed to repeat its self-destruction *ad infinitum*. Rather, Miller's novel is brought to life by the inversely correlated intellectual and moral development of humankind. As knowledge and power are accumulated and consolidated by the elite, the bulk of human society descends into an era during which mankind grows bellicose, suspicious, and self-centered. Inevitably, petty squabbles erupt into full-scale wars, and empires crumble, leaving the survivors to start down the path to self-destruction once again. I would hesitate to suggest that Miller consciously and deliberately models the temporal structure of his novel on specific aspects of the cyclical conception of history one may trace through Hesiod, the Pythagoreans, Plato, Ovid, and the Stoics.[7] But Miller's vision of human development is certainly consistent with those of his Greco-Roman antecedents, if taken synchronically as an ancient worldview to be contrasted with the linear view dominating contemporary historical theory. An understanding of the classical worldview, then, may enable readers to better appreciate the profoundly troubling tenor of the fatalism of *Canticle* by comparing it with the similarly deterministic tone found in classical accounts of humanity's moral entropy.

While in no way limited to Greco-Roman thought, the prominence of cyclical history's place in later Western European philosophy owes much to its place in the works of Hesiod, the Pythagoreans, Plato, Ovid,

---

[6] Dunn (1988: 107).
[7] See, for example, Johnston (1933).

and the Stoics. Arguably, the origins of cyclical history in Hellenic thought may be located in the Pythagoreans' concept of the "great" or "perfect" year, which Plato describes in the *Timaeus* (*Tim.*) as the completion of a grand cosmological cycle when all astronomical bodies have returned to their respective points of origin, and the universe is once again configured as it was at the beginning of time (39c4–39d6):

Mankind, with hardly an exception, have not remarked the periods of the other stars, and they have no name for them, and do not measure them against one another by the help of number, and hence they can scarcely be said to know that their wanderings, being infinite in number and admirable for their variety, make up time. And yet there is no difficulty in seeing that the perfect number of time fulfills the perfect year when all the eight revolutions, having their relative degrees of swiftness, are accomplished together and attain their completion at the same time, measured by the rotation of the same and equally moving.[8]

Later, the Roman Stoics borrowed the concept of the great year (in Latin, *magnus annus*) to describe the period of time between the reconstruction of the world (*renovatio*) following the conflagration that marked the end of a previous historical cycle and the unavoidable future flooding and conflagrations that would eventually destroy the present. According to Seneca (*Quaestiones Naturales* [QN] 48–49),

So just as, when the moon and sun are in conjunction, the equinoctial tide rises higher than all others, so this tide which is unleashed to occupy the land is more violent than the normal highest tides, brings more water with it, and it does not recede until it has risen above the summits of the mountains it is going to inundate . . . on that occasion the tide is not bound by laws, and its advance is unlimited . . . In the same way as the conflagration will occur. Both events occur when God has decided to inaugurate a better world and to end the old. Water and fire lord it over all terrestrial things; they bring about creation, they bring about destruction. So whenever the world has decided on revolution, the sea is sent crashing down over us, just as heat and fire are when another form of extinction is approved.[9]

[8] Trans. Jowett (2009).
[9] Trans. Hine (2010).

Importantly, both the Pythagorean and Stoic cosmogonies emphasize renewal and a return to an original, even purified, state. Still, neither philosophical camp devotes much discussion to the place of mankind during the great year. Rather, for a fuller consideration of humanity's role in the perpetual cycle of destruction and renewal one finds outlined in the scientific and philosophical realms, one must turn to the poets, particularly Hesiod and Ovid.

In his *Works and Days* (*WD*), Hesiod outlines what he identifies as the successive ages of mankind: the Golden Age, the Silver Age, the Bronze Age, the Heroic Age, and the Iron Age. During the Golden Age, "the firstborn race of articulate men" were a "[g]odlike" race impervious to the pain of earthly worry and physical suffering (107, 109).[10] Without effort of any kind, "everything worthwhile / Came to their hand, as the grain-growing earth bore fruit without tilling" and the men and women of Hesiod's Golden Age lived a life of leisure (113–114). "After this whole first generation was finally buried," Hesiod informs us, "those that inhabit Olympus fashioned a second, / Silver race, which was very inferior, worse than the first one" (121–122). Lacking both the size and intellect of the prior race of men, the second age of man "lived only the tiniest time, and moreover they suffered / Much in their folly" and "could not keep themselves back from their wicked / Violence on one another" (128–129). Frustrated by the violent tendencies of the second race of men, as well as their refusal "to serve the immortals" (130) or even "worship the gods who inhabit Olympus" (134), Zeus destroyed them. Even more violent than the men of the Silver Age, the "new third race of articulate mankind" grew preoccupied with "Ares' / Noisy employment" and spent much of their lives fighting wars (138–139). After the Bronze generation "went down to the underworld's cold rot" as a result of the unceasing violence they brought into the world, Zeus created "a godlike race of heroical men who were known as / Demigods" (153–154). The men and women of the Heroic Age, unlike the races living during the three previous ages of man, continue to inhabit the Earth in "a / Dwelling place far from men at the furthermost ends of the earth" (161–162). Following the temporary reversal of mankind's moral disintegration during the Heroic Age, however, humanity resumes its downward trajectory and enters into the Iron Age, the era in which Hesiod claims we live.

---

[10] Trans. Hine (2005).

The Iron Age, to Hesiod, is tainted by such depravity and suffering that he pities the individual born into it (*WD* 172–176):

How I would wish to have never been born one of this fifth generation!
Whether I'd died in the past or came to be born in the future.
Truly of iron is this generation, and never by day will
They intermit hard labor and woe; in the night they will also   175
Suffer distress, for the gods will give them unbearable troubles.

The denizens of the Iron Age, Hesiod continues, "will show no respect to their elders" (183) but rather "they'll only respect evildoers, / Monsters of violence" (189). Moreover, the world will be inhabited by "Wretches who don't acknowledge the face of the gods and who will not / Pay back ever the cost of their upbringing to their old parents" (185–186). As the value of religion and family erode, so will any vestiges of morality (190–194):

Might will be right, all shame will be lost and   190
All inhibition. The wicked will try to ruin the good man,
Shamelessly uttering falsehoods, wickedly bearing false witness.
Noisy, discordant Envy, malicious, delighting in mischief,
Hateful-faced will accompany all us unfortunate humans.
Evil will reign and, disgusted, the gods will cleanse the Earth.

Significantly, despite employing the future tense to describe the men and women of this era, Hesiod places himself (and, by extension, modern humankind) in the Iron Age.

Human history is also represented as a series of successively inferior ages in Ovid's *Metamorphoses* (*Met.*). Unlike Hesiod, however, Ovid sees little more than unidirectional movement from near-divine to quasi-bestial and, accordingly, dispenses with the Heroic Age. In Ovid's version, "The Golden Age was . . . a time that cherished / Of its own will, justice and right" (*Met.* 1.88–89).[11] Since "People were unaggressive and unanxious" (1.96–97), they "were content at home, and had no towns / With moats and walls around them. . . . No one needed soldiers" (1.99). The world was a paradise: "And Earth, untroubled, / Unharried by hoe or plowshare brought forth all / That men had need for, and those men were happy" (1.101–103). While humankind retained its generally peaceful nature in the subsequent Age of Silver,

[11] Trans. Humphries (1983).

"Jove made the springtime shorter, added winter / Summer, and autumn" (1.116–117), rendering it necessary for "men [to build] houses for themselves" (1.120). Furthermore, the natural abundance of the Earth no longer provided enough food for its human inhabitants, and humankind developed agriculture and animal husbandry. During the Age of Bronze that followed, men of all "dispositions / Took on aggressive instincts" and were "quick to arm" (1.125–126), but in Ovid's estimation were "not entirely evil" (1.127). Ovid's Age of Iron, like that of Hesiod, is characterized by "trickery and slyness, plotting, swindling, / Violence and the damned desire of having" (1.131–132). Humanity's increasing avarice and selfishness led to "Men spread[ing] their sails to winds unknown to sailors" (1.132) in search of new land, and that land, "Free, once, to everyone, like air and sunshine, / Was stepped off by surveyors" (1.135–136). As mankind sought to extract ever more sustenance from the earth and continued parceling out land, tensions mounted, "And War came forth" (1.138), while "Justice, last of all immortals, / Fled from the bloody earth" (1.148–149).

In both Hesiod and Ovid, mankind undergoes a gradual process of moral erosion over the course of a given "great year." As mankind moves from the Golden Age into the Silver, Bronze, and Iron Ages, greed and aggression become increasingly prevalent, while a reverence for the gods and a respect for humanity disintegrates. As I suggested earlier, a similar pattern of moral erosion and escalating animosity occurs in *Canticle*. The steadily entropic breakdown of human compassion in the novel suggests that Miller shares with writers such as Hesiod and Ovid a pessimistically fatalistic view of a devolving mankind. In the years following the Flame Deluge that has decimated the planet's population and the Simplification that ensures post-holocaust humanity will be thrust into a dark age, one can find elements of Golden and Silver Age traits among the scattered remnants of humankind populating Miller's novel. Much like Golden Age men and women who have become "pure spirits inhabiting earth and / Noble protectors of mankind, warding off evils from mortals" (*WD* 119–120), the monks of the Albertian Order of Leibowitz become protectors of humankind in the form of "bookleggers" and "memorizers" who seek "to preserve human history for the great-great-great-grandchildren of the children of the simpletons who wanted it destroyed" (*Canticle* 64). Such preservation of human knowledge is, for the Leibowitzian monks, an act of religious devotion, a hallmark of Golden and Silver Age morality lauded by both Hesiod and Ovid.

By the time Thon Taddeo arrives at the abbey in "Fiat Lux," however, the erosion of Golden and Silver Age ideals has become a source of conflict in Miller's future Renaissance as Bronze and Iron Age surfeits begin corrupting mankind. Indeed, the court of Hannegan II is practically overflowing with the "trickery and slyness, plotting, swindling, / Violence and the damned desire of having" that Ovid identifies as central to Iron Age humanity (*Met.* 1.131–132). Hannegan II, Miller's embodiment of humanity at its most power-mad and land-hungry, not only tricks a nomadic people into waging war against an enemy while secretly spreading disease among the nomads' cattle, he also arranges for the execution of a key religious figure in order to undermine the authority of the Catholic Church and seize control of the bulk of the southern region of what is, in our time, the United States, and declare himself "Hannegan II, by Grace of God Mayor, Viceroy of Texarkana, Defender of the Faith, and Vaquero Supreme of the Plains" (*Canticle* 214). Concurrently, Thon Taddeo, Hannegan's relative and beneficiary, seeks knowledge at the Abbey while rejecting wholesale the Christian morality the monks have tried so hard to preserve alongside the Memorabilia. Thus, when Dom Paulo, the abbot of the Leibowitz abbey, argues that Thon Taddeo must choose "[t]o serve God first, or to serve Hannegan first," it should come as no surprise that "[t]he scorn in [the scholar's] voice" (222) recollects Hesiod's account of Silver and Bronze Age humanity's not being "willing to serve the immortals" (*WD* 130) or "worship the gods who inhabit Olympus" (*Canticle* 134).

In "Fiat Voluntas Tua," whatever traces of Golden, Silver or Bronze Age humanity one sees in "Fiat Lux"—save for the modicum one finds preserved among the brothers in the monastic community, which Lewis Fried claims "now represents self-reflexive humanity in its embrace of mankind"[12]—have completely evaporated in favor of the sort of selfish and violent desires Hesiod and Ovid identify as hallmarks of the Iron Age. By the time "the last Canticle of the Brethren of the Order of Leibowitz" (*Canticle* 244) begins in the year 3781, Dom Jethrah Zerchi complains that the "world's been in a *habitual* state of crisis for fifty years" (259, Miller's emphasis). "Shamelessly uttering falsehoods" and "wickedly bearing false witness," to borrow Hesiod's language (*WD* 192), Miller's government-appointed talking head, answering reporters' questions regarding a nuclear detonation, has little difficulty lying to a

[12] Fried (2001: 367).

panicked public about its nation's involvement in an incident that "scorched a city out of existence" (*Canticle* 300). Likewise, moral codes influenced by the atheism, agnosticism, and secular humanism of Miller's Iron Age have superseded the theologically derived morality one associates with earlier ages. To this end, the military-industrial complex has adopted an image of a man with a "sweet-sick face, blank eyes, simpering lips, and arms widespread in a gesture of embrace," drawn from "some of the most effeminate images by which mediocre, or worse than mediocre, artists had traditionally misrepresented the personality of Christ," as the mascot for the euthanasia clinics the government builds to put victims of radiation poisoning to death, thereby perverting an image of Christian kindness to lure people into a decidedly non-Christian activity (313). In the end, Miller seems to believe, such a lack of faith-based morality, combined with the proliferation of greed and violence in Miller's Iron Age, results in a second Flame Deluge. Tellingly, Dom Zerchi foresees the destruction and processes it in terms reminiscent of the increasingly greedy human society as it progressed through the Ages of Man, as envisioned by Hesiod and Ovid (285):

The closer men came to perfecting for themselves a paradise, the more impatient they seemed to become with it, and with themselves as well. They made a garden of pleasure, and became progressively more miserable with it as it grew in richness and power and beauty; for then, perhaps, it was easier for them to see that something was missing in the garden, some tree or shrub that would not grow. When the world was in darkness and wretchedness, it could believe in perfection and yearn for it. But when the world became bright with reason and riches, it began to sense the narrowness of the needle's eye, and that rankled for a world no longer willing to believe or yearn. Well, they were going to destroy it again, were they—this garden Earth, civilized and knowing, to be torn apart again that Man might hope again in wretched darkness.

And so, Miller's version of the "great year" begins again and mankind sets about re-ascending the heights of human reason, only to be damned once more by the same greedy ambition that sets it on its way.

Once one grasps Miller's understanding of humanity as a race doomed by its desire for knowledge first to strive to build paradise with accumulated learning, then to be overcome by greed for that paradise, and finally to resort to violence to snatch up ever more parcels of that Eden, one recognizes Miller's affinity with the Greco-Roman thinkers who first articulated a vision of mankind in which humanity devolves, through a series of ages, from a godlike race to a greedy, violent one. Just as Seneca foresees humanity repeatedly wiped away by "the conflagration and the flood" marking the conclusion of each great year, the Flame Deluge repeatedly destroys human civilization in Miller's world (*Canticle* 49). With such strong similarities between Greco-Roman models of cyclical history and Miller's vision of human development, I would argue, it is probably not coincidental that readers will observe the parallel the author implicitly draws between his twentieth-century world and that of Rome. Indeed, as we liken the human race in "Fiat Voluntas Tua," "Fiat Lux," and "Fiat Homo" to the twentieth century, the Renaissance, and the Dark Ages, respectively, we realize that the only logical parallel for the "once-mighty civilization" preceding the first Flame Deluge is Rome, the last mighty Western civilization to fall before the Middle Ages. Miller even hints at this parallel when Thon Taddeo refers to the "ancients" as "the European-American civilization" (121). Here, the hyphenated conflation of European and American civilizations into a single "ancient" civilization resembles the contemporary tendency to lump ancient Greece and Rome into a single historical-cultural unit whose apex was the height of the Roman Empire. In inviting readers to make the connection between Thon Taddeo's "ancients" and our own ancients, then, Miller's text appears to take on the trappings of a cautionary tale. In other words, if the late Roman Empire, with all its famous excesses, falls into the end of Hesiod's Iron Age, and if our own modern society parallels that of Rome, we may be closer to self-destruction than we think.[13]

ECHOES OF THE ANCIENTS: NAMING AND LANGUAGE IN *A CANTICLE FOR LEIBOWITZ*

Several critics, most notably John A. Stoler, have examined Miller's use of historically and literarily allusive names throughout *Canticle*. While Stoler's study examines possible historical and religious sources for several of the novel's key characters, the scope of his analysis is limited by his

---

[13] For another SF parallel between (Imperial) Rome and contemporary (American) society, see the discussion of Suzanne Collins's *The Hunger Games* in Makins (this volume, chapter thirteen).

assumption that "[i]n order to emphasize [the novel's] spiritual theme and at the same time delineate the functions of his characters, Miller has carefully drawn the names of several of his most important figures from Christian lore."[14] While I generally agree with Stoler's reading of the novel, I would argue that Miller's use of names to reinforce the thematic content of *Canticle* extends beyond those borrowed from Judeo-Christian lore to include names drawn from the Greco-Roman tradition as well. The presence of characters bearing names drawn from the languages and literature of the Greco-Roman world provides Miller's text with a playfully unobtrusive means of maintaining the reader's awareness of the classical world's relevance to the novel. Similarly, Miller's liberal use of Latin words and phrases throughout *Canticle* both reveals a profound concern for verisimilitude in depicting ecclesiastical affairs and, in the language's displacement of English as the dominant tongue of the educated world, serves as an additional mark of the cyclical nature of human history.

Significantly, Miller's first classically allusive name appears on the novel's first page, immediately attuning the reader to the Greco-Roman echoes that appear throughout the text. In this instance, Francis offers "a hasty prayer to Saint Raul the Cyclopean" for protection against attacks from the mutated humans he fears will attack him (*Canticle* 3). On the surface, one may interpret the reference to the mythological one-eyed race of giants to be little more than a convenient way for Miller to hint at the radiation-induced mutated appearance of Saint Raul (as well as the appearances of Francis's imagined attackers) without describing his ocular abnormality in any great detail. However, given the fact that Francis utters this prayer after he "had begun to build a wall," it is possible that Miller also intends for the saint's name to evoke images of the Cyclopean masonry found in Mycenae and Tiryns (9). To be sure, while Russell Hillier describes Brother Francis's structure as "a miniature St. Peter's 'dome'" because of its shape,[15] the fact that the young monk "hoped that by a careful selection of rocks and a certain amount of juggling, dirt-tamping, and pebble-wedging" (10) he could complete his project suggests the novice's stonework actually resembles that which Pausanias, for example, describes as Cyclopean in his *Description of Greece*: "the walls of the city, which are the only ruins left, are the

---

[14] Stoler (1984: 77).
[15] Hillier (2004: 170).

work of the Cyclopes made of rude stones. . . . And in ancient times small stones were inserted so as to dovetail with the large stones" (2.25.8).[16] Brother Francis's prayer to Saint Raul, then, may very well be the first of Miller's many allusions to the classical world.

Miller's use of allusive names is not limited to figures buried in the future monks' hagiographies. For instance, at the beginning of "Fiat Lux," the introduction of Marcus Apollo, a high-ranking Catholic priest living in Texarkana, invites us to associate his surname with the eponymous Greco-Roman god. While Stoler claims that "[i]n order to lend prophetic force to the priest's warning [about man's inability to learn from his mistakes], Miller named him after Apollo, the classical god of prophesy," he devotes considerably more time and space to examining the fact that the priest's surname "also brings to mind the biblical Apollos, a preacher of the gospel contemporary with St. Paul."[17] His discussion does not mention that Apollo is also the god of light and truth, two of the most important themes in "Fiat Lux." Just as Miller uses St. Raul the Cyclopean's name to bring a classical mythological connotation to Brother Francis's masonry, the author invites readers to draw connections between Marcus Apollo's era—a time in which Thon Taddeo seeks truth and the light of reason under Brother Armbruster's electric arc-lamp—and the concepts championed by his divine namesake.

Similarly, Miller draws upon the ancient Greek and Latin vocabularies to underscore the characteristics of several key figures in *A Canticle for Leibowitz*. For instance, the author names the abbot heading the Leibowitz abbey during Francis's tenure as a novice "Arkos." Given the fact that the abbot's repeated flogging of Francis accompanies his routine denial of the young monk's vows, his surname is almost certainly derived from ἄρκος, the Greek word for "bear," which, as James Strong has suggested, carries with it the added implication of "obstructing by ferocity" (*Strong's Exhaustive Concordance* s.v. *arkos*). Likewise, the monk who carves the statue of Saint Leibowitz that appears in all three sections of Miller's novel has the rather odd surname of "Fingo." Like his abbot, the woodworking monk bears a name drawn directly out of an ancient language. In Latin, *fingo* refers to the act of "form[ing] or fashion[ing] by art

---

[16] Trans. Shilleto (1886).
[17] Stoler (1984: 78).

(in wax, clay, stone, etc.).”[18] Later, in “Fiat Voluntas Tua,” Miller introduces Dr. Cors, a member of the Green Star Relief task force charged with evaluating radiation cases. Dr. Cors, who requests permission to “bring [radiation victims] into [the abbey’s] courtyard” (*Canticle* 294), shares his last name with a derivative form of the Latin word *cohors*, one of whose meanings is “a place enclosed around, a court, enclosure, yard, pen.”[19] In each of these cases, the Greek or Latin word Miller borrows to name his character serves the dual function of adding nuance to the author’s characterization and ensuring that readers continue to contemplate the book’s relationship to the classical world throughout the text.

Finally, it would be easy to dismiss the copious Latin phrasing with which Miller tessellates *A Canticle for Leibowitz* as merely the author’s attempt to enhance the verisimilitude of his fictional Christian community by immersing both his fictional monks and his real-life readers in the traditional language of the Church, but such a dismissal would be hasty. It is true that the overwhelming majority of the Latin phrases appearing in *Canticle* are either spoken among the monks or as part of a religious ceremony, but the language’s significance in the text resides less in the content of the words than in the language’s survival in the first place. Unlike the “pre-Deluge English” appearing in the Memorabilia, Latin is a living language in the novel (17). The very fact that what we regard as contemporary English has become a dead language while Latin has reassumed its position as the world’s dominant *lingua franca* suggests that, in some very real ways, Miller’s post-apocalyptic world is more closely related to that of ancient Rome, with whom Miller’s humanity shares a language and its accompanying thought processes, than to modern America, from whom they have inherited a world most of us would find utterly alien. This linguistic continuity, evident both in the novel’s onomastics and in the characters’ speech, serves to reinforce Miller’s cyclical view of history: our future is our past and our past is our future. Our desire for growth, our penchant for violence, our greed, and our wrath are no different from those of the ancient Greek and Roman peoples from whom we, like Walter M. Miller, Jr., inherited the concept of cyclical history.

[18] Lewis and Short (1879: s.v. *fingo*).
[19] Ibid. (1879: s.v. *cohors*).

7

Time and Self-Referentiality in the *Iliad* and Frank Herbert's *Dune*

Joel P. Christensen

Swift-footed Achilles stood among them and spoke.
(*Iliad* 1.58)

Now Paul's training is our only hope, she thought, *his youth and swiftness*. (*Dune* 225)

Frank Herbert's *Dune* has been called "epic" since its first publication in 1965.* And, with its wide-ranging themes, basic narrative of the maturation of Paul Atreides and its violent clash of cultures, it merits such acclaim in the modern sense of the word. But *Dune* also shares some characteristics with ancient Greek epic itself. From the "swiftness" ascribed to Paul, both symbolic of his vibrant strength and reminiscent of the Homeric Achilles, so famously fleet of foot, to the obstacles that beset hero and audience alike as *Dune* and Homer's *Iliad* (*Il.*) challenge

* I would like to thank the editors of this volume, Oxford University Press's anonymous referees, and David Luce and Donald Karr for careful reading and comments. In this chapter all citations of *Dune* refer to the 1965 edition of the novel.

assumptions about heroism, Herbert's work is both indebted to and a revision of the ancient epic genre.

This relationship should not be wholly surprising at first glance. Modern science fiction (SF) and ancient narrative myth occupy similar cultural positions—a phenomenon perhaps anticipated by the anthropologist Claude Levi-Strauss's articulation of the overlapping spheres of science and myth.[1] Both storytelling traditions, while providing entertainment,[2] facilitate the exploration of individual identity and psychology, the examination of social structures, and the search for humankind's place in the universe.[3] On these similarities alone, we can profitably identify the influence of classical myth on modern SF of the sort exemplified by *Dune* through the motifs and narrative patterns of the stories like those of the estranged hero Orestes (who avenges his father's murder) or of Oedipus (who takes his father's place). Yet modern novels like Herbert's are not simple retellings of Greco-Roman myth (any more than *our* versions of the myths are ever simple tales). However, the comparison of Homer's *Iliad* with Herbert's *Dune* provides an opportunity to explore the appropriation of myth and to observe affinities of a literary nature that capitalize on mythical traditions and inherited narrative patterns. Striking similarities in works drawn from different worlds illustrate both the closeness of their genres and what helps establish the appeal and exceptionality of each work.

In narrative function, especially, these two works run parallel. The *Iliad* and *Dune* similarly conceptualize and instrumentalize the future and the past, subordinating both to their needs as they position *their* stories as both culmination of the past and midwife to a

[1] " . . . the kind of logic in mythical thought is as rigorous as that of modern science . . ." (Lévi-Strauss 1963: 230). Sutton and Sutton (1969: 231) protest that SF is the "myth of modern technology."

[2] For the "fantastic" as entertainment, see Aristotle's *Poetics* (*Poet.*) 1460a. Aristotle labels the "fantastic" (*to thaumaston*) a species of the illogical (*alogon*), but modern critics may be more severe: Broderick (2003: 51) characterizes fantastic literature in part as "adolescent craving for imaginary worlds." For SF as "escape literature," see Rabkin (1976: 44).

[3] For the psychological function of SF and myth, see Jung (1959) and Sutton and Sutton (1969). For SF's critical examination of social structures and norms (including taboos), see Todorov (1975: 138–139); Rabkin (1976: 133–137); Angenot and Suvin (1979); Theall (1980); and Sullivan (2001: 89). For such examination as a common ground between SF and ancient mythical literature, see Georgiadou and Larmour (1998: 46–47).

derivative future. In addition, each work also comments on the nature of storytelling to warn that the stories we tell shape and limit the lives that are lived according to them. In this chapter, I will examine these ideas by first exploring the characteristic similarities of these texts (and how they fulfill aspects of what some call the "fantastic"). Then, I will focus on two themes: (1) time, or the relationship between "history" and the narrated tale; and (2) self-reflexive knowledge of the power of storytelling.

THE FANTASTIC

How does one justify comparing Homer's epic with Frank Herbert's novel when they are so separated by style and time? The narratives share certain superficial similarities (from the name "Atreides" to the attribution of swiftness to both heroes).[4] Another starting point is that the *Iliad* and *Dune* both stand as exemplary works in genres with similar functions. So, the common cultural functions of narrative myth in Homeric epic and SF may shape and motivate their general characteristics. One way to conceptualize the shared foundation of ancient epic and novelized SF—even if as an imperfect adaptation of a literary theory—is to understand both works as displaying features of a "genre" called the "fantastic." Brief consideration of this category helps us reframe these shared qualities and focus on their effects.

First, some generic similarities help set the stage. For one, ancient epic and SF narrative overlap in the cultural function of mythmaking. The *Iliad* evolved within an oral tradition of narrative myth.[5] SF is a type of modern mythmaking that arguably developed to fill a void created by cultural change.[6] Indeed, both traditions provide frames through which

---

[4] For *Dune* as epic, see Kafka (1975: 51) and Cirasa (1984).
[5] For an overview of mythical influence on the Homeric epics, see Graf (2011); cf. Edmunds (1997). For the oral tradition and the *Iliad*, see Schein (1984: 1–44) and Foley (1991: 135–189).
[6] Bakhtin (1986: 43), in discussing Goethe's "perfect" conception of historical time, sees myth as a system of thought that prized and created the "otherworldly" before the world was "rounded out" by realism. Accordingly, Gothic fiction (and its later genes in SF; see Brantlinger 1980) is a reaction against the historical vision of the Enlightenment, a return to the otherworldly.

their cultures structure and endeavors to "understand" the universe.[7] In this parallelism, SF storytelling replaces a mythical/historical past peopled by gods and heroes with a mythologized science, a space where the unbelievable is achieved through "scientific" instead of divine means. A second parallel, then, is the strategy both genres employ to surmount audience reaction to the impossible through the creation of *other* worlds.[8] Both forms make the unbelievable more palatable through adherence to basic laws, the cultivation of lexical and visual connection points, and a basic "grammar" of the heroic narrative and folktale motifs.[9] More significantly, narrative myth and SF also locate the unbelievable in alternate timescapes that are marginal to the time of main narratives.[10] The value of such displaced settings for the examination of features of the audience's real world should not be discounted: these distanced constructions furnish opportunities for social and cultural reflection as recognizable features of the audience's world, reconfigured in the fantasy, are brought into critical relief.[11]

Indeed, both Herbert's *Dune* and Homer's *Iliad* blend reality and fantasy critically. The *Iliad* is a fantasy of a historical past: its players are gods and demigods, but its landscape, objects, and concerns reflect and refract those from the world(s) of its audiences.[12] Just as Herbert's *Dune* blends elements from our historical world with mythologized names in a consciously heroic narrative, the *Iliad* blends historical layers, disparate elements, and story patterns from earlier and contemporary narratives. Both texts are essentially *simulacra*, refractions of disparate real-world elements. These "copies" do not demand the fidelity of our more realistic fictions, yet the combination of the real and the unreal

---

[7] See Sutton and Sutton (1969) and notes 1–3 above.

[8] Sullivan (2001) labels this a "second world," perhaps following Tolkien (1966); Bakhtin (1986: 43) prizes the term "otherworldly"; and Todorov (1975) presents "supernatural."

[9] For the creation of common ground between the supernatural world of the text and the ordinary world of the audience through lexical and archetypal contingencies, see Sullivan (2001). Tolkien (1966) focuses on the internal consistency of the unreal worlds.

[10] Cf. Eizykman (1985: 67–68).

[11] See Georgiadou and Larmour (1998: 46–48). For the general social functions of fantastic literature, see Todorov (1975: esp. 92–93) and Rabkin (1976: 53–74). Cf. Sullivan (2001: 279–289). For more personal effects, see Tolkien (1966).

[12] For the *Iliad* as a "fantasy" of the past, see van Wees (1992); for its refraction of historical layers, see Wilson (2002: 122).

seduces and entertains audiences even while inducing them to reflect critically upon the world outside the narrative.[13]

As *simulacra* (or alternate worlds), *Dune* and the *Iliad* exhibit features of what some modern literary theorists have called the "fantastic."[14] While there is debate about whether or not the fantastic is a genre, works with fantastic characteristics have common effects in creating new worlds that are similar to our own.[15] Understanding that both Homer's *Iliad* and Herbert's *Dune* are "fantastic" helps in part to justify their comparison. But so viewing these works also helps us understand the temporal strategy of each narrative and its relationships to its own narrative traditions. Both the *Iliad* and *Dune* are mythical in their qualities, but they stand out within the realm of the fantastic because they are also anti-myths. Roland Barthes (1989: 65) sees myth as converting sociocultural norms into the natural and thereby cementing dominant ideologies in "insidious" ways; yet both of our texts, while transmitting the ideologically derived forms of their genres and their cultures, also question the naturalness of their assumptions.[16] For example, the narratives of each work implicate their audiences in the worst offenses of their "heroes." Homer's Achilles confounds audiences by inviting them to understand or even identify with a man whose choices destroy his own people. Herbert's Paul Atreides, moreover, invites the reader to cheer for a heroic pattern that produces an annihilating jihad. Hence, the *Iliad* and *Dune* both use conventional forms to examine, not only the

---

[13] Where Baudrillard sees the simulacrum as a negative object that bears no relationship to any reality (1994), Deleuze (1995) envisions it as offering a realm where dominant ideology may be challenged (cf. Butler 2003: 141). Rabkin has similarly identified in fantastic works an ability to affect our interpretation of the known world radically through what he calls "fantastic reversal" (1976: 117).

[14] Todorov's definition of the fantastic as a genre is a tad slippery: "Genre represents, precisely, a structure, a configuration of literary properties, an inventory of options. But a work's inclusion within a genre still teaches us nothing as to its meanings" (1975: 141). See Rabkin (1976: 118 n. 1) for comments on his definition's similarity to Todorov's (1975).

[15] Todorov has described the "fantastic" as creating a world that "has no reality outside language" but is still fundamentally "not of a different nature" (1975: 92).

[16] For the extent to which epic contains (while also subtly probing) its own ideology, see Rose (1997); see Thalmann (1988) for rival ideologies within the *Iliad*. For ideology in SF, see Angenot and Suvin (1979). For SF's progressive and liberal "bias" (one transgressed by *Dune*), see Macleod (2003: esp. 236 on *Dune*). Eizykman (1985: 81–82) allows for more general fluidity in SF ideology.

worlds they reflect, but also how that reflection is contained and how it relates to the external world.[17]

TIME

The futuristic movie *Star Wars* begins "A long time ago . . .," even as the rebooted *Battlestar Galactica*'s advanced civilization devolves to the audience's primitive forebears.[18] The distanced time-setting of these narratives helps show by comparison that the fantastic character of Homer's *Iliad* and Herbert's *Dune* resides partly in their liminal, marginalized, and distant temporality. Such distancing can go forward, backwards, or sideways: what matters is that the fantastic narrative occurs elsewhere in time. Homer's *Iliad* is set in a past just beyond the memory of the audience but whose geography, genealogies, and objects are recognizable; Herbert's *Dune*, set over twenty millennia in the future, blends speculative technology (spaceflight, ornithopters, personal force-shields) with a relatively familiar Bedouin-type culture (the Fremen) and severe limitations. By collapsing past and future into the present tale, both narratives also endeavor to set their stories at moments of foundational transformation.

Suffusing this liminal temporality, importantly, is a boundlessness of time in the consciousness of both narratives. By this I mean that, while the temporal perspective of the external audience is bound by contemporary concerns and individual experience, the conceit offered by narrative myth (especially epic) and SF is of a world where narrators and characters, and through both the audience, may transcend normative temporal boundaries.[19] In this, both works are implicitly concerned with establishing a relationship between the synchrony of the tale being told and the (constructed) history that precedes it. Such focus also keeps

---

[17] See Todorov (1975: 6) for the way that the fantastic crosses generic boundaries. Cf. Rabkin (1976: 133–137).

[18] Distance from the "time" of the audience may be described as "adventure time," which carves a space outside "history and biography"; see Bakhtin (1986: 15). On *Battlestar Galactica* and the classics, see Tomasso (this volume, chapter eleven).

[19] Rabkin (1976: 95–108) argues convincingly that fantastic works offer escape from history. By creating a time *outside* real time and evoking a sense of timelessness, fantastic works relieve some of the psychic pressure of impending death. Tolkien (1966) offers a similar focus on fantasy as escape and consolation.

in mind both the future and how, in part, *these* narratives will replace the pasts expropriated within them.

To retrace this logic a bit: both Homeric poetry and Herbert's *Dune* create worlds that are at first glance synchronic (stories that happen during *one* period of time) but whose details and conventions depend on a diachronic consciousness ("history"—the stories and events that precede the narrative). The narrative devices used to effect these tensions fall on an axis that contrasts myth and science. Time is expanded in Homeric poetry into the past through the repository of knowledge of storytelling, and into the future through prophecy.[20] In *Dune*, time is enlarged through science fantasy: characters possess ancestral memories (the ability to recall and inhabit past lives), and the use of the spice mélange enables partial prognostication in some and perfect prescience in Paul Atreides.

We may uncover the depth of this correlation by considering the narrative strategies of each text more fully. Time in Homer's *Iliad* is deceptively simple.[21] Homeric characters display a conception of time we could call *deictic*—the present tense correlates with the time of an utterance; the past indicates what came before, and the future what comes after.[22] Through storytelling, the world prior to our *Iliad* is always shaping and informing its synchronic world. Often its contents are implicitly judged by the measure of prior tales, as when Phoenix tells Achilles the story of Meleager and the Calydonian Boar Hunt (*Il*. 9.433–605), or Agamemnon attempts to exculpate himself by telling how Zeus was also deceived (19.87–134).[23] Even the future seems written: fate and the gods shape the tale (even while leaving room for choice and deviation).[24] Zeus'

[20] For more on prophecy in SF and ancient epic, see Cirasa (1984).

[21] As Bakker (2005: 92–113) argues, the epic's origin in a performance-genre complicates time-expression. For a basic overview of issues of the narrative time of the epics, see Bakker (2011). For narratological evaluations of Homer, see de Jong (1987).

[22] Consider poets, prophets, and fools: Calchas knows "what is, what will be and what was before" (*Il*. 1.70). The Trojan advisor Polydamas "saw the before and after" (*Il*. 18.250), a talent in which Agamemnon, according to Achilles, is deficient (*Il*. 1.343).

[23] In the *Iliad,* heroes and gods use the past to measure the present. See, for examples, the stories told at *Iliad* 4.370–400, 5.381–415, and 6.125ff. See Willcock (1964) for the classic presentation of this; Edmunds (1997) for a thorough discussion and bibliography; and Alden (2011) for a short but insightful survey. Often, however, such tales can produce dissonance if they are too closely compared to their contexts; see Barker and Christensen (2011).

[24] There is debate about the degree to which Homeric heroes have free will. For an overview and basic arguments, see Gaskin (1990) and Lesky (2004).

prophecies act as fate for the participants within the narrative and as prolepsis (foreshadowing) for the audience external to the narrative.[25]

Despite this neat system, the *Iliad*'s sense of time is curtailed and expanded. Character consciousness of history extends backward only a few generations—perhaps the length of Nestor's life (three generations; *Il.* 1.250–252); at times, the narrator breaks the temporal limitations in a different direction, gesturing forward to the world of the audience.[26] In short, the *Iliad* creates a temporal realm that enables both its participants and the external audience to peer behind and ahead in defining the here and now of the narrative.

In *Dune* we also find a deictic sense of time extended into the past through various means.[27] The past is invoked through personal (e.g., grandfather Leto) and archival history (the records of the Bene Gesserit). Paul's transformation into the Kwisatz Haderach (*Dune* 456) combines with his genetic memory (or race consciousness) to create poetic devices that replace epic's poetic tradition and convention of prophecy.[28] Genetic memory allows the past to impinge on the present, while prescience gives Paul glimpses of shifting and uncertain futures.[29] Through his ability to see into the past and the future, Paul creates a synchronic present where time and space are one (288).[30] Familiar narrative techniques and the inclusion of recognizable names (Atreides), figures (e.g., Mahdi,

[25] Several of Zeus' speeches map out the course of the epic (8.4–28, 8.469–483, 15.47–77, 17.451–458, 20.13–30, and 24.64–79); see Heiden (1996).

[26] Homer points forward when he describes how Diomedes picks up a stone larger than any contemporary man could pick up (*Il.* 5.302–304; cf. 12.380–383; 20.285–287). This scene is expanded for Hector when he breaks through the Greek wall (12.445–450).

[27] Herbert summarizes Paul's deictic time sense: ". . . he could view time, sensing the available paths, the winds of the future . . . the winds of the past: the one-eyed vision of the past, the one-eyed vision of the present and the one-eyed vision of the future—all combined in a trinocular vision that permitted him to see time-become-space" (*Dune* 288).

[28] Genetic memory (in *Children of Dune*, 1976) is described as "race consciousness" in *Dune*. It both allows the Bene Gesserit to connect with their past to represent a single line conjoining past, present, and future, and sets Paul (and later his son Leto) apart from other men. There is a negative side: race consciousness is Paul's "terrible purpose" (*Dune* 467).

[29] For Paul's prescience and its significance for history, see DiTomasso (1992: 319–322).

[30] Paul's prescience appears variously as "a kind of Heisenberg indeterminacy" (*Dune* 88), but then a vision of "available paths" (190). It is the present that becomes murky for Paul (e.g., "the here-and-now existed as a place of mystery," 223). Because he joins past and future, Paul unites all time; see DiTomasso (1992: 320).

105) and motifs (heroic pattern: exile, great deeds and return, etc.) allow *Dune* to develop a time-sense similar to that of the *Iliad*: recognizable elements connect briefly to the "real" world of the audience, while Paul performs the role in the narrative of prophets, poets, and gods.[31]

Some differences, perhaps culturally bound, do arise. Where the *Iliad*'s temporal gestures are limited in duration both forward and backward, *Dune*'s scope is more far-reaching. In both cases, however, the authority of the synchronic tale derives from the diachronic consciousness evinced by the text and imparted to the audience. Each narrative develops its meanings by collapsing past and future into an unstable present.[32] By disintegrating diachronic time, each narrative appropriates its patterns, its lessons, and its essence by creating a synchronic moment that is diachronic in scope—a moment that acknowledges the importance of the past but reconfigures it for present ends. By harnessing the future through prophecy on one hand and prescience on the other, each text attests to its own status as a fulcrum: what follows will be dependent on it and implicitly derivative or degenerative in comparison.

The synchronic emphases of each work lead to a secondary similarity between them. As each narrative positions its tale as a fulcrum over which past and future balance, they also position the events of their tales as definitive moments of transformation. Where the Greek poetic tradition conceives of the war at Troy as an event of ultimate change (the end of the race of heroes), *Dune*'s Paul sees his existence and subsequent wars as ruptures of rebirth. In the proem to the *Iliad*, the destruction of Achilles' rage is framed as being part of Zeus' plan (*Il.* 1.5), one framed elsewhere as aiming for the destruction of the race of heroes through war. According to other ancient sources, Greek myths envisioned the war at Troy as part of Zeus' effort to destroy humankind or eliminate the race of heroes—to

---

[31] For an extensive examination of the "monomyth" and its attendant patterns (following Campbell 1949) in the *Dune* series, see Palumbo (1998).

[32] On the *Iliad*, Lynn-George (1988: 272) writes: "In its tale of the past for the future—already belated, after the event, and always ahead of itself, telling what is still to come—the epic compounds a sense of finitude with a sense of the indefinite. The work of immortal glory was already accomplished and is never yet fully completed." Similarly, but less positively, Paul Atreides is conscious of the collapsing boundaries of time; and he fears it: "Yet, he could not escape the fear that he had somehow overrun himself, lost his position in time, so that past and future and present mingled without distinction. It was a kind of visual fatigue and it came, he knew, from the constant necessity of holding the prescient future as a kind of memory that was in itself a thing intrinsically of the past" (*Dune* 370).

transform the world into one more like that of the audience by separating the spheres of god and human. The *Iliad*, in its presentation of mortality as the definitive feature of humanity and its contemplation of the dangers of demigods like Achilles and too-close commerce between gods and men, both motivates and dramatizes this process.[33]

Dune's Paul similarly sees his place in time as a fulcrum where the generations before his birth culminate in a jihad in his name to achieve rebirth for mankind.[34] Paul's actions lead to the end of Fremen culture (as dramatized in the sequel *Dune Messiah*), a radical transformation of imperial politics and economics, and the birth of a terrifying religion that will unify while destroying. Paul himself, in fact, comes to understand with remorse that mankind has become stagnant and that only jihad would allow it to be reinvigorated (*Dune* 467). Indeed, in its narrative, the *Iliad* imagines the destruction of the walls of the Greek camp and of Troy (*Il.* 12.1–35), the punitive destruction of unjust human beings by Zeus (16.384–393), and through such obliteration the foundation of the world to follow. Thus, both narratives position themselves at crisis points in imagined histories where one epoch ends in flames to give birth to a new one. These works invite their audiences into narratives that are positioned as the end and the beginning of history, enjoining them to see themselves at such critical moments.

SELF-REFERENTIALITY

Both the *Iliad* and *Dune* probe the limits and dangers of storytelling. In this reflection on the efficacy of narrative, both works also reflect on

---

[33] This plan probably has several referents (see Clay 1999), but it may correlate to the plan mentioned in fragment 1 of the lost epic *Cypria*: a plan to destroy the race of heroes that is similar to Zeus' plan in Hesiod's *Works and Days* (156–165). For the incompletion of the plan, see Lynn-George (1988: 38). See Clay (2011: 26 and 58) on the extinction of the race of heroes. Cf. Graziosi and Haubold (2005); Barker (2008).

[34] During one of *Dune*'s ecological discussions, Herbert describes the struggles of humankind as "the need of their race to renew its scattered inheritance, to cross and mingle and infuse their bloodlines in a great new pooling of genes. And the race knew only one way for this—the ancient way, the tried and certain way that rolled over everything in its path: jihad" (195). For Herbert's environmental concerns as contrasted with inconsistent regard for other scientific fundamentals, see Slonczewski and Levy (2003: 175).

their own status as narratives, to varying degrees of explicitness. Such
self-referentiality also depends in part on positioning the telling of the
story at the end of the past and the beginning of the future. In fortifying
this territory, each narrative contemplates its own repeatability and, in
turn, the consequences of storytelling (especially heroic tales). Both
offer their audiences various stories told and interpreted by their characters, through which these texts establish the parameters by which
their characters live—that is, the stories that influence the decisions
their characters make—indicating where narratives corrupt or condemn characters, where the tales characters tell constrain and inform
the decisions they make. The result is that each work explores the nature
of its own form while also endeavoring to establish itself as an exemplary (or final) permutation of that form.

Before considering this theme further, we can again note some basic
correspondences. Both narratives develop an image of eternal fame for
heroic deeds and that which persists after death.[35] In addition to valida-
tions of glory, however, each narrative also implies that death comes
equally, regardless of fame (*Il.* 9.318–320; *Dune* 208). This relationship
between the promises of glory and the realities of mortality provides
only a secondary tension as each narrative explores the nature of mythmaking. A second correspondence is perhaps more sinister, as each
work positions the use of storytelling as essential to own narrative. In
both cases, we witness central characters, especially Paul and Achilles,
facing up to the paradigmatic and manipulative power of stories.

The *Iliad* is filled with stories from its own past, offering positive or
negative examples for the people who tell them.[36] In Book 9 of the *Iliad*,
for example, Phoenix invokes the "famous stories of men" (*klea andrôn*;
Il. 9.524–528) as the realm from which the Achaians draw their lessons;
Achilles himself seems to be reciting tales prior to the arrival of the

[35] In the *Iliad*, Hector claims compensatory fame for a man whom he kills (7.87–91).
Similarly, *Dune* offers fame (memory) as an exchange for sacrifice: "If it is the Lisan
al-Gaib you serve, as you have said it, why raise mourning cries? The memory of one who
died in this fashion will live as long as the memory of man endures" (211). In both narratives, fame remains paramount when a central hero faces death. Hector wishes not to
"die without a fight and ingloriously, but only after doing something great for those who
will come after to learn" (*Il.* 22.303–305); Paul considers that *"And if I die here, they'll say
I sacrificed myself that my spirit might lead them. And if I live, they'll say nothing can
oppose Muad'Dib"* (*Dune* 468; italics in original).
[36] See above, note 23.

embassy that fails to persuade him to return to war (9.189–191).[37]
Homeric characters use these narratives to measure their accomplishments (so Agamemnon compares Diomedes to his father Tydeus from the famous "Seven Against Thebes," 4.370–400) or to motivate decisions in their story (as Nestor uses a tale from his past to persuade Patroclus to replace Achilles, 11.655–803). Achilles' reflections on the tales from the past seem less profitable—he resorts to inaction.

In addition, the *Iliad* claims a place for itself among earlier tales. The narrator asserts that *only* the Muses could know the *kleos* ("fame") of the catalogue he is about to recite (*Il.* 2.484–487) and Achilles recognizes that his strife with Agamemnon—already the topic of complaints and rumor—will be remembered long after his death (19.56–64). Remembrance and exemplarity, contemplated by the *Iliad* from the past as it presents it, are the very things supplied by its present narrative and anticipated as objects for men of the future. The additional implication is that the story being told—the *Iliad*—is the one the external audience should appeal to for lessons, since it shows Achilles and others drawing ineffectively from other traditions.

Dune offers lessons of a somewhat different sort: its sense of itself is similar, but offers a contrast in its consciously cynical manipulation of the heroic pattern in prophecy and myth. In a way, it spells out the menace that is only just felt in the *Iliad*. Throughout *Dune*, its participants also see their actions as the material of future tales.[38] But narrative myth is used manipulatively in the form of prophylactic religious propaganda distributed by the Bene Gesserit.[39] Paul's mother, Jessica, calls this program a "sham" (*Dune* 53), and Paul's father, Duke Leto, sensing the correlation between the Fremen myths and his son, advises Paul to "capitalize" on this strategically (105).

---

[37] For *klea* denoting heroic poetry, see Beck (2011: 443). For *kleos* as the glory conferred by poetry, see Nagy (1979). For *klea andrôn* as the "traditional expression for the themes" of the oral tradition, see Ford (1992: 59–67). For Achilles' singing, see Nagy (1996: 71–73).

[38] Paul reflects on mythmaking before he rides the great worm: *"I cannot do the simplest thing without it becoming a legend. They will mark how I parted from Chani, how I greet Stilgar—every move I make this day. Live or die, it is a legend. I must not die. Then it will only be legend and nothing to stop the jihad"* (*Dune* 378; italics in original).

[39] The first reference is early in the narrative: "Jessica thought about the prophecy—the Shari-a and all the panoplia propheticus, a Bene Gesserit of the Missionaria Protectiva dropped here long centuries ago . . . the protective legends implanted in these people . . . " (*Dune* 54; cf. 277, 287).

In a way, Herbert's novel addresses the emphasis of Homer's *Iliad* on paradigmatic examples. Paradigmatic tales remain, but they more often function as admonition, as in the image of Duke Leto's father hung in the palace on the planet Arrakis facing the bull who gored him—we and the characters know this is a warning about facing danger and an allegory for Duke Leto's attempt to spring the trap set for him by Baron Harkonnen and the Emperor (*Dune* 51–52, 154). That Leto (and Paul) cannot take this lesson to heart points to the futility of "good" stories that just cannot apply, good models that cannot be followed.

Dune also illustrates that when myths are so clearly instrumentalized, unintentional consequences follow as myth and science are mixed into a toxic poultice and parallel prophecies coalesce around Paul. While the Bene Gesserit prophecies about the Kwisatz Haderach (an evolutionary figure whose qualities Paul displays) wear the guise of scientific experimentation—their messiah is *hypothesized*—they lose control of their experiment and enter the unknown when it combines with the "indigenous" messiah prophecies of Arrakis (*Dune* 129, 193). *Dune*, though, creates an initial ambiguity about Paul's status: Jessica first suspects and then fears that her son might be the culmination of their breeding program, while Paul seems to follow his father's advice in using legends strategically. As he embraces one aspect of his own nature (the superhuman skills of the Bene Gesserit breeding program), he also accepts the trappings of the native Arrakian legends as a matter of survival (219).[40]

The initial ambiguity of Paul as prophesied messiah and/or evolutionary accomplishment is resolved only by the fact that he does the things he is supposed to do. Pervading this process, however, is both ambivalence—as Pardot Kynes says, "no more terrible disaster could befall your people than for them to fall into the hands of a Hero" (*Dune* 269)—and a sense of the indeterminacy of prophecy, perhaps of narrative itself (". . . prescience, Paul realized, was an illumination that incorporated the limits of what it revealed—at once a source of accuracy and meaningful error," 88). So, in one way, the novel indicates the uncontrollability of myth and, at the same time, undermines its own tale (insofar as it is built on the same narrative patterns as myth). Once deployed, stories take on new permutations and new meanings—those

---

[40] This acceptance is tentative, but grows steadily. Jessica panics when Paul openly embraces *both* prophetic strains (*Dune* 413). Near the end of the novel, he embraces both uncertainly when he undergoes the ritual of the water of life (423).

who tell the stories become hemmed in by the boundaries set within them. As the Fremen, Jessica, and Paul accept the roles presented to them by the stories that they have told and embraced, they become part of a narrative whose end they cannot choose. In *Dune*, the *participants* of a narrative become trapped by the stories that have already been told about them: they hear the stories; they try to control them; and, in the self-fulfilling act of narrative, they perform them.

The *Iliad* and *Dune*, furthermore, share this essential ambiguity regarding their messages, or, to put it differently, they produce polysemies that resist positivistic interpretations.[41] The key characters of Homer's *Iliad* and Herbert's *Dune* are all keenly aware of the power of storytelling and their own potential to become narrativized.[42] For Homeric heroes, these tales can serve as positive (or negative) examples for the future, just as they hope to be performing deeds that will win them eternal renown (and roles in later educational narratives). For *Dune's* aristocrats, myths are a way to exert strategic control over large populations. In both cases, myth functions to establish the parameters by which the life of the characters (and subsequent generations) will be lived.

Even as the narratives contrast in the valence—positive or negative— they attach to this mythical process, each also participates in a bit of "curtain-drawing." It is in unveiling the restrictive power of narrative that Homer and Herbert resonate together most and reflect the impact of narrative on life *outside* the texts. Famously, Achilles has a choice of two fates (to die young and receive immortal fame, or to live out his days in ignominy; *Il.* 9.410–416); much has been made of this articulation, but on some level, Achilles has no choice. From the audience's perspective, Achilles' story has already been told: he will never leave the war because he never has left the war. Similarly, Paul articulates a choice between fates (to address his grandfather the Baron, or unleash a jihad on the universe; *Dune* 195). Just as Achilles looks to his past, through the *klea andrôn*, and his future, through divine prophecy, Paul gazes into time only to find that the past and the future narrow to tremendously limited options. Paul forestalls the decision consciously, but moves steadily forward until there is no choice; Achilles also refuses to

---

[41] For this as a central part of SF's engagement with "the crisis of modernism," see Broderick (2003: 62).

[42] For metapoetic consciousness as part of SF tradition, see Butler (2003: 138–139).

choose—he does not go home to enjoy a long life, but he does not rush to embrace glory. Both Achilles and Paul, then, find themselves ultimately without a choice, hemmed in by the stories told around them and that they themselves also tell.

In the *Iliad,* part of what condemns heroes to repeat mistakes is the limited nature of their precedents—the stories they know constrain what they think they can do—a fact Achilles may be struggling with while singing the *klea andrôn* in *Iliad* Book 9. The additional implied warning by both the *Iliad* and *Dune* is that the *audience* is similarly hemmed in and shaped by the stories it knows. Our world is thus constrained by the stories we have heard about it. In this way, both the *Iliad* and *Dune* comment implicitly upon the nature of storytelling. The stories we tell condition our interpretation of the past and constrain our understanding of the future.

There are some abiding differences in this process. Where the *Iliad* is arguably ambivalent about the "hero" (if not subtly negative about Achilles), *Dune* is antagonistic towards him while still inviting its readers to identify with Paul. Where the *Iliad* seems complicit and competitive in its attempts to expropriate from earlier traditions in the creation of a new narrative, *Dune* appears cynical about the effects of heroic narrative even as it masters the form. Even as the *Iliad* anticipates its future reception optimistically, *Dune* laments the hegemonic dangers of narrative.

While much of the difference I have indicated is contextual and generic—the history of literature has changed the way readers and writers think and talk about storytelling—the oral character of the Homeric poems deserves as much credit for their shape as the literary–science fantasy nature of Herbert's time merits for his. But the sophisticated triangulation and manipulation of time, combined with an essential commentary on the foundation of their respective genres, constitutes significant common ground for the *Iliad* and *Dune*, and perhaps an explanation for their preeminence in their respective genres. These similarities, in addition, have as much to do with the pervasive literary influences of the Western tradition as with the putative genre of the fantastic. As examples of fantastic literature, both works break generic boundaries and create new narrative worlds (and problems) for their audiences.

8

Disability as Rhetorical Trope in Classical Myth and *Blade Runner*

Rebecca Raphael

If, for the unconscious, the robot is the perfect object that sums up all the others, this is not simply because it is a simulacrum of man as a functionally efficient being; rather, it is because, though the robot is indeed such a simulacrum, it is not so perfect in this regard as to be man's double, and because, for all its humanness, it always remains quite visibly an object, and hence a slave. In the last analysis, robots are always slaves.

—Jean Baudrillard[1]

One might think of disability as the master trope of human disqualification.

—David Mitchell and Sharon Snyder[2]

---

[1] Baudrillard (1996: 130).
[2] Mitchell and Snyder (2000: 3).

Our cinematic culture teems with artificial life: robots, cyborgs, androids, replicants, artificial intelligence, artificial organisms, undifferentiated but hostile machines. Since the motif expresses real concern about technological possibilities that become more probable every year, one might suppose that this bestiary began in the modern era. Yet the concept of humanlike artificial-mechanical beings appears in the myths of many cultures. In this article, I examine two loci—Greco-Roman myths about artificial beings and the Ridley Scott film *Blade Runner* (1982)—in order to assess how artificial beings rhetorically define the human.[3] This is not a study of direct influence, but rather a comparative analysis of two phases of Western civilization's engagement with the idea of artificial life. Jean Baudrillard locates the source of contemporary anxiety in the robot's close approach of simulated humanity, while its deficits mark it as an object. The role of deficit, in turn, often appears as disability, such that the more closely an artificial life simulates the human, the more it begins to resemble disqualified human beings. Thus, Mitchell's and Snyder's observation can be amplified as "disqualification from the human," not only for humans who do not have an ideologically normal body, but also for artificial life that is ideologically barred from crossing into adequate similarity. By examining selected classical myths and *Blade Runner* side by side, we shall more easily grasp these two related aspects of our imaginings of artificial life: artificial life rhetorically defines the human, and it does so primarily through tropes of hyper-ability and disability.

In contemporary discussions of artificial life, particularly salient is Donna Haraway's work on the cyborg. She focuses on the cyborgs of contemporary mythology, arguing that their human-machine hybridity defies the possibility of a unitary origin. That is, a composite of such disparate parts cannot have a simple or single birth, nor a myth of origin.[4] On account of these multiple origins and plural nature, the cyborg threatens to destabilize boundaries between the binaries human/animal, organism/machine, and physical/non-physical. Thus, cyborgs evoke horror. Haraway, instead, proposes a positive disposition toward

---

[3] *Blade Runner* is based on Philip K. Dick's *Do Androids Dream of Electric Sheep?* (1968). The film has had four versions: the 1982 U.S. Theatrical Cut, the 1982 International Theatrical Cut, the 1992 Director's Cut, and the 2007 Final Cut. I refer to the 1982 U.S. version, unless otherwise noted. (As long as Ridley Scott lives, I am skeptical that anything is a "final" cut.)

[4] Haraway (2004: 7–45).

the cyborg. Liveley has explored Haraway's transvaluation in terms of classical precedents, and finds that the most attractive and repulsive quality of the cyborg is its hybridity.[5] Liveley notes a tension between Haraway's use and denial of classical myth, and between ancient and post-modern concepts and valuations of the cyborg. While I find much value in Haraway's treatment of contemporary cyborgs, a close reading of the key classical passages shows that classical myth was not negative about artificial, hybrid beings—or unitary in its treatment of human origins. Furthermore, the direct classical-to-modern comparison attempted here can elucidate significant differences in concepts of the human *vis-à-vis* artificiality.

A less direct but perhaps more fruitful analysis of artificial life forms comes by way of disability studies.[6] Disability scholars have explored those variations of human embodiment in which physical, emotional, and cognitive impairments or differences are constructed as socially disabling—that is, as not quite fully human. Garland-Thomson proposed the term *normate* for the ideological (as distinct from statistical) norm for human bodies, from which women, people of color, and persons with disabilities were judged to differ in a way detrimental to their value.[7] To the extent that artificial life also varies from the normate, it comes into the company of these other devalued bodies or persons. The contrast between classical myths and the replicants of *Blade Runner* parallels the trajectory of the unusual bodies from wonders to freaks, which Garland-Thomson elucidates elsewhere.[8] Moreover, Mitchell and Snyder forcefully argue that nearly all forms of discounting discourse—of race, ethnicity, class, gender, sexual orientation—have used disability in order to represent the discounted category as less than an ideological norm. With respect to artificial life, the connection I draw is that artificial beings are consistently represented as distinguishable from, and sometimes dangerous to, humans on the grounds of some deficit. Yet they also

[5] Liveley (2006: 275–294). For another example of hybridity in the classics and SF film, see Rogers (this volume, chapter ten).

[6] See David (2010) and Snyder (2002) for introductions to the field. For an historical survey of classical sources on disability, see Garland (1995).

[7] Garland-Thomson (1997).

[8] Garland-Thomson (1996: 1–19). Monster theory will need to augment disability analysis for a full understanding of the replicants and other cyborgs.

have some exceptional abilities that evoke powerful emotional responses of wonder or fear, for these hyper-abilities also question or mark human identity. How they do so is explored for each of the primary sources treated here.

Finally, since artificial life is unavoidably a simulation of organic life, Baudrillard's analysis of simulacra proves cogent.[9] First of all, in both classical myth and science fiction (SF), artificial life forms tend to perform certain types of labor, especially martial and sex work. The use of simulacra (or robots) reflects a desire to separate "real" humans from these types of work, even as the nature of the labor requires the human form and scale. In that context, the more-real-than-real quality of simulacra, which may entice in some ways, appears existentially threatening when humanity itself is being simulated. After all, if a simulacrum is a copy for which there is no original, and if artificial life simulates humanity, then the existence of the copy seems to erase the original—or at least to render it less "originary." Simulacra as such are not necessarily monstrous or disabled, but simulated humans tend to be treated, by specific cultural productions, as if they were one or both of these. The trope of disability reins in this potential erasure by representing the simulacrum as a disqualified human.

CLASSICAL SIMULATIONS

The notion of artificial life begins, in Western literature, with the Greeks. Several relevant myths provide the early stock of possibilities, with which contemporary SF continues to play. *Blade Runner* and *Do Androids Dream* do not explicitly rework the classical material, but rather continue variations on a theme, working with the structural possibilities implicit in the concept of artificial life in relation to humans. In the discussion below, I take, in each case, the most developed literary form of a myth, while conceding at the outset that the available sources probably rest on numerous older variants. Our cases are Hephaestus' Golden Maidens, Talos the bronze giant, and Galatea.

---

[9] Baudrillard (1994). In particular, see the chapters "The Precession of Simulacra" (1–42) and "Simulacra and Science Fiction," (121–127).

Arguably, the first androids in Western literature appear in the *Iliad* (*Il.* 18.367–617), and they are female.[10] In this scene, the Titaness Thetis visits Hephaestus, the lame smith god, to request new armor for her human son, Achilles.[11] Here we have an originary association of disability and artificial life: Hephaestus, whose standard epithet is "the renowned double-lamed" (περικλυτὸς ἀμφιγυήεις), is the only god with a disability, and he is assisted in his work by these impressive automata. (The *Iliad* does not directly assert that he made them, but if not he, then who?) Incidentally, he is also the only Greek god who does anything we would recognize as productive labor. In a culture that saw leisure as belonging to the aristocracy on one hand, and skilled, productive labor as the mark of lower social status on the other, disability and work together signal his difference from the other Olympians.[12]

The scene between Thetis and Hephaestus contains several descriptions of his body. At his first appearance, he recalls one of his two falls from Olympus (*Il.* 18.394–397):

> Thetis saved my life
> when the mortal pain (ἄλγος) came on me after my great fall,
> thanks to my mother's will, that brazen bitch,
> she wanted to hide me—because I was a cripple (χωλόν).[13]

His story implies an initial condition that so dissatisfied Hera that she threw him from Olympus, and in the fall, he sustained painful injuries.[14]

[10] We would more properly call them "gynoids" or perhaps "parthenoids." Without referring to this passage, Haraway (2004: 29–31) observes that females are problematic for unitary origin myths and encourages feminism to embrace cyborg hybridity.

[11] For a comprehensive discussion of the linguistic connection between Daidalean artifice and armor, see Morris (1992), especially chapter 1.

[12] For the low status of laborers, including skilled craftsmen, see Murray (1993: 55–56). He comments on Hephaestus (and Demodocus the blind bard), "The mythic prototypes of human skills are themselves physically marred." See also Vernant (1982: 72–75) for social stratification in the eighth century, and Burkert (1992: 1–25) on the Near Eastern context for craftsmen.

[13] English quotations from the *Iliad* are from Fagles (1998), from which these are lines 461–464. For the Greek, I consulted Monro and Allen (1902).

[14] The *Iliad* includes two instances in which Hephaestus was thrown from Olympus; he narrates both of them. In the first one mentioned (*Il.* 1.586–594), Zeus throws him out because he took Hera's side in a quarrel. He falls for a day and the landing knocks the *thumos* out of him. Lameness is not mentioned, but it may be a result of injury. In the second (*Il.* 18.394–409), he appears to have been born lame, and Hera disposes of him out of shame. Parental anger is common to both versions, and both seek to explain his affiliation with the Titanesses. Whether his disability is congenital or acquired is an interesting ambiguity.

Hephaestus then describes his occlusion, hidden in the sea-cave of Thetis and Eurynome, where he becomes a master craftsman. So he owes her, and readers/listeners know this before she makes her request. After this speech, Hephaestus gets up from his tools to see to his guest (18.410–417):

> With that
> He heaved up from the anvil block—his immense hulk
> hobbling along but his shrunken legs moved nimbly.
> (. . .πέλωρ αἴητον ἀνέστη / χωλεύων· ὑπὸ δὲ κνῆμαι ῥώοντο ἀραιαί.)
> . . .Then he sponged off his brow and both burly arms,
> his massive neck and shaggy chest, pulled on a shirt
> and grasping a heavy staff, Hephaestus left his forge
> and hobbled on.[15]

The description draws attention both to his disability ("hobbling," χωλεύων, brackets the passage) and to his enormous strength and agility; indeed, the implied surprise that someone with "shrunken legs" can move well suggests an able-bodied expectation of poor locomotion (a "normate attribution," to use Garland-Thomson's term).

Before the host asks his guest what she wants, we meet the Golden Maidens (*Il.* 18.417–420):

> ὑπὸ δ' ἀμφίπο λοι ῥώοντο ἄνακτι
> χρύσειαι, ζωῇσι νεήνισιν εἰοικυῖαι.
> τῇς ἐν μὲν νόος ἐστὶ μετὰ φρεσίν, ἐν δὲ καὶ αὐδὴ
> καὶ σθένος, ἀθανάτων δὲ θεῶν ἄπο ἔργα ἴσασιν.

> Handmaids ran to attend their master,
> all cast in gold but a match for living, breathing girls.
> Intelligence fills their hearts, voice and strength their frames,
> From the deathless gods they've learned their works of hand.[16]

They seem to be household servants and personal assistants; nothing in the passage suggests that they help him at the forge (and elsewhere in classical myth, we see that Hephaestus is in fact helped there by the Cyclopes). The passage dwells on both their artificiality and their lifelike minds and

---

[15] Fagles (1998: 479–488).
[16] Ibid. (488–491).

motion. Indeed, this combination is the basis of their fascinating quality. Since this passage immediately follows the description of Hephaestus above, it sustains the tone of wonder at beings with paradoxical qualities, or at least qualities that the narrator and audience found paradoxical. Hephaestus' Golden Maidens set the standard for artificial life: human intelligence (νόος) and bodies indistinguishable from the real thing. Finally, the narrative represents the Maidens as marvelous, as exemplars of the artificer's skill; they are not presented as a threat, nor does the narrator seem at all troubled by them. If anything, the Maidens set the stage for the creation myth that follows: Hephaestus makes an artificial world on Achilles' shield, complete with motion, sound, and lifelike figures. The Maidens thus foreshadow this artificial cosmogenesis: as Hephaestus is implied to have made the Maidens, so will he make an artificial world in motion on the shield.

In the Hephaestus–Maidens association, then, we have a disabled male god and artificial women. Both combine hyper-ability and disability. Hephaestus does so in his combination of immortal creative power and lameness. The Maidens are exceptional in that they are composed of metal but have humanlike abilities. However, the Maidens are divine artifacts that cannot themselves make artificial life. Indeed, with respect to the gods, all other life forms, including human beings, are artifactual; whether the artifact can make other artifacts is dubitable, Daedalus notwithstanding.[17] If the maidens are like mortals, then mortals are perhaps like them in important ways.

A second major instance of an artifactual being that combines hyper-ability and disability is the bronze warrior Talos in the *Argonautica* of Apollonius of Rhodes (*Argon.* 4.1638–93).[18] On their journey home, Jason and the Argonauts, trying to make landfall in Crete after two days of windless rowing, encounter the bronze giant. Talos defends the island by hurling rocks at the ship, rocks that he is able to break off from mountain cliffs (4.1638–40). That detail vividly establishes his impressive size and strength. Apollonius has rendered concrete the Hesiodic myth of a bronze race, emphasizing the metallic

<hr/>

[17] The accounts of his automata do not present anything quite this impressive, in my view. Morris (1992: Chs. 1–3) notes the first occurrence of Daedalus' name in *Iliad* Book 18 and argues that the passage provides the origin for the character and his myths.

[18] For the Greek, I have used Seaton (2003). In addition, I consulted Seaton's English translation and also that of Rieu (1959).

composition of his body (4.1638, 1641, 1646, 1676).[19] The initial description includes a notice of his weak spot, a place where thin skin covered a vein. The sailors, of course, do not see this, and the bronze giant's rock-throwing is enough to make them back water rather than attempt to land and engage in combat. Medea insists that she can defeat Talos, with two interesting provisions. Even if he is bronze all the way through (*Argon.* 4.1655–56), she can defeat him; the clause suggests that neither she nor the sailors know if he is completely bronze. Her second qualification is that her magic will work, unless Talos is immortal (4.1656). Again, she does not know, and no one else does. Since the gods could assume many forms and since the mythical Mediterranean was populated with all manner of beings, this provision makes sense. It does not seem to be prompted by anything except the possibility that such an exceptional being is a god, and a sensible precaution against brash claims to power. Medea then casts a death spell, fueled with malice; it causes Talos to scrape the area of thin skin, collapse, and die. The ship successfully makes harbor at Crete.

The account contains several ambiguities about Talos. First, Apollonius alludes to the bronze race's origin from ash-trees, and may also speak of them, in an ambiguous construction, as demigods (*Argon.* 4.1641–42):

τὸν μὲν χαλκείης μελιηγενέων ἀνθρώπων
ῥίζης λοιπὸν ἔοντα μετ᾽ ἀνδράσιν ἡμιθέοισιν . . .

He was of the stock of bronze, of the men spring from ash-trees, the last left among the sons of the gods . . .[20]

While ῥίζης λοιπὸν seems clearly indicative of descent from the bronze race, it is less clear whether μετ᾽ ἀνδράσιν ἡμιθέοισιν classifies the whole race as demigods or only places them at the time of and in company with demigods. At any rate, the Hesiodic source credits Zeus with the creation of the bronze race. Talos also seems to be at Zeus's disposal, for the latter makes a gift of him to Europa, so that he may guard the island. Finally, there is the matter of his life fluid. The narrative refers at first to

---

[19] The Hesiodic progression of metals is clearly metaphorical. With respect to the bronze race, the metal is used in weapons and building, but not for their bodies (Hes. *WD* 143–155).
[20] Seaton (2003).

his blood vessels (σύριγξ αἱματόεσσα; 4.1647), and then, when he bleeds
out, to ἰχώρ (4.1679). One term suggests mortality, the other immortality. Talos is a hybrid entity, for Apollonius includes at least the divine
feature of ἰχώρ in a being that is clearly an object made for work. Since it
is not clear who made him, we cannot categorize him as an artificial life
form without qualification. He is, however, metallic, like Hephaestus'
Maidens; he combines exceptional ability (size, strength) with an
unusual and fatal weakness; and defeating him requires unusual means.
Evidently, he has no richer life, inner or otherwise, than hurling rocks at
strangers who threaten the domain he is set to protect. Talos is a slave
laborer, something of a drone, and very like Baudrillard's robot. In his
size, strength, and potential lethality, Talos conforms well to Gilmore's
definition of a monster; he is a hostile leftover from an earlier stage of
cosmogenesis.[21]

   Ovid's story of Pygmalion and Galatea in *Metamorphoses* (*Met.*)
Book 10 is our single case of man as creator of an artificial being, except
that he creates only the artifact, not the life. (The statue-turned-girl is
not named in the text, but later tradition gave her the name Galatea.)
Pygmalion is a bachelor disgusted by real women, so he carves his ideal
woman in ivory (10.247–255)[22]:

Interea niveum mira feliciter arte
sculpsit ebur formamque dedit, qua femina nasci
nulla potest, operisque sui concepit amorem.
Virginis est verae facies, quam vivere credas
et, si non obstet reverentia, velle moveri;
ars adeo latet arte sua. miratur et haurit
pectore Pygmalion simulati corporis ignes.
Saepe manus operi temptantes admovet, an sit
corpus an illud ebur, nec adhuc ebur esse fatetur.

During that time he created an ivory statue,
A work of most marvelous art, and gave it a figure
Better than any living woman could boast of,
And promptly conceived a passion for his own creation.
You would have thought it alive, so like a real maiden

---

[21] For Gilmore's definition, see below, note 34.
[22] Text: Hill (1999).

that only its natural modesty kept it from moving:
Art concealed artfulness. Pygmalion gazed in amazement,
Burning with love for what was in likeness a body.
Often he stretched forth a hand to touch his creation,
attempting to settle the issue: *was* it a body,
or was it—this he would not yet concede—a mere statue?[23]

There is a double likeness to the statue: its body is like a real body, so much so that its real lack of motion simulates modesty. This is the very trait in which Pygmalion found real women lacking. He is quickly confused about the nature of his own artifice, touching it, giving it gifts, and dressing it. That is, the narrator makes a strong claim for the *visual* resemblance of the artificial maiden to a real one,[24] but Pygmalion enters an *emotional* relationship with the statue, endowing it with fictive life. He knows what it is, but willfully sustains his fantasy. George Hersey elaborates on the tactile quality of the statue and the role of touch in bringing her to life; he situates all of these relational elements in a long history of statue-love.[25]

The motif of simulation appears in several ways throughout the events that bring Galatea to life. Pygmalion prays to Venus, not for the transformation of the maiden into a real woman, but for a wife "similar" to her (*Met.* 10.274–276):

. . . "Si di dare cuncta potestis,
sit coniunx, opto," non ausus "eburnea virgo"
dicere, Pygmalion "similis mea" dixit "eburnae."

"If you in heaven are able to give us whatever
We ask for, then I would like as my wife—" and not daring
To say, "—my ivory maiden," said, "one like my statue!"[26]

Feldherr argues that there is little textual support for the idea that Pygmalion wants the statue to come to life.[27] The strange petition does not specify in what way the wife should be *like* the statue, and it could mean another statue like her; i.e., a duplicate. His statue is like real women in

[23] Translation: Martin (2010: 10.316–326).
[24] Feldherr (2010: 252–254) analyzes Ovid's use of visuality as a narrative transposition of the tension between stasis and motion in visual art and also as a representation of cultural metamorphosis from East to West.
[25] Hersey (2009) discusses Ovid's passage in chapter 6.
[26] Martin (2010: 10.347–349).
[27] Feldherr (2010: 262).

appearance, but unlike them in (simulated) modesty; evidently he wants a real woman who is like the statue in appearance, but unlike her in being alive. Would not such a being be a real woman? But that is not what he wants: he desires this regress of simulation. Venus knows his unspoken wish and decides to give it to him; she signals an omen at the altar. Pygmalion then goes home to "the replica of his girl" (*simulacra suae petit ille puellae*), a phrase that suggests the statue is a simulation of the girl he loves, presumably an imaginary one. He begins to make love to it, and is surprised to feel it becoming warm under his touch. Feldherr notes that the transformation is narrated from Pygmalion's perception: *visa tepere est*.[28] Once again, he does not know what to believe; interestingly, the narrator does not describe the warm flesh as lifelike, but rather as similar to wax. Shortly after this image, we have *corpus erat*: Galatea then awakens to real modesty (blushing), sight, and consciousness. Narratively, however, she is represented primarily as Pygmalion perceives her, and not as an independent agent. Hephaestus' Maidens more clearly possess agency.[29] So is she real, or just a better simulation? This passage easily lends itself to Baudrillard's precession of simulacra: Pygmalion begins by confusing his desires with reality, and ends with the hyper-real.[30] Whether the statue/girl ever passes through "reality," she is clearly an artifactual being created for sex.

The Maidens, Talos, and Galatea all have artificial qualities, either clearly stated or suggested by description. In each case, there is a combination of exceptional ability or power and some deficiency or lack, relative to the divine or the human norm. They are all god-made, either completely or in the crucial respect. In that feature, they do not differ from human mortals, who are also god-made. Here, the Hesiodic accounts of Pandora provide a useful differential. In both accounts (*Theogony* [*Theog.*] 561–612; *Works and Days* [*WD*] 54–105), Zeus orders the creation of Pandora as a punishment to men in retribution for Prometheus' gift of fire. Hephaestus acts as direct creator, shaping the maiden from earth (*Theog.*) or earth and water (*WD*), while other gods provide aspects of personality and clothing.

---

[28] Ibid. (263–264). Overall, he argues that the narrative places readers with Pygmalion, in the position of viewers of artworks.

[29] This discussion is not intended to enter the debate about interiority and its historicity and representation. I only mean to point out that the narrative is strongly from Pygmalion's view and does not use its techniques of representation for agency, intention, and desire to represent the maiden.

[30] Baudrillard (1994: 22).

Pandora differs from the Golden Maidens, Talos, and Galatea in having a body formed from earth, rather than metal or ivory; Hesiod also presents her as the etiology for women and the troubles men endure. Furthermore, the account in *Theogony* gives her a fascinating crown on which wondrous moving creatures appear quite lifelike (578–584). In relation to our theme, Pandora is both closely associated with and clearly distinct from what we might call non-animal beings. In the terms of classical myth, all mortals are Pandoras; that is, products of divine artifice.[31] Nevertheless, these myths make a distinction between an organic human and an artificial "human," with the composition of the body being the necessary differential. Artificial life, in these myths, is made of the same substances that human craftsmen use for tools, buildings, and artworks. The functions of these beings are labor, defense, and sex.

None of the narratives represents the artificial life's interiority, even given the limited ways in which any kind of inner life is represented in classical sources. They are never the point-of-view characters, nor are their interests the central ones. In this respect, these artificial forms are treated quite differently from the humans in the stories in which they appear, but the texts never betray an awareness of the different treatment. That is, there is no narrative interest in reassuring us that they cannot compete with humans. (I do not mean that Talos does not threaten Jason's men, only that he does so by throwing rocks, not by being the sort of thing he is and thereby throwing humanity's nature into question.) We do find a fascination with their bodies, and especially a fascination with likeness, deceptive appearances, and the possibilities arising from these.[32] If the key identity binaries of classical thought were god/human, human/animal, and male/female,[33] then the Maidens, Talos, and Galatea do not threaten any of these. They simply exist outside of the first two, subservient to the gods and similar to human slaves; all *are* clearly placed in gender categories. Perhaps part of the fascination evident in these texts is the simulation of something

[31] Like a cyborg, Pandora is a composite work, both as she is represented in either account and also in her multiple, non-identical textual origins. However, I believe that she points to a weakness in Haraway's account of the cyborg: it is not unique in having multiple, composite origins. Greek creation myths about human beings, male and female, also have these qualities, and biblical myth is less unitary than Haraway seems to assume.

[32] I not mean to suggest that the conception of the body was mechanistic, only that these simulations were made of different materials. For a discussion of mechanistic explanations and automata, see Berryman (2003).

[33] See DuBois (1991).

that belongs in one of the categories, where the simulation nevertheless defeats the desire to categorize. Thus they are not a threat to Greco-Roman concepts of humanity itself, although they do play, a bit salaciously, with lacunae in the categorical schema. By contrast, in modern SF, particularly in *Blade Runner*, we see structural similarities but a very different sense of boundary threat. To put it concisely, contemporary cyborgs are monsters, and classical artificial life forms are not.

To be sure, classical myths had many monsters, but artificial life forms do not seem to be among them. On the basis of a global inventory of myths, anthropologist David Gilmore has developed a cross-cultural definition of monsters as hybrid, hostile, and hungry.[34] His treatment favors archaic material in which monsters are usually animal/human hybrids left over from whatever cataclysm created the current world. Classical examples would include Typhoeus, the Hydra, the Chimera, and the Minotaur. Hostility toward human life and civilization is a requisite; gods or heroes must defeat monsters precisely because they destroy human life. None of the classical artificial life forms shows monstrous destructiveness. Talos is only a superficial exception, for defense of a location is his work, and he does not appear hostile to human beings as such. Therefore, classical myth did not associate artificial bodies and minds with dangerous hybridity, threats to human civilization, or existential threats to the nature of humanity. In contrast, film cyborgs are strongly associated with all of these elements. They are our monsters, and to a major instance of them we now turn.

CONTEMPORARY REPLICANTS

As do the classical myths, *Blade Runner* has many versions. Ridley Scott has released four versions of the film (U.S. Theatrical Cut and International Theatrical Cut, both 1982; the Director's Cut of 1992; and, in 2007, the Final Cut).[35] I shall refer to these in the singular, as *Blade Runner*, with the

---

[34] Gilmore (2003: 1–10); see also his discussion of classical myths (37–46). See also Cohen (1997), Beal (2001), and Asma (2009).

[35] At the 2010 Austin Film Festival, I attended a session featuring David Peoples, one of the screenwriters, who was honored that year for lifetime achievement in screenwriting. When asked which version of *Blade Runner* he preferred, Peoples impishly reminded the audience that he has seen versions that were never released, and then suggested that it was not yet a finished film.

1982 U.S. cut as the primary reference. In addition, its literary source is the Philip K. Dick novel *Do Androids Dream of Electric Sheep?* (1968). Since the film differs in significant ways from the novel, each shall be discussed in its own right. In particular, the nature and function of the artificial life forms differ in Dick's novel and in Scott's film(s), and indeed, among the several versions of the film. Yet all of the variations show motifs carried over from classical myth as well as distinctively twentieth- and twenty-first–century anxieties about the boundaries between human beings and machines.

Do Androids Dream of Electric Sheep? presents a post–nuclear war dystopian future in which humans on Earth live in varying states of ability and disability, and android laborers are a privilege of able-bodied, off-world colonists.[36] Empathy and the lack of it provide the definitive distinction between humans and androids (as the artificial life forms are called in the novel).[37] Beyond its definitive role in the human–android distinction, empathy is central to the novel both thematically and dramatically. The major religion on Earth is Mercerism, for which empathy is the cardinal virtue. Oddly, humans manipulate their own emotions, including empathy, through a mechanical device; it is unclear whether this feature of the fictional world is intentionally ironic or inadvertently inconsistent. Finally, the central drama of the hero, Deckard, focuses on his ability to feel empathy, especially for the androids he hunts. In short, empathy is the major theme, and it supersedes the interlocking question of reality versus simulation. Dick's own statements and essays reinforce the significance of empathy: he has claimed to represent empathy as the definitive human quality, and he complained publicly about Ridley Scott's choice to turn the androids into characters who might feel empathy and for whom others might feel it.[38] In spite of the author's protestations, however, the novel's treatment of empathy is not so straightforward.

---

[36] Dick engaged the concept of androids many times, including, most prominently, in *Vulcan's Hammer* (1960), *The Simulacra* (1964), and *We Can Build You* (1972). Artificial intelligence is prominent in *VALIS* (1981), and the theme of simulation—of experiences, life forms, and whole universes—is pervasive in Dick's corpus. I do not intend my discussion of this one novel as a full exploration of his thought on artificial life forms or these related topics.

[37] In discussing the novel, I shall use its own term, "androids," for the artificial life forms. The film's memorable coinage, "replicants," should not be retrofitted to the novel. Nevertheless, the Dick's androids and Scott's replicants are both artificial *organic* life forms, not inorganic machines.

[38] Sammon (1996: 285); Landon in Kerman (1991).

The social-symbolic structure of the fictional world includes humans of various sorts, animals faux and real, and androids. The last must be understood in the context of this larger symbolic world and social hierarchy. First, humans are highly stratified by physical and mental fitness, which function as criteria for highly valued positions as space colonists. Second, wealth differences among Earthers are evident, especially as these enable or hinder conspicuous displays of empathy toward animals.[39] Animals are scarce, and caring for them in one's home is an act of both religious devotion and wealth display. Accordingly, the society develops a market in artificial animals, to allow those who cannot afford a real one to keep up appearances. For all the religious and social injunctions to empathy for animals, not all human beings seem to qualify. People with acquired cognitive disabilities are called "chickenheads" (bad) and "antheads" (worse). These humans are denied jobs, shunned socially, and routinely subjected to microaggressions. No character ever seems aware of this lack of empathy for fellow humans; on the contrary, becoming a "chickenhead" or worse is a dreaded fate. Thus all animals are treated as worthy of empathy, but not all humans are.[40]

Thus the human society into which the androids are introduced is stratified around cognitive and emotional ability. These androids are not mechanical, but rather artificially constructed *organic* life forms. For all that, the capacity to *feel* empathy is the definitive distinction between humans and androids. Androids are designed to simulate empathy and other emotions, but the Voight-Kampff test administered by Deckard and other bounty hunters is supposed to find the biological reflexes of empathy at thresholds beyond the abilities of androids. It is interesting that Dick represents both empathy and its simulation as physically based so as to be measurable, for this raises the possibility that humans and androids could become indistinguishable. At any rate, the androids have an emotional difference that is disabling in this fictional world. Just as

---

[39] My parallelism to Veblen's well-known phrase is intentional. One of the fascinating aspects of this fictional world is the way wealth is required to obtain and support an organic ("real") animal, but the main purpose of animal ownership is the social display of empathy.

[40] I do not detect any disapproval of this attitude in the implied author; on the contrary, the implied reader's agreement seems to be assumed. Gwaltney in Kerman (1991) argues that the novel makes a case for animal rights, an interpretation I find rather farfetched.

contemporary society recognizes emotional differences among human beings and categorizes such differences as illnesses, disabilities, or both, so the ideology of this post-apocalyptic Earth treats the androids' lesser capacity for empathy as a disqualification from humanity. They also have certain hyper-abilities, such as strength and endurance. And they kill humans. In short, they are monsters.

Since willingness and ability to kill are common to Deckard and the androids, his capacity to feel empathy becomes his only distinguishing feature from them, and a fragile one at that. Some critics view Deckard's ability to feel empathy for the androids he kills, painful as it is, as evidence that he has not yet lost his humanity. With this point, however, we reach another of the book's aporiai: the androids do appear to feel empathy for each other, if not for humans. If that is so, then Deckard's empathy for androids renders his status more, not less, ambiguous. In a world in which people use machines to regulate their emotions, it is entirely murky what a "real" emotion is. We are left with a detectable biophysical difference between humans and androids, but its meaning is not at all clear. What is clear is that the humans vest great significance in the *idea* that they feel emotions in general, and empathy in particular; whether they actually feel such empathy is another question. One possible construal of the novel is that the urge to use emotion as the site of human–machine difference may be mistaken.

Ridley Scott's 1982 film *Blade Runner* adapted Dick's novel for a SF feature film. The filmmakers coined the term *replicant* for the androids.[41] Scott originated two major changes from the novel: he wanted the replicants to be characters with whom audiences would empathize, and he downplayed empathy as a distinguishing feature of humanity in favor of the replicant's quest for longer life. Much attention has been given to Deckard's status, but the film's response to this question is subtle and, in my view, secondary. Thus, I focus on the replicants and their qualities as artificial life forms.

The film orients us to these figures just after the opening credits: text scrolling over a black screen introduces the Replicants, organic artificial life forms engineered for space colonization but illegal on Earth. They

---

[41]Screenplay by Hampton Fancher and David Peoples. Peoples, brought on late, contributed significantly to humanizing the replicants and coined the term. See Bukatman (1997: 17).

are defined by reference to their variations from human abilities: "The Nexus 6 Replicants were superior in strength and agility, and at least equal in intelligence, to the genetic engineers who created them."[42] This introduction highlights their hyper-abilities; their disability is a short lifespan, approximately four years. The short lifespan is central to the plot. The replicants, led by Roy, are on a quest for a longer lifespan, which they believe their maker can provide. Furthermore, the replicants have rebelled before: they are banned from Earth on account of their slave revolt some years before the time of the action. Like monsters, then, replicants can be indiscriminately violent; yet they are also given a very human and understandable justification for that violence.

The short lifespan provides the motivation for the replicants' quest to find their designer, Tyrell. It also figures into the human–replicant distinction. In an early expository scene, Bryant, Deckard's boss, says that replicants were designed to mimic humans in every way except emotions, but the designers thought they might develop emotions over time. This is a more developmental representation than we find in the novel, where the androids are made with some level of emotional simulation that does not change. In any case, Bryant claims that the designers created the short lifespan as "a fail-safe device" against the replicants' emotional development. They will not have, in the words of Roy's first line, "time enough." What would be so bad about replicants with an emotional life? Bryant does not say, but the likely problem is that replicants would then become indistinguishable from humans. This explanation for the short lifespan is revisited when Roy is confronting Tyrell. The two have a rapid exchange about artificial cellular design, and Tyrell clearly states that he could not solve a particular problem in cellular decay. This explanation is quite different from Bryant's, and is probably the true one. Tyrell, after all, knows more about replicants than Bryant does, and is actively trying to make a replicant "more human than human," with an emotional life based on implanted memories—Rachael. Implanted memories are, essentially, simulated time. But Roy wants real time and, finding that his creator cannot provide it, kills him by pressing out his eyes. In the end, Roy must come to terms with his short lifespan and the cessation of consciousness it brings. His time-on-film is bookended by references to time, from his opening

---

[42] Scott (2007). The collection contains DVDs of the U.S. and International 1982 theatrical releases, and the 2007 Final Cut, in addition to production and archival material.

"time enough" to his final line, "time to die." Time—the experience it brings, and the conscious sustenance of memory—is represented as the necessary substrate of emotional life, for both humans and replicants. Perhaps time evades effective simulation, for experiences are not mere data. They are, rather, the dynamic and relational nexus in which subjectivities grow. The dying Roy shows a keen sense not just of experiences, but of himself as perceiver. Indeed, his recognition of Deckard as another, distinct subjectivity may be the empathy he finally acquires and the reason he refrains from killing Deckard, too.

The character J. F. Sebastian was created for the film; he fills the dramatic function of the novel's Isidore, a "chickenhead" who shows a remarkable capacity for empathy with humans, animals, and the androids. Both characters have disabilities, cognitive (Isidore) or physical (Sebastian), and both provide crucial assistance, even empathy, for the androids/replicants. Sebastian is a genetic engineer and recluse, more at home with his menagerie of automata than with other humans. The man is brilliant, but not quite at Tyrell's level. He also suffers from "Methuselah syndrome"—premature aging.[43] (Priss's question in reply, "Is that why you're still on Earth?" is the only allusion in the film to the novel's spatial-social stratification by ability.) Like Isidore in the novel, Sebastian mediates between humans and replicants, but Scott, Fancher, and Peoples have sharpened this role into an isomorphic one. Like the replicants, Sebastian lives a shorter life; but like other humans, he lives long enough for emotional development. He is different enough not to be at home with other humans, so he "makes friends," literally. We often see the replicants blend into human social settings, and Sebastian's place provides the counterpart setting in which Priss hides among the automata. Finally, the climactic sequence in which Deckard and Roy hunt each other begins in this intermediate place created by Sebastian inside a near-ruin from the pre-apocalyptic era. In his nature and in the spaces

[43] Progeria is a real but extremely rare condition. This condition and other variants of usual aging appear in the myths of the Sibyl; in Jonathan Swift's Struldbruggs (*Gulliver's Travels*, 1726); in F. Scott Fitzgerald's *The Curious Case of Benjamin Button* (1922), adapted to film under the same title (2008), in which the hero is born old and grows younger; in the *Star Trek* episode "The Deadly Years" (1967) as an effect of radiation exposure; and in the form of forced aging in the *Doctor Who* episode "The Sound of Drums" (2007). The real condition has an organizational and media presence as the Progeria Research Foundation, http://www.progeriaresearch.org/. To my knowledge, the most ancient reference to infants born with the features of advanced age occurs in Hesiod (*WD* 181).

he creates, Sebastian further obscures the difference between human and replicant, precisely by his replicant-like yet natural disability.

Perhaps the greatest anxiety represented in the film is not the possibility of replicants who are indistinguishable from humans, but rather the possibility of not knowing oneself correctly. In Deckard's early trip to the Tyrell Corporation, he intuits that Rachel is an even more sophisticated replicant who does not know what she is. Deckard marvels at the lack of self-knowledge, but the same question is raised later, by Rachel, to him: "You know that Voight-Kampff test of yours—did you ever take that test yourself?" He does not answer. I do not think the question is resolvable, or is supposed to be. Indeed, the variant versions of the film have provided fuel for this interpretive fire. The 1992 Director's Cut lacks the voiceover of the original releases, employs the symbol of the origami unicorn more prominently, and shows Deckard driving away with Rachel at the end. All of these details seem to make Deckard more probably a replicant who does not know himself. Yet the very multiplicity of variants, which parallels mythic (re)composition, also undermines attempts to stabilize an interpretation of Deckard as either human or replicant. If we viewers could "know" what Deckard is, his case would fall on the side of recognizing the other's nature. Representing a figure who probably does not know what he is, even when he can know what others are, presents the anxiety of self-knowledge in a fuller form. In short, it matters less what he is, and more whether he can know what he is. And if he cannot, does it matter?

PARALLEL MOTIFS: DISABILITY, ARTIFICIALITY, AND THE RHETORIC OF THE HUMAN

We can now step back and examine the continuities and discontinuities between classical myths and *Blade Runner*. The notion that artificial life forms will be used as a labor pool, specialized for work, war, and sex, is quite persistent, and is quickly losing its fictionality.[44] Not to attribute prophetic powers to Greco-Roman myths, but classical sources anticipate the major purposes to which artificial life forms will be put—and to which

[44] Robots are already used, to some extent, in advanced warfare, and Japan in particular has pursued the development of caretaker robots for its aging population. Sex robots remain some years in the future, but they have moved from the hypothetical to the soon-possible.

human beings, then and much later, even now, were and are put. Second, the trope of disability occurs in the myths and in *Blade Runner* (and much other SF, too): artificial life forms are defined by a combination of simulation of humanity and disqualifying disability. Indeed, defining an artificial life form as "dis-abled," in some way, relative to an alleged human norm has become a stock trope in SF.[45] In the instances discussed here, the proximity of another kind of disabled being, god or human, underlines the major role of ability in defining humanity. Conversely, the disabling discourse that supports enslavement of humans can be viewed as a means of representing some humans as simulations of the non-human; that is, as not "real" or "complete" human beings. Finally, a sense of the wondrous spans from classical myth to *Blade Runner*, from the narrative tone for Hephaestus' Maidens, to Sebastian's amazed exclamation "You're so different . . . you're so perfect." The simulation is more wondrous than the reality it simulates. It is against the backdrop of these continuities that we can see the differences between artificial life in classical myth and in *Blade Runner*.

The discontinuities are quite revealing of contemporary anxieties. First, classical myth locates difference in bodily substance and performance: the Maidens are gold and move on wheels, Talos is made of bronze, and Galatea of ivory. Their bodies are made of different substances, not of human flesh, and yet their simulation of human bodies is an occasion for wonder. The myths do not seem to attribute a deficiency of mind or emotion to these other substances, nor does the simulation of human surfaces disturb human identity. As modernity adopted a Cartesian view of the body as a machine, an essentialist human identity had to reside elsewhere, in some non-physical mind.[46] Then, as belief in anything non-physical eroded, this identity had nowhere to go, at least nowhere that could not, in principle, be constructed as an artifact. Late twentieth-century SF returned repeatedly to the emotions as the locus and identity of the human, and Dick's novel and Scott's film(s) are cases

---

[45] A few major examples are Asimov's robots of the *Foundation* series; Commander Data of *Star Trek: The Next Generation*; and HAL 9000 of *2001: A Space Odyssey*, both the Arthur C. Clarke novel (1968) and the Stanley Kubrick (1968) film. The last item is more properly classified as artificial intelligence rather than artificial life, but this boundary is not clear.

[46] For Descartes, the mind is a non-physical, identity-bearing consciousness, while the body is a physical, non–identity-bearing machine. See his *Sixth Meditation* and the *Treatise on Man*.

in point. The substance of the body, literally what it is made of, has been lost as a possible differential.[47]

Furthermore, confronted with physically and mentally superior artificial life, the human is defined by means of disabling the artificial being: the artificial being is by nature emotionally disabled, and it may contain deliberately programmed disabilities. This is a differential that we do not find in classical myths, which seem uninterested in emotionality as a definition of human or artificial identity. (It does arguably enter into the distinction between gods and mortals, not as an absolute distinction but insofar as they have very different emotional registers, with death being the key variable.) *Blade Runner* strongly suggests that even these emotional boundaries are unstable, an instability that would threaten the identities of both terms. Moreover, one of the major criteria for being monstrous is anthropophagy, and many SF machines and cyborgs do seek to exterminate human life forms. But the cyborg as perfect simulation, "more human than human," hyper-real at the terminus of the precession of simulacra, represents a very subtle form of destructive consumption: it eats up the possibility of an essentialist human identity. This anxiety even infects the criticism of the film, as we see in the attention to Deckard's nature.

Finally, in the fixation on the human–artificial distinction, I find a rhetorical quality. Here, Deckard's own conflict takes center stage: in his capacity to intuit before he can measure, to feel empathy for replicants, and perhaps to bring Roy Batty to his final understanding of their common, mortal nature, Deckard enacts an encomium to the human as emotional being. At the same time, although an audience may identify with the replicants' quest, their four-year-old emotional development in very powerful bodies is frightening. They function as cautionary examples of what humans can be, but should not be. Tyrell, likewise, represents the engineer so detached as to have lost his emotional capacity for anything other than excitement at his own inventive prowess. If the artifact in some way contains or represents its maker, our artificial life forms are ourselves. The monstrous, disabled, near-perfect simulated beings of *Blade Runner* embody the post-modern fear that we have become too completely artificial.

---

[47] This statement is intended descriptively of the film's world, not definitively of the metaphysical questions.

Part III

Classics in Space

9

Moral and Mortal in *Star Trek: The Original Series*

George Kovacs

"Athena, you were right. The time has passed. There is no room for gods!"[1] With his dying words, Apollo, last of the Greek gods, identifies a fundamental ethic at the heart of the rationalized universe of *Star Trek: The Original Series* (*TOS*). Defeated by Captain James T. Kirk and the crew of the USS *Enterprise*, Apollo must give way to *TOS*'s human future, and he is not alone. Over the course of its five-year mission, the *Enterprise* encountered several immortal and/or omnipotent beings, typically revealed to be morally bankrupt.[2] The series associated immortality with stagnation and a depletion of moral fiber. The future it depicted was a humanistic utopia, beyond the reach, or even the understanding, of the extremely long-lived. It is no accident that this correlation between moral and mortal is exposed in a figure of Greek myth.

[1] Transcripts for all episodes of *TOS* can be found at http://www.chakoteya.net/StarTrek.

[2] The *Enterprise*'s "five-year mission" lasted two and a half years, or forty, depending on one's reckoning. *TOS* ran on NBC from Sept. 8, 1966, to June 3, 1969, when it was cancelled by the network. It has never been off the air since, however; it has survived in syndicated reruns, and spawned several television series and film franchises.

In this chapter, I wish to explore the deployment of myth and moral instruction in *TOS*, a process that in important ways replicates the origins of myth in antiquity. One of the strategies by which contemporary relevance was built into futuristic space adventures was to evoke the historic and mythical past shared by both the fictional characters of the series and its viewers of the present.[3] Three episodes in particular offer explicit and sustained examples from antiquity in order to explore the moral potential and responsibility of humanity's future. These will, after a brief theoretical overview of the functioning of myth in *TOS*, serve as my case studies.[4] In "Who Mourns for Adonais?"[5] the crew of the *Enterprise* encounter, and eventually defeat, the Greek god Apollo. In "Plato's Stepchildren,"[6] the Starfleet officers discover a civilization claiming to be a direct descendent of Plato's *Republic*. And finally, the Roman Empire is found alive and well in the twentieth century in "Bread and Circuses."[7] The plot of this final example revolves around the Prime Directive of non-interference, the nigh-unbreakable code that governs the behavior of Starfleet's human officers. The Prime Directive evolves throughout the run of *TOS*, developing a little further with each episode in which it appears.

TOS presented an optimistic vision of mankind's future in the twenty-second century as part of a clear, didactic agenda for its present. Deployed by the United Federation of Planets (a cipher for the present-day United Nations), the Starship *Enterprise* and its crew explored a wide variety of ethical situations, even as they physically explored the universe. As often as they battled alien monsters, the crew wrestled with a wide range of moral conundrums. In these, they were

[3] Kreitzer (2004) catalogues a vast list of literary and artistic allusions in *TOS*.
[4] Greek myth and Roman history are the two distinct starting points for antiquity in popular culture and have generated very different reception histories. Nisbet (2008) and Cyrino (2005) provide sustained analysis of each, respectively.
[5] Episode 2.33; Sept. 22, 1967, by Gilbert Ralston and Gene L. Coon. I provide two modes of ordering. The first number (here, 2) is the season, followed by the episode number (here, 33), with episodes numbered consecutively throughout the series. Hence "Who Mourns for Adonais?" is in the second season, and the thirty-third episode of the series (but only the second of the season). Following is the original airdate of the episode (here, Sept. 22, 1967). The sequences differ slightly (episode were aired out of their production order). I include official writing credits, though input in the form of story-plotting and rewrites came from creator Gene Roddenberry and other showrunners.
[6] Episode 3.67; Nov. 22, 1968. Meyer Dolinsky.
[7] Episode 2.43; March 15, 1968. Gene Roddenberry, Gene L. Coon, and John Kneubuhl.

often guided by the Prime Directive. The crew were conspicuously inter-racial for their time, and their mission was one of peaceful exploration, motivated neither by financial greed nor by aggressive expansionism. In other words, they were meant to depict the best of humanity, evolved from the barbarities of its past (which include the television viewer's present). The *Enterprise* crew encountered a wide variety of challenges to their ideological underpinnings: mighty aliens seeking to test human morality, distant civilizations demonstrating negative examples of behavior, and paradise planets offering competing scenarios of utopia.

Both in modern science fiction (SF) and in antiquity, myth may dis-seminate ideology through the demonstration of moral principles and models of behavior (both positive and negative), but it is always incum-bent upon the recipient to infer such moral lessons. It is by no means a new idea to think of the *Star Trek* universe in mythological terms.[8] Like any popular and longstanding fictional realm, the *Star Trek* universe is constructed of interlocking narrative strands, recurring themes and motifs, and allusions both within its own corpus and without. It is gov-erned by rules and assumptions: how space travel is accomplished, for instance, or how societies are structured. On a macro-level, these rules behave consistently and predictably: this is the internal logic of the fic-tional universe, a logic that allows the viewer to accept the unreal tales told therein. To put it another way, the universe of *Star Trek* sustains the credibility of its fictions by following set patterns. As any serious fan will tell you, a disruption of those patterns is a disruption of the immer-sive viewing experience; it exposes the fictional nature of these stories in a too-explicit way. If a crew member spacewalks without a protective suit, for instance, the illusion is compromised.

There is, however, a great deal of flexibility structured into those rules and assumptions. This flexibility derives from *TOS*'s organic evolution and the nature of its fictive content. The universe of *TOS* is not subject to actual physical laws, but speculative, creator-driven agendas. The rules may be changed or suspended for the purposes of individual narratives. For an episodic series like *TOS*, which has no macro-narrative to guide story construction, this flexibility is impor-tant. More significantly, this mythographic malleability bestows upon

---

[8] Kapell (2010) collects many of the articles on *Star Trek* as myth published in the past four decades.

these stories an applicability beyond the speculative boundaries of their fictive universe: they serve as parable, as allegory, or in other didactic capacities (consider Hesiod's *Works and Days* [*WD*], for example, in which Hesiod instructs his brother through mythological paradigms).

In the case of *TOS*, the didactic impulse is incredibly important, both as integral to creators' agendas and as the key to *TOS*'s long-term success. Gene Roddenberry, especially, had specific ideologies to express in his stories, but other showrunners, such as Gene L. Coon and Dorothy Fontana, had agendas, too.[9] These impulses were often inhibited, modified, or sometimes abetted by the series' financial concerns, represented by the production studio (Desilu Studios) and the broadcasting network (NBC). It was financial reasons, exploiting the series' post-run popularity, that kept *TOS* in widespread syndication, cementing its position in the public consciousness and enabling the close fan scrutiny that has made *Star Trek* such a cultural force today. The didactic element fueled fan interest: viewers at the time were convinced they were seeing something deeper than the mere space tales of competing series, such as the contemporary *Lost in Space*.[10]

I limit myself to examples from *TOS*, which aired across three seasons and seventy-nine episodes, partly for reasons of space, but primarily because this series was the (very messy) crucible for the *Star Trek* mythos. Constraints of time and budget meant episodes were often written and produced quickly. Writers were only loosely concerned with standards of continuity and consistency of detail—the obsessive examinations of the series' fans had not yet manifested. When fan response did materialize, this, too, guided the writing, hence the greater emphasis on the relationships among the three principles—Kirk, Spock, and McCoy—as the series (and films) progressed. These conditions produced irregularities in everything from the physics of star trekking to the operating protocols of Starfleet.

---

[9] Hark (2008: 22–23). Of these, Coon is particularly relevant to my discussion. He wrote several episodes and served as series producer from "Miri" (1.12; Oct. 27, 1967) to "Bread and Circuses" (2.43; March 15, 1968). It was during his tenure that the Prime Directive was developed, and six of the nine episodes that feature it are clustered near the end of his run, late in the second season.

[10] Taplin (1999: 55) suggests a very similar perception that contributed to the rapid spread of Athenian tragedy throughout classical Greece.

I therefore liken the myth-building of *TOS* to the development of Greek myth, particularly in the Archaic (800–490 B.C.E.) and Classical (490–323 B.C.E.) periods, when narratives were being told according to related demands of genre (epic, melic, dramatic, etc.) and context (ritual, public performance, sympotic, etc.). Like *TOS*, this period supplied later writers (painters, sculptors, etc.) with a broad mythical universe, rife with unique narrative challenges and distinct options, as competing versions of different myths existed side by side. In this analogy, the later series and films perform the function of Hellenistic (323–146 B.C.E.) writers, still building the mythos of *Star Trek*, but now far more self-consciously, with deliberate attempts to expand earlier ideas and to reconcile perceived contradictions.[11]

TOS not only generates myth, it applies what it finds. Allusions to Greco-Roman myth and history abound. The interface between Greek myth and *TOS*, however, is often cosmetic referencing at best, a dressing to imply a depth that the writers did not have the time to develop.[12] This is not unusual in SF, or indeed in any other genre of mass media. An hour-long format and pressed weekly writing schedules limited artistic world-building, as did the assumed public demand for regular action sequences. Sustained intellectual discussion had to be limited; few conversations on *TOS* last more than a minute or two before concerns of pacing move the viewer to a new scene. Nevertheless, the writers of *TOS* deployed high concepts of SF that frequently interrogated human nature and the type of societies that human nature was considered wont to produce.

To this end, mytho-historical allusions function as shorthand suggestions of intellectual depth and historical continuity, grounding episodes in the Earth of *TOS*'s past (and the past/present of the viewer).[13]

[11] Baker (2001: 82–84). Baker cites the *Deep Space Nine* episode "Trials and Tribble-ations" (*DS9* 5.6; Nov. 4, 1996), which sought not only to embed *Deep Space Nine* more deeply into franchise continuity, through the incorporation of *TOS* episode "The Trouble with Tribbles" (2.42; Dec. 29, 1967), but also to engage directly the dynamics of that series' fandom. In addition to the later series, there are countless spinoff novels, "official" guides, fan fictions, and fan-generated debates at conventions and online forums, each with differing degrees of canonicity in the *Star Trek* Universe.
[12] The terminology of appropriation of classical antiquity by modern popular culture is not rigorously defined. Keen (2006), focused on SF, and his term "allusion," which I use below, is a good start. I borrow "cosmetic referencing" from Marshall (forthcoming). See also Kovacs (2011: 15–24) and Rogers and Stevens (2012a: 142).
[13] Such "historical" continuity is often established in *TOS* (and in later series) through a formula of three examples, two real and historical, one speculative but on the same

This is typical of *Star Trek*'s pop-psychologizing and pared-down social allegory. Such allusions are not limited to antiquity, of course, and include broad references to many periods of (mainly) Western history and culture. Plot lines and story ideas were borrowed from competing television genres, and often recycled within the series itself. Both Roddenberry and Coon had previously written for television Westerns and police procedurals. Elements of horror (especially in the case of predatory aliens), crime fiction, and other genres are prevalent as well.[14] These allusions work to situate *TOS* in the broader intertext of Western culture, not only adding to the series' credibility but also granting to the viewer greater interpretive scope in considering the series' intellectual and philosophical intimations.

Allusions permeate all levels of *TOS*, beginning, almost literally, with the titles of each episode.[15] Assigned episode titles implied cultural weight and an intellectualism that was rarely delivered in any meaningful way, but left it incumbent on the reader to infer meaning. My first case study provides a good example. "Who Mourns for Adonais?" features neither Adonis nor Aphrodite, his mythical lover and mourner. The title is derived from a line of Percy Bysshe Shelley's "Adonais" (line 415); the unique spelling of Adonais, unknown before Shelley, confirms the allusion.[16] Composed upon the death of Keats in 1821, "Adonais" is, among other things, a commentary on the immortality of poets and their work. In this sense, "Adonais" has resonance for *TOS*, which also examines, here and in other episodes, the limits of mortality. "Adonais" itself is heavily steeped in the classical tradition—Shelley used Bion's *Death of Adonis* as a model (he had translated the first forty-seven lines some years before).[17] Vergil's tenth *Eclogue* is another influence, and

---

continuum. In "Bread and Circuses," for instance, Spock and McCoy debate the merits of the expanded Roman Empire and its institution of slavery. Spock points out that "They seem to have avoided the carnage of your first three world wars," citing "the six million who died in your first world war, the eleven million who died in your second, the thirty-seven million who died in your third."

[14] Baker (2001: 82–3).

[15] Each episode of *TOS* featured a "cold open" or "teaser": a short hook before the opening credits. The title of the episode was then prominently displayed immediately after the first commercial break.

[16] Knerr (1984: 55–56).

[17] The lines were not published until 1976; Everest and Matthews (2000: 697–698).

both Plato's and Moschus' eulogies of Bion are quoted as epigrams to the poem.[18]

"Who Mourns for Adonais?" makes no attempt to engage antiquity through these literary avenues; it cites the poem in its title, probably for its implications of literary and philosophical *gravitas* (in other words, it *sounds* profound). This may explain the use of line 415 even though the refrain of mourning for Adonais is repeated throughout the poem. Only here in the poem is the refrain posed as a question: the interrogative invites further contemplation, and therefore implies greater philosophical weight.

Nevertheless, the power of allusion is on display in the title of this episode. Though the writers are using a cultural shorthand, the gap between reference and meaning provides the viewers the interpretive space to develop their own reading of the episode. The literate, classically informed viewer is best positioned to fill in these gaps, even as they are best aware of its contradictions and possible shortcomings. Since "Who Mourns with Adonais?"—along with many other *TOS* episodes—rejects immortality as intellectually and morally depleting, the title of this episode is imbued with a certain irony. Shelley's unorthodox spelling of Adonais introduces even greater possible relevance. If Wassermann's speculation that "Adonais" puns on *Adonai*—a Hebrew

---

[18] Here are the quotations as Shelley printed them; see Knerr (1984: 24). The lines of Moschus have seen much emendation since "Adonais" was published, and I have translated his version. The translation of Plato is Shelley's own from "To Stella" (1821).

Plato, *Epigrammata* 670:

Ἀστὴρ πρὶν μὲν ἔλαμπες ἐνὶ ζωοῖσιν Ἑῷος·
νῦν δὲ θανὼν λάμπεις Ἕσπερος ἐν φθιμένοις.

Thou wert the morning star among the living, / Ere thy fair light has fled; / Now, having died, thou art as Hesperus, giving / New splendour to the dead.

Moschus, *Idyll* 3.109–112:

φάρμακον ἦλθε, Βίων, ποτὶ σὸν στόμα, φάρμακον εἶδες.
πῶς τεῦ τοῖς χείλεσσι ποτέδραμε κοὐκ ἐγλυκάνθη;   110
τίς δὲ βροτὸς τοσσοῦτον ἀνάμερος ἢ κεράσαι τοι
ἢ δοῦναι λαλέοντι τὸ φάρμακον; ἔκφυγεν ᾠδάν.

A poison, Bion, came to your mouth, poison you knew.
How could it approach your lips and not turn sweet?   110
What mortal so wild could mix or provide
a poison to you singing away? He has shunned music.

For an example of Virgil's *Eclogues* as a source of inspiration in modern SF, see Stevens on Jules Verne's *Journey to the Center of the Earth* (this volume, chapter three).

word for god—is correct, then we have a new implication for an episode that literally ends with the death of a god: "Who Mourns for God(s)?"[19]

The plot of "Who Mourns for Adonais?" is not complex.[20] While on a routine mission charting the planet Pollux IV (our first hint of a classical presence), the *Enterprise* encounters a powerful being who claims to be Apollo. He explains that, when the ancient Greeks grew weary of worshipping them, he and his fellow gods returned to their home. There they have been waiting for humans to cross the stars to worship them once again. One by one, however, the other gods grew weary of waiting and allowed themselves to dissipate into the "cosmic winds"—not exactly death, for the gods are immortal, but "a point of no return" as Apollo describes it.

It is Kirk who puts together the episode's central conceit: Apollo and his fellows were extremely powerful and long-lived aliens who visited Earth and, in the context of early Greek culture, were taken for gods. Kirk's revelation was not a new one in SF. It is a common trope, best articulated by Arthur C. Clarke's Third Law: "Any sufficiently advanced technology is indistinguishable from magic."[21] Clarke first articulated this Law some months after "Who Mourns for Adonais?" first aired, but it was already functioning as a narrative device in SF—one that allowed SF writers to circumvent clunky explanations of advanced but speculative technology.

Clarke's Third Law, which permits any seemingly supernatural event to be categorized as advanced science, is also in keeping with the theology of *Star Trek*, which is, like creator Gene Roddenberry himself, essentially atheistic, though "secular humanist" might be a better phrase, and in keeping with the *Zeitgeist* of 1960s culture and media.[22] Encounters with the divine

[19] Wasserman (1959: 311–313). See also Knerr (1984: 55–56) for other possible etymologies.

[20] Asa (1999) and Winkler (2009: 86–90) also provide independent analysis of this episode.

[21] Clarke (1968); see also Prucher (2007: 22). All three Laws are included in Clarke (1999: 1–3). Also published in 1968 was Erich von Däniken's *Chariots of the Gods* (translated into English in 1970; see Winkler 2009: 87), though aspects of the "ancient astronaut" theory date back at least as far as the stories of H. P. Lovecraft and his Cthulhu *mythos* (on whose receptions of antiquity see Walter 2014).

[22] Barrett and Barrett (2001: 141–157) traces attitudes toward religion in the first four series as well as many of the films. In *TOS*, acknowledgements of Judeo-Christian values occasionally appear. Two of the most notable examples appear in my focus episodes. In

are consistently "rationalized" within *Star Trek*'s science fictional parameters, in this case by assimilating the Greek gods into an advanced, but technologically attainable, civilization. In the case of Apollo, the Greek gods are further assimilated into a continuity of world history, retroactively debunking the superstitions of the past through "rational" explanation.

In "Who Mourns for Adonais?" the status of the gods does indeed prove to be technologically attainable. Apollo's power is attributed to an otherwise inexplicable organ in his body, his only physiological distinction from human anatomy, which allows him to channel power from an outside source. The power source, it turns out, is housed inside his temple. The difference between god and man is reduced to a minor anatomical anomaly, almost an appendix, and overcome by mortal scientific ingenuity. Spock works out how to penetrate Apollo's force field with the ship's phasers and destroy the power source (similarly, Spock and McCoy use science to match the power of the Platonians, see below). This of course means destroying Apollo's temple; the symbolism is not subtle. Apollo, defeated and confronted with his own consequentiality (which he can only measure from a human perspective), fades away into the "cosmic winds."

With Apollo's demise, the *Enterprise* crew expresses regret, acknowledging the contribution he and his fellow gods made to Greek culture, and by extension their own. Kirk pontificates: "Would it have hurt us, I wonder, to have gathered just a few laurel leaves?" Kirk's rhetorical question undercuts the hostility to god-worship exhibited earlier by the crew, especially by Kirk himself: "Accept him, and you condemn all of us to slavery, nothing less than slavery." This closing line, however, perhaps resonates with the episode's title and was surely written for its strong rhetorical flavor (as was the title itself). Ultimately, the humans' regret inverts the dynamic of Shelley's model. Ostensibly written as "an evocation of the Adonia,"[23] an annual rite of mourning for the death of

---

"Who Mourns for Adonais?" Kirk rejects pantheism, claiming "We find the One sufficient." At the conclusion of "Bread and Circuses," Uhura reports the rise of Christianity. Even here, however, the parallel nascent belief-system is described as a "philosophy of total love and total brotherhood," not a religion. See Asa (1999: 39, 48). The reference may owe more to the tradition of Hollywood depictions of ancient Rome, which frequently pitted the Romans against early Christians, with whom audience members were meant to identify. On this phenomenon, see Wyke (1997) and Cyrino (2005) *passim*.

[23] Reed (1997: 15).

Aphrodite's lover, Bion's poem focuses on the lamentations of Aphrodite: the immortal mourns for the passing of her mortal lover. Here, however, it is the mortal crew of the *Enterprise* who mourn the loss of the god. Rather than regretting a loved or worshipped personage, their lamentations are couched in terms of scientific and cultural loss.

Apollo's behavior in "Who Mourns for Adonais?" is consistent simultaneously with many depictions of Apollo in Greek myth and with the concept of immortality as it is understood in *TOS*.[24] This Apollo is an emotionally volatile character, one who longs to be worshipped and loved, but is prone to fits of anger and jealousy when the humans deny him. He lusts after the human female Carolyn Palamas, the ship's "A and A expert."[25] Apollo's volatility conforms to both epic and tragic manifestations of the hero, as does his pursuit of a mortal woman who ultimately rejects him. *TOS* is famously capable of killing off single-appearance characters (usually red-shirted security personnel), and therefore the viewer may genuinely fear the fate of Palamas. In the final battle against Apollo, Palamas helps destabilize Apollo by rebuffing his advances and treating him like a scientific specimen: "I'm not some simple shepherdess you can awe. I could no more love you than a new species of bacteria." Apollo's response is mythically typical: he proceeds to rape her.[26] Thus Palamas takes her place alongside her mythological counterparts, including Daphne, Coronis, Cassandra, Creusa; Apollo is unambiguously without moral compass. When he sees his temple destroyed, Apollo expresses his love for Palamas, but it is clear that he does not understand that action in moral terms, nor does he understand why the humans have found it necessary to reject him. He initially offers the humans an idyllic paradise, but it is utopia on his terms, not theirs, requiring worship of him and a rejection of human

[24] Oddly, he is only semi-divine: Palamas identifies his mother, Leto, as mortal, and Apollo later uses this heritage to justify his advances toward Palamas. Winkler (2009: 87) supposes the change was made for viewers unfamiliar with the sexual habits of the Greek gods.

[25] The two A's apparently stand for "Archaeology, Anthropology, and Ancient Civilizations." McCoy, who applies the title to Palamas, is not a master of abbreviations. He is, in fact, a doctor.

[26] Given the standards of 1960s television, the episode is circumspect: we see Palamas thrown to the ground by Apollo's storms and winds, and he grows in size to loom and stare down at her. The camera cuts away to the *Enterprise* attacking Apollo's temple, but when Palamas is next seen, she is dazed and disheveled.

technological advancement, effectively a reversion to the Golden Age of Hesiod (*WD* 109–120) in which humanity, though provided for, has no agency of its own. Apollo plans to destroy the *Enterprise* and bring its crew to the planet, where they will work with only the crudest technologies as farmers and shepherds.

Apollo is one of a number of omnipotent characters in *TOS* who are depicted as emotionally and morally inferior to the mortal protagonists. In the ethical logic of *TOS*, conditions of immortality and omnipotence, as well as situations of paradise, lead to stagnation (on the individual level, as with Apollo, or the societal, as with the Platonians below) and therefore a negation of humanity's natural development.[27] The world of *Star Trek* is itself utopian, but it is a dynamic utopianism that accommodates, and even encourages, humanity's need to grow and explore. Technological and scientific development form the imperative of a healthy society, and such development is never done. The implication is that moral development, linked with human activity, is never complete. Immortal beings in *TOS* either fail to develop the self-discipline of a moral conscience, such as Apollo here, Trelane in "Squire of Gothos," or the Onlies of "Miri,"[28] or they suffer a moral decline, such as the Platonians in "Plato's Stepchildren" (see below).

Many of these examples evoke elements of the television viewer's past (Trelane's house is stocked with antiques primarily from the Napoleonic era). This *mise-en-scène* serves as an environmental signifier of their failed moral development: it is the mortal *Enterprise* personnel who exist in humanity's future, while the immortals are stuck in its past. Several episodes that invoke the Prime Directive as a plot point likewise feature iterations of the viewer's past ("Bread and Circuses," "The Omega Glory," "Patterns of Force") or its technology ("A Private Little War").

---

[27] Stagnation as the souring consequence of utopia is a frequent motif of twentieth-century SF; see James (2003: 222). *TOS*'s recurrent trope of the emotional and moral inferiority of omnipotent aliens has proved irresistible to satire; see, e.g., the *Futurama* episode "Where No Fan Has Gone Before" (4ACV11), featuring an omnipotent alien who "collects" the cast-members of *TOS*.

[28] Trelane, though omnipotent, is a child. There has been fan speculation that he is a Q, the race of immortal beings who appear in the later series. The *Voyager* episode "Death Wish" explicitly tackles the stagnating effects of immortality. The Onlies are children who live as children for hundreds of years, but die almost immediately upon reaching adolescence. If Apollo offers a Hesiodic Golden Age, the Onlies occupy the Silver Age.

Apollo's longevity and power leave him unable to understand dynamic change or evolution. Though he is prepared for the humans to resist his compulsions to worship (he is constantly handing out "lessons," shows of force to keep the humans in line), it does not occur to him that the humans, despite mastering space travel, may have advanced in power. In the episode, Kirk explains to Apollo, "We've outgrown you. You asked for something we can no longer give."

In the third-season episode, "Plato's Stepchildren," the *Enterprise* responds to a medical emergency and encounters another group of humanoid aliens who, like Apollo, have lived in classical Athens. A small band of genetically engineered Sahndarans had to flee when their sun went nova. Seeking a new home, they made their way to Earth, where their leader Parmen was impressed by the teachings of Plato. When that civilization came to an end (this terminus is vague, but they make no mention of Aristotle), they left Earth and established a new home for themselves on an unknown planet. Rechristening themselves as "the Platonians," they constructed a new society based on the ideals of Plato's philosophy, with Parmen as self-declared philosopher-king. They call their society a "Republic" and refer to each other as "Academicians," though no clearer reference to Plato's works is given.

The Platonians are functionally immortal, though highly susceptible to mortal injury after millennia away from sickness and bacteria. Since their time on Earth, the Platonians have developed psychokinetic abilities, removing the need for physical exertion and providing them with the ability to control any non-Platonian. Immortal and nearly omnipotent, the Platonians are virtually gods. Only a single Platonian, the dwarf Alexander, has failed to develop these superhuman abilities, and has been treated as a slave and plaything by the others for centuries.[29] The episode spends a great deal of time establishing the totality of the Platonians' power over Kirk and the crew of the *Enterprise*.[30]

Naturally, the godlike status of the Platonians means they are also morally corrupt. Parmen justifies his status as near-tyrant of the

---

[29] Why the Sahndarans chose to genetically engineer a single dwarf is a question left unexplored, but perhaps we are meant to think of Hephaestus, who is lame and a frequent source of entertainment to the other Olympian gods. On disability as a trope in SF, including discussion of Hephaestus, see Raphael (this volume, chapter eight).

[30] It is under the compulsion of the Platonians that Kirk and Uhura kiss, famously the first interracial kiss on television.

Platonians by citing his strength of mind. Parmen, however, conflates his intellectual capacity with his telekinetic abilities, which manifest as physical force. The Platonians' application of Plato's teaching is an example of distortion through reception: it would be very difficult, if not impossible, to properly reconstruct the philosophy of Plato through analysis of the Platonians' own actions.[31] Both Roddenberry and Coon served in the Second World War, and hence were familiar with other historical misappropriations of antiquity for self-validating purposes, notably Nazi neoclassicism.[32] Kirk, Spock, and McCoy suspect the Platonians' dubious intentions quickly. Indeed, the Platonians have determined that McCoy must remain among them, as insurance against future medical emergencies, and they psychically manipulate and torture Kirk, Spock, Uhura, and Nurse Chapel in an effort to coerce McCoy.

The Platonians, like Apollo in "Who Mourns for Adonais?" are alien visitors to, and then refugees from, classical Athens. In a reversal from that earlier episode, where Apollo and his fellow aliens have demonstrated powers that shape Greek (and therefore Western) society, the Platonians have been influenced by the Greeks and shaped their own society accordingly (their telekinetic power developed later). But as immortals, they cannot understand the basic emotional impulses of lesser humans, so the need for Plato's teaching is lost upon them. As Kirk points out, Parmen uses his abilities to control and manipulate others. In a society of free and empowered citizens, Parmen becomes a tyrant. Ironically, the Platonians therefore follow the degenerative path from democracy into tyranny identified by Socrates in Plato's *Republic* book 8 (562b–c). Their Republic becomes an example of flawed classical reception: it becomes the very thing against which their model text warned them.

As in "Who Mourns for Adonais?" the power of the gods is not unassailable in "Plato's Stepchildren." McCoy and Spock are able to replicate the telekinetic powers of the Platonians (though not their longevity) by synthesizing a mineral to which the Platonians have been exposed. They are so successful that Kirk is able to completely overpower Parmen and

---

[31] Such a reversal may be signaled by the name of Parmen, which seems to be a play on Parmenides, whose pre-Socratic teachings influenced Plato. Here, it is Parmen who claims to have learned from Plato.

[32] There is a good deal of scholarship on this topic, most of it German. Schein (2008: 84) is a good place to start.

set his own terms for the Platonians' surrender. The episode's moral lesson comes from the dwarf, Alexander, who is offered the telekinetic abilities of his fellow Platonians and rejects them, even after an immortal lifetime of ill treatment. Alexander's reward is to be taken aboard the *Enterprise*, to be conveyed out to the galaxy at large,[33] while the other Platonians are quarantined in their stagnant society.

Repeatedly throughout *TOS*, the *Enterprise* encounters alien life forms who, through their own longevity, advanced power, or paradisiacal location, are able to offer to the human crew of the *Enterprise* an alternative utopic environment. These offers of wholesale paradise are invariably turned down, as each offer requires a halting of human progress, a denial of human evolution (though the *Enterprise* crew will often appropriate elements of alien technology). The human impulse of exploration and the dangers of mortality bring a heightened sense of morality and independence of self. This, of course, is a strong antithesis to the generally more pessimistic world of Greek myth, where the best course of conduct is thorough worship and avoidance of divine encounters. The allegorical figures of, say, Icarus or Bellerophon demonstrate the futility (and fatal consequences) of human presumption (*hubris*) in Greek myth.

In *Star Trek*, the human race imposes its own moral parameters in the form of the Prime Directive. In fact, the Prime Directive is a direct extension of *TOS*'s humanist project: "One fascinating feature of *Star Trek*'s optimistic humanism is that it also expressly denies to humanity the qualities traditionally ascribed to God, such as immortality, omniscience, and omnipotence."[34] Rather than forbidding contact with superior beings (indeed, the *Enterprise* seeks out these beings), the Prime Directive is intended to protect lesser civilizations from human influence—those beings susceptible to the injunctions of Clarke's Third Law and therefore disposed to view technologically advanced humans as gods. In other words, humanity must not even be perceived to be godlike. In its earliest conception, the Prime Directive was specifically intended to enable development and growth in other species, but such

---

[33] Kirk promises Alexander a new world of experience in which physical appearance is irrelevant. As usual, he undercuts this noble sentiment in his final line of the episode, when he commands Lieutenant Commander Scott to beam up a "little surprise."

[34] Asa (1999: 58).

growth was obligatory. In "Return of the Archons,"[35] the first episode to
mention the Prime Directive, Kirk and Spock debate the forced removal
of Landru, a computer that has psychically forced peace and tranquillity
upon the population of Beta III, at the expense of free will or societal
development. When Spock raises the question of the Prime Directive,
Kirk replies, "That refers to a living, growing culture. Do you think this
one is?" In its earliest articulation, the Prime Directive imposed humanistic principles of self-motivated development on the races that are to
survive. Again the theme of immortality occurs: Landru is a machine
programmed by a philosopher of planet Beta III's distant past, intended
by its creator as a personal legacy, and a provider of peace and harmony
for his people. Without a soul, however, and nearly omnipotent (like the
Platonians, it can assume total control of lesser beings), the computer
Landru enforces mindless compliance to a hive mind.

One of the foundational features of the *Star Trek* mythos, the Prime
Directive undergoes several iterations over the course of *TOS*, and is
further refined in later *Star Trek* series. Kirk's description in "Return
of the Archons" is far too subjective—he must personally judge
whether a civilization is progressing sufficiently (too godlike a position)—and adjustments are made throughout the series. As with any
element of the mythical universe, the Prime Directive can be ignored
by writers if it might obstruct the plot, and indeed several episodes
omit discussion of it, where a hard adherence to continuity would otherwise require it.[36]

The Prime Directive is given its fullest *TOS* definition in "Bread and
Circuses" as the Enterprise officers discuss the constraints on their mission. *Kirk*: "No identification of self or mission. No interference with the
social development of said planet." *McCoy*: "No references to space, or
the fact that there are other worlds, or more advanced civilizations." The
Prime Directive in this episode serves as a foil to the capabilities of the
technologically superior *Enterprise*, and prevents an otherwise easy

[35] Episode 1.22; Feb. 9, 1967, Roddenberry. The episode's title, another classical dressing, refers to a lost Starship whose crew was assimilated into the planet's population. The
crew of the *Archon* were the first to resist Landru's total psychic control. The crew of the
Enterprise, wearing similar uniforms, are identified as "Archons," and complete the liberation of the populace from Landru's control.
[36] Later series are more diligent about the definition and application of the Prime
Directive, starting with *The Next Generation*. Hark (2008: 76).

Figure 9-1 In a twentieth-century "Rome" on an unidentified planet, gladiatorial matches are broadcast for the amusement of the Empire. Here, Spock and McCoy are forced into the arena (a.k.a. the television studio) to do battle. "Bread and Circuses," *TOS*, Paramount Pictures.

escape by Kirk, Spock, and McCoy.[37] The episode features a "complete Earth parallel," a *TOS* trope in which a world develops exactly according to Earth history, though with some key difference. In this case, the Roman Empire has survived into the twentieth century, televising gladiatorial fights (as we see in Figure 9-1) and marketing products like the "Jupiter 8" automobile and "Mars" toothpaste.[38] Here, the brutality of the viewers' past, a world that admitted (as McCoy argues) "slavery, gladiatorial games, despotism," is compared to, and explicitly fused with, the viewer's present. Failed Starfleet officer Merik (who had landed

---

[37] "Bread and Circuses" was the last episode produced under the guidance of Gene L. Coon, and the last in a cluster of episodes using the Prime Directive as a plot device (it is only mentioned twice in the third season).

[38] Many ciphers for the Roman Empire exist in modern SF. For a partial list (mainly in novels), see Brown (2008: 416–422); for particular examples, see Makins (this volume, chapter thirteen, and 2014) and Harrisson (2014).

on the planet before Kirk and crew) and Spock, who often plays devil's advocate to McCoy's judgemental tirades, point out that this world has, however, experienced little or no war since Rome's conquering of the world—a *Pax Romana* on a global scale (though they themselves do not use the term). This episode's exploration of the Prime Directive is arguably the most complex, in which the Roman consul, Claudius Marcus, has learned of the Directive and exploits it to manipulate Kirk.

As a self-imposed mandate, the Prime Directive becomes one of the moral centers of the *Star Trek* universe, a buttress against mortal *hubris*, one that grows in mythical terms, evolving through several iterations generated by different narrative needs within *TOS* (and later *Star Trek* series).[39] It becomes a marker of *Star Trek*'s fundamental humanism (even as it is applied to alien species), demanding that each civilization find its own way in the universe. It also demarcates the humans of Starfleet from many of the technologically or physically superior races it encounters. Apollo and his race in "Who Mourns for Adonais?" have influenced human civilization, though their motives were clearly not altruistic. They desired worship that the humans eventually denied them. The Platonians, too, had no qualms about occupying ancient Earth, though in a reversal of the formula, it was they themselves who were affected. Even in "Bread and Circuses," the proconsul Claudius Marcus is aware of the Prime Directive through the failed Starfleet officer Merik, who is depicted as weak and corrupt. Claudius Marcus, for his part, is uninterested in the technology of Starfleet, except to the extent that it can secure his own despotic power.

In the *Star Trek* mythos, the Prime Directive imposes limits on the actions of humanity, parameters that are defined to prevent the excesses of the behavior seen in immortal beings. Interference constitutes playing God, and Starfleet has learned, both through its own actions and by observing the actions of others, that such behavior leads to suffering on the part of the lesser species and degrades the moral integrity of the more powerful species.

The importance of the Prime Directive to the *Star Trek* universe begins small but develops, both through *TOS* and especially in the later series, to become one of the fundamental elements of a vast mythology. As

[39] One episode of *Star Trek: Voyager*, "The Omega Directive" (4.21; April 15, 1998; Jimmy Diggs, Steve Kay) introduces a superseding command.

I have argued throughout this chapter, the mythos of *Star Trek* developed in an organic fashion, as writers of *TOS* took scattered elements of narrative, plot motifs, and other cultural models to piece together their own episodic stories. Those writers were making it up as they went along, and, like the bards and poets of archaic and classical Greece, they were not composing for long-term narrative demands, but on an episodic basis. The resultant inconsistencies, which have maddened obsessive fans and later series writers alike, have produced a flexible mythology that is able to reach beyond its immediate intended context. When deployed superficially as they are in *TOS*, the mythical and historical paradigms of classical antiquity are immediately recognized by the audience and quickly establish a continuity between the viewer's past and present and *TOS*'s humanist and utopian future. But it is exactly this superficiality that grants the greatest interpretive scope to *TOS*'s use of antiquity, opening space for allegorical and didactic readings of many episodes (exactly as the writers planned). This broad but shallow scope demands little of the viewer in an academic sense, but paradoxically compels the viewer to work harder as they meaningfully decipher each episode.

After forty years, with the fan-base still working hard, *Star Trek* remains one of the major accomplishments of mainstream SF of the twentieth century. Not incidentally, *Star Trek* also represents an important and influential moment in modern SF's receptions of classical antiquity.

10

Hybrids and Homecomings in the *Odyssey* and *Alien Resurrection*

Brett M. Rogers

"ODYSSEYS"

I've seen acts of every shade of terrible crime from man-like
    creatures,
And I've had the breath of liars blowing me off course in my sails.

—Andy Partridge[1]

Along with the terms "classic" and "epic," perhaps no classically derived term is used (and abused) more in contemporary narrative than "odyssey."[2] This remains true in the case of science fiction (SF). From Stanley G. Weinbaum's short story "A Martian Odyssey" (July 1934), to the

[1] From the XTC song "Jason and the Argonauts," *English Settlement* (1982).

[2] I extend my gratitude to James Evans, Amy Fisher, Aislinn Melchior, and the students in my Classical Traditions course (University of Puget Sound, Spring 2013) for insightful comments on earlier stages of this project. My deepest thanks go to my co-editor, Benjamin Eldon Stevens, who has patiently read several drafts of this chapter, offering many valuable insights both here and during many other shared odysseys. All errors are mine.

recent Odyssey Writing Workshops Charitable Trust for writers of fantasy, SF, and horror,[3] modern authors have regularly used the term "odyssey" to denote "a long series of wanderings" or "a long, adventurous journey."[4] Such use and abuse has been driven in part by the immense popularity of *2001: A Space Odyssey* (1968), directed by Stanley Kubrick and co-written by Kubrick and Arthur C. Clarke,[5] who understood "odyssey" to be concerned with "wandering, exploration, and adventure."[6] However, the identification of Homer's *Odyssey* (eighth century B.C.E.) as a narrative primarily occupied with a "journey" has influenced SF since its arguable origins in the *True History* by Lucian of Samosata (second century C.E.); in *True History*, an unnamed narrator sails to the ends of the inhabited world, traveling as far as the moon and sun, encountering along the way numerous bizarre, hybrid creatures.[7] Regardless of the precise source or influence—whether Kubrick, Lucian, or Homer "himself"[8]—many contemporary SF authors and narratives

[3] See "Odyssey Writing Workshops Charitable Trust" at http://www.sff.net/odyssey/. Accessed February 23, 2013. Cf. the theme of the 2001 meetings of the International Association for the Fantastic in the Arts, "Once and Future Odysseys," cited in Hall (2008: 85).

[4] Such extended use of *odyssey* in the English language goes back at least as far as the late nineteenth century (according to *Oxford English Dictionary* [OED], possibly back to Robert Louis Stevenson), and even further back in the French language, perhaps as early as 1798; see *OED* s.v. "Odyssey" 2, with etymology.

[5] The screenplay is based on Clarke's short story "The Sentinel" (1948), reprinted in Agel (1970: 15–23). Hall (2008: 82–87) emphasizes the particular importance of *2001: A Space Odyssey* in firmly linking the Homeric epic to space travel.

[6] Kubrick, cited in Agel (1970: 25). As Jeremy Bernstein reported in the *New Yorker* (and the article is reprinted in Agel 1970: 24–26), Kubrick came up with the idea for the title in April 1965, with the (unwittingly ironic) intention of setting it apart from contemporary SF films that focused on "monsters and sex." Kubrick explained that "[i]t occurred to us that for the Greeks the vast stretches of the sea must have had the same sort of mystery and remoteness that space has for our generation" (quoted in Agel 1970: 25). Interestingly, Clarke is cited as an exemplum in the *OED* entry (s.v. "Odyssey" 2) for his use of the term in *Songs of the Distant Earth* (1986): "The four-billion-year odyssey from amoeba to Man." On the "journey" in SF more generally, see Roberts (2006a). On elements of Homer's *Odyssey* in *2001*, see the brief treatment in Hall (2008: 85–6).

[7] On Lucian's *True History* as SF, see, e.g., Fredericks (1976), Swanson (1976), Georgiadou and Larmour (1998), Brown (2008: 415), and Keen (this volume, chapter four). Felton (2012: 130) describes the creatures Lucian's narrator encounters as "parodies in being hybrids more bizarre that those found in previous authors."

[8] For our purposes here, I remain agnostic on the thorny "Homeric question," and I use the name "Homer" here simply to denote "the poet(s) of the *Odyssey* as the text survives today." I do not assume that Homer was a real historical personage, or that "he" was an individual singer, transcriber, or editor (as opposed to, e.g., a fictional, hybrid

have drawn upon the *Odyssey* to describe their own journeys and encounters with some form of physical or conceptual Other: Weinbaum's "The Lotus Eaters" (1935) and "Proteus Island" (1936); R. A. Lafferty's *Space Chantey* (1968); Brian Stableford's *In the Kingdom of the Beasts* (1971) in the *Dies Irae* series; "What Fools These Mortals Be" in *Star Trek* #53 (July 1978);[9] the Franco-Japanese cartoon series *Ulysses 31* (1981–1982); Lannah Battley's "Cyclops" (1985); and the *Star Trek: Voyager* episode "Favorite Son" (3.20, March 1997).[10]

And yet the *Odyssey* (*Od.*) cannot be reduced to the status of mere travelogue. The *Odyssey*'s journeys and encounters with the Other, limited to the first half of the epic, work in the service of a somewhat grander theme, a theme that is also fundamental to much SF: what it means, or could mean, to be human. The very first word of the *Odyssey*, ἄνδρα ("[a/the] man"; 1.1), invites audiences to meditate on the definition of "man" in the world, as opposed to—and in tandem with—immortal gods, monsters, even women.[11] In this light it is possible to view Odysseus' famous narrative to the Phaeacians about his ten-year journey (in books 9–12) not only as a catalogue of places visited and beings encountered, but also as a thought experiment[12] that meditates on a number of possible ways one could combine aspects of human, divine/superhuman, and

---

Chimera representing centuries of a poetic tradition). On the problems concerning the reception of "Homer," see Graziosi (2002, 2008).

[9] The cover not only features a picture of the Cyclops carefully observing Kirk, Spock, and a third man held in his enormous hand, but also features the bold proclamation "Ancient Greek deities force Kirk and Spock on an odyssey of peril!"

[10] This list is compiled from Hall (2008: 83–87) and Brown (2012: 210). Hall, following Suvin (1979: 155), includes Jules Verne's *Twenty Thousand Leagues Under the Sea* (1869) as proto-SF that is informed by the *Odyssey*. Hall argues for the inclusion of *David Starr: Space Ranger* (1952) and the subsequent *Lucky Starr* novels by Isaac Asimov (under the pen name "Paul French"), although many critics point to the dominant (intermediary) influence of the Lone Ranger stories. Brown (2012: 212–216) reads Margaret Atwood's *Penelopiad* as SF. We might add the recent SF-inspired graphic adaptation of the *Odyssey* by Seymour Chwast (2012), who fuses images inspired by Greek vases with a mid–twentieth-century aesthetic inspired by such comic strips as *Flash Gordon*. I leave it to finer minds to examine the SF wonder *2069: A Sex Odyssey* (dir. Georg Tressler, 1977), for which see Hall (2008: 190).

[11] Contrast this with the opening of the *Iliad*, which focuses on "the wrath . . . of" a specific, named individual, "the son of Peleus, Achilles" (μῆνιν ἄειδε, θεά, Πηληϊάδαο Ἀχιλλῆος; 1.1).

[12] Cf. Fredericks (1980), who, in identifying Promethean and Odyssean archetypes in SF, argues that "Odyssean SF emphasizes the openness of the universe to mankind's speculative intelligence" (101).

animal/subhuman existence.[13] The presence of such Others, of such alternate ways of being and doing, in turn casts doubt on the certainty of "man" himself.

Moreover, the *Odyssey* is not merely a poem about a journey or journey-as-thought-experiment, but a thought experiment about a particular place: "home." Most SF narratives that draw on the *Odyssey* emphasize the outbound journey into the unknown, the encounter with the alien or Other, the act of discovery,[14] but they do not necessarily include a return homeward, a reapplication of discovery to the self in one's original context.[15] (*Space Chantey* and *Ulysses 31* offer exceptions.) To be sure, in our contemporary age of widespread diaspora and scientific exploration of the human body and mind, many contemporary SF narratives locate the ideas of "man" and "home" within the autonomous individual.[16] Such an individualistic view of "man," however, stands in stark contrast to the *Odyssey*, whose ethical thought articulates the "man"

---

[13] Despite my use of the term "monster" above, as well as its general importance in this article, I deliberately omit it from this list. Monsters are often considered Others sitting at the interstices of the other notional categories in this list, and are, in the useful formulation of Lada-Richards (1998), figures whose "prerogatives and . . . essence are powerfully interlocked with the perennial dialectic of 'Otherness' with respect to the 'Norm'" (46). It should become clear throughout this article that there is much overlap between "monsters" and "hybrids" or "hybrid creatures," although these categories in themselves are not necessarily identical. On the complexities of defining "monsters" and the "monstrous," see, e.g., Lada-Richards (1998: esp. 42–49), Gilmore (2003), and Felton (2012). See also DuBois (1991), who provides important discussion about *difference* (in terms of race, sex, species, and citizenship) in early Greek taxonomic thought. For application to the classics and SF, see Raphael (this volume, chapter eight).

[14] In this vein, it is worth noting that the name of the spaceship in *2001: A Space Odyssey* is *Discovery*.

[15] Fredericks (1980) similarly argues that "Odyssean SF focuses on the assimilative and adaptive element of intelligence," such that the hero in Odyssean SF "adapts . . . thrives, again becomes *the* dominant species" (101, his emphasis). However, Fredericks focuses almost exclusively on the SF hero's "journey" in terms of *intellect* (e.g., "modern man's scientific adventures . . . are the spiritual kindred of Odysseus' exotics adventures in the unknown," 100) and his discussion of assimilation and adaptation does not explore at sufficient length the way in which man's own "home" or humanity may come under scrutiny.

[16] For many authors, "home" is not a physical location, but a frame of mind, and one that is also susceptible to instability and change, as well as the vagaries of memory. In his reading of Derek Walcott's poem "Homecoming: Anse La Raye," Gregson Davis (2008) makes the point eloquently:

> What is "permanent," for Walcott, is the underlying emotional ambivalence, revealed in each iteration of the arrival/departure syndrome, that yields painfully acquired insight into the experiential paradox which beclouds all "homecomings"—the perception that the very notion of "homecoming" may be, at bottom,

in terms of his physical location and social relationships. Humans in the *Odyssey* declare their identities in terms of place of origin and social (patrilineal) affiliation: "I am Odysseus, son of Laertes . . . [who] inhabits shining Ithaca" (Εἴμ᾿ Ὀδυσεὺς Λαερτιάδης . . . ναιετάω δ᾿ Ἰθάκην εὐδείελον; *Od.* 9.19–21). There lurks a certain discomfort with individuals who are insular, including literal island-dwellers and others who hold little regard for social relationships, such as Polyphemus the Cyclops, Aeolus, Circe, and Calypso. Thus, in the proem of the *Odyssey*, Homer may defer identifying the "man" as Odysseus (1.21), but refers to the importance of "homecoming" (*nostos*) four times in the first seventeen lines (νόστον 5, νόστιμον ἦμαρ 9, νόστου 13, νέεσθαι 17).[17] The *Odyssey* emphasizes its commitment to exploring "man" in motion in a particular direction, in the process of the journey homeward, attempting to situate anew the shape of the human within one's original social context.

We are accustomed to reading the *Odyssey* teleologically—that is, we read with the knowledge that Odysseus will indeed reach Ithaca and his wife Penelope by the end of the poem.[18] Some critics have subsequently viewed Odysseus' refusal of the immortality offered by the goddess Calypso and return home as a sign "of [his] return to normality, of his deliberate acceptance of the human condition," of his return to, and valorization of, human existence.[19] However, we the audience might resist hastening to such conclusions. We might find ourselves at odds with Odysseus' choice, gawking at his rejections of

---

an oxymoron. As the disillusioned speaker of "Homecoming: Anse La Raye" comes to understand, "there are homecomings without home." Given the transforming mirror of time, "home" cannot be recuperated, and despite nostalgic desire for a pristine wholeness, it remains an unstable, if not destabilizing, concept that is constantly challenged by the shadow of memory (405).

[17] Foley (1999: 115–168) usefully examines the *Odyssey* as a *nostos* song within context of the oral tradition.

[18] Famously, there are two problems with this common, teleological reading of the *Odyssey*. First, Alexandrian critics debated where exactly the "end" of the *Odyssey* should be; it is possible, but not certain, that Aristarchus may have athetized the part of the poem coming after the reunion of Odysseus and Penelope (*Od.* 23.296); see Heubeck, in Russo et al. (1992: 342–345). Second, despite the opinions of the Hellenistic editors, we know from the prophecy of Teiresias during the *Nekyia* (*Od.* 11.100–137) that Odysseus' travels will not end with his return to Ithaca, but that he must leave Ithaca again and establish an inland cult of Poseidon; cf. Hansen (1990).

[19] Vidal-Naquet (1996: 39). Compare the more compelling formulation of Segal (1992) that Odysseus' rejection of Calypso's offer "refuses the possibility of a world . . . where the barriers between god and mortal could be fluid" (498).

the simple life of the Lotus Eaters, the pastoral existence of the monstrous Cyclops,[20] or the quiet seclusion of Calypso. Furthermore, Odysseus' return home to Ithaca in Book 13, only halfway through the poem, does not actually conclude the thought experiment; not only does Odysseus continue to encounter many "man-like creatures"[21] whose precise humanity remains suspect, but on Ithaca Odysseus himself continues to be a body in motion, susceptible to physical changes and performing superhuman, perhaps even monstrous, actions that render his own humanity suspect in his ongoing quest for *nostos*. In other words, we might suspect that Odysseus is returning home to Ithaca not as a "man" who has accepted his own stable humanity, but as a hybrid entity in a constant state of flux, both in physical form and in ethical orientation, whose identity resists closure and is subject to ongoing interrogation.

In what follows, I pursue such a reading of the *Odyssey* by placing it in dialogue with one SF film that demonstrates a similar concern with definitions, configurations, and hybridizations of the human and Other during the journey homeward: *Alien Resurrection* (dir. Jean-Pierre Jeunet, 1997). In *Alien Resurrection* (*AR*), Lieutenant Ellen Ripley (played by Sigourney Weaver), the protagonist of the *Alien* film series, is "resurrected" from the dead, cloned aboard the secret space station/ship *Auriga* from a combination of human and Alien DNA recovered from the original Ripley.[22] (In the previous film, *Alien³* [dir. David Fincher, 1991], Ripley committed suicide in order to destroy the

[20] For example, the dithyrambic poet Philoxenus of Cythera (c. 435–380 B.C.E.) composed a poem in which a romantic Polyphemus sings of his love for the sea nymph Galatea (fragments 815–824 Campbell). The Cyclops as bucolic lover appears again in *Idylls* 6 and 11 of Theocritus (c. 270s B.C.E.), then famously becomes a hybrid of both lover and killer in Ovid's *Metamorphoses* 13.719–897 (8 C.E.).

[21] I "riff" here on the quotation from the epigraph, a couplet from the XTC song "Jason and the Argonauts" (1982), in which songwriter Andy Partridge rejects the traditional teleological narrative of the Argonaut myth ("There may be no golden fleece / but human riches are released"), and focuses instead on the "journey" and the opportunity it offers to interrogate the boundaries of "man." Though the song invokes the hero Jason, the narrator's repeated references to his own observations ("I've seen"; "I've watched") strike a rather Odyssean note; cf. "Odysseus saw the cities and learned the minds of many men" (πολλῶν δ᾽ ἀνθρώπων ἴδεν ἄστεα καὶ νόον ἔγνω; *Od.* 1.3). Later in the song, Partridge offers a hauntingly Odyssean line: "I have watched the manimals go by / Buying shoes, buying sweets, buying knives. / I have watched the manimals and cried / Buying time, buying ends to other peoples' lives."

[22] See Kaveney (2005: 190–191) for criticism of the film's plausibility in SF terms.

last surviving Alien, a fetus implanted inside her.[23]) As the Ripley clone confronts her own "corrupted"/"enhanced" hybrid self, she must simultaneously confront various Others, both human and monstrous: the military scientists who resurrected her in order to resurrect the Alien species, a crew of cutthroat mercenaries, and, of course, the Aliens themselves.[24] Events turn bloody, and *Auriga* begins an emergency return to Earth. Although Ripley's journey "homeward" to Earth is not an intentional goal as it is for Odysseus—nor, for that matter, has this Ripley clone previously been "home" to Earth[25]—the imminent *nostos* raises important ethical questions about what kind of creature Ripley will be and what kind of society she will be fit to inhabit if and when she returns. I argue that Ripley's confrontation with her own physical and ethical hybridity in turn offers a productive analogue that helps articulate the ways in which Odysseus, too, at the ethical level, comes home more hybrid than human.

CLASSICAL INFLUENCES IN *ALIEN RESURRECTION*?

> A book's influence is never straightforward. Common readers, unrestricted by the rigours of academe, allow their books to dialogue with one another, to exchange meanings and metaphors, to enrich and annotate each other. In the reader's mind, books become entwined and intermingled, so that we no longer know whether a certain adventure belongs to Arsilaous or to Aquiles, or where Homer ends Ulysses' adventures and the author of Sinbad takes them up again.
>
> —Alberto Manguel[26]

---

[23] Mulhall (2002: 119) rightly argues that we cannot simply call *AR* a "sequel" to *Alien³*, since neither Ripley nor the Aliens are actually the same species as in the previous *Alien* films.

[24] As Murdock and Aberly (1997) report, Tom Woodruff, Jr., the actor in the Alien suit in *AR*, has said that Ripley "is more human corrupted by alien DNA," whereas Sigourney Weaver considered Ripley and the Queen Alien "enhanced" by each other's DNA (32).

[25] The original Ripley has not returned to Earth since the beginning of *Aliens* (dir. James Cameron, 1986). Even in *Aliens* she did not make planetfall, remaining aboard a space station.

[26] Manguel (2007: 88).

One possible objection to this project is that no obvious relationship exists between the *Odyssey* and *AR*. I wish to address this concern in three different ways. First, I point to the complexity in attempting to determine any direct or indirect "genetic" relationship between the *Odyssey* and *AR*. Second, I examine evidence suggesting that the *Odyssey*, though not directly present in *AR*, may have indirectly or unconsciously influenced ideas about hybridity and the monstrous in the wider corpus of *AR*'s screenwriter, Joss Whedon.[27] Finally, I discuss the few direct classical references in the *Alien* series.

One of the most serious problems facing any study in the classical reception of the *Odyssey* lies in its monumental influence and pervasive presence. As Edith Hall has observed, the enormousness of the *Odyssey*'s influence on our imagination and cultural values makes it difficult to track and detect all of its "spinoffs."[28] Protean in form, the *Odyssey* has been received, resurrected, and retold in countless poems, plays, novels, paintings, sculptures, films, television episodes, cartoons, comic books, and children's books.[29] As Manguel contends in the epigraph above, it becomes difficult to discern where one story ends and another begins as the *Odyssey* travels more freely than its famed protagonist from telling to retelling, across the boundaries of space, time, and culture.

Furthermore, different aspects of the poem, different "meanings and metaphors," as Manguel puts it, might make the passage at any given point: a character, an action, a theme, a style, an image, a symbol or entire symbolic system. Consequently, the *Odyssey* is Protean not just in form, but also in meaning; as Italo Calvino speculates, "If I read the *Odyssey* I read Homer's text, but I cannot forget all that the adventures of Ulysses have come to mean in the course of the centuries, and

---

[27] According to McIntee (2005: 120), Whedon's first complete draft of the screenplay "wasn't much different from that of the finished movie." For accounts of the differences between the original draft and the finished film, see McIntee (120–122) and Greenberg (2012: 433–434).

[28] Hall (2008: 3).

[29] Hall attributes this phrasing to Kenner. Hall (2008: 3–4) goes on to note that there have been numerous studies of the influence of the *Odyssey* and, more commonly, the figure of Odysseus/Ulysses. For further discussion, see, e.g., Highet (1949); Stanford (1964); Rubens and Taplin (1989); Bloom (1991); Boitani (1994); MacDonald (1994); Schwartz (2004); Graziosi (2002); Hurst (2006); Graziosi and Greenwood (2007); Manguel (2007); and the essays of Davis, Graziosi, Roisman, and Vajko in Hardwick and Stray (2008); Myrsiades (2009); Greenwood (2010); and Montiglio (2011).

I cannot help wondering if those meanings were implicit in the text, or whether they are encrustations or distortions or expansions."[30] We must therefore exercise caution in identifying the difference between a specific "reception" (i.e., that X receives Y or something specific from Y) and a shared cultural idea or belief (i.e., that X and Y merely happen to talk about the same thing or in the same style).[31]

Given these complexities, I do not aim here to claim that *Alien Resurrection* is a conscious or deliberate reception of the *Odyssey*. Rather, I am interested in the profit that comes from placing these texts in dialogue with one another, from considering the relationship Lorna Hardwick describes as "a two-way relationship between the source text or culture and the new work and receiving culture" in order to "frame new questions or retrieve aspects of the source which have been marginalized or forgotten."[32] In short, I am interested in the ways Odysseus and Ripley might be "cultural companion[s]" who shed light on each other.[33]

That said, I wish to note that there are two pieces of evidence—one circumstantial, one more direct, albeit chronologically later—to suggest the *Odyssey* has had at least an indirect influence on the work of Joss Whedon. As for the circumstantial evidence, in twentieth-century Anglo-American education, the *Odyssey* appeared in high school and college curricula with great frequency, a hallmark of the West's deep interest in its own legacy in "Great Books."[34] If Whedon had

---

[30] Calvino (1986: 128).

[31] "Style" here is inspired by Cicero in *De Optimo Genere*, who advises translating "in the same sentiments and forms as much as figures, with words fitted to our own disposition. I consider it necessary to translate not word for word, but I preserve the whole form and force of the words" (*sententiis isdem et earum formis tamquam figuris, verbis ad nostram consuetudinem aptis. In quibus non verbum pro verbo necesse habui reddere, sed genus omne verborum vimque servavi*; 14). For further discussion, see Hardwick (2003: 19–20).

[32] Hardwick (2003: 4). Cf. Hardwick (1992) for discussion specifically about, and possible models for, the reception of Homer.

[33] For the phrase "cultural companion," see James (2009: 239). My tactic here is similar to that of Christensen (in this volume, chapter seven) and offers a compelling contrast, I hope, to the study of Homer as a direct source for reception in *Ilium* as we see in Grobéty (also in this volume, chapter twelve).

[34] I am presently unaware of, but would be very interested in, any study that tracks with relative precision the presence of the *Odyssey* in the curricula of secondary and higher educational institutions; for a starting place, see Tomcho, Norcross, and Correia (1994). That Anglo-American students read (parts of) Homer's *Iliad* and *Odyssey*, however, is such a truism that an author on the website *Exaggeration and Blank Verse* writes "Some would argue that comparing Joss Whedon to Homer is an insult to Homer.

226 Classics in Space

not encountered the story of the *Odyssey* in his early youth in some mythological compendium, then it is likely that he encountered the *Odyssey* in his studies at several prestigious institutions: Riverdale Country School (New York City), Winchester College (England), or Wesleyan University (Middletown, Connecticut).[35]

The direct piece of evidence comes a little more than a decade after Whedon wrote *AR*, from the musical commentary, *Commentary! The Musical* (December 2008), written for the musical *Dr. Horrible's Sing-Along Blog* (July 2008). In the commentary, Whedon sings "Heart, Broken," in which he laments the culture of commentary and criticism that has developed in contemporary television and film. As the song begins, he traces a history of storytelling beginning with cave paintings and the *Odyssey*: "Homer's *Odyssey* was swell / A bunch of guys that went through Hell / He told the tale but didn't tell / The audience why / He didn't say, Here's what it means / And here's a few deleted scenes / Charybdis tested well with teens. . . . " Whedon's references to the *Odyssey* allude to books 11–12 in particular—the Underworld, Charybdis—suggesting that, for Whedon, the most recognizable core of the *Odyssey* lies in its difficult journey and monsters (as opposed to, e.g., its gods or romantic reunions). Moreover, there has been some suggestion that traces of the *Odyssey* can be detected in Whedon's "space western" television drama *Firefly* (2002).[36] It is perhaps relevant for our discussion here that *Firefly* and its continuation in the film *Serenity* (2005) are considered by many fans and critics to be Whedon's "second

---

(Others, mostly high school students forced to read *The Iliad* or *The Odyssey* against their will, would call it an insult to Joss Whedon. If they knew who that was.)" See "Firefly as the *Odyssey* (In Space)," at the website http://inlovewithnight.tripod.com/id53.html. Accessed March 12, 2013.

[35] Dear Joss Whedon: If you read this, please do let me know when you remember encountering the *Odyssey*.

[36] The anonymous author of the web post "Firefly as the *Odyssey* (In Space)" argues that the main plot of *Firefly* traces the pursuit of war veteran Captain Malcolm Reynolds after not "home" but peace in a state of serenity. The author also identifies several allusions to Odyssean characters and scenarios throughout the series: the Lotus Eaters (in the episode "Ariel"), the Cyclops (in the figure of Niska from "The Train Job" and "War Stories"), Circe (in the figure of Saffron from "Our Mrs. Reynolds" and "Trash"), the voyage to Hades (in "The Message" and "Out of Gas"), the Sirens (in "Heart of Gold"), and Scylla and Charybdis (in "Bushwhacked"). See the website http://inlovewithnight.tripod. com/id53.html. Accessed March 12, 2013. The arguments as presented are not strong, but do merit consideration.

pass" (as it were) at many of the characters, images, and themes found in *AR*.[37] Thus, even if there are no explicit references to the *Odyssey* in *AR*, it is clear Whedon knows the *Odyssey* and has devoted some thinking, in particular, to its monsters.

There are also a few classical references in the *Alien* series itself. In the first film, *Alien* (dir. Ridley Scott, 1979), the planetoid on which the human crew of the spaceship *Nostromo* discovers the aliens is identified as LV-426; in early drafts of the script and the novelization (as well as in the extended universe), the planetoid is specifically identified as Acheron LV-426. The allusion here to the river Acheron, one of the rivers of the Underworld in Greek myth, suggests that the humans have crossed a major threshold into the realm of the dead, or, at least, the monstrous. To borrow Whedon's phrase from *Commentary!*, *Alien* becomes the story of "a bunch of guys who went through Hell" although, crucially, one of the "guys" survives, the female protagonist Ellen Ripley. Furthermore, the most recent *Alien* film, the "prequel" *Prometheus* (dir. Scott, 2012), explicitly engages with (and rewrites) the myth of the Titan Prometheus in order to re-envision the *Alien* franchise as a narrative about the unintended consequences of, and terrible suffering resulting from, techno-scientific discovery and humankind's confrontation with its own creator.[38] This second classicizing reference comes after *AR* and therefore is not useful for our discussion; nevertheless, it is worth noting that, together, these two references suggest that Ridley Scott, in originating and developing the Aliens universe, is specifically drawn to icons in Greek myth that explore and articulate human suffering.

HYBRIDS AND HOMECOMING IN
ALIEN RESURRECTION

CALL: "What should we do?"
RIPLEY: "I don't know. I'm a stranger here myself."
—*Alien Resurrection* (alternate ending)

---

[37] Gallardo C. and Smith (2004: 170) call the crew of the *Betty* the "prototype" for the crew of *Serenity*; cf. Greenberg (2012: esp. 438).
[38] For one such reading of *Prometheus*, see Rogers and Stevens (2012b).

Often deemed "postmodern" and "parodic," *AR* makes numerous references to the previous *Alien* films,[39] such that the film exhibits an almost Odyssean obsession with its position at the "end" its tradition.[40] Nevertheless, Jeunet and Whedon did not import from *Alien* Ridley Scott's particular interest in the Acheron myth. Whedon does, however, anticipate Scott's later interest in the Prometheus myth in *AR*'s most explicit classical reference, found in the name of the space ship/station upon which the events of the story transpire, the USM *Auriga*.[41] In this section, I examine how *Auriga* evokes a number of classical myths that cluster around particular themes: techno-scientific innovation; travel; death, betrayal, and murder; and human/animal hybridity.[42] *Auriga*, I suggest, not only provides a liminal setting for the encounter between human and Other at the edge of the universe, but also, in its classicizing reference, cooperates in multiple forms of hybridity. Although *Auriga* does not allude to the *Odyssey* itself, I suggest that the various meanings of *Auriga* for *AR* become more coherent when we view them through the lens of the *Odyssey*. *AR* can be usefully understood, not only as a tale concerned with the definition of the "human" and hybridity, but also as a thought experiment about the ethical place of such hybrids in the context of homecoming.

Latin for "charioteer" or "helmsman," *Auriga* alludes to the constellation Auriga (Greek, Ἡνίοχος, or "Rein-holder"). At the very least, the allusion foreshadows the role of the *Auriga* as a "chariot" in conveying Ripley and the Aliens to Earth. Since the ship is sentient, controlled by the

[39] On *AR*'s multiple engagements with the earlier *Alien* films, as well as other film narratives and genres, see, e.g., Mulhall (2002: 121–122, 128, 130–131), Gallardo C. and Smith (2004: 157–163).

[40] Most (1992b) argues that the *Nekyia* scene (Book 11) in the *Odyssey* sets the poem against its predecessors and competitors in the hexameter tradition. Cf. Martin (1993), who discusses the *Odyssey* as a metatext about "the *end* of a poetic tradition" (his emphasis, 240), calling it "the last hero song."

[41] For discussion of the conception and design of the *Auriga*, see Murdock and Aberly (1997: 14–19, 22–25). Jeunet initially requested two different designs for the *Auriga*: one design treated it as a spaceship and emphasized horizontal lines; the other design treated *Auriga* as a space station, emphasizing vertical lines in order to invoke the image of surgical tools. Together, these competing designs emphasize that the audience is meant to think of *Auriga* initially as a floating laboratory, but, once the Aliens escape, *Auriga* becomes a moving vessel, heading towards Earth.

[42] No previous study I am aware of has explored the classical meanings of *Auriga*, although Kaveney (2005: 195, 201) does draw attention to ancient Christian mythology and imagery in the film. Joss Whedon's oeuvre shows an ongoing interest in how vehicles reflect and shape human identity; see, e.g., Rogers and Scheidel (2004).

artificial intelligence "Father," *Auriga* is both "chariot" and "charioteer," vessel and driver.

There are several myths associated with the charioteer's catasterism— that is, how the charioteer became a constellation.[43] Some ancient authors took the charioteer to refer to Erichthonius (or Erechtheus), the son of the lame god Hephaestus who was raised by the goddess Athena.[44] Erichthonius is said to have invented the four-horse chariot (*quadriga*), which enabled him to win acclaim as an athlete.[45] If *Auriga* refers to Erichthonius in this guise, then, in Promethean fashion, the name hints at the human desire to use technology to compensate for humanity's own natural shortcomings. Such is the explicit intention of the scientists on *Auriga*, as Dr. Wren (played by J. E. Freeman) tells Ripley: "The potential benefits of this [the Alien] race go way beyond urban pacification. New alloys, new vaccines. . . . "

Other ancient sources emphasize the charioteer as not the inventor of the chariot, but its driver, as well as the consequences that befall him. Some took the constellation to refer to Myrtilus, the son of Hermes and charioteer of Oenomaus: Myrtilus was first bribed to cause the death of Oenomaus in a chariot accident so that the hero Pelops could win Oenomaus' daughter, Hippodamia; Myrtilus was subsequently killed by Pelops.[46] Similarly, others saw the constellation as the catasterism of Hippolytus (the son of Theseus killed in a chariot accident),[47] Bellerophon (who is struck down

[43] On the constellation in general, see Aratus *Phaenomena* (*Phaen.*) 156–166, Pseudo-Eratosthenes (Ps.-Eratosth.) *Catasterismoi* (*Cat.*) 13, Germanicus (German.) *Aratea* (*Arat.*) 157–173, Manilius *Astronomicon* 1.361–7, Hyginus (Hyg.) *Poetica Astronomica* (*Poet. Astr.*) 2.13; cf. Allen (1899: 83–92), Kidd (1997: esp. 239–243), and Condos (1997: 49–54). Kidd (1997: 239) notes that the actual origin of the name for the constellation is unclear, but the identification of the constellation seems to be Babylonian in origin; cf. Condos (1997: 53–54).

[44] On the myth of Erichthonius and its variants, see Gantz (1996: 77, 233–237). In some accounts, Erichthonius is "earth-born" (Herodotus 8.55) but raised by Athena (e.g., Euripides *Ion* 265–274). In contrast, Ps.-Eratosthenes (*Cat.* 13) claims his birth is the result of Hephaestus' spilling his seed during an attempt to rape Athena; cf. Hyg. *Poet. Astr.* 2.13, *Fabulae* (*Fab.*) 166.

[45] For Erichthonius as inventor of the chariot, see Ps.-Eratosth. *Cat.* 13, German. *Arat.* 157–159, Hyg. *Poet. Astr.* 2.13. In a similar vein, Allen (1899: 85) offers that *Auriga* may allude to Trochilus, whose name means "running" or "turning" ("turning wheel"?).

[46] Ps.-Eratosth. *Cat.* 13, Hyg. *Poet. Astr.* 2.13.2, German. *Arat.* 159–162. On the myth of Myrtilus, see Gantz (1996: 541–543).

[47] So Pausanias (2.32) claims about the Troezenians. On the myth of Hippolytus, see Gantz (1996: 285–288).

attempting to fly to the heavens),[48] and Phaëthon (who crashes the chariot of the Sun).[49] Together, these myths suggest that the name *Auriga* in *AR* signals [self-]destruction; the scientists and military personnel of *Auriga* are willing to kill other humans (the kidnapped hosts, the crew of the *Betty*, Ripley) in order to drive their Alien-based research project forward, only to annihilate themselves in the process.

Interestingly, the constellation *Auriga* is itself a hybrid of human and animal figures, including not just the charioteer, but also the (Olenian) Goat (the star Capella), fastened to the Charioteer's left shoulder, and the Goat's Kids, located on the Charioteer's wrist.[50] In some ancient astronomical texts, the Goat is identified with Amalthea, a goat (or nymph) who nourished the infant Zeus.[51] We also find the notion of human/animal hybridity extended to the charioteer's own body; the fabulist Hyginus (first or second century C.E.?) claims that Erichthonius, the product of Vulcan's attempt to rape Minerva, was born a hybrid, "a boy . . . who was a serpent below the waist" (*Fabulae* [*Fab.*] 166; cf. *Poetica Astronomica* [*Poet. Astr.*] 2.13).[52]

These different images of hybridity in *Auriga* may be read into *AR* in several ways. First, as noted earlier, the scientists clone the Aliens with the desired goal of producing "new alloys, new vaccines," but with the actual result of producing new hybrid beings[53]—not just the human/Alien Ripley, but also the Alien/human Queen Alien, who gives birth to both more (hybrid) Aliens and, through the human uterus the Queen

---

[48] Allen (1899: 85) includes Bellerophon, ascribing the suggestion to La Lande. Hyginus reports (*Poet. Astr.* 2.18) that Aratus and others also associated Bellerophon with the constellation Equus, known more famously as "Pegasus"; cf. Allen (1899: 323). On the myth of Bellerophon, see Gantz (1996: 313–316); for a minor role played by the name in *Forbidden Planet*, see Bucher (this volume, chapter five).

[49] Nonnus *Dionysiaca* 38.424–428. On the myth of Phaëthon, see Gantz (1996: 31–34). Allen (1899: 84–85) also includes in his catalogue Absyrtus (whom Medea dismembered as she and the Argonauts fled Colchis), but offers no source for this claim.

[50] Aratus *Phaen.* 156–166, with Kidd (1997: 239–243). Cf. German. *Arat.* 169–173.

[51] See Ps.-Eratosth. *Cat.* 13, Hyg. *Poet. Astr.* 2.13.4, Kidd (1997: 242), and Condos (1997: 53).

[52] Trans. Smith and Trzaskoma (2007: 152–153). On the problems of Hyginus' identity, as well as the title and date of the *Fabulae*, see Smith and Trzaskoma (xlii–xliv).

[53] Greenberg (2012: 437–439) notes that an interest in the theme of oppressive authoritative agencies that lose control pervades Whedon's later work, including *Buffy the Vampire Slayer* (the Initiative in season 4), *Angel* (Wolfram and Hart), *Firefly* (the Alliance), and *Dollhouse* (the Rossum Corporation).

has inherited from her "mother" Ripley, the more monstrous Newborn.[54] Through the lens of the Erichthonius myth, *AR* looks like a struggle between the human scientists (Vulcan) and the androgynous, warlike Ripley (Minerva),[55] who together produce the renewed race of Aliens and the wholly unique Newborn (Erichthonius). Or, we might instead attempt to establish a correspondence between the constellation and *AR's* plot, which offers some interesting possibilities: Is *Auriga* the ship, Ripley the Goat/Amalthea, and the Aliens the Goat Kids? Or are we to consider Ripley the charioteer, the Queen as the Goat, and the Newborn as the Goat Kids? Such a diverse array of possible meanings, I suspect, is the point. At any rate, the appearance of the hybrid *Auriga* should be a warning sign to audiences: the Goat and the Kids became famous in antiquity as weather signs indicating the onset of rough weather in mid-to-late September, and thus became synonymous with storms, disasters, and even deaths at sea.[56] *Auriga* in *AR* thus foreshadows the "stormy weather" that lies ahead, signaling the many deaths to come.[57]

My objective here is not to pinpoint Whedon's precise intention in choosing this name for the ship, but rather to demonstrate how *Auriga* is a vehicle for several possible symbols and meanings for *AR*. Scholars have spent much ink on the importance of the notion of hybridity in *AR*, observing how Ripley, the "posthuman" subject, exists in a liminal state,[58] transgressing and bringing together several notional boundaries: she is, variously, a living "clone" of a dead woman,[59] a virgin

---

[54] All of the Aliens are in fact hybrids who share genetic characteristics with the host species, which point we learn from the hybrid dog/Alien in *Alien³* and is confirmed in the final scene of *Prometheus*.

[55] Gallardo C. and Smith (2004: 164) observe that "the Ripley clone is a being conceived by a father alone. She is Athena, Galatea."

[56] For an extensive catalogue of sources, see Kidd (1997: 240–241).

[57] Gallardo C. and Smith (2004: 164–165) miss this destructive connotation to *Auriga*, but see it in Ripley herself (as part of the SF tradition), "whose presence prefaces chaos, destruction and death, as did the femmes fatales in *Lifeforce* (1995) and *Species* (1995)," as well as the creature of Mary Shelley's *Frankenstein*.

[58] Kaveney (2005: 189–204) particularly emphasizes *AR's* interest in liminality, threshold states, and double natures.

[59] Mulhall (2002: 121) usefully distinguishes between Ripley as "clone" and "hybrid":

> Cloning suggests replication, qualitative indistinguishability, whereas hybridity suggests the cultivation of difference, a new creation. In *AR*, cloning engenders hybridity; even genetic replication cannot suppress nature's capacity for self-transformation and self-overcoming, its evolutionary impulse.

mother (and grandmother), a masculine female (if not quite as androgynous as in the previous *Alien* films),[60] a laboratory-grown child with the experience of a war veteran, an individual "human" with the blood, mixed DNA, hive mind, and collective racial memory of an Alien species. It has, however, gone unrecognized how *Auriga*, not just in its location—on the edge of the universe, in the liminal space where human meets Other—but also in its name, shares in, and provides the environment for, these multiple forms of hybridity. Simultaneously, *Auriga* adds a level of complexity to *AR*'s notion of hybridity, for *Auriga* is also a literal chariot—that is, a vehicle for bringing Ripley, the scientists, the crew of the *Betty*, the resurrected Alien species, and the Newborn "back home" to Earth. Unlike its multiple possible classical referents—Erichthonius, Myrtilus, Hippolytus, Bellerophon—*Auriga* in *AR* is crucially not a symbol of departure or exile, but of the return "home."

At this juncture, it is therefore productive to view *AR* through the lens of Homer's *Odyssey*. It is possible to describe *AR* in terms of many of the *Odyssey*'s plot points and themes: after a long absence, a war veteran has been "resurrected from the dead," although (s)he is being held captive in a solitary location. The veteran begins the voyage home, confronting various forms of Others as (s)he tries, as leader, to keep an increasingly diminished crew alive. The survival of the war veteran—both a long-standing custodian of, yet also a "stranger" to, home—depends crucially on recognizing who possesses the values that will preserve the community, and who must be eliminated as a threat to a successful homecoming and the integrity of the home.[61]

The joke, of course, is that "home" or "home base" (as various characters call Earth) is not very nice. Much as Ithaca is rocky and too rugged for owning horses (*Od.* 4.600–608), Earth in *AR*, we are repeatedly reminded, is a "shit hole." Indeed, in an alternate version of the final scene, Ripley and Call (played by Winona Ryder) sit in a dusty field filled with junk, gazing at a crumbling Eiffel Tower looming over post-apocalyptic Paris

[60] On gender and the tension between masculinity and femininity in the *Alien* series and action films more broadly, see Tasker (1998: 67–72).
[61] Benjamin Eldon Stevens raises the interesting question of how much modern (SF) revisions of Homer are filtered through (Dante's vision of) Virgil's already-reception, or more specifically, through an Aeneidic vision of homecoming after war. On the reception of Virgil's Underworld in Jules Verne, see Stevens (this volume, chapter three).

Figure 10-1 Ripley and Call return home to find a post-apocalyptic Paris. Ripley: "I'm a stranger here myself." From Jeunet, Jean-Pierre, director, 1997. *Alien Resurrection*, Twentieth Century Fox.

(see Figure 10-1).[62] This raises the additional question of whether "home" was really worth saving in the first place: after all, this is the same Earth, as Wren informs Dr. Gediman (played by Brad Dourif), where the once-treacherous Weyland Yutani corporation—responsible for human-kind's imbrication with the aliens from the very beginning—has been bought out by Walmart.

There is also a more serious point to *AR*'s *nostos* plot. If *Auriga* simply remained at the edge of the universe, the Ripley hybrid could, in theory, exist indefinitely without fully confronting the question of her own humanity. Like the Ripley hybrids (#1–7) discovered in the clone-storage facility (seen in Figure 10-2), our Ripley (Ripley #8) could remain indefinitely outside of time, as if in stasis, on Calypso's island, or even in the Underworld.[63] However, the moment *Auriga* itself begins the journey back to Earth, the

[62] Jeunet displays a general fascination with post-apocalyptic or derelict urban land-scapes in his other early films, *Delicatessen* (1991) and *The City of Lost Children* (1995). The city is almost itself a character in these films, as well as in the sunnier *Amélie* (2001) (e.g., in the comic orgasm montage).

[63] Benjamin Eldon Stevens has suggested a parallel in the (unfulfilled) possibility of Odysseus' accepting Calypso's offer and a prolonged life, albeit a life of suffering; cf. Ripley #7 in the clone storage facility, who begs Ripley #8 to kill her. Alena Karkanias, a student in my Classical Traditions course, suggested that the clone-storage facility is like

Figure 10-2 The clone-storage facility contains early attempts to "resurrect"
Ripley, now in stasis, including Ripley #1 (center foreground), #3 (right), #5
(left), and #6 (center background). Murdock and Aberly (1997: 114).

question "Who/What is Ripley?" gains added urgency. At that moment the
Ripley and Alien hybrids no longer exist in a vacuum—the vacuum of a laboratory, the vacuum of space—but suddenly threaten to rejoin human society
and test the definition of "humanity" on its home turf, Earth itself.

With the transition into the homecoming plot, *AR* becomes an even
more ethically complicated narrative. On one hand, as Raz Greenberg
has observed, "Ripley portrays indifference towards the other human
characters, not caring whether they live or die."[64] More to the point,
Ripley comes into conflict with all of the human characters at one point
or another, such that the audience can imagine her choosing her allegiances differently. After all, Ripley has just cause to seek revenge on the
scientists and military crew of *Auriga*, who have "resurrected," surgi-
cally invaded, and imprisoned her. Ripley also has cause to break from
the mercenary crew of the *Betty*, who engage in human trafficking and
initially threaten to harm her. There is some suggestion that the Ripley
hybrid could join with her genetic "family," the Aliens with whom she
shares a hive mind and memory (such that she can hear the Queen in
pain),[65] or join with the Newborn, who, upon its birth, kills the Queen

the Underworld. Mulhall (2002: 130) frames this perhaps more in Oedipal terms, seeing
Ripley in this scene as discovering "the riddle of her own identity."
  [64] Greenberg (2012: 435).
  [65] On Ripley and collective memory, see also Mulhall (2002: 120).

and licks "grandmother" Ripley affectionately. (As Gediman creepily intones, "Look, it thinks you're its mother.") In other words, Ripley could very well not be the heroine of the first three *Alien* films who single-handedly wiped out the Alien race, but remain the very "it" or "meat by-product" the scientists and military consider her to be.

On the other hand, the Ripley hybrid nevertheless chooses to ally herself with the humans, although she aligns herself most closely with another Other, the android Call. Crucial to Ripley's decision is her memory, which, in the worldview of the *Odyssey*, is a central feature of homecoming. Although she shares the Alien hive mind and memory, Ripley resists the Sirenic call that could lure her to the Aliens and the past. Instead, her memory of her earlier encounters with the Aliens dominates her ethical thinking, so that she never considers rejecting the human community for the Aliens or the Newborn. Indeed, soon after Ripley starts speaking, she warns Wren that the past threatens to repeat itself: "It'll breed. You'll die. Everyone in the . . . fucking . . . company. Will die." What is compelling, then, is how dependent the Ripley hybrid is on her own (constructed) memory in order to make moral decisions, despite the fact that no single moral value or code seems to bond the humans fighting to escape the *Auriga* and return to Earth. Ripley does not fight to preserve human goodness, or a particular vision of community, or even motherhood (killing her own "child").[66] At best, she acts out of self-interested survivalism based on past actions, as if a reflex of her former self.[67]

What will happen, then, if Ripley, the Aliens, or the Newborn make it to Earth itself? As it turns out, neither the Aliens nor the Newborn survive the journey—nor, for that matter, does the crew of the *Auriga* and its artificial intelligence, "Father."[68] The hybrid Ripley, however, does reach Earth alive, along with a handful of Others: the wheelchair-bound pirate Vriess (played by Dominique Pinon), a hybrid of human and

---

[66] See ibid. (125–135).

[67] Greenberg (2012: 435) suggests that Ripley is even indifferent to her own survival, but never explains why Ripley chooses survival over any other option.

[68] In one of the film's more pointed feminist gestures, Call tells Wren, "Father's dead, asshole." Greenberg (2012: 436–437) usefully discusses the relationship between Ripley and the android Call in terms of "the victory of two oppressed female characters over their male oppressors" (i.e., Father and the scientists), drawing parallels with Whedon's portrayal of the Buffy–Dawn sisterhood relationship in *Buffy the Vampire Slayer*.

technology;[69] the monstrously hyper-masculine and violent pirate Johner (played by Ron Perlman); and the morally driven android Call.[70] Although the film concludes with one hybrid Other (the Aliens) eliminated, it openly acknowledges that the journey for this surviving group of hybrid Others is far from over, leaving an important question unanswered. Call gives voice to this question as "she" and Ripley first gaze upon Earth: "What happens now?" Strikingly, in the alternate ending of the film, Call's question becomes "What should we do?" gaining both an ethical pointedness and a sense of agency. Ripley's response—"I don't know. I'm a stranger here myself"—poignantly captures the problem of her situation.

As Greenberg suggests:

> Ripley fully realizes that she herself is not completely human, and she obviously has her fears about (re)integrating into human society. But Ripley is also another kind of "stranger"—she now embarks on a journey back to the same human society that almost brought the monster apocalypse upon itself. Will it happen again?[71]

We might say then that, looking through the lens of the *Odyssey*, Ripley has only completed the first half of her homecoming; her *nostos* remains incomplete.[72] Like Odysseus waking up in a state of confusion as a "stranger" on the shores of Ithaca (*Od.* 13.194–216), Ripley arrives on Earth uncertain about what comes next. As Call observes in the alternate ending, the military are likely to come "sniffing around here pretty soon," like Penelope's suitors waiting to ambush Telemachus or Odysseus. Will Ripley surrender to the military? Or will she use her Alien attributes to fight the military and scientists?[73] Although Ripley's

---

[69] Cf. Marc Caro's concept art for Vriess' costume (in Murdock and Aberly 1997:46–47), which originally involved mechanized leg braces, and only later became the wheelchair that so clearly marks Vriess as Other-bodied.

[70] In the reading of Mulhall (2002: 125–127, 135), the childlike Call represents spiritual integrity in contrast to fecund/maternal embodiment, which Ripley rejects in her willingness to kill the Aliens and the Newborn.

[71] Greenberg (2012: 439).

[72] In a recent interview about the possibility of a subsequent *Alien* film set on Earth, Sigourney Weaver confessed that the *Alien* saga "does feel slightly unfinished to me," although Weaver did not like a proposed script written by Whedon; see Carroll (2009).

[73] *AR* seems to valorize this kind of action, as we see in the instance of the kidnapped human Purvis, who uses the Alien gestating in his own body to take vengeance on Dr. Wren and ensure escape for the surviving Others.

survivalist instincts have, up to this point, conveniently dovetailed with her willingness to kill the Aliens hostile to the human race, the actions of the Ripley hybrid aboard *Auriga*—violence against the scientists and military, the murder-genocide of her own monstrous offspring—do suggest that greater violence looms ahead in her homecoming.

"THERE'S A MONSTER INSIDE YOUR CHEST": READING ODYSSEUS THROUGH RIPLEY

> Wer mit Ungeheuern kämpft, mag zusehn, dass er nicht dabei zum Ungeheuer wird. Und wenn du lange in einen Abgrund blickst, blickt der Abgrund auch in dich hinein.
>
> Whoever fights with monsters should see to it that he does not thus become a monster. And if you stare too long into an abyss, the abyss stares back into you.
>
> —Friedrich Nietzsche[74]

AR suggests that, broadly speaking, heroes in the process of homecoming face monsters from every side: some appear to be Other (Aliens, the Newborn); some appear like the hero in form, but are no less dangerous (the scientists, military, mercenaries). How the hero could act is complicated by the hero's own hybrid status. Since Ripley comprises both human and Alien, she has potential allegiances to both communities, although in the film she privileges human existence over Alien existence. She ultimately finds herself keeping community with Others (the android, the Other-bodied) while further conflicts with normative humans probably loom on the horizon. Moving forward, it is unclear whether the humans or the Ripley hybrid will end up being the "monster." In this section, I use this reading of *AR* to return to the discussion started in the first section of the chapter and suggest that we view Odysseus' homecoming in terms of his status as an ethical hybrid.

It is important to start with a caveat: unlike Ripley in *AR*, Odysseus is not a genetic hybrid, although genetic hybrids are not foreign to ancient Greek thought. Not only are there human/animal hybrids (Erichthonius, Typhoeus/Typhon, Pan, centaurs, etc.), there are also human/god

[74] *Jenseits von Gut und Böse* ("Beyond Good and Evil"), Aphorism 146 (my translation).

238   *Classics in Space*

hybrids—that is, demigods or *heroes* (in the Greek sense of the term), the offspring of one mortal and one god. As the poet Hesiod (c. 700 B.C.E.) relates in *Works and Days* (*WD*), his poetic guide to human suffering and farming, these demigods (ἡμίθεοι; *WD* 160) populated the Generation of Heroes (157–175), which preceded Hesiod's and our own Iron Generation (176–201). From a genetic perspective, Odysseus does not quite belong to this race; both his parents, Laertes and Anticleia, are mortal.[75] Nevertheless, from a social and ethical perspective, "godlike" Odysseus does belong to the hybrid Generation of Heroes, insofar as he fought at Troy, side by side with demigods in battle; he and his men also engaged in other activities that Hesiod ascribes to heroes (*WD* 162–165), such as a great sea journey in order to engage in warfare and piracy (*Od.* 9.39–61) and cattle raiding (*Od.* 12.298–373).[76] With the aid of Athena, Odysseus is not just a master of disguise, but a veritable shape-shifter.[77]

Furthermore, Homer invites the audience to think of Odysseus as being like, or having the ethical disposition of, an animal, such that Odysseus can *seem* like a human/animal hybrid.[78] Similes compare Odysseus to, for example, a lion stalking sheep (*Od.* 6.130–134) and a lion who has devoured an ox (22.402–406). Portents similarly associate Odysseus with (violent) animals. Helen reads a portent, an eagle carrying a goose (15.160–165), to mean that "Odysseus . . . will come home and take revenge; or he is now home, and prepares evil for all the suitors" (15.176–178). Here the term for "portent" (πέλωρον; 15.161) also aligns the eagle, and therefore Odysseus, with other monstrous prodigies in the *Odyssey*, such as the Cyclops, "a monster knowing lawlessness" (πέλωρ, ἀθεμίστια εἰδώς; 9.428) and Scylla, "an evil monster" (πέλωρ κακόν; 12.87).[79] Likewise, Penelope dreams that

[75] Some later traditions held that Odysseus was actually the bastard son of the famous trickster Sisyphus; see Gantz (1996: 175–176).
[76] Buchan (2004: 135) observes that, when Athena exhorts Odysseus to prepare to fight the suitors, she couches it in terms reminiscent of a heroic contest (*aethlos*), a cattle raid: even if he were facing fifty battalions of men, he would drive away their cattle and sheep (*Od.* 20.49–51).
[77] *Od.* 13.429–438, 16.172–185, 16.454–459, 23.156–163; cf. 16.207–212.
[78] Heath (2005) examines archaic and classical Greek thinking about the difference between humans and animals, focusing in particular on the importance of speech and silence; for his discussion of the *Odyssey*, see ibid. (39–118).
[79] The Greek adjective πέλωρος, and its nominal form πέλωρ, denote a "prodigy" or "monster" (as Liddell and Scott's lexicon [LSJ⁹] charmingly notes, "mostly in a bad sense"); see LSJ⁹ s.v. πέλωρ, πελώριος, and πέλωρος, as well as Heubeck and Hoekstra (1989: 242).

an eagle kills twenty geese and declares itself a portent of Odysseus' imminent return home and the death of her suitors (19.535–553).

Intriguingly, Homer compares Odysseus' heart to "a bitch, standing
over her feeble puppies, [who] barks at a strange man and rages to fight"
(ὡς δὲ κύων ἀμαλῇσι περὶ σκυλάκεσσι βεβῶσα / ἄνδρ᾽ ἀγνοιήσασ᾽ ὑλάει
μέμονέν τε μάχεσθαι; 20.14–15). Immediately following the simile,
Odysseus exhorts his heart to "endure" (τέτλαθι δή, κραδίη; 20.18), as if
he must master "a monster inside [his] chest" (to quote Ripley).[80] We
might say that Odysseus here resonates with two characters in *AR*: Ripley
in her struggle to understand her hybridity;[81] and Purvis (played by
Leland Orser), in whom an Alien embryo has been implanted and whose
ability to exercise self-mastery over the monster in his chest is crucial to
his survival and ability to kill Dr. Wren in revenge for the implantation.
It is perhaps no coincidence that Odysseus also reminds his doglike
(Scylla-like?) heart of its endurance in the cave of another human/ani-
mal hybrid, the anthropophagic Cyclops (20.18–21), inviting the comparison between his heart/himself and the Cyclops while asserting his
mastery over the monster within himself.[82]

The precise contours of Odysseus' humanity when he reaches home,
then, are indeed questionable. Perhaps no single deed exemplifies this
better than Odysseus' murder of the suitors and execution of the maidservants. Noting the general condemnation of murder throughout the
Odyssey, Robin Hankey observes:

Odysseus is the human being who kills by far the most fellow humans in the
whole epic. His revenge is nothing short of a bloody massacre or atrocity. . . .

---

[80] On this passage, as well as passages related to the monstrosity of the Cyclops
throughout the *Odyssey*, see Clare (1998: esp. 2).

[81] Exemplary is the mess hall scene, during which Wren expresses his intention of
taming the Aliens. Ripley's reply ("Roll over, play dead. Heel? . . . You can't teach it
tricks") exposes the disjunction between Wren's expectation (the Aliens can be treated
like dogs) and the reality (the Aliens cannot be tamed but will turn on the scientists).
Wren replies, "Why not? We're teaching you," attempting to cage Ripley within the same
logic (Ripley = Alien = dog).

[82] "Doglike" could also positively evoke the faithful patience of the hero's aged dog,
Argus, who dies upon recognizing the returning Odysseus in disguise (*Od*. 17.317–360).
On the hero's self-control in the second half of the *Odyssey*, see, e.g., Segal (1992: 492,
514–517), who argues that, in contrast to the murderous feasting of the Cyclops, as well
as the bloody revenge envisioned by Athena (*Od*. 13.395–396), Odysseus exhibits some
concern for piety in his murder of the suitors (22.411–416, 480–481); Segal nevertheless

Not only does Odysseus himself kill the leading suitors and many others, he knowingly and mercilessly kills an apparently quite genuine suppliant . . . personally orders the torture of Melanthius in meticulous detail . . . personally orders the execution of the disloyal slave women. . . . It is appropriate that, when the killings have ended, Odysseus is described as spattered in blood and gore, hands and feet alike, like a lion that has eaten an ox ([22.]402–406). The picture sums up the inhuman savagery of the whole revenge.[83]

Nor does the death of the suitors end Odysseus' killing spree. Once they learn of their children's murder, the parents of the suitors lead an (unsuccessful) attack against Odysseus, Telemachus, and Laertes (24.413–548). It requires the intervention of Athena to force the Ithacans to relent from battle (24.528–536); in contrast, to stop Odysseus from attacking, "screaming in his fury like a lofty eagle" (οἴμησεν δε ἀλεὶς ὥς τ' αἰετὸς ὑψιπετήεις; 24.538),[84] there must come both a threat from Athena (24.539–544) and a thunderbolt cast down by Zeus (24.539–540). Animal-like and godlike in his bloody vengeance, the ethical hybrid Odysseus—indeed, the action of the poem itself—can only be stopped through the intervention of the king of the gods, the arbiter of order in the *kosmos*.

The ethically hybrid hero in the *Odyssey* ultimately problematizes the poem's very attempt to define "man." In the proem, Odysseus is indeed a moving target, "a man of many turns" (ἄνδρα... πολύτροπον; 1.1), not just because of his many travels, his cunning intelligence, and his physical transformations, but also in his ethical orientation, shifting between man, god, and animal. Odysseus even becomes "NoMan" (Οὖτις ἐμοί γ' ὄνομα, 9.366–367), negating identity and self in order to survive the encounter with the Cyclops. Mark Buchan has suggested that the failure to name Odysseus in the proem points to the hero's resistance to classification, arguing that "man" (ἄνδρα) is "radically inassimilable to sense, to language," and that such resistance to classification equates the hero with death, itself unknowable.[85] Odysseus may not be Hades or death itself, but, like the hybrids Ripley and *Auriga* in *AR*, he delineates the

---

maintains that, despite such piety, "the possibility of a surd, malevolent, amoral blocking force or of uncontrollable violence . . . never fully disappears" (517).

[83] Hankey (1990: 92–93). In the *Penelopiad*, Atwood (2005) gives voice to the dozen (disloyal?) maidservants whom Odysseus orders to be executed; cf. Brown (2012).

[84] Stanford (1962: 430) compares Odysseus here to "a berserk Norseman."

[85] Buchan (2004: 139). For fuller discussion of the links between the *polytropos* hero, Hermes, and Hades, see ibid. (136–141).

end(s) of humanity for countless other characters, becoming a harbinger of death and slaughter. Although most members of his own household survive (including his son Telemachus), the returning king
commits an egregious act of murder; his victims, the suitors, comprise
more than one hundred youths of the next generation. Much as "mother"
Ripley kills the Aliens and the Newborn in order to guarantee that she
reaches home, so, too, does "father" Odysseus wipe out an entire generation of Cephellanian nobility, as well as many of their parents, in order
to guarantee his *nostos*. As Buchan eloquently puts it, "[h]is survival is
dependent . . . on the failure of others to survive."[86]

I do not intend in this chapter to exonerate the suitors, whose reckless
behavior in wooing Odysseus' wife (ἀτασθαλίαι; *Od.* 21.146)[87] and
offenses against *xenia* (the "guest–host relationship" that protects
strangers and guests) threaten the social ideology Homer seems to promote.[88] From Odysseus' perspective, the suitors not only resemble the
monstrous Cyclops, but, perhaps more terrifyingly, point to the unre-
solved contradiction between "civilized" and "Other" represented by
the Laestrygonians (10.80–132), who inhabit the far edges of the world
and are so culturally illegible to Odysseus' men that these giant canni-
bals are able to annihilate Odysseus' crew, destroying eleven of his
twelve ships and killing hundreds of men.[89] Nevertheless, in his slaughter of the suitors, Odysseus not only violates the communal values of
xenia (killing his guests), but himself becomes culturally illegible and

---

[86] Buchan (2004: 142).

[87] For accusations of suitors' recklessness, see also *Od.* 23.67, 24.458.

[88] Hankey (1990: 91–5) notes that the several justifications for the murder of the suitors in the *Odyssey*: (1) the suitors have committed offenses against *xenia*, domestic fidelity, due honor and respect, and Odysseus' property; (2) the murder of the suitors brings
Odysseus glory akin to that gained by Orestes, who (as we are repeatedly told throughout
the *Odyssey*) avenged the murder of his father Agamemnon, a war veteran also killed
upon his return home; (3) the heroic ethos allows vengeance, for "helping one's friends
and harming one's enemies"; (4) Homer depicts the gods as approving Odysseus' actions.

[89] The Laestrygonians have no tilled fields or pastures (*Od.* 10.98), but they do use fire
(as suggested by smoke, 99) and a spring (105–107), and possess sufficient social organization for a city (104–105, 118), marketplace or place of assembly (114), a lofty royal palace
(111–112), and collective military action (118–122). They seem to Odysseus' men to practice *xenia* (111), but much like the famous *Twilight Zone* episode "To Serve Man" (Bare
1962), the Laestrygonians do not serve ("assist"), but rather serve ("eat") their guests
(116). Cf. Clare (1998), who observes a broad similarity between the Cyclops and
Laestrygonian episodes, yet argues that the difference in the stories generates "shock
value" for the monstrosity of the Laestrygonian episode (8).

unrecognizable, a human being most capable (in Hankey's words) of "inhuman savagery." In the course of his homecoming, Odysseus internalizes the "eat or be eaten" ethos of the Cyclops and the Laestrygonians, as if—heedless of Nietzsche's warning in the epigraph—he has stared into the abyss and become the very monsters he once saw and fought. Here the "companion" figures of Ripley and Odysseus converge, pointing to an unsettling possibility: the hybrid hero, the embodiment of humanity's uncertain and often dangerous shape in its relentless journey forward in space and time, comes as a harbinger exposing the fiction of "homecoming" itself, the fiction of returning without serious, even deadly, consequence for individual, collective, and human "homes."

11

Classical Antiquity and Western Identity in *Battlestar Galactica*

Vincent Tomasso

In the first season of the science fiction (SF) television series *Battlestar Galactica* (2003–2009 [*BSG*]), Lieutenant Kara "Starbuck" Thrace travels to the planet Caprica in order to obtain the Arrow of Apollo ("Kobol's Last Gleaming, Parts I and II," 1.14–15).[1] She undertakes this mission on the orders of President Laura Roslin, who, inspired by a prophecy in the sacred Book of Pythia, believes that the Arrow will show them the way to Earth and, ultimately, the salvation of humankind. Caprica is a charred wasteland, having been devastated by nuclear weapons used by the Cylons, the robot civilization that annihilated much of human society at the start of the series. The Arrow is housed in the Delphi Museum of the Gods, which Thrace finds in ruins: rubble

[1] I would like to thank Brett M. Rogers and Benjamin Eldon Stevens for organizing the innovative panel (American Philological Association, San Antonio, Texas, 2011) from which this chapter originated, and for making helpful comments on drafts. Audience members at that meeting and at a version of this chapter presented at Stanford University responded thoughtfully. Mark Pyzyk, Toph Marshall, and Erin Pitt read and commented on drafts at various stages. Two anonymous readers for the Press raised stimulating questions and issues. Any remaining infelicities are my own.

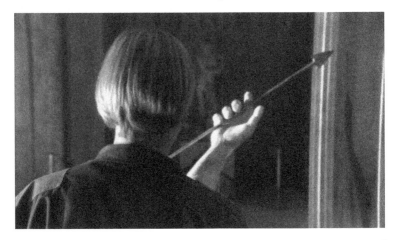

Figure 11-1 Kara "Starbuck" Thrace prepares to take the Arrow of Apollo from its display in the Delphi Museum of the Gods. From Michael Rymer, dir. 2005. "Kobol's Last Gleaming Part II," *Battlestar Galactica*, NBC Universal.

strewn on its front steps and throughout its galleries, exhibits smashed and mutilated, and broken pipes leaking water. It has become a tomb for religious artifacts, many of which, though badly damaged, are vaguely identifiable as statues and vases from classical antiquity.[2] From these ruins Thrace is able to retrieve the Arrow (as seen in Figure 11-1), which is a key step in the teleology of the series: the search for an inhabitable planet and the resolution of the endless cycle of violence between humans and Cylons.

This scene demonstrates how *BSG* meditates on the construction and meaning of human, and more particularly Western, identity via classical antiquity. Humans in the series articulate their identities in part through religion, which is predicated on what the series' audience associates with classical myths. Using classical myths in this way creates what literary critic Darko Suvin calls "cognitive estrangement," a central aspect of the SF genre as he defines it: "SF is, then, a literary genre whose necessary and sufficient conditions are the presence and interaction of estrangement and cognition, and whose main formal device is an

---

[2] This depiction of classical ruins is a prevalent motif in SF; see Brown (2008: 416–422).

imaginative framework alternative to the author's empirical environment."[3] "Estrangement" means that the text's narrative universe is distanced from the audience's knowledge of their own world—that there are some similarities with the "real" world, but also a "new set of norms."[4] "Cognitive" means that the estrangement impels the audience to reflect on the differences between their world and the narrative world. *BSG*'s cognitive estrangement is achieved via a setting distant in time and place from the audience's own, populated by beings whose culture and society are both similar to and different from the audience's, as well as a variety of technological factors that have parallels in the audience's world, especially space travel and the creation of artificial intelligence that becomes self-aware. Indeed, the finale strongly implies that the latter process is already underway in the audience's contemporary world through footage of various kinds of robots, including one that mimics the human form and appearance very closely.[5] In short, *BSG*'s cognitive estrangement causes the audience simultaneously to identify with and to be distanced from the series' human culture.

In this chapter, I argue that *BSG* uses cognitive estrangement to give its audience a broader perspective on themselves and their Western identity, and that this perspective is informed by the series' message that the mythic approach to the universe, rather than the cognitive one, will save humanity.[6] Classical antiquity is thus positioned in a complex way as both a source of salvation through its myths, and a source of destruction through ancient Greece's cognitive inquiry and Rome's decadence. This attitude reflects uncertainties about the Western tradition and its future role in the formation of identity.

BSG aired for four seasons on the SyFy cable channel from 2003 to 2009. It is a reimagining by Ronald Moore of a 1978 television series of

---

[3] Suvin (1979: 7–8). Despite Suvin's language, SF is not limited to literature; see Roberts (2006a: 2), who argues that the genre is a "cultural discourse" that includes literature, television programs, films, comic books, and video games.

[4] Suvin (1979: 6).

[5] One of the pieces of footage is stamped with the MSNBC logo, a global television news channel in the audience's world.

[6] I have borrowed the terms "mythic" and "cognitive" from Suvin's definition of the SF genre's approach to the universe (1979: 7): "The myth is diametrically opposed to the cognitive approach since it conceives human relations as fixed and supernaturally determined. . . . Conversely, SF . . . focuses on the variable and future-bearing element from the empirical environment. . . ."

the same name and premise that was created by Glen Larson; this chapter will focus on the later series exclusively.[7] The narrative of Moore's series begins with the destruction of a human civilization called "the Colonies" by the Cylons, a society of robotic organisms that were created by humans as servants. The nuclear attack is the culmination of several years of conflict between the two sides after the Cylons became self-aware and waged war on the Colonies. The series chronicles the journey of the attack's survivors in a fleet of spacecraft composed of the military ship *Galactica* and a number of civilian ships as they try to find another inhabitable space while surviving the pursuit of the Cylons.

The Colonials are polytheists, worshipping beings that they call the Lords of Kobol, whose basic attributes, spheres of influence, and relationships with one another are almost identical to those that are attributed to the deities depicted in classical myths. For instance, the call sign of Lee Adama, a high-ranking Colonial officer, is "Apollo," whom another character identifies as a son of Zeus, "good with a bow, god of the hunt, and also of healing" ("Bastille Day," 1.3); similarly, various classical texts also attribute these characteristics to the Greek and Roman god Apollo.[8] Gods mentioned and/or directly worshipped in the series are Aphrodite, Apollo, Ares, Artemis, Asclepius, Athena, Aurora, Hera, Poseidon, and Zeus (which we see, for example, in Figure 11-2). Characters call these deities by their ancient Greek names almost exclusively, but in a few cases they use the Roman equivalent. "Aurora" is the Roman name for the goddess of the dawn (Grk. "Eos"); and although characters most often refer to the king of the gods as "Zeus" and the god of war as "Ares," in a few cases they use the Roman equivalents "Jupiter" and "Mars." These exceptional cases could be mistakes made by the producers and writers, but they also demonstrate that in American popular culture ancient Greece

---

[7] *Caprica* (2010) and *Blood and Chrome* (2012) are prequel series to the reimagined *BSG* that exist within the same narrative continuity but deal with somewhat different issues; this chapter does not take them into account.

[8] Another instance of this phenomenon is in the episode "The Passage" (3.10), when a Cylon Hybrid calls the Eye of Jupiter "the eye of the husband of the eye of the cow." Gaius Baltar deduces that the latter part of this riddling description alludes to "Hera, sometimes referred to as 'cow-eyed Hera'." This is a common description, or epithet, of the goddess in classical texts (βοῶπις in Greek), which demonstrates the complex nature of Moore and his team's engagement with classical antiquity.

Figure 11-2 Kara "Starbuck" Thrace prays to statuettes of Artemis and Athena. From Brad Turner, dir. 2004. "Flesh and Bone," *Battlestar Galactica*, NBC Universal.

and Rome are often conflated. For this reason I speak of *BSG*'s engagement with classical antiquity, classical myths, and the classical tradition generally rather than with ancient Greece specifically.

The series' connection with classical antiquity extends beyond narrative to practice. Oracles—Colonial religious personnel who are integral to the teleology of the series—articulate knowledge received from the Lords of Kobol in much the same way as oracles did in classical myth and ancient life.[9] In the episode "Exodus, Part I" (3.3), the Colonial oracle Dodona Selloi plays an important role. Her name is derived from the ancient site of an oracle of Zeus in northwestern Greece, and the names of the priests who worked there. The Greek warrior Achilles describes Dodona in Book 16 of Homer's *Iliad* (*Il.*): "Zeus, Pelasgian lord of <u>Dodona</u>, dwelling far away, ruler of wintry <u>Dodona</u>, around you the <u>Selloi</u> dwell, oracles with unwashed feet who sleep on the ground" (Ζεῦ ἄνα <u>Δωδωναῖε</u> Πελασγικὲ τηλόθι ναίων / <u>Δωδώνης</u> μεδέων δυσχειμέρου, ἀμφὶ δὲ <u>Σελλοὶ</u> / σοὶ ναίουσ' ὑποφῆται / ἀνιπτόποδες χαμαιεῦναι; 233–235). Dodona Selloi connects Colonial spirituality and the classical legacy it represents with the future survival of mankind when she prophesies about Hera Agathon,

[9] For an in-depth look at oracles in the ancient Greek world, see Burkert (1985: 114–118).

a human-Cylon hybrid child who will be central to the conclusion of the series. Although long deceased by the time the series begins, the Pythia is another oracle whose advice Laura Roslin, the President of the Colonies, follows ardently. The Pythia's writings in the Sacred Scrolls guide Roslin, just as in antiquity the Pythia's prophecies at Apollo's temple at Delphi in northern Greece guided visiting suppliants; they are also similar to the Sibylline books consulted by the Romans.

The Lords of Kobol and the myths about them are important aspects of Colonial identity for many characters in the series, including non-humans. To Sharon Agathon, a Cylon who falls in love with, marries, and has a child with Colonial captain Karl Agathon, Colonial religion is a bridge between the world that she wishes to leave and the one she wishes to enter. In the second season, she joins Karl on the *Galactica* but is promptly thrown into the brig because the crew do not trust her. When Commander William Adama realizes that Sharon can be a useful ally in a rescue operation, he officially commissions her as an officer (in the episode "Precipice," 3.2). In spite of this, the majority of the human crew still does not trust her, and throughout the rest of the series Sharon suffers from periodic racist attacks, though it is clear that she has gained some status in human eyes when she takes on a traditional pilot call sign. In the episode "Torn" (3.6), Karl solicits a call sign for his wife from their fellow officers. Sharon settles on Brendan Costanza's proposal of "Athena": "You know—the goddess of wisdom and war, usually accompanied by the goddess of victory?" This moment demonstrates the important role that Colonial religion and myth can play in some segments of Colonial society. Before this moment, Sharon was counted among the humans' antagonists, a status that begins to change with Adama's official recognition of her as an ally. Yet she embraces her new human identity fully only when she takes on the name of a divinity worshiped by her race's enemies. The question of belief is irrelevant here: what matters is that Colonial myths are supporting the formation of a human identity; thus they are cultural markers rather than markers of belief, necessarily.

Not all Colonial officers view these myths positively, and there is a wide spectrum of belief among both the civilian and military populations, from atheists like Commander William Adama, to ardent believers like Roslin, to the cautiously faithful like Thrace, to opportunists like Gaius Baltar. Some characters vociferously assert their skepticism of religion and the myths that accompany it. When Roslin, guided by the mythic hermeneutic, suggests that a myth about the Arrow of Apollo detailed in Colonial scripture will be the key to the fleet's salvation, in keeping with the cognitive hermeneutic Adama protests, "they're just stories, myths, legends. Don't let it blind you to the reality we face" ("Kobol's Last Gleaming," 1.12). Despite his dim view of the truth-value of such narratives and skepticism toward the mythic approach that they support, however, Adama nevertheless uses these same stories to achieve his own ends. In the second episode of the miniseries, he recites the legend of Earth from the Book of Pythia in order to give the fleet purpose, despite his later revelation to Roslin that he does not believe in the planet's existence.[10] Whatever the beliefs held by individuals, Colonial myths are used to direct the teleology of the series, demonstrating that they are an important and defining part of human culture in the series.

These references to classical myth are recognizable to the target audience on some level as a result of the Western production and reception context of *BSG*. SyFy is an American cable channel owned by the large American media conglomerate the National Broadcasting Company (NBC). The creator of the series, Ronald Moore, is an American, as are the writers. Most of the cast members are North Americans, and most of the filming was done in British Columbia, Canada. The target audience of SyFy is primarily in the English-speaking Western world: the United States, Canada, the United Kingdom, and Australia. Audiences in these countries tend to be somewhat familiar with classical myths through modern retellings like Edith Hamilton's *Mythology* (1942), Ingri and Edgar Parin d'Aulaires' *Book of Greek Myths* (1962), and Bernard Evslin's *Heroes, Gods, and Monsters of the Greek Myths* (1966), which are used frequently in secondary and post-secondary education.[11] The ubiquity of classical myths in modern popular culture similarly attests to their popularity.[12]

BSG's inclusion of classical myths into the belief system of a society as technologically advanced as the Colonies allows the series to explore the ontology and future of humanity via the conflict between the mythic hermeneutic (represented by the classical tradition) and the cognitive

---

[10] Ironically, Pythia's prophecy about Earth turns out to be true in the final episodes.

[11] Meckler (2006: 10, 176).

[12] Recent, high-profile film releases include *Clash of the Titans* (Leterrier, 2010), *Immortals* (Singh, 2011), and *Wrath of the Titans* (Liebesman, 2012). Classical myths have also formed the basis for highly successful television programs like *Hercules: the Legendary Journeys* (1995–1999) and *Xena: Warrior Princess* (1995–2001).

hermeneutic (represented by SF). The classical tradition, in which cultural products created after antiquity refer to or adapt the worlds of ancient Greece and Rome, on the surface contrasts with SF. Whereas the former looks to the past in order to bring the present into better focus, SF speculates based on the scientific methodology so characteristic of the modern period to make sense of the present moment.[13] While some scholars trace the roots of SF as far back as the Greek writer Lucian's second century C.E. satire *True Histories* (and in a few cases, to the one of the oldest Greek texts we have, Homer's *Odyssey*), in modern popular culture SF is usually associated with modern scientific and technological advancement.[14] Although, as the chapters in this volume show, SF has deep connections with antiquity,[15] for modern audiences the classical tradition and SF nevertheless appear to be on opposite ends of history, since the latter is predicated on the conditions that belong to or stem from the audience's own moment, whereas the former is predicated on the cultural conditions that prevailed thousands of years ago.[16] I want to stress that popular culture often *imposes* this opposition between the classical tradition and SF; the two modes of thought are in fact quite similar, since both strategies reflect the concerns of the present by reflecting on another time period.[17]

---

[13] Franklin (1978: vii) argues that the SF genre results from the mindset created by the rapid and continual scientific and technological progress at the start of the Industrial Revolution. Cf. Suvin (1979: 64–65): "[t]he *novum* is postulated on and validated by the post-Cartesian and post-Baconian scientific *method*" [emphasis in the original].

[14] See Suvin (1979: x, 87, and 97–98) and Georgiadou and Larmour (1998: 45–48) for assessment of and further bibliography on Lucian's place in science fictional genealogies. See also Rogers and Stevens (2012a: 141–142), who argue that we might search for common strategies between classical texts like Homer's *Odyssey* and Lucian's *True Histories* and SF, rather than a literal origin. For a connection between Lucian and a particular modern exemplar, H. G. Wells, see Keen (this volume, chapter four).

[15] Witness the subtitle of Mary Shelley's *Frankenstein; or, The Modern Prometheus*, on which see Rogers and Stevens (2012a: 127–129); cf. their introduction to this volume. I would argue however that part of the pleasure for the reader here is the *frisson* generated by the juxtaposition of title and subtitle.

[16] Bukatman (1993: 4) further links technology to the American ideal of progress: "Technology . . . defines the American relation to manifest destiny and the commitment to an ideology of progress and modernity."

[17] Cf. the formulation of the relationship between past, present, and future in SF by Rogers and Stevens (2012a: 129): "modern SF has, from its very beginnings, as it were looked forward to the future and around at the present *in part* by looking further back. . . ." (emphasis mine). Cf. also Brown (2008: 416), who states that there is "an obvious ostensible mismatch between the 'classics' (high status, elite, *ancient*) and SF (low status, popular, *modern*) . . ." (emphases mine).

This artificial division between classical tradition (ancient) and SF (modern) is sometimes conceptualized as a series of negotiations that occurs within the SF genre itself between two approaches to understanding what it means to be human in the wider universe. The mythic hermeneutic is rooted in knowledge obtained through supernatural sources, religious practice, and tradition, while the cognitive hermeneutic derives from empirical knowledge, scientific methodology, and progress. Mendlesohn argues that, in the twentieth century, SF "treated [religion] . . . with at best polite contempt: religion was essentially of the 'Other,' the backward and primitive. . .."[18] In science fictional receptions of classical antiquity, this conflict is often presented as the myth-obsessed ancient Greek and Roman cultures, which worshipped fickle and jealous deities, versus cognitive modern cultures, which are "enlightened" about the nature of the universe through empirical observation. Of course this dichotomy is not an accurate representation of reality—after all, ancient Greek philosophy and science were the precursors of modern scientific methodology, and likewise there are modern myths—but this is often the *popular* perception of the conflict in SF.

An example is the 1967 episode of *Star Trek: The Original Series* "Who Mourns for Adonais?" (2.2), in which Captain Kirk and crew encounter a being that claims to be the god Apollo.[19] The crew determines that Apollo is a member of an alien race that visited Earth 5,000 years previously and used their technological knowledge to elicit worship from the ancient Greeks. In the conclusion of the episode, Kirk disavows Apollo, and the alien perishes.[20] After Apollo's death, Kirk reflects that the

[18] Mendlesohn (2003b: 264). Cf. Roberts (2006a: 3), who locates the genesis of SF in the conflict between science and religion: "The specificity of this fantasy is determined by the cultural and historical circumstances of the genre's birth: the Protestant Reformation, and a cultural dialectic between 'Protestant' rationalist post-Copernican science on the one hand, and 'Catholic' theology, magic and mysticism, on the other." Roberts also identifies the genre along a continuum spanning the avowedly realistic ("hard SF") and the completely mystical (fantasy). The conclusion of *BSG* causes the series to fall closer to the latter category, but it was still very much on the SF continuum for the majority of its run.

[19] The title of the episode is derived from Percy Bysshe Shelley's 1821 poem "Adonais." Some scholars have thought that Shelley's title is a merging of the name "Adonis," the Greek youth who is a lover of Aphrodite and killed out of jealousy by Ares, and the Hebrew word "Adonai," which means "Lord"; see, e.g., Wasserman (1959: 311–312). On the episode, see further Kovacs (this volume, chapter nine).

[20] Kirk's rejection of Apollo is mysterious: "Mankind has no need for gods. We find the one quite adequate." The philosophy implicit in this statement is never elaborated,

Greek "gods" were important: "Much of our culture and philosophy
came from a worship of those beings." In this vision of the glorious and
progressive future, humans have no more place for the mythic approach,
despite the acknowledged fact that this system eventually allowed culture (and by implication, science) to advance. Ancient Greek religion
and myth are important stepping stones that humanity no longer
needs—indeed, they literally threaten to halt the *Enterprise*'s mission
"to seek out new life and new civilizations" and to trap Kirk and company in the unenlightened and servile past.

"Who Mourns for Adonais?" is pertinent to the present argument
because of its influence on Ronald Moore, the creator of the reimagined
BSG. Moore was a fan of *Star Trek* as a young man and became a writer
for three subsequent series, *Star Trek: the Next Generation* (1987–1994),
Deep Space Nine (1993–1999), and *Voyager* (1995–2001).[21] As a result, he
studied and absorbed *Star Trek*'s attitudes and philosophies, and *BSG* is
in part his response to those worldviews. Whereas *Star Trek* in general
praises the cognitive hermeneutic over the mythic one, Moore's series
does the reverse; not only is the cognitive approach viewed negatively
because it is responsible for the creation of the Cylons and the near-total
destruction of humanity, but the mythic approach is an integral part of
the series' teleology.

The mythic hermeneutic in *BSG* is advocated by a group of Colonials,
the most prominent of whom is Laura Roslin, the President of the Colonies.
She uses Colonial myths, via scripture and artifacts, to make sense of the
post-apocalyptic universe. The series consistently validates the mythic
mode of interpretation because it plays a crucial role in the search for and
ultimate discovery of a new home after the destruction and occupation of
the Colonies. By contrast, the cognitive hermeneutic is embraced by
William Adama, the military commander of the fleet, who explicitly
rejects myth as an approach to solving problems and understanding
humanity's place in the universe.[22] The exponents of these two extremes

---

but one possibility is that the writer/producers formulated it to placate the majority
Christian audience members while also expressing a kind of pantheistic view of the universe; cf. Asa (1999: 45), who dismisses the implications of the comment. The creator of
the series, Gene Roddenberry, was in any case an avowed atheist; see Pearson (1999: 14).

[21] Cf. Porter and McLaren (1999b: 2–3).

[22] Pache considers classical reception in the series primarily with regard to the
romantic relationship between Adama and Roslin. She analyzes the figure of Adama

frequently clash over how to proceed. The opening of this chapter contains an example of this clash: Roslin is guided by the priestess Elosha to seek the Arrow of Apollo that the Sacred Scrolls claim will point the way to Earth ("Kobol's Last Gleaming, Part I," 1.12). Adama forbids this, but Roslin secretly orders Lieutenant Kara Thrace to retrieve the Arrow. Because she directly contravened his orders and subverted one of his officers, Adama removes Roslin from the presidency, and the conflict between these two characters is a major plot line in the first half of the second season. Eventually, a team from the *Galactica* successfully uses the Arrow to open the Tomb of Athena on the planet Kobol ("Home, Part II," 2.7), which correctly identifies the next stop in the search as the Eye of Jupiter, an astronomical phenomenon that directs the Colonials to the Ionian Nebula, a supernova remnant near Earth. These events validate the mythic hermeneutic that Roslin ascribes to, as opposed to the cognitive approach that Adama propounds. Without the Sacred Scrolls, the Arrow of Apollo, and the Eye of Jupiter, Earth would never have been discovered.[23] In fact, without Colonial myth and religion, Earth might have never been a goal for the fleet in the first place. There is no empirical knowledge about the existence of Earth at the opening of the series; it is a matter of faith in the Sacred Scrolls, the Colonials' book of scripture, which contain the legend of Earth.

The cognitive hermeneutic loses out in the struggle between Adama and Roslin, and this valorization of the mythic hermeneutic occurs in many other places in the series. Science is responsible for the major problems of the narrative: scientists created the Cylons, nuclear weapons annihilated Colonial civilization, and the Colonies' most prominent scientist, Gaius Baltar, allowed the Cylons to penetrate Colonial defenses.[24] All of these negative connotations, combined with the

---

through Aeneas, and of Roslin through Dido, to argue that *BSG* is "a feminized version of Virgil's *Aeneid* that focuses on love and compromise as the basis of the new empire" (2010: 132). Other sources for aspects of *BSG* have been identified in Hesiod's *Theogony* and *Works and Days* (Garvey 2014) and, indirectly, Xenophon's *Anabasis* (L'Allier 2014); see generally Bataille (2014).

[23] The first Earth that the Colonials reach is a barren planet that has been destroyed by nuclear war. The second, inhabitable Earth is discovered only through the intervention of Thrace, who is implied to be an angel of "God," the all-powerful being behind the events of the series that is identifiable neither as the Cylon God nor as the lords of Kobol. Thus Earth is finally attained through a non-Colonial spiritual force, but the mythic approach was necessary to get the fleet to the point where Thrace could intervene.

[24] On the subject of the series' depiction of scientists, particularly Baltar, see Jowett (2008).

success of Roslin's mythic hermeneutic, lead to a controversial move in the finale. Lee Adama pathologizes technology and boldly suggests that the Colonials destroy all of their equipment and begin their new lives on Earth *tabula rasa*. This suggestion represents the ultimate triumph of mythic over cognitive hermeneutics: "our brains have always outraced our hearts. Our science charges ahead, but our souls lag behind. Let's start anew" ("Daybreak, Part II," 4.20). Following Lee's advice, the Colonials send all of their technology into the sun and provide the indigenous humans with language ("we can give them the best part of ourselves")—and presumably the culture that is implied by language. This solution to the considerable problems posed throughout the series has angered many critics, but in some ways it is a valid response to the frustrating cycle the Colonials find themselves trapped in.[25] If technology is what renews the destructive cycle, it is logical that the cycle will be broken if technology is abandoned. The final moments of the finale, in which modern American society is on the same brink of total collapse because of its heedless pursuit of (robotic) technology, call into question the success of Lee's plan. In *BSG*'s vision of history, the route to humanity's salvation is the mythic one, not technological progress—even though the latter resulted from the materialist inquiries made by Greek philosophers who participated in the same culture that also invested in the mythic approach. Although the Colonials attempted to jettison technology, humans eventually discovered it again, due in part to ancient Greece's contributions. By locating humanity's downfall in science and technology and its salvation in spirituality, *BSG* positions the classical past as simultaneously solution and problem.

The series creates this picture of classical antiquity by causing its audience both to identify with and to be distanced from Colonial religion. Identification encourages the audience to see similarities between themselves and the Colonials, while distancing provides them with a broader perspective on their own identities. We have already seen how Colonial religion creates identification through its strong associations with classical myth, but identification is also achieved through the religion's differences from ancient Greek and Roman religions. While

---

[25] Stoy and Kaveney (2010) have made the most vitriolic outbursts regarding the finale. Kaveney (2010) criticizes the series on the basis of her own definition of SF ("literature of reason, not faith"; 230) and on the notion that the episode was the result of lazy writers.

classical myths are familiar to Western audiences, ancient religions, with their extensive use of sacrifice and lack of organizational structures and dogmatic religious texts, are not. Colonial religious practices are modeled on those of modern Judaism and Christianity. For instance, the personnel consists of priests, priestesses, brothers, and sisters; priests wear stoles and brothers wear black habits; and Galen Tyrol sees Brother Cavil for a version of confession ("Lay Down Your Burdens, Part I," 2.19). Moore and his team did not use classical religious practices as the basis for Colonial religious practices, probably because doing so would distance the audience too much. *BSG*'s combination of classical myths with modern religious rituals incorporates classical antiquity into a future human culture that Moore's audience could recognize and identify with to some extent.[26] Colonial culture is not ancient Greece or Rome, nor is it any modern Western culture; it is an amalgam of all of these cultures and thus signifies Western-ness on an abstract level.

The audience is distanced through Colonial religion's most central feature, polytheism. The Cylons, by contrast, are monotheists: the Cylon God is omnipotent and omniscient, his worshippers spread his gospel, and he is equated with love and salvation from sin.[27] Because Western cultures are heavily influenced by Judeo-Christian thought—whether audience members identify themselves as members of those faiths or not is irrelevant—this aspect of Cylon culture creates some measure of identification. Both Colonials and Cylons thus evoke identification and distancing, a situation that Marshall and Potter analyze in terms of American and Muslim identities in the first decade of the twenty-first century.[28] They conclude that Colonials and Cylons embody different aspects of these two groups at different points in the series, a situation that destabilizes the audience's assumptions about their own identities. This is similar to what I am saying about the series' use of cognitive

[26] A misunderstanding of this may lie behind the criticism of Stoy (2010): "the odd and ultimately pointless use of Greek and Roman deities to stand in for the Colonial ones . . ." (20). Although she never fully explains what she means by this, her comment suggests that she feels that classical myths were tacked onto a Judeo-Christian system of religious practices without deep significance for the narrative or for the audience. Cf. Ryman (2010: 41): "The few concessions to [the SF] setting are inexpensive substitutes. . . . These fool no one; and are readable as jokes."

[27] Six: "Don't you understand? God is love" (Miniseries). Cf. 1 John 4:8: "God is love" (ὁ θεὸς ἀγάπη ἐστίν).

[28] Marshall and Potter (2014).

estrangement through classical antiquity: the audience's identification with and estrangement from Colonial culture result in a broadened perspective on the audiences' Western identities.

Sandra Joshel and her co-authors write in the introduction to *Imperial Projections* that this principle also holds true for cinematic receptions of ancient Rome: "popular representations allow audiences simultaneously to distance themselves from that past and to identify with it."[29] This similarity makes SF's receptions of the classics as worthy of analysis as cinema's, but it is important to note that the two phenomena are not exactly parallel. Joshel's cinematic receptions allow for both identification and estrangement in order to confirm the present audience's notions of self, whereas SF (and *BSG*'s reception of antiquity) does this in order to cause the audience to reexamine their preconceived ideas about their own identities. The series encourages its audience to both identify with and be estranged from the classical tradition to give them a different perspective on the Western tradition that informs their identities. Cognitive estrangement thus paves the way for the audience to accept one of the ultimate messages of the series: that humanity must embrace a mythic approach to the universe in order to break the historical cycle of destruction, which has been exacerbated by the cognitive approach based on science and technology.

Although the Colonials' mythic hermeneutic points the way to a future, it cannot ensure that future because it is incapable of ending the cycle of violence by itself. Although science certainly contributed to it, the conflicting religious systems of Cylons and Colonials are also at the heart of the problem. The solution, the series ultimately posits, is hybridity, which is embodied in Hera Agathon, the child of Colonial Karl Agathon and Cylon Sharon. Despite the hybridity of Hera's human and Cylon DNA, her name derives solely from Colonial myth and culture: her first name is identical with the name of Zeus' wife, and her last name means "good" in ancient Greek.[30] We learn in the finale that Hera is absolutely critical to the survival of humanity. In "Daybreak, Parts I and II" (3.19–20), the Colonials reach Earth and merge with the native population, a very early form of *Homo sapiens*. The narrative skips

---

[29] Joshel, Malamud, and Wyke (2001: 4); cf. Brown (2008: 416).
[30] Agathon is the first name of a Greek tragic poet of the mid-to-late fifth century B.C.E. It may resonate for a modern Western audience familiar with "Agatha" as a first name.

ahead 150,000 years and reveals that Hera was the "mitochondrial Eve," an ancestor of modern humans. Hera is thus a major part of the solution to the conflict between humans and machines and the interminable cycle of destruction in that she merged the genes of Cylons and humans into an indistinguishable common heritage.

Despite her name's pedigree, Hera is far from a pure embodiment of Colonial spiritual tradition. Her mixed blood makes her an alteration of tradition, a realignment of the past to accord with the exigencies of the future, which is necessary if there is to be a future at all for humans or Cylons. The fact that all of this took place in human prehistory—with the implication that ancient Greece and Rome somehow received aspects of their culture from the Colonial and Cylon survivors—demonstrates how Westerners have moved and continue to move away from Colonial religious tradition toward technological hedonism and destruction. This swerve from tradition is embodied in the erasure of Hera's original name by modern scientists, who replaced it with two new cultural referents, an adjective derived from a microscopic structure in cells that is discernible only with advanced technology, and the name of the first woman in the Old Testament. "Eve" may suggest that there is a glimmer of hope that Colonial tradition has not been lost completely, but many scientists express regret that their observation was ever associated with that name.[31] Hera's rechristening suggests that modern humans have forgotten the Colonials' decision to reject the cognitive and embrace the mythic and are no longer aware of the cultural compromise that produced Hera. Her name and function have been lost to time, and with this loss, so, too, the ability to recognize humanity's dark past and compromised future.[32]

In the final moments of the last episode, two mysterious "angel" figures, who claim to be servants of an omnipotent being and who are identical in appearance to Baltar and Cylon model Six, stroll through a modern city and ruminate on the fate of humanity. "All of this has

[31] See, e.g., Wills (2010: 130–31).
[32] A scene from episode 4.4 ("Escape Velocity") makes the point that the Colonial/classical tradition is not enough to ensure humanity's survival. Lily, a member of Baltar's monotheistic cult, hesitantly reveals that she believes in Baltar and his one God as well as in Asclepius, the god of healing in both the Colonial and classical traditions. Head Six, a spiritual entity whom only Baltar can see, remarks, "Old gods die hard." The Colonials' gods die hard because they are an important part of the series' teleology—and indeed, since Colonial society provided the basis for later ancient societies, as the final episode suggests, the old gods continue to live in different forms throughout human history.

happened before—" Six begins, and Baltar finishes her sentence, "—but the question remains: does all of this have to happen again?" This exchange recapitulates the central question of the series: does the mythic, represented in the series by the classically inspired Colonial religion, weigh down and destroy humanity, rendering it incapable of breaking out of the historical cycle of violence, or does it have the power to save? Baltar is skeptical that the modern Earth can survive, referring to the destroyed planets Kobol, Earth, and Caprica, but Six is hopeful ("Let a complex system repeat itself long enough and eventually something surprising might occur")—which is ironic, given the Corinthian capitals clearly visible behind her. This scene reminds us of the important part that classical antiquity plays in *BSG*'s major themes. On one hand, classical/Colonial myths are indispensable for locating a place where life can continue. On the other hand, classical antiquity is revealed to be the cause of humanity's inability to escape the cycle, not only through the clash of Colonial and Cylon civilizations, but also through the scientific and technological advances of ancient Greek thinkers and the decadence of the Roman Empire.[33]

To break out of this destructive cycle, *BSG* suggests, humanity must embrace a mythic hermeneutic and hybridize its traditions, as well as reject the technology that leads to arrogance and decadence. Deriving many of its elements from classical myth, Colonial religion creates cognitive estrangement by anchoring its audience's identities in their Western heritage, while also distancing them by depicting these myths as the basis for the polytheistic religious practice. Through cognitive estrangement, *BSG* seeks to give its audience a broadened perspective on themselves as well as argue the necessity to return to a mythic tradition. The series never explicitly states why humanity diverged from the path towards the mythic set by the Colonials, but an inevitable conclusion is that the classical civilizations were partly responsible for the swerve. Colonial spirituality gave way to technology and science, which were developed in the West by Greek empirical thinkers and philosophers,

---

[33] Moore paralleled Colonial civilization with the Roman Empire before its fall on his Scifi.com blog on 15 March 2005; this comment is no longer available in its original form. His notion of (American) society mirroring the past of the Roman Empire is common in SF (see Brown 2008: 416–422) as well as in early American thought (see Winterer 2002: 79); see the chapters by Makins and Kovacs (this volume, chapters thirteen and nine, respectively).

most famously on the western coast of Asia Minor in the sixth century B.C.E., and to the hedonistic decadence of the Roman Empire.[34] The series thus presents a deeply conflicted picture of classical antiquity and its legacy as vital for Western identity, culture, and continued existence, and simultaneously as part of the cycle of conflict and destruction.

---

[34] This view of the legacy of classical antiquity is ironic since, according to Vernant (1982: 11), myths played a major role in enabling Greeks to create democracies that were based on materialist thought.

Part IV

Ancient Classics for a Future Generation?

12

Revised Iliadic Epiphanies in Dan Simmons's *Ilium*

Gaël Grobéty

RAGE

Sing, O Muse, of the rage of Achilles, of Peleus' son, murderous, man-killer, fated to die, sing of the rage that cost the Achaeans so many good men and sent so many vital, hearty souls down to the dreary House of Death. And while you're at it, O Muse, sing of the rage of the Gods themselves, so petulant and so powerful here on their new Olympos, and of the rage of the post-humans, dead and gone though they might be, and of the rage of those few true humans left, self-absorbed and useless they may have become.
[. . .]
Oh, and sing of me, O Muse, poor born-again-against-his-will Hockenberry—poor dead Thomas Hockenberry, Ph.D., Hockenbush to his friends, to friends long since turned to dust on a world long since left behind. Sing of *my* rage, yes, of my *rage*, O Muse, small and insignificant though that rage may be when measured against the anger of the immortal gods, or when compared to the wrath of the god-killer, Achilles.

> On second thought, O Muse, sing of nothing to me. I know you.
> I have been bound and servant to *you*, O Muse, you incomparable
> bitch. And I do not trust you. Not one little bit.
> If I am to be the unwilling Chorus of this tale, then I can start the
> story anywhere I choose. I choose to start it here. (*Ilium* 1)

These are the first lines of the science fiction (SF) novel *Ilium* (2003) by
the American author Dan Simmons.[1] I will comment later on this opening, but no further explanation is needed in order to realize either how
aggressive the narrator Thomas Hockenberry is towards the usually
respected Muse and her authority, or, consequently, how rebellious
Ilium itself appears compared with its "model," the *Iliad* (eighth century
B.C.E.). Dan Simmons has always been inspired by classical and canonical literature from the past (among others by Homer, Shakespeare,
Keats, Dickens, and Twain),[2] but he also takes an interest in modern
authors from the beginning of the twentieth century, including Ernest
Hemingway, James Joyce, and William Faulkner.[3] In that regard, I read
Simmons as a bridge between antiquity and contemporary literature.

This chapter will consider some scenes in *Ilium* and analyze its struggle to replace Homeric values and beliefs with new preoccupations valued by modern society. As demonstrated by Hockenberry's insults
against the Muse, the main field of opposition is religion and the relationship between men and gods. For that reason, I focus on the notion
of "epiphany," which has always represented privileged instances of

---

[1] This chapter is derived from a contribution I made at the Corhali Conference held at
Princeton University in 2009. I am very grateful to David Bouvier, Pietro Pucci,
Constanze Güthenke, Renate Schlesier, Christian Wildberg, Andrew Ford, and Froma
Zeitlin for their insightful remarks on my work. I warmly thank the two editors of this
volume for their attentive revision of this chapter at a later stage.

[2] Homer's and Shakespeare's lives and/or works are used in *Ilium* (2003) and *Olympos*
(2005), John Keats's in the *Hyperion* series (1989, 1990, 1995, 1997), Charles Dickens's in
Drood (2009), Mark Twain's in *Fires of Eden* (1994), and Ernest Hemingway's in *The
Crook Factory* (1998). It is worth adding that Simmons makes extensive use of ancient
mythologies, whether they are Hindu (*Song of Kali*, 1985), Egyptian (*Summer of Night*,
1991; *A Winter Haunting*, 2002; *Drood*, 2009), Hawaiian (*Fires of Eden*, 1994), Greek
(*Ilium*, 2003; *Olympos*, 2005), Inuit (*The Terror*, 2007), or Sioux (*Black Hills*, 2010). In
most of these works, the ancient beliefs interact with the contemporary world in a crucial
and often threatening way.

[3] For instance, James Joyce and William Faulkner are mentioned in *Olympos*, along
with Marcel Proust, Walt Whitman, and Emily Dickinson, as a way for robots to know
more about human psychology: Simmons (2005: 497).

divine encounters, and will examine how its two non-Christian meanings collide as two representations of the world—ancient and modern—
are opposed.

If we are to believe the *Oxford English Dictionary*, the word "epiphany" appeared in the English language, along with the French word
"épiphanie," sometime between the twelfth and fourteenth centuries. It
only referred to the Christian festival observed on January 6th, com-
memorating the visit to the infant Jesus by the Magi (or Three Kings).[4]
Only in the early seventeenth century was the meaning widened to any
manifestation of some divine and superhuman being,[5] thus encompassing the apparition of the gods in archaic epic. Finally, two centuries
later, by the mid-1800s, a third meaning divested the epiphany of its
divine component, simply defining it as any sudden and important
manifestation or realization.[6]

The epiphany taken in its second sense has been widely accepted by
classical scholars as a good designation for the self-revelation of
Olympian gods to mortal eyes or perceptions. These epiphanic moments
have always been considered privileged loci for studying the interaction
between men and gods in Greek antiquity. Divinity exposes itself and
offers, or so it seems, a possibility for humankind to understand it
better.

But things, as they are, are not so simple: interpretation of divine
epiphanies is one of the most controversial subjects in Homeric scholarship. Despite numerous takes and ambitious readings by prominent
scholars, Iliadic epiphanies never completely reveal the mystery of the
deity, which is kept even when the gods appear. In general terms, the
function of most divine interventions remains strangely ambiguous,
and even the most recent answers to the question are elusive. For
instance, Slatkin argues that "[t]he role of the gods might be seen as a
structure of explanation for what is beyond individual human control"
and "anticipates our modern awareness that all our undertakings. . . are
shaped by an array of forces, some manifest, others inaccessible to our
mortal comprehension"[7]—which does not explain a lot. Following

---

[4] Brown (1993: 837).
[5] Ibid. (837).
[6] Ibid. (837).
[7] Slatkin (2011: 321).

Tsagarakis, we can wonder "to what extent is divine intervention in Homer an artistic or a religious phenomenon,"[8] and look for the meaning in narratological rather than (or as well as) in theological or anthropological terms.

A fascinating answer to Tsagarakis's interrogation is provided by Pietro Pucci's brilliant analysis of Athena's epiphany in *Iliad* Book 1,[9] which reveals that the mystery concerns not only the external appearance of the goddess but also the narrative reasons underlying her coming. Pucci insinuates that Athena's apparently purposeless epiphany is a textual strategy developed by the poem in order to justify itself:

> If we ask, in fact, who gains from the solution that the goddess offers to Achilles' dilemma, we will have to respond that the gain is the reader's and the reader's only. For from the goddess's solution arises the wrath of Achilles, that is, the poem itself. It is only by condemning Achilles to impotent rage that the *Iliad* fulfills itself as a poem.[10]

Pucci's interpretation is very subtle in the way it explains Athena's epiphany as the result of a combined necessity engendered by religious beliefs, as well as textual strategies and narrative developments. By starting the narration of the epic, Athena's epiphany becomes a paradigmatic representation of the power of the gods, and of their ability to control and decide human fate.

In contrast, the third meaning of the word "epiphany" is strictly opposed to the first two, as it seems to imply that human realization or even "inspiration" can occur without any intervention of a superhuman being. The inner epiphany, born in a time of religious contestation, was mostly explored and popularized at the beginning of the twentieth century by modern authors such as James Joyce and William Faulkner (whose books, according to one character in Simmons's *Olympos*, are supposed to help one to know more about human psychology).[11] In *Epiphany in the Modern Novel*, Morris Beja describes this type of epiphany as

[8] Tsagarakis (1977: viii).
[9] See Pucci (1998: 71–80).
[10] Pucci (1998: 77).
[11] See above, note 3.

a sudden spiritual manifestation, whether from some object, scene, event, or memorable phase of the mind—the manifestation being out of proportion to the significance or strictly logical relevance of whatever produces it.[12]

For instance, a famous occurrence of the word "epiphany" is found in James Joyce's unfinished novel *Stephen Hero*:

He believed that it was for the man of letters to record these epiphanies with extreme care, seeing that they themselves are the most delicate and evanescent of moments.[13]

Even if the causes are completely different, it would be hard not to notice that the effects mentioned here are the same as those produced by a divine epiphany: the suddenness of the event, its evanescent dimension, the near-impossibility of rationalizing it and understanding it. Over time, the same sort of event, named "epiphany"—the sudden enlightenment of the human mind—has come to be incorporated within two opposite ideas about the metaphysical world.

It is not surprising, then, that this evolution of the word's definition is reflected by most contemporary rewritings or adaptations of the *Iliad*, which often simply suppress the gods, or displace them as characters' beliefs that the narrator does not share.[14] *Ilium* proves to be original and interesting in the way it extensively problematizes the question of what an epiphany is, rather than simply setting that question aside or passing it by.

Before beginning an analysis of *Ilium*, it is necessary to say a few words about the story's narrator and explain the context of the beginning of the novel. The fictional character Thomas Hockenberry lives at the beginning of the twenty-first century, in the United States; he is a scholar, whose specialty is Homer's *Iliad*.[15] Thousands of years later, in a far future, he is mysteriously cloned by beings very similar to the Greek

[12] Beja (1971: 18).

[13] Joyce (1963: 211).

[14] Many examples can be found, and in multiple media (literature, comics, and cinema): *An Iliad*, by Alessandro Baricco (2006); the *Troy* trilogy, by David Gemmell (2006, 2007) and David Gemmell and Stella Gemmell (2008); *Age of Bronze*, by Eric Shanower (2001, 2004, 2007); *Troy*, by Wolfgang Petersen (2004).

[15] On scholarly figures in *Ilium* and *Olympos*, see Laimé (2014).

gods, who watch over a Trojan War very similar to the one described in the *Iliad*. The Muses give him a very specific mission: to spy on the Trojan War, make a daily report, and establish whether the events follow the course of the *Iliad* he studied during his first life. Hockenberry will discover that these futuristic Greek "gods" are nothing but genetically modified human beings.

The origin of the Trojan War they watch over is interesting: it is implied in *Ilium* that human geniuses, such as Homer or Shakespeare, can create real worlds with their minds. Their narrative and imaginary worlds, transmitted to us by texts and books, do exist somewhere as alternative universes. In the future, humans gain the possibility to travel through time and space and open doors to those worlds created by the power of the human mind. This science-fictional trick allows Thomas Hockenberry, reborn Homerist, to walk among the "real" heroes of the Trojan War.

As an independent narrator, he says, he can start the story anywhere he chooses (*Ilium* 1). In chapter 1, here is the scene where he decides to start (4):

Tonight is the assembly at Agamemnon's tent and the confrontation between Agamemnon and Achilles. This is where the *Iliad* begins, and it should be the focus of all my energies and professional skills, but the truth is that I don't really give a shit. Let them posture. Let them bluster. Let Achilles reach for his sword—well, I confess that I'm interested in observing that. Will Athena actually appear to stop him, or was she just a metaphor for Achilles' common sense kicking in? I've waited my entire life to answer such a question and the answer is only minutes away, but, strangely, irrevocably . . . I . . . don't . . . give . . . a . . . shit.

This provocative indifference towards the "great" *Iliad*, initiated by Hockenberry's rejection of the Muse, is justified in the narrative by the fact that he can no longer endure to live in that strange world; he feels deeply depressed due to his years of slavery and routine service to the gods. In other words, the story of the *Iliad*, as Homer had compiled it, has literally become Hockenberry's prison.

Moreover, showing indifference here allows him to draw the reader's attention to the only point that makes Hockenberry really curious: the thought that he will witness Athena's epiphany. There is a voyeuristic dimension to such a remark, a desire to know what really hides behind the epiphany. Hockenberry is a specialist in Homer, and like so many Homerists, he is particularly intrigued by the epiphanic question. More interestingly, the way the question is asked explicitly conveys the opposition between the last two definitions of the epiphany, as presented above: the physical presence of Athena as an external power and influence, or the internal decision made by Achilles alone. The scholar Hockenberry understands the double nature of the epiphany, and implicitly refers to the academic debate on that precise question.[16] For the lay reader, his interrogation also implies that Athena's appearance, more than anything else in Book 1 of the *Iliad*, can be crucial.

Hockenberry then uses a magical power of disguise given by the gods in order to witness the assembly in Agamemnon's tent. He takes the form of, or "morphs" into, Bias, an Athenian captain serving Menestheus (mentioned in *Iliad* 13.691), and watches the growing tension between Agamemnon and Achilles.

The rewriting of the epiphanic passage by Simmons is much longer than the original text. It is therefore interesting to see which elements differ. On one hand, some sentences, or parts of sentences, are almost literally copied from the Iliadic text (underlined in both texts; see below). Other passages have been reformulated, certainly to give a (supposedly) more modern rhythm to the quarrel. On the other hand, there are three entirely new paragraphs in Simmons's text (marked in *italics*). They do not exist at all in the *Iliad*, and consist only of descriptive passages, indicating a strong presence and the intervention of the narrator, Hockenberry. I focus here on the first half of the scene, the last part being less relevant to my point.

I divide the text into three parts (a, b, and c), in order to clarify my analysis. I quote first the translation of the *Iliad* by Richmond Lattimore (1961), then the corresponding passage from *Ilium*. We will see how Dan Simmons, while choosing the first hypothesis and making Athena really appear, dismisses her divine power by transforming her epiphany into a technological masquerade.

---

[16] Faced with the enigma of Athena's epiphany, some scholars have argued in favor of the second hypothesis, considering Athena's actions as an external image of Achilles' own decision. For examples of that tendency, see Dodds (1951), Snell (1953), MacCary (1982).

(a)
. . . But here is my threat to you.
Even as Phoibos Apollo is taking away my Chryseis.
I shall convey her back in my own ship, with my own
followers; but <u>I shall take the fair-cheeked Briseis,</u>
your prize, I myself going to your shelter, that you may learn well   185
<u>how much greater I am than you</u>, and another man may shrink back
from likening himself to me and contending against me.
So he spoke. And the anger came on Peleus' son, and within
his shaggy breast the heart was divided two ways, pondering
whether to draw from beside his thigh the sharp sword, driving   190
away all those who stood between and kill the son of Atreus,
or else to check the spleen within and keep down his anger.
Now as he weighted in mind and spirit these two courses
and <u>was drawing</u> from its scabbard <u>the great sword</u>, Athene descended
from the sky. For Hera the goddess of the white arms sent her,   195
who loved both men equally in her heart and cared for them.
(*Iliad* 1.181–196)

But know this, Achilles, Agamemnon goes on, his shout dropping to a terrible whisper that can be heard by all the hundreds of men assembled here, whether you leave or stay, I will give up my Chryseis because the *god*, Apollo, insists—but <u>I will have your Briseis in her stead</u>, and every man here will know <u>how much greater man is Agamemnon</u> than the surly boy Achilles!

Here Achilles loses all control and <u>goes for his sword</u> in earnest. *And here the Iliad would have ended—with the death of Agamemnon or the death of Achilles, or of both—and the Achaeans would have sailed home and Hector would have enjoyed his old age and Ilium would have remained standing for a thousand years and perhaps rivaled Rome in its glory,* but at this second the goddess Athena appears behind Achilles. (*Ilium* 15)

In (a), the detail of Achilles' inner thoughts, of his *mermêrizein*, has been replaced by an insight into the potential future of the situation. Hockenberry speaks of the three main elements that could cancel the Iliadic narration: the departure of the Achaeans, the survival of Hector, and the survival of Troy itself. As Hockenberry points out, if Achilles dies, or Agamemnon, or both, the first (and main) consequence would be the end of the *Iliad* as we know it, the end of Homer's poem. All that could have happened, but, writes Simmons, at this second the goddess

Athena appears behind Achilles. The word *but* emphasizes the role played by Athena, as an opposition to that hypothetical future and a condition of Hector's death and the fall of Troy. Simmons is fully conscious of the fundamental role of Athena's epiphany, as analyzed by Pucci: even before the goddess's appearance, Hockenberry mentions that Athena's epiphany is a precondition for the existence of the poem itself. It is a way to warn us about the significance of the scene.

(b)
The goddess standing behind Peleus' son <u>caught him by the fair hair</u>,
appearing to him only, for <u>no man of the others saw her</u>.
Achilles in amazement <u>turned about</u>, and straightway   200
knew Pallas Athene . . . (*Iliad* 1.197–200)

I see her. Achilles <u>reels around</u>, face contorted, and obviously also sees her. <u>No one else can.</u> *I don't understand this stealth-cloaking technology, but it works when I use it and it works for the gods.*

No, I realize immediately, this is more than stealth. The gods have frozen time again. It is their favorite way of talking to their pet humans without others eavesdropping, but I've seen it only a handful of times. Agamemnon's mouth is open—I can see spittle frozen in midair—but no sound is heard, no movement of jaw or muscles, no blinking of those dark eyes. So it is with every man in the circle: frozen, rapt or bemused, frozen. Overhead, a sea bird hangs motionless in mid-flight. Waves curl but do not break on the shore. The air is as thick as syrup and all of us here are frozen like insects in amber. The only movement in this halted universe comes from Pallas Athena, from Achilles and—even if shown only by my leaning forward to hear better—from me.

Achilles' hand is still on the hilt of his sword—half drawn from its beautifully tooled scabbard—but <u>Athena has grabbed him by his long hair</u> and physically turned him toward her, and he does not dare draw the sword now. To do so would be to challenge the goddess herself. (*Ilium* 15–16)

Just after Athena's appearance, we come to the second and longest added passage. It appears as an attempt to answer an important question couched in the Homeric text: what is the real "procedure" of the epiphany? How is it possible that Athena makes herself visible to Achilles alone? Were she only invisible, the other men in the assembly would have seen Achilles acting strangely and talking alone. The Homeric text does not comment on what we could call the external witnesses of the epiphany.

Dan Simmons tries to explain it using the concept of frozen time, whose early examples can be traced back to Christian sources such as the apocryphal *Infancy Gospel of James*,[17] yet I would suggest that the reason for this choice is not to allude to the first definition of the epiphany, considering Simmons's rejection of all that is divine or religious, as we shall see hereafter. It is, more likely, a nod to frozen time as a well-known science fictional trick made famous by, e.g., *The Matrix* (directed by Wachowski and Wachowski, 1999). He describes the scene with several significant details that create the "sensation of the moment" (the air as thick as syrup, frozen like insects in amber) or intensify the strangeness of the visual elements (the frozen spittle, the motionless bird in the air, the waves that curl but do not break). This long description makes the stopping of life and time paradoxically alive.

But consequently, Simmons only describes the outside particularities of the phenomenon: he gives us no explanation, no deep understanding of what clearly is an epiphany produced by technology. All that Hockenberry can say is "I don't understand." From that, it is easy to see that Simmons's technological propositions are not an answer. They present a new alternative idea for what could visually have been Athena's epiphany, but keep mysterious, superhuman, the nature of the power capable of such a great deed. In a way, the frozen-time concept itself is far too abstract to be considered as anything other than an elusive miracle—it is still outside our own experience in such a way that it does not promote a scientific understanding of the hypothesis, but keeps an element of mysticism in play in the scene. In SF, technological extravagance, created by human genius, is a new form of "divine" might, even if it is explicitly deprived of any "real" supernatural or magical power, as we will see hereafter.[18]

(c)
. . . and the terrible eyes shining.   200
He uttered winged words and addressed her: <u>Why have you come now</u>,
<u>O child of Zeus</u> of the aegis, once more? <u>Is it that you may see</u>

---

[17] See chapter 18 of the gospel, where Joseph, looking for a midwife for Mary, witnesses the same kind of frozen time when the midwife comes to him: the birds in the air are still, people who are eating do not move, a shepherd raises his hand to strike the sheep, but his hand remains up. Only Joseph, the midwife, and Mary are able to move in this frozen world. For the complete text, see Miller (1994: 380–396).

[18] On technology and/as "divine might" or "magic," see the discussion by Kovacs (this volume, chapter nine) about the *Star Trek* episode "Who Mourns for Adonais?"

the outrageousness of the son of Atreus Agamemnon?
Yet will I tell you this thing, and I think it shall be accomplished.
By such acts of arrogance he may even lose his own life. (*Iliad* 1.200–205)

But Achilles' eyes are blazing—more mad than sane—as he shouts into the thickened, syrupy silence that accompanies these time-freezes, Why! Damn, damn, why now! Why come to me now, Goddess, Daughter of Zeus? Did you come to witness my humiliation by Agamemnon?

Yield! says Athena.

If you've never seen a god or goddess, all I can do is tell you that they are larger than life—literally, since Athena must be seven feet tall—and more beautiful and striking than any mortal. I presume their nanotechnology and recombinant DNA labs made them that way. Athena combines qualities of feminine beauty, divine command, and sheer power that I didn't even know could exist before I found myself returned to existence in the shadow of Olympos.

Her hand stays wrapped in Achilles' hair, bending his head back and making him swivel away from frozen Agamemnon and his minions.

I'll never yield! shouts Achilles. Even in this frozen air that slows and mutes all sound, the man-killer's voice is strong. That pig who thinks he's a king will pay for his arrogance with his life! (*Ilium* 16)

The third paragraph emphasized above proposes an answer to another question asked by the Homeric text: what does Athena look like? For in Homer, we find that the physical presence of Athena is not sketched or represented in any way.[19]

For that matter, Hockenberry uses the same strategy as for the time-freezes: he chooses to reveal some things, but ultimately does not dispel the enigma of epiphany. What we know is that Athena is seven feet tall. But what do phrases like "larger than life" or "more beautiful and striking than any mortal" truly mean? It is an impression rather than a description. Even if Hockenberry wants to say more to us, his entire text shows his own limits and his incapacity to describe what he sees. "All I can do is tell you, Athena combines qualities of feminine beauty, divine command, and sheer power that I didn't even know could exist." In (b), many details allow us to visualize the scene, not to

[19] Pucci (1998: 69).

understand its functioning; in (c), on the contrary, the visual elements themselves are clouded by Hockenberry's incapability to say more about them. The epiphany mostly keeps its secret.

One last word ought to be said about the departure of Athena, which concludes the scene. I have not included the entire quotation here, because on this point Simmons's text is closer to Homer's than in any of (a), (b), and (c). In the *Iliad*, Athena simply goes back again to Olympos (*Iliad* 1.221), in confusingly simple terminology that says nothing about the real manner of her travels. In *Ilium*, she winks out of existence— "QTing" back to Olympos (*Ilium* 17).

Simmons enjoys building literary blendings, and making genres collide. A SF novel about the *Iliad* is by itself a kind of provocation, and Simmons stresses this point in the text. An expression like "QTing back to Olympos" brings out a deep feeling of strangeness: what could be more opposed to the very traditional Olympos, House of the Gods, than a mysterious SF word, meaning *quantum teleporting*?

It is one more way by which the technological mystery progressively replaces the divine, magical mystery. By using an invented abbreviation that cannot be understood without reading the explanation several pages later, Simmons uses the same kind of textual strategy and creates the same feeling of "blank" epiphany[20] as the Homeric text. Paradoxically, whatever its type, the epiphany holds a contradiction in itself: it is a revelation whose precise nature never reveals itself.

What that entire epiphanic scene gives us when reading *Ilium* is the answer to Hockenberry's double hypothesis, corresponding to two different definitions of the epiphany: Will Athena actually appear to stop him, or was she just a metaphor for Achilles' common sense kicking in? (*Ilium* 4). But neither would be the right answer. For if the second possibility—corresponding to the "modern" epiphany—is clearly neglected, the actual presence of Athena does not imply by any means the existence of any "real" divinities similar to those in the *Iliad*. As I stated above, the gods in *Ilium* are genetically modified humans who played with science and willingly decided to become gods. In that regard, it is easy to understand that the warning implied in the *Iliad* against *hubris* has been ignored, and that those god-humans in *Ilium* are fully hubristic. They

---

[20] See Pucci (1998) for the description of Athena as a blank figure (69) or a blank presence (74).

deceive the heroes on the plain of Troy and use their technology as a means of imposing their authority.

Simmons then rejects any form of true polytheistic religion and creates a new foe who only imitates the Greek gods to gain their divine advantages. The epiphany, taken in the second meaning given by the *Oxford English Dictionary*, is no longer the manifestation of a superhuman power that rules the universe, but of technological arrogance and its blindness. In that regard, *Ilium* can easily be interpreted as a warning against contemporary scientific excesses, modern forms of what has been called *hubris*. The divine epiphany is used as a means to talk about the present, not the past.

But Simmons goes much further, because he does not want to stick to that pessimistic vision and to describe a world where the human race is desperately subjected to the megalomaniac pseudo-deities he describes; he wants to show the independence of humans and their ability to escape from any form of totalitarian authority. In other words, he does not want to narrate the same *Iliad* a second time, because the respective position of men and gods in the epic never changes.

In order to fulfill that purpose, he will bring to the forefront, in a very consistent fashion, the third definition of epiphany, the only one that accords to men the complete mastery of their fate. Just after Athena's epiphany, in the same chapter (and I doubt it is a coincidence), we find the following scene:

It's at this instant, remembering the murderous gaze that Achilles had turned on Athena in the instant before she wrenched his hair back and cowed him into submission, that a plan of action so audacious, so obviously doomed to failure, so suicidal, and so wonderful opens before me that for a minute I have trouble breathing. [. . .]

I will do this thing. The decision comes with the exhilaration of flying—no, not of flying, but in the thrill of that brief instant of zero gravity one achieves when throwing oneself from a high place and knowing that there is no going back to solid ground. Sink or swim, fall or fly.

I will do this thing. (*Ilium* 18–19)

The thought Hockenberry has at this instant is his plan to rebel against the gods. His idea is to unite Trojans and Achaeans against the deities of Olympos, and to destroy their tyranny with the help of the human heroes. We can see it as a symbol: the human being getting rid of the ancestral divinities—or their technological surrogates—and taking his own responsibilities. The Iliadic narration will be completely modified.

But here lies the most important point: later in the text, Hockenberry will remember that moment, and will call it "my moment of epiphany" (*Ilium* 36), a word clearly used here in its third meaning, and never used elsewhere in *Ilium* for the apparition of the gods. But it is interesting to note that the metaphor of the frozen movement, the zero-gravity image felt by Hockenberry, strongly echoes the frozen time that accompanies Athena's epiphany. The words he uses to describe the beginning of his experience are "It's at this instant that . . ." : it is sudden and unexpected, not unlike Athena's appearance. These two different epiphanies have the same impact on the human mind.

In his definition of the modern epiphany, Morris Beja writes that the manifestation is out of proportion to the significance or strictly logical relevance of whatever produces it.[21] In the case of Hockenberry, the initial impulse is precisely the vision of the murderous gaze that Achilles had turned on Athena, and that shows that the hero hates the goddess. Interestingly enough, that particular detail finds its origin in a philological mystery of the Homeric text. In the *Iliad*, it is impossible to settle whether the *deinô oi osse* ("terrible eyes," *Iliad* 1.200; see the first line of both texts in section c) belong to Athena or to Achilles. Some have strongly argued for the first possibility,[22] which seems to have become the canonical and mainly accepted reading.[23] However, these arguments depend on personal interpretations, and no objective evidence that might settle the matter has been discovered to this day.

[21] Beja (1971: 18).

[22] Most notably, Nicole Loraux (1982) has analyzed the similarity between the *deinô osse* and Athena's recurrent epithets such as *glaukôpis* ("shining-eyed," which first appears six lines later, in *Iliad* 1.206), in order to show that it must be the goddess's eyes. To that argument, Pietro Pucci answers that in *Iliad* 19.16–17, the eyes of Achilles are described as "blazing at the sight of arms" in terms reminiscent of our passage (1998: 74). The debate has still not ended.

[23] Indeed, the *deinô osse* as Athena's description seem to have become "obvious," non-problematical, for most recent general works on Homer, from the chapter on the gods in *The Cambridge Companion to Homer* (Kearns 2004: 72) to the gods' entry in *The Homer Encyclopedia* (Slatkin 2011: 319).

Whereas Lattimore follows the consensus and chooses the first possibility, Simmons decides that the eyes are Achilles'; obviously, he does
not possess any scientific evidence unknown to the entire academic
community. As a literary author, he uses scientific questions and hypothetical answers in order to fulfill his artistic purposes. In this case, his
choice proves to be fundamental for the fulfillment of the narrative, for
he makes this hateful gaze the very heart of his own tale. If Achilles
hates Athena, as his eyes reveal, he would be willing to declare war
against the gods.

Thus *Ilium*, taking advantage of the interpretational doubt of the
Homeric text—the "predecessor" it needs to redefine—imposes its own
interpretation, which leads directly to the complete destruction of the
Iliadic narrative. At the moment when Athena's epiphany starts the
Iliad's narration, Simmons uses the third kind of epiphany to start the
specific narration of *Ilium*, which must rebel against the original epic in
order to find its own identity. Of course, modifying the narration of the
Iliad cancels the long-term effects of Athena's epiphany. It can be considered as a paradigmatic struggle between these two kinds of epiphany: ultimately, the inner epiphany, the modern one, will symbolically
lead Hockenberry to his final victory.

This also confirms Hockenberry was right not to trust the Muse. At
the beginning, he rejects a first manifestation of the divinity, a first
epiphany, which is the inspiration given by the Muse to tell the story.
From the beginning, Hockenberry only trusts his own inner will in taking responsibility for the tale he is about to narrate.

In Hesiod's *Theogony* (22–34), when the Muses instruct and inspire
the poet, a double reading results from the uncertainty about how
Hesiod wished to represent the Muses: do they cut and give the laurel
branch to the poet themselves, thus giving him the entire work already
completed? Or do they ask Hesiod to cut the laurel branch by himself?
The question of the physical presence of the Muse dates back to
antiquity.

Hockenberry only asks the same question in a modern context: does
the Muse really possess a power of inspiration, or does the poet, who can
only count on himself, have to find in his own inner strength the means
by which he can tell his tale? Hockenberry answers the question with a
double refusal. First of all, he tells the Muse: "I do not trust you" (*Ilium*
1); then, although he is curious about Athena's epiphany, he concludes: "I

don't give a shit" (4). That double refusal of the old deities' influence clearly cancels the power of their epiphanies in the reader's mind.

Moreover, it will allow the specific narration of *Ilium* to exist. Without having rejected the Muse's inspiration, Hockenberry would never have told that story to the reader; and without his inner epiphany, which gave him the idea and the courage to cancel Athena's epiphany by modifying the narration of the *Iliad, Ilium* would have remained a clone of the *Iliad*, and would not have had its own existence. Hockenberry's rebellion turns out to be the rebellion of Simmons's novel itself against its source text.

But Simmons goes even further in his demystification of the divine epiphany. Fully conscious of the real influence of the gods on the characters of the epic, Thomas Hockenberry will create a second (and false) epiphany of Athena, in order to make Achilles change his mind. I have already stated that Hockenberry had the technological power to take the form of someone else: he will use that power to take the form of Athena herself, and make Achilles believe that the goddess killed Patroclus. Mad at Athena, Achilles will call upon his mother Thetis. And then Hockenberry will talk to Achilles in disguise for the second time, this time as Achilles' mother Thetis, to persuade him to make peace with Hector, and to defy the gods. Hockenberry uses, very consciously, the same strategy for *Ilium* as Homer or the Homeric instance of narration did for the *Iliad*, which is an epiphany in order to start the narration.

So the Homeric epiphany, at first mysterious, then demystified via technology, becomes the tool of a masquerade whose purpose is to affirm the greatness of the human mind. The original power of the divine epiphany (first and second definitions of the word) has been transferred into a new type of epiphany (third definition), better suited to a science-fictional vision of our time as one of religious disinterest, psychology, and individualism. We have seen that a great mystery was hiding the complete understanding of the Homeric epiphany. That mystery seems to have jumped from one epiphany to the other. For what is more powerful and more mysterious nowadays than the human brain, soul, or mind, able to conceive its own epiphanies? Who can pretend to have explored it all? As did Homer, many writers, from James Joyce to Dan Simmons, tried (and still try) to explore the phenomenon further by literary means.

By its subject itself, *Ilium* acknowledges the *Iliad*'s authority as a classical model and praises Homer's genius: creator of worlds—literary *and* physical. At the same time, it contradicts and even defies its model in order to transmit its own values based on free will, thus rejecting the divine epiphany in favor of the inner one, which better illustrates the sensibility of our time.

13

Refiguring the Roman Empire in
The Hunger Games Trilogy

Marian Makins

Nothing about the packaging of *The Hunger Games* trilogy suggests that it depicts a society based on ancient Rome. The covers feature no classical details; there is nothing overtly classicizing about the titles—*The Hunger Games, Catching Fire, Mockingjay*.[1] Indeed, narrator and protagonist Katniss Everdeen specifically locates the action in a dystopian future version of the United States. In an early scene, she hears her mayor recite the story of their country's birth: after a series of ecological disasters, competition for scarce resources escalated into war; when the dust had settled, a new nation "rose up out of the ashes of a place that was once called North America" (*The Hunger Games* [*HG*] 18). Katniss later reports learning in school that the ruling Capitol "was built in a place once called the Rockies," while her own coal-mining district "was in a region known as Appalachia" (*HG* 41).

But classically minded readers encounter tantalizing details at every turn. The country that succeeds the United States is called "Panem," as

---

[1] Collins (2008), (2009), and (2010) (cited as *HG, CF,* and *M,* respectively). Unless otherwise noted, all translations from ancient authors are my own.

in the Latin phrase *panem et circenses* ("bread and circuses," Juvenal [Juv.] 10.81). Capitol citizens have Latin(ate) names like Caesar, Flavius, and Octavia. In the districts, where residents subsist on supplies allocated by the state, children from poor families sign up for extra distributions called "tesserae"—*tessera* being the Latin word once used to denote tokens entitling Roman citizens to the grain dole. And, by signing up for tesserae, these children raise their odds of being condemned to fight other children in an annual spectacle reminiscent of Roman gladiatorial shows. This is the Hunger Games, in which the Capitol takes two children from each district, imprisons them all in a high-tech outdoor arena, and makes them fight to the death on national television. The government instituted this practice, Katniss explains, as punishment for the districts' one attempt to gain independence, some seventy-five years before the story opens (*HG* 18).

The premise of a tyrannical power exacting living, breathing tribute from conquered neighbors comes from Greek myth. Like Theseus, who chose to join a group of young Athenians sent as tribute to King Minos of Crete, Katniss volunteers to take her younger sister's place as female "tribute" from District 12. And, just as Theseus dared battle the Minotaur and escape from the Labyrinth, Katniss defies the Capitol from start to finish, not only surviving the Games, but ultimately helping to eradicate them forever through participation in a new district rebellion.[2]

Author Suzanne Collins has acknowledged that the Hunger Games "were inspired by" the *Greek* legend of Theseus.[3] She has also said, however, that she did not want to "do a Labyrinth story," and indeed, the Theseus paradigm becomes less operative once the plot gets underway.[4] In its place, the story of a legendary *Roman* underdog looms ever larger: Spartacus, the Thracian-born gladiator who led a slave uprising against Rome in 73–71 B.C.E.[5] Collins has described researching "not only the historical Spartacus

[2] On Theseus as volunteer, see Plutarch *Life of Theseus* 17.2; on Katniss's defiance, see Muller (2012: 59).

[3] Quoted in Blasingame (2009: 726–727).

[4] "Labyrinth story" is quoted in Margolis (2008). For a definition of "paradigm," see Hardwick (2003: 90): "Myths, legends and episodes have provided paradigms, that is, tales told and retold through individual works or successive texts providing models or contrasts either with other characters and events within the work or, more broadly, with the treatment of the same theme in other works."

[5] Cf. Margolis (2010).

and the popular media about him, but many of the historical gladiators from pre-Christian times."[6] These investigations helped her shape the society of Panem according to the "gladiator paradigm": "(1) a ruthless government that (2) forces people to fight to the death and (3) uses these fights to the death as a form of popular entertainment."[7] In other words, while Katniss's initial predicament and courageous self-sacrifice cast her as a "futuristic Theseus," the metropolis into which the "tribute train" (*HG* 42) delivers her is a futuristic version of Rome, not Knossos; and the danger awaiting her is not a monster in a maze, but a gladiatorial contest *sine missione* ("without release") in a futuristic Colosseum.

This chapter explores Panem's "Romanness" in order to illuminate the contours and effects of Collins's reception of ancient Rome. I begin by mapping out correspondences between Collins's fictional "Rome" and several source texts.[8] Just as the plot of the trilogy combines elements of two paradigms, so my analysis will show that Panem is a "hybrid" refiguration, fusing elements of the historical Roman Empire with an archetype that originated in ancient moralizing and satirical texts and has been developed in American popular culture.[9] Then, after examining the nature of Collins's refiguration, I consider its logic.[10] What are the implications of refiguring an already-distorted vision of Rome in this way? What work can *this* Rome accomplish, that another could not? I approach these questions, first, by locating the books in the subgenre of the young adult critical dystopia.[11] Like other such works,

[6] Quoted in Blasingame (2009: 727).

[7] Ibid. (727). For a discussion of the "gladiator paradigm" in *The Hunger Games* trilogy and in *Star Trek*, see Harrisson (2014).

[8] According to the provisional framework laid out by Lorna Hardwick for discussing reception, "correspondences" are "aspects of a new work which directly relate to a characteristic of the source" (Hardwick 2003: 9). Like Hardwick, too, I intend the word "text" "in its broadest sense," here encompassing film and television in addition to "oral sources, written documents and works of material culture" (4).

[9] "Refiguration" in this context is "selecting and reworking material from a previous or contrasting tradition" (Hardwick 2003: 10). For ancient archetypes, cf. Winkler (2001: 50): "late republican and especially imperial Rome has . . . come to be an almost archetypal—as well as stereotypical—society characterized by might and vice."

[10] Cf. Wyke (1997: 13).

[11] Lyman Tower Sargent defines a "critical dystopia" as "a non-existent society described in considerable detail and normally located in time and space that the author intended a contemporary reader to view as worse than contemporary society but that normally includes at least one eutopian enclave or holds out hope that the dystopia can be overcome and replaced with a eutopia" (quoted in Baccolini and Moylan 2003: 7).

The Hunger Games trilogy challenges readers to confront dystopian trends in society, while holding out hope that improvement is still possible.[12] Ultimately, I argue, Collins's revision of the archetypal Rome "intervenes" on two fronts: it appropriates a paradigm from Hollywood's Roman epics to encourage reflection on issues of social justice and political self-determination, and it problematizes aspects of contemporary media culture by establishing a three-way parallel between Panem, ancient Rome, and twenty-first-century America.[13]

MAPPING THE ETERNAL DYSTOPIA

This section delineates the principal correspondences between Panem and two Romes—one historical and consonant with modern scholarly ideas about the Empire, and the other archetypal, resembling distorted images of Imperial society found in both ancient literature and Hollywood films.

Geopolitics

The political geography of Panem resembles the Roman Empire in that the seat of imperial authority is located in a metropolis surrounded by territories it controls.[14] Panem's capital shares its name with the temple that served as Rome's "public face" and symbolized its destiny as "the head or capital of the world."[15] Like Rome, too, the Capitol deploys a professional military force to maintain order. Citizens joining the Peacekeepers sign up for a fixed term of twenty years (*Mockingjay* [*M*] 83), the same commitment required of recruits to the Imperial Roman legions.[16] And, just as the Roman army limited personal attachments among its soldiers, Peacekeepers cannot marry or have children (83).[17]

---

[12] Baccolini and Moylan (2003: 3–8).

[13] "Intervention" in this context is "reworking the source to create a political, social or aesthetic critique of the receiving society" (Hardwick 2003: 9).

[14] The mayor of District 12 describes Panem as "a shining Capitol ringed by thirteen districts" (*HG* 18).

[15] Gowers (1995: 26).

[16] Scheidel (2007: 417).

[17] On limited personal attachments in the Roman army, see ibid. (417–419).

The Capitol also follows Rome in keeping a symbolic presence in each district through architecture. Like a typical Roman provincial city with forum and basilica at its heart,[18] the main town of each district is organized around a square ringed with shops and dominated by a monumental marble edifice called the Justice Building, which serves as the regional seat of imperial administration. As some have argued in regard to Roman provincial architecture, the urban form repeated throughout Panem "act[s], in a highly symbolic manner, to project the character of the relationship" between individual communities and the capital that controls them.[19]

However, the character of the relationship between the Capitol and the districts differs from that between Rome and its provinces. Panem's government uses the monumental city centers in the districts as venues to reassert its dominance over the population. For example, district residents are required to attend the annual "reaping" ceremony, in which a government representative stands on a "temporary stage . . . before the Justice Building" to select tributes for the Games (*HG* 17). Officials manage the crowds, signing people in as they reach the square, directing latecomers to adjacent streets to "watch the event on screens," and imprisoning truants unless they are "on death's door" (16–17). "The reaping," Katniss observes, "is a good opportunity for the Capitol to keep tabs on the population" (16).

Totalitarian interventions of this kind were foreign to the Roman administrative mindset, leading historian J. E. Lendon to remark that "outside the capital itself the Roman empire was a libertarian's dream."[20] Even the development of the characteristic provincial urban centers depended on the involvement of local elites, rather than being centrally orchestrated.[21] But the conception of Rome as a totalitarian state has a long history, nowhere more evident than in film.[22] Many of Hollywood's Roman epics presented the Empire as a parallel to a modern totalitarian regime like Nazi Germany or the Soviet Union, while others pilloried a repressive element within American society, such as the House Un-American

---

[18] Hingley (2005: 85).
[19] Ibid. (77, with bibliography).
[20] Lendon (2000: 403).
[21] Hingley (2005: 77–82).
[22] See ibid. (402); cf. Winkler (2001: 51): "In the United States, the negative view of imperial Rome has received its widest dissemination in the cinema."

Activities Committee (HUAC).[23] Indeed, the 2012 film adaptation of *The Hunger Games* announced its allegiance to this tradition by imbuing the architecture and iconography of the Capitol with the neoclassical aesthetic favored by modern fascist regimes, which was famously depicted, in glorious Technicolor, in *Quo Vadis* (1951), *Ben-Hur* (1959), and other films.[24] In portraying Panem as a totalitarian version of the Roman Empire, therefore, Collins hews more closely to modern popular-cultural stereotype than to ancient history.

Economics

In a similar vein, Panem's economic structure both resembles and distorts the historical situation in antiquity. The Roman Empire relied on imports from the provinces to supply its crowded capital, a city whose "requirements . . . far outstripped the local resources."[25] Over time, certain commodities came to be associated with particular provinces, such as papyrus from Egypt and purple dye from Syria. Likewise, Panem's Capitol imports both staples and luxury goods, with each district filling an economic niche: District 3 makes electronics, District 10 raises livestock, and so on (*Catching Fire* [*CF*] 213). Katniss eventually learns that the Capitol would not be able to sustain its population without the districts (*M* 169).

But the government maintains an iron grip on Panem's food supply, exerting a degree of control unparalleled in antiquity. The Capitol's annual distributions of grain and oil to district residents recall monthly grain rations distributed to Rome's urban poor; yet, whereas Roman magistrates purchased imported grain to supply their own citizens, the government of Panem confiscates what the districts produce and doles it back out to them in dribs and drabs.[26] In other words, the Capitol's economic interventionism is punitive as well as pragmatic, keeping the districts subservient by threatening them with starvation.

[23] On Germany in US film, see Winkler (2001: 54–72); on the Soviet Union, see Wyke (1997: 142–144); and on HUAC, see ibid. (23, 66–68). Some films contain both anti-fascist *and* anti-Communist symbolism, an elasticity that reflects the Cold War–era tendency to conflate fascism and Communism into "one overriding totalitarianism" (Joshel, Malamud, and Wyke 2001: 7).

[24] Winkler (2001: esp. 58–59 [*fasces* and eagles], 59 n. 14 [architecture]).

[25] Aldrete and Mattingly (2010: 195); cf. Juv. 5.92–98.

[26] Aldrete and Mattingly (2010: 201–203); cf. *HG* 202.

The authenticity of the word assigned to the Capitol's "bonus" distributions underscores this ambiguity.[27] When a district child turns twelve, her name is entered once into the tribute-selection lottery. She can then add her name again as many times as there are people in her family, in exchange for tesserae. In Latin, *tessera* could be applied to any small object serving as a "token or voucher."[28] A *tessera frumentaria*, for example, was "a ticket . . . entitling [the bearer] to a free supply of corn," while other *tesserae* guaranteed admission to theaters and amphitheaters.[29] Knowing these definitions adds poignancy to Collins's use of the term: a tessera might help a district child feed her family, but it could also be her "ticket" into the arena.

Culture

Panem is thus broadly similar to the historical Roman Empire with respect to geopolitical and economic organization, differing primarily in the degree of control exerted by the imperial authority. The totalitarianism attributed to the "Romans" in *The Hunger Games* trilogy evokes the archetypal Rome depicted in film, not the historical Rome. Capitol society is likewise characterized by a degree of moral debasement recalling stereotypical depictions of the Empire.

To say that Katniss experiences culture shock upon arrival in the Capitol would be an understatement. In District 12, everyone works hard, and most still struggle to get by. In contrast, Capitol citizens seem frivolous, excessive, even depraved. But Capitol culture may not seem so strange to contemporary readers, because the vices Katniss observes—extravagance, gluttony, licentiousness, cruelty—coincide with those attributed to Imperial Rome in popular media like the film *Gladiator* and Home Box Office's (HBO) television series *Rome*. This unsavory vision can then be traced back even further, to the Romans themselves.

The idea that life among Rome's upper classes consisted of an endless round of banquets, orgies, and spectacles derives not from archaeological

---

[27] "Authenticity" is "close approximation to the supposed form and meaning of the source" (Hardwick 2003: 9).

[28] *Oxford Latin Dictionary*, s.v. "tesserae" (2.a).

[29] Ibid. (2.c); with Fagan (2011: 100–101).

remains or other "hard" evidence, but from literature—the exaggerated satirical tableaux of Horace, Juvenal, and Petronius; the sensationalized Imperial portraiture of Suetonius and Tacitus; the philosophical moralizing of Seneca; the ascetic treatises of Christian apologist Tertullian. These writers (among others) sought to expose degeneracy, moral blindness, and hypocrisy in society. Their extreme characterizations shocked and entertained while slyly prompting readers to wonder, "Could that be *us*?"

Many of those authors launched their critiques from the (assumed) perspective of an outsider or bystander, imparting an aura of detached objectivity to their views and inviting the audience to make common cause. A similar dynamic operates in many of Hollywood's widescreen Roman epics. During the Cold War, Hollywood projected images of a decadent Rome characterized by might (tyrannical leaders, militarism, slavery, fondness for blood sport) and vice (luxury, lust, persecution of minorities).[30] The protagonists in these films tend to be members of oppressed groups—Christians, Jews, slaves. Katniss's jaundiced perspective on the excesses of Capitol society is similarly informed by her marginal identity. As a tribute from the poorest district, her life depends on her ability to navigate and manipulate a hegemonic culture that she both envies and despises. She is an outsider trapped inside a social world from which she is simultaneously alienated.[31]

The Hunger Games, like many dystopias, opens *in medias res* in the "terrible new world," with Katniss resigned to her place within what is, for her, normal life.[32] The reader's struggle to adjust to the post-apocalyptic setting is then duplicated in the narrative when Katniss is plunged into Capitol society, reeling at the extravagance she encounters. Extreme body modification practices and outlandish attire are routine, to the extent that when Katniss first meets Cinna, her stylist for the Games, she is shocked by how normal he looks (*HG* 63).

Capitol citizens are equally excessive in their consumption of food and drink. In *Catching Fire*, Katniss attends a banquet that would have impressed even Trimalchio, the freedman in Petronius' *Satyricon* (*Sat.*) whose lavish dinner party became the stuff of movie legend with 1969's

[30] Winkler (2001: 51).
[31] Cf. Larmour (2007: 181): "[Juv. 1.95–126] dramatizes the 'outsider' status of the satiric wanderer locked inside a cityscape from which he is alienated."
[32] "Terrible new world" is quoted from Baccolini and Moylan (2003: 5).

Fellini Satyricon.[33] With horrified fascination, Katniss describes a spread containing "everything you can think of, and things you have never dreamed of": whole cows, pigs, and goats turning on spits; fowl stuffed with fruit and nuts; "waterfalls of wine, and streams of spirits that flicker with flames" (*HG* 77).

The scene then takes a turn highlighting the indebtedness of Capitol culture to distorted representations of Roman life. When Katniss and fellow-tribute Peeta Mellark let fall their forks in surrender, Cinna's well-meaning but oblivious assistants give them a lesson in local etiquette that signals the vast gulf of experience separating the Capitol from the starving outer districts. It seems denizens of the Capitol never allow mere fullness to keep them from enjoying a feast. Instead, they pick up one of the "tiny stemmed wineglasses filled with clear liquid" set out on a special table, retire to the lavatory to drink the purgative, and then return to the banquet (*HG* 79).

Collins here alludes to the well-known fact that every upscale Roman house featured "a special room, adjoining the dining hall, where gluttonous eaters who had swilled too much rich and exotic food might throw up the contents of their stomach in order to return to their couches empty enough to enjoy the pleasures of still more food."[34] Except that this "fact," blithely reported by architectural critic Lewis Mumford, is actually fiction, a myth probably stemming from a passage of Seneca excoriating Romans so corrupted by luxury that "they vomit in order to eat, eat in order to vomit, and do not even deign to digest the banquets for which they scour the whole world" (*vomunt ut edant, edunt ut vomant, et epulas quas toto orbe conquirunt nec concoquere dignantur*; *De Consolatione ad Helviam* 10).[35] Even if Seneca's hyperbolic, moralizing tone did not warn against taking his words too literally, there is also the absence of corroborating evidence: Romans did sometimes throw up on purpose, but generally not for this reason; and in any case, they did not do it in a special "vomit-room."[36] Late Latin's *vomitoria* only ever referred to the corridors that "spewed" spectators into or out of an amphitheater.[37] Like Seneca the Stoic philosopher—and like

[33] Petronius *Sat.* 26–78.
[34] Mumford (1961: 224).
[35] Cf. Day (2008: 4).
[36] Cf. Cicero *Pro Rege Deiotaro.* 21; Suetonius *Life of Nero* [*Ner.*] 20.1, *Life of Vitellius* 13.1.
[37] *Lewis and Short*, s.v. "vomitorius" (II).

Juvenal, whose third *Satire* influenced later dystopian depictions of Rome's urban landscape—Mumford had his own agenda, guiding his presentation of Rome as a city whose architecture reflected its decadence.[38]

Ancient authors and Hollywood filmmakers alike have endowed the Romans with lasciviousness to match their culinary and sartorial extravagance.[39] *The Hunger Games* trilogy contains little sexual content, but the experience of handsome victor Finnick Odair hints at a similar degree of depravity in the Capitol. Katniss learns in *Mockingjay* that Panem's president, Coriolanus Snow, used threats of violence against Finnick's family to coerce him into staying in the Capitol and allowing himself to be prostituted to the rich and powerful (170). Finnick chose to take payment for his "work" in secrets. Though Katniss does not give details, she communicates the general idea with references to "strange sexual appetites," "betrayals of the heart," and "charges of incest" (171).

Panem's Capitol also shares with Rome a tolerance or even appreciation for violence. Capitol citizens keep slaves—the so-called Avoxes, condemned criminals whose tongues have been cut out.[40] They also accept that politics is a brutal business. Finnick informs Katniss that President Snow came to power young and stayed there thanks to a combination of ruthlessness, paranoia, and the judicious use of poison (*M* 171–172). Finnick's chilling portrait of Snow's reign recalls both references to poisoning in Juvenal's *Satires*[41] and hair-raising tales bruited about in antiquity concerning Nero, some of which have been dramatized in films like *Quo Vadis* (1951).[42]

---

[38] On Juvenal, see Laurence (1997: 14); for Mumford, see Laurence (1997: 5–10).

[39] Classic accounts from antiquity include Suetonius *Life of Tiberius* 43–44 (Tiberius' orgies on Capri) and Juv. 6 (adultery among Roman wives); on the cinematic side, the *Penthouse*-produced *Caligula* (1979) stands out, but even in *Spartacus* (film, 1960) "the theme of Roman sexual 'deviance' is inextricably tied to the theme of corruption of absolute power" (Cyrino 2014: 619).

[40] From Gk. *a-* ("without") + Latin *vox* ("voice"). In her first encounter with an Avox, Katniss draws a parallel between the maimed girl's situation and her own (*HG* 80): "She has reminded me why I'm here. Not to model flashy costumes and eat delicacies. But to die a bloody death while the crowds urge on my killer."

[41] E.g., Juv. 1.158, 6.610–626, 14.6–24.

[42] For example, Nero famously had his stepbrother poisoned at the dinner table (Tacitus *Annales* 13.15–16; Suetonius *Ner.* 33.2–3). *Quo Vadis* (1951) follows Suetonius *Ner.* 38 in having Nero set fire to Rome and watch happily from a height while singing. On this and other filmic representations of Nero, see Wyke (1997, ch. 5).

But violence is more than a fact of life for the people of Panem's Capitol; it forms the basis for their highest form of entertainment. The Hunger Games correspond to Roman gladiatorial shows (*munera gladiatoria*) in many respects. First, just as intense excitement preceded the opening of the Roman games, with the gladiators publicly feasted and led into the arena in a parade, so the run-up to the Hunger Games starts with a parade in which costumed tributes ride out in horse-drawn chariots—an occasion so spectacular even Katniss gets carried away by it (*HG* 70).[43] Then come three days of intensive training in combat and survival skills. Like gladiators learning from specialists hired by their head trainer (*lanista*), the tributes train together in one gym, taking instruction from experts.[44] Their training is surreptitiously observed by the Gamemakers, "twenty or so men and women dressed in deep purple robes" (97), who resemble the prominent citizens (called *editores* or *munerarii*) who financed and organized gladiatorial shows in Rome.

It falls to the Gamemakers to design and equip a venue for the Games. Although the venue is always simply called "the arena," a new one is built each year, in a different location and with different terrain. On the day the Games are due to start, the tributes are transported to the site and sequestered in individual "Launch Rooms" under the arena. Collectively known as the catacombs, these substructures recall those under the Roman Colosseum, which were used as holding cells for prisoners and waiting areas for performers.[45] Each Launch Room is equipped with a clear-sided cylinder that lifts the tribute into the arena through a trapdoor—another feature reminiscent of the Colosseum.[46] Unlike ancient amphitheaters, however, the Hunger Games arenas have no seating. Instead, ubiquitous hidden cameras capture the action, with selected footage broadcast nightly.

Audience response is important. There is no formal process of appealing to the audience for mercy, like in the Roman amphitheater, but viewers do participate in the drama, becoming, if not quite the "masters" (*domini*) to whom Roman *editores* were beholden, then at least something

---

[43] On the intense excitement preceding the games, see Fagan (2011: 214–215).
[44] On gladiators learning from specialists, see Wiedemann (1992: 117) and Fagan (2011: 220).
[45] Harley (1999: 46). The tributes, of course, are both.
[46] Ibid. (46).

like "associate directors."[47] The Gamemakers monitor viewers' responses and edit the broadcasts to emphasize popular characters and storylines, such as Katniss and Peeta's romance (*HG* 362). At the end of those Games, viewer sentiment even compels the Gamemakers to crown an unprecedented *two* victors.[48] Nor is the arena a closed system: the Gamemakers can intervene at any time to make things more interesting or palatable for the audience. Some of their interventions indicate that there are, in fact, limits to what Capitol viewers will accept, just as Roman spectators expected unwritten codes of gladiatorial etiquette to be enforced "on the sand."[49] Dead tributes' bodies are promptly removed, for example; Katniss says that once, when a tribute named Titus "went completely savage," the Gamemakers "had to have him stunned with electric guns to collect the bodies of the players he'd killed before he ate them" (143).[50] On the other hand, the audience bores easily—"the one thing the Games must not do," Katniss wryly observes, is "verg[e] on dullness" (173)—and the Gamemakers often employ violent methods of hurrying things along.[51] Katniss remembers past Games that were unpopular with viewers because (quoting Vivienne Muller) they offered "limited entertainment value," like "failed, poor quality television drama[s]."[52]

Interested parties can also intervene in the Games by sending gifts to individual tributes, either to give favorites an edge or simply provide encouragement. The turning point in Finnick's Games, for instance, was the arrival of a silver parachute bearing what Katniss says may be the costliest gift she has ever seen given in the arena, a trident (*CF* 209):

[It] was a natural, deadly extension of his arm. He wove a net out of some kind of vine he found, used it to entangle his opponents so he could spear them with the trident, and within a matter of days the crown was his.

[47] On the appeals process, see Fagan (2011: 137–138, 215 n. 78); on *domini*, see ibid. (130, 133, 142–144); and on associate directors, see Muller (2012: 55–56).

[48] Muller (2012: 60).

[49] Fagan (2011: 193–194).

[50] The reference here is probably not to the Roman emperor but to the titular character of Shakespeare's *Titus Andronicus*, who bakes the flesh of two young men into a pie and serves it to their mother (Act 5, scene 3). Like the Rome constructed on the great sound stages of mid–twentieth-century Hollywood, Shakespeare not infrequently functions as a mediating influence in contemporary receptions of antiquity; see Martindale and Martindale (1990).

[51] E.g., the "muttations" (*HG* 331).

[52] Muller (2012: 55); cf. *HG* 39.

Readers familiar with the Roman games will realize that Finnick, as seen in Figure 13-1, effectively transformed himself into a *retiarius* ("net-man"), a type of lightly-armed gladiator who wielded a weighted net (*rete*) and trident.[53] Given Finnick's physical beauty and later stint as a courtesan, it may be amusing to note that while the scantily clad *retiarii* were often admired for their good looks, their nakedness also made them symbols of effeminacy and lewdness.[54]

In another parallel with Roman gladiators, the social position of those who survive the Hunger Games is ambiguous. Victors enjoy celebrity status in the Capitol and are hailed as heroes in their own districts, where their triumph entitles the populace to extra distributions of food for a year. But the fact that they are now permitted to move their families into the upscale "Victors' Village," combined with the lingering effects of their traumatic experiences, sets them apart from their fellow citizens. Nor are they really welcome in other districts, where their survival serves as a reminder that none of the other tributes will be coming home.[55]

Arena fighters occupied an equally uncertain position in Roman society. On the positive side, successful gladiators could become celebrities or sex symbols, and particularly good *munera* were remembered with nostalgia.[56] Some citizens even entered the arena voluntarily.[57] While these "contract-fighters" (*auctorati*) might be motivated by the desire to rescue a family member, like Katniss, or by economic necessity, many seem to have risked their lives for nothing more than a chance to prove themselves before an adoring crowd.[58] But not even the most renowned fighters could achieve complete social respectability. Gladiators were classed as "disreputable" (*infames*), a social category that also included actors, prostitutes, and convicted criminals.[59] The

---

[53] Fagan (2011: 219–220).

[54] Carter (2008); cf. Juv. 2.143–148, 8.199–210.

[55] Katniss and Peeta experience this firsthand during their Victory Tour; see esp. *CF* 47–72.

[56] On gladiators as celebrities and sex symbols, see Wiedemann (1992: 26), Kyle (1998: 85), and Fagan (2011: 213–215), and cf. Martial 5.24. To give one (comic) example of nostalgia, at Petronius *Sat.* 29, Encolpius asks about the three frescoes in Trimalchio's atrium and learns that they depict the *Iliad*, the *Odyssey*, and "Laenas' gladiatorial show" (*Laenatis gladiatorum munus*), respectively.

[57] Kyle (1998: 87–90); Fagan (2011: 212–213).

[58] Cf. Fagan (2011: 212).

[59] Wiedemann (1992: 28–29); Fagan (2011: 152 n. 74, with further bibliography).

Figure 13-1 Detail from a publicity poster for *The Hunger Games: Catching Fire* (2013), featuring Finnick Odair (Sam Claflin) as a sort of *retiarius*, trident in hand, standing beside fellow-tribute Mags (Lynn Cohen). Credit: Lionsgate.

294 Ancient Classics for a Future Generation?

infames were thought untrustworthy and, as such, denied certain legal and civic privileges.[60] Finally, the Hunger Games echo the Roman games in possessing a strong ideological component. "Most gladiators," notes Donald Kyle, "became so against their will," including those captured during wars of territorial expansion or while Rome was quelling insurrection.[61] Condemning captives to almost-certain death before a cheering and jeering crowd sends powerful messages. Such displays may have reassured Roman citizen spectators about national security and reaffirmed their moral superiority over conquered nations.[62] To Rome's enemies, the message would have been more pointed, for all that it was transmitted in the guise of entertainment: resistance to Roman hegemony was not only futile, but potentially (and spectacularly) fatal.[63] And despite the fact that theirs is an irretrievably lost perspective, it stands to reason that at least some of the victims themselves understood what the example of their death might signify.[64]

The majority of Panem's "gladiators" certainly read the Hunger Games as a coded message from the Capitol (*HG* 18–19):

Taking the kids from our districts, forcing them to kill one another while we watch—this is the Capitol's way of reminding us how totally we are at their mercy. How little chance we would stand of surviving another rebellion. Whatever words they use, the real message is clear. "Look how we take your children and sacrifice them and there's nothing you can do. If you lift a finger, we will destroy every last one of you."

Interestingly, though—and despite Katniss's strong words—it later becomes plain that the Capitol's "real message" is not received with equal clarity everywhere. Districts 1 and 2 have been largely assimilated

---

[60] E.g., the right to witness a will or appear in court on another's behalf (Wiedemann 1992: 28).

[61] Kyle (1998: 79). Spartacus himself is said to have come to Rome as a prisoner-of-war (Wiedemann 1992: 102–103).

[62] Kyle (1998: 82); cf. Wiedemann (1992: 3).

[63] Futrell (1997: 46–47). At the same time, Wiedemann argues that condemnation to a gladiatorial school (*ad ludos*) actually signaled Rome's clemency, in that men whose rebellion merited death were given an opportunity to win their lives back (Wiedemann 1992: 103–105).

[64] Cf. Futrell, who argues that Roman gladiators were "essentially irrelevant to the overall message" of gladiatorial *munera*, being "simply a means to an end, a channel through which ritual [was] accomplished" (1997: 210).

into the dominant culture, a difference reflected in local naming conventions: whereas most outer district citizens have names derived from nature (e.g., Katniss,[65] Primrose) or from their district's chief industry (e.g., Finnick[66] from the fishing district, Thresh and Chaff from the agricultural district); three of the five District 2 tributes named in the trilogy have Latin(ate) names—Cato, Brutus, and Enobaria—like Capitol citizens.[67] The inner districts' close relationship with the Capitol has also earned them a correspondingly high standard of living. As a result, they produce stronger, healthier tributes, who train in secret before ever reaching the Capitol (94).[68]

In addition to their tributes' superior preparation (and correspondingly high odds of winning), the inner districts' enthusiasm for the event is real, not feigned. According to Katniss, winning the reaping (*HG* 22) or the Games themselves is considered an honor in the wealthier districts (22). While the symbolic "reaping" of children from conquered territories may not echo ancient Roman practice, the phenomenon of differential acculturation does: the northern and southern regions of Italy, considered an integral part of the state by the Imperial period, were once independent nations that resisted assimilation.

In sum, there is much that is authentic in Collins's refiguration of gladiatorial *munera*, as well as of Roman Imperial culture generally. The overall effect, however, is distorted by exaggeration of negative elements and omission of more positive ones. For example, while some wealthy Romans undoubtedly served decadent feasts upon occasion, they would not have done so every day, and a large percentage of the urban population was vulnerable to deprivation via frequent food shortages.[69] Likewise, while gladiatorial combat could be brutal and often did end in death, this was by no means always the case.[70] Some skilled fighters had

---

[65] Fittingly, given her archery skills, *katniss* is a another name for the arrowhead plant (*HG* 52).

[66] A phonetic spelling of "finnoc," "white trout," from the Gaelic *fionnag* (*OED*, s.v. "finnoc").

[67] These characters' first appearances are at *HG* 182, *CF* 191, and *M* 224, respectively. The name Enobaria may have been inspired by Domitius Enobarbus, a character in Shakespeare's *Antony and Cleopatra*, loosely based in turn on Gn. Domitius Ahenobarbus (cos. 32 B.C.E.).

[68] These "Career Tributes" are "always favorites" in the Games, and one of them usually wins (*HG* 69).

[69] Aldrete and Mattingly (2010: 198).

[70] Wiedemann (1992: 34).

long careers and earned the respect accorded today's sports stars.[71] Many had wives and children.[72] And injured gladiators always had the option of appealing to the *editor* (and the crowd) for release.[73] By eliding such possibilities, Collins imbued her gladiatorial paradigm with aspects of the public executions (*summa supplicia*) carried out in the Roman arena at midday.[74]

Collins's characterization of Capitol spectators is just as black-and-white. They may balk at cannibalism, but their enthusiasm for televised violence is considerable, occasioning many astringent remarks from Katniss.[75] In contrast, they struggle when confronting hardship and violence in their own lives. Katniss witnesses this dichotomy firsthand during the rebellion, first, when she rescues her traumatized prep team from a rebel prison (*M* 47–49), and again, when the sight of her jagged scar "triggers [TV producer Fulvia Cardew]'s gag reflex" (61–62).[76] Tertullian reports a similar phenomenon among Roman arena-goers (*De Spectaculis* 21.3–4):

> Qui in plateis litem manu agentem aut compescit aut detestatur, idem in stadio gravioribus pugnis suffragium ferat; et qui ad cadaver hominis communi lege defuncti exhorret, idem in amphitheatro derosa et dissipata et in suo sanguine squalentia corpora patientissimis oculis desuper incumbat; immo qui propter homicidae poenam probandam ad spectaculum veniat, idem gladiatorem ad homicidium flagellis et virgis compellat invitum.

> The same person who checks or curses someone carrying on a violent quarrel in the streets, casts a vote for more serious blows in the stadium; and the same person who shudders at the corpse of a man who has died a natural death, lingers in the amphitheater with the most patient eyes on bodies bitten and dismembered and stiff in their own blood; the same person, indeed, who comes to the games to show approval for the punishment of murder, drives a reluctant gladiator to murder with whips and beatings.

---

[71] Kyle (1998: 84–85); Fagan (2011: 194–196).

[72] Wiedemann (1992: 119–124).

[73] Fagan (2011: 137, 142–143, 222–223).

[74] Kyle (1998: 53–55); Fagan (2011: 133–137, 174–187).

[75] For example, when Peeta speculates that Capitol citizens may not be happy to see them returned to the arena for the special 75th Anniversary Games, Katniss replies, "I'm guessing they'll get over it once the blood starts flowing" (*CF* 194).

[76] Ironically, Fulvia insists the scar be covered up for the propaganda clip they are filming, but suggests covering it with "a bloody bandage ... to indicate [Katniss has] been in recent combat" (*M* 70). Cf. Muller (2012: 58–59).

Roman spectators could be bloodthirsty, especially when prejudiced against the combatants, and some probably did react differently to violence encountered in other settings.[77] Yet many went to the arena for reasons other than savagery—say, out of appreciation for gladiatorial skill[78]—and an even greater number never went at all.[79] Moreover, just as many Romans were neither well dressed nor well fed, so, too, were many intimately familiar with violence, pain, and death.[80] Tertullian, like Katniss herself, exaggerates for effect.

THE PROVOCATIONS OF PANEM

Maria Wyke has written that cinema, informed by various nineteenth- and twentieth-century historiographic genres, "has long provided its own distinctive historiography of ancient Rome that has vividly resurrected the ancient world and reformulated it in the light of present needs."[81] But the ancient world was subject to continual reformulation already in antiquity by writers who crafted representations of society to suit their own aims. Tertullian, for example, hoped his lurid portrait of Roman arena-goers would persuade fellow Christians that the games encouraged "lack of restraint and baseness of behavior."[82] Horace, with his account of an extravagant dinner *chez* Nasidienus (*Satires* 2.8), both inculcated in his readers the Epicurean value of moderation and lampooned the vulgarity and pretensions of social climbers. Hollywood screenwriters then elaborated on these stereotypes of a vice-ridden Rome in order to vilify modern authoritarian regimes or, more recently, to diagnose a perceived decline in traditional American values.[83]

I argue that Collins's futuristic version of the "Eternal Dystopia" aims both to reinforce the ideological opposition between democracy and totalitarianism for a young adult audience, and to provoke reflection on certain aspects of American media culture. To support these claims,

---

[77] On prejudice against combatants, see Fagan (2011: ch. 5).

[78] Ibid. (215–217).

[79] Ibid. (276–278).

[80] Ibid. (25–27, violence; 30–32, pain/death).

[81] Wyke (1997: 8).

[82] Fagan (2011: 123).

[83] Day (2008: 7), with bibliography.

I first examine the series' generic affiliation as critical dystopia, then triangulate between Rome, Panem's Capitol, and contemporary America on the basis of desensitization to media-purveyed violence and consumption of exploitative entertainment.

Critical Dystopia

Critics invariably label Panem a *dystopia*. It is not, however, the same kind of dystopia as (for example) Airstrip One in George Orwell's *1984*. "Classical" dystopias feature protagonists who end up crushed by their authoritarian societies in spite of attempts to escape or alter them; any utopian hope offered by such texts exists only outside their pages.[84] By contrast, "critical" dystopias "allow both readers and protagonists to hope by resisting closure: the ambiguous, open endings . . . maintain the utopian impulse *within* the work."[85] The ending of *Mockingjay* fits this description to a tee. The rebels overthrow the government, but the reader cannot know whether or not their new republic will prosper. And although Katniss finds a kind of peace with Peeta, she is too deeply scarred to experience unalloyed happiness. This ambiguity is characteristic of critical dystopias: characters may succeed in changing society as a result of awareness and knowledge they have gained, but open endings typically leave them struggling to deal with the consequences of their choices.[86]

Critical dystopias are often marketed to adolescents, who relate to narrative tropes such as loss of innocence and rebellion against authority.[87] Adolescence is also a time when young people start to view society with critical eyes, confronting endemic social problems like discrimination and class inequality.[88] Developing political consciousness then leads to anxiety over more global challenges, such as nuclear proliferation, scarcity of resources, and the ramifications of technological advances.[89] These are precisely the tropes, problems, and anxieties

---

[84] Baccolini and Moylan (2003: 7).
[85] Ibid. (7).
[86] Baccolini (2003: 130); cf. Muller (2012: 61).
[87] Hintz and Ostry (2003: 9–11).
[88] Ibid. (7–9).
[89] Ibid. (11–2).

typically found in young adult dystopian fiction, mixed with one last crucial ingredient: hope that improvement is still possible.[90]

Yet, despite preserving a "utopian impulse," critical dystopias are generally not prescriptive. They do not pinpoint a specific threat or solution, but only reveal cracks in the social foundations of the world,[91] leading the reader to what Fredric Jameson has called "fruitful bewilderment."[92] The mechanism is one of estrangement.[93] Once distanced from the familiar by the novelty of a fictional world, readers struggle to comprehend that world's strangeness, only to realize that their own reality has been concealed beneath the strangeness all along. The shock of recognition compels readers to come to grips with the author's vision of the future and determine how it could evolve from their present. What cracks, then, does Collins's refigured Rome reveal in the social foundation of contemporary America?

Themes of social justice and political self-determination are undeniably important in the trilogy. The opposition between the districts and the Capitol raises questions about social challenges like the equitable allocation of resources and the balance between political cohesion and individual freedom. Moreover, the narrative arc culminates in the struggle to found a republic, with representation for all. Katniss and Haymitch Abernathy, her mentor in the Games, hear about the rebels' plan from former Gamemaker–turned–rebel leader Plutarch Heavensbee (*M* 83–84):

"We're going to form a republic where the people of each district and the Capitol can elect their own representatives to be their voice in a centralized government. Don't look so suspicious; it's worked before."

"In books," Haymitch mutters.

"In history books," says Plutarch. "And if our ancestors could do it, then we can, too."

---

[90] Ibid. (10).

[91] Ibid. (8): "Utopian fiction reveals the social foundations of our own world—and the cracks that form in them."

[92] Quoted in Hintz and Ostry (2003: 4).

[93] For an in-depth look at the history of the term as applied to SF by Suvin and others, see Parrinder (2001); on the displacement of contemporary concerns onto antiquity in film, see Joshel, Malamud, and Wyke (2001: 4).

Frankly, our ancestors don't seem much to brag about. I mean, look at the state they left us in, with the wars and the broken planet. Clearly, they didn't care about what would happen to the people who came after them. But this republic idea sounds like an improvement over our current government.

For all her skepticism, Katniss plays a key role in determining the character of the new state. Disobeying orders to shoot the already dying President Snow, she assassinates President Coin of District 13 instead, realizing that she would be no less a tyrant than Snow and that the citizens of communitarian District 13 are no freer than the other districts have been. This is the climax of *Mockingjay*—when Katniss achieves the insight that leads her to take aim at Coin instead of Snow, ensuring the deaths of *both* despots and affording the infant republic a chance to put its ideals of social justice into practice.

Casting the Capitol as the archetypal Rome makes sense in a plot culminating in the victory of republicanism over totalitarianism, because it allows Collins to leverage the familiarity of an us-vs.-Rome dynamic commonly found in film. Hollywood has traditionally vilified the Roman Empire while glorifying the Roman Republic, which served as an important model for the Founding Fathers. Rome essentially reverted to a monarchy with the rise of Julius Caesar, and that form of government—the one from which the American colonists sought to liberate themselves—is thought to lead to tyranny.[94] Many cinematic portrayals of the Empire even conform to the so-called linguistic paradigm, in which despotic or decadent Romans are played by British theater actors while American actors star as the heroic, marginalized protagonists.[95] It has been suggested that these choices reflect a desire to project onto antiquity the historical antagonism between the colonies and the British Empire.[96]

Plutarch's reassuring words to Haymitch and Katniss suggest that he thinks of the district rebellion as a second American Revolution. Unlike the colonists, however, the district rebels have no need to invent a tradition connecting them to the Roman Republic and casting their oppressors in the role of the wicked Empire; the Capitol already *is* (a version of) the (archetypal) Empire, and the rebels, like the Capitol citizens, already

[94] Winkler (2001: 50).
[95] Wyke (1997: 23).
[96] Joshel, Malamud, and Wyke (2001: 8–9).

belong to the invented tradition that partially guarantees the success of Collins's refiguration of them as such.[97] The narrative arc thus acquires a certain inevitability, potentially affirming readerly conviction that the right to self-determination must be protected and that resources should be fairly allocated.

Media Desensitization

Despite the prominence of these themes, however, the desire to make general points about social organization would not by itself motivate intense concentration on violent spectacle, which is where I believe Collins's refiguration works the hardest. Her high-tech version of the Roman games suggests a timely parallel between the stereotypically Roman delight in bloody spectacle and contemporary consumption of violent, exploitative media.

Collins herself has explained the genesis of the trilogy in terms of concern over media desensitization. The idea came to her while channel-surfing between the evening news and a reality show:

On one channel, there's a group of young people competing for I don't even know; and on the next, there's a group of young people fighting in an actual war. I was really tired, and the lines between these stories started to blur in a very unsettling way.[98]

Collins links this experience with the terror she felt as a child, when, in spite of her mother's efforts to protect her, she glimpsed some footage of the war in Vietnam—"[news coverage] at that time was much more graphic in illustrating the fate of our soldiers"—where her father was deployed.[99] Nowadays, Collins fears, "people see so many reality shows and dramas that when real news is on, its impact is completely lost on them":[100]

I worry that we're all getting a little desensitized to the images on our televisions. If you're watching a sitcom, that's fine. But if there's a real-life tragedy

[97] On invented traditions, see Wyke (1997: 14–15).
[98] Quoted in Margolis (2008).
[99] Blasingame (2009: 727).
[100] Quoted in ibid. (727).

unfolding, you should not be thinking of yourself as an audience member. Because those are real people on the screen, and they're not going away when the commercials start to roll.[101]

The topic of desensitization remains controversial, but some studies suggest that exposure to media violence produces "desensitization-related outcomes," both on a physiological level and when it comes to tolerating aggressive behavior in others.[102] It is probably safe to say, too, that most of Collins's readers would not respond to real-life violence with the same equanimity as a violent film or first-person shooter, let alone with the competence of an action hero or video game avatar.[103] While we might like to think we would be as brave and resourceful as Katniss if placed in a similar situation, we might just as easily fall to pieces, like Katniss's prep team imprisoned in District 13. In other words, no matter how much we sympathize with or root for the tributes and the rebels, we *recognize* ourselves in the citizens of the Capitol; in spite of attempts to distance ourselves from the "Romans" in the story, we are thus unwittingly identified with them.[104] For this reason, readers may derive comfort from the compassion Katniss shows to those whose experience of hardship has only ever been virtual. Certainly her attitude is more sympathetic than that of Tertullian, who described a similar phenomenon at the Roman games over two thousand years before.

Reality Television

In keeping with the dreamlike juxtaposition of documentary and "reality" programming that inspired the trilogy, Collins's refiguration of the archetypal Rome addresses the current vogue for video vérité voyeurism alongside the issue of desensitization.[105] The Hunger Games combine advanced surveillance technologies with aspects of gladiatorial *munera* and the *summa supplicia* to produce a dystopian version of a *Survivor*-type reality show.

---

[101] Quoted in Margolis (2008, n.p.).
[102] Bushman and Anderson (2009), with bibliography.
[103] Cf. Fagan (2011: 263).
[104] Cf. Joshel, Malamud, and Wyke (2001: 6).
[105] On video vérité voyeurism, see Calvert (2004: 5-6).

In the Games, as in *Survivor*, a single winner must emerge from a diverse group of strangers stranded in a hostile environment to compete for a prize. However, there are also three crucial differences between the two. First, while thousands clamor to appear on *Survivor*, the "cast" of the Games is conscripted, and the technology that renders cameramen unnecessary in the arena leaves tributes simultaneously devoid of privacy and very much alone. Second, modern production teams strive to ensure participants' safety, standing by to evacuate injured or ailing contestants, while the Hunger Games' equivalent of a Medevac unit shows up only after someone has died. And third, the diversity of each year's "cast" of tributes reflects, not a neoliberal interest in accentuating interaction between populations and probing the limits of democratic comity, as critics have argued for *Survivor*, but an authoritarian strategy for punishing past disobedience and deterring it in the future.[106] *Survivor*'s structure promotes teamwork and group governance, at least up to a point.[107] But teamwork between tributes in the arena is discouraged, both implicitly (by the rules) and explicitly (by the Gamemakers' interventions and selective editing of footage for broadcast).

These divergences from the *Survivor* pattern suit the stereotypically Romanized context of the Hunger Games, since they accentuate the ruthlessness of Panem's rulers and the detached avidity of the spectators. The Games thus represent a possible result of endowing the archetypal Rome with technology enabling covert surveillance and, by extension, reality programming. Such technology enhances the feeling of intimacy between viewer and subject while simultaneously intensifying the desensitization effect, both by increasing the physical distance between spectators and participants and by permitting increased manipulation by producers.[108] Ironically, the technological element—which sets Panem apart from even the archetypal Rome and moves the trilogy into the realm of SF—probably does the most to ensure that Collins's primary audience recognizes their own society in Panem.

[106] Ouellette and Hay (2008: 186).

[107] Ibid. (185); with Cavender (2004).

[108] It also potentially deprives citizens of an opportunity for expressing opinions and flexing political muscle, as Wiedemann has argued for the crowd in the Roman amphitheater (1992: 165–176).

Americans already live in a republic, and violent reality shows are, at least for now, uncommon.[109] But invasive technology enabling surreptitious surveillance and the creation of voyeuristic entertainment? There is nothing virtual about *that* reality.

PLUTARCH'S HISTORY LESSON

I hope I have shown that Collins's Panem, far from being an uncritical reception of popular culture stereotypes, is a carefully constructed hybrid refiguration that implicates aspects of contemporary society. In conclusion, I suggest that Collins underscores the deliberate and productive nature of her refiguration by embedding in the story a character who himself models the process of classical reception.

As a former Head Gamemaker, Plutarch Heavensbee possesses a wealth of privileged information that the Capitol has kept secret, including the origins of the country's name. The Capitol has in fact suppressed almost all knowledge of antiquity, simply appropriating what they needed—names and vocabulary, monumental architecture, the games and the rituals surrounding them—to sanction their model of imperial domination.[110] Only once the rebellion is underway does Plutarch enlighten Katniss (*M* 223–224):

"Oh, the city might be able to scrape along for a while [without the districts to supply it]," says Plutarch. "Certainly, there are emergency supplies stockpiled. But . . . in the Capitol, all they've known is *Panem et Circenses*."

"What's that?" I recognize *Panem*, of course, but the rest is nonsense.

"It's a saying from thousands of years ago, written in a language called Latin about a place called Rome," he explains. "*Panem et Circenses* translates into 'Bread and Circuses.' The writer was saying that in return for full bellies and entertainment, his people had given up their political responsibilities and therefore their power."

---

[109] Fagan (2011: 233).

[110] "Appropriation" is "taking an ancient image or text and using it to sanction subsequent ideas or practices (explicitly or implicitly)" (Hardwick 2003: 9). For additional application to *The Hunger Games* trilogy, see Makins (2014).

I think about the Capitol. The excess of food. And the ultimate entertainment. The Hunger Games. "So that's what the districts are for. To provide the bread and circuses."

"Yes. And as long as that kept rolling in, the Capitol could control its little empire. Right now, it can provide neither, at least at the standard the people are accustomed to."

Plutarch's explication of what "the writer was saying" is actually fairly accurate, as a look at the original context will show (Juv. 10.77–81):

> Iam pridem, ex quo suffragia nulli
> vendimus, effudit curas; nam qui dabat olim
> imperium, fasces, legiones, omnia, nunc se
> continet atque duas tantum res anxius optat,   80
> panem et circenses.

It's a long time now since [the populace] shed their responsibilities, since we sold our votes for nothing; for they who once had it in their power to grant *imperium*, the rods of high office, legions, everything, now hold themselves back and wish anxiously for only two things—bread and circuses.

Plutarch, however, uses this passage in a way its author would probably have abhorred. Juvenal aimed to spotlight his fellow citizens' willingness to surrender their right to political self-determination in exchange for food and entertainment, mentioning neither the provenance of the "bread and circuses" nor the people expected to produce them. Moreover, as an Italian native, he would have been unlikely to champion a provincial revolt. But Katniss naturally applies Plutarch's explanation to the relationship between Snow's regime and the *districts*, not that between the government and the Capitol citizens, as a strictly analogical reading would require. Plutarch (just as naturally) encourages her interpretation; after all, he needs her to continue serving as the face of the rebellion.

Like Collins herself, Plutarch presents a reception of Roman Imperial society inspired by a distorted source text and tailored to help a young adult audience gain insight into the receiving society. He succeeds in this, as his etymology crystallizes Katniss's understanding of the way the Capitol views the districts—not as people, but as commodities to exploit. In addition, her district-centric interpretation of Juvenal indicates a suggestive reading of the way the Roman Empire related to its possessions: the capital *did* rely on the provinces for grain, and most arena fighters were *not* citizens, nor even free-born. Plutarch with his history lesson thus reaffirms what students of classical reception already take for granted: that accuracy is neither the only nor the best criterion by which to judge receptions, and that analyzing "misrepresentations" of antiquity can illuminate both the "ideological impulses" of the receiving society and even, at times, antiquity itself.[111]

[111] On such "ideological impulses," see Day (2008: 4).

14

Jonathan Hickman's *Pax Romana* and the End of Antiquity

C. W. Marshall

"We can take comfort in the fact that, as usual, most people remain ignorant of how aggressively we have been funding scientific research," Cardinal Beppi Pelle tells the Pope in 2053, as part of his report on the Roman Catholic Church's recent discovery of time travel (*Pax Romana* [*PR*] 1.10).[1] This vision of the church, which is created in Jonathan Hickman's *Pax Romana*, is meant to confound readers' expectations,

---

[1] *Pax Romana*, written and illustrated by Jonathan Hickman, was published by Image Comics in four single issues from Dec. 2007 to Nov. 2008 and collected as a trade paperback in 2009. The collected edition is the most easily available format, but pages are unnumbered. The following conventions are therefore used for reference. Divisions between the four chapters are clearly marked (e.g., "end one" appears by itself on a page preceding a page with the words "chapter two"). If we exclude these title pages, chapter 1 has 30 pages, chapter 2 has 24 pages, chapter 3 has 28 pages, and chapter 4 has 28 pages. Reference is made to chapter and page number (chapter headings appear on 1.3, 2.1, 3.1, and 4.1; 1.1–2 and 4.30–32 serve as bookends, as they repeat the phrase, "Destroy the Past, Create the Future"). Because of Hickman's artistic style, which often challenges the expected reading-order of panels, reference is made to the page and not to the individual panel. The collected edition also contains an 11-page appendix offering a (revised) timeline of the years 337–1108 (from the death of Constantine to the "Reestablishment"), which was not part of the serial comic release. A consequence of this numbering is that

and in Pelle's audacious claim about the ecclesiastical investment in science, we see the foundation of the apparently outrageous premise of the four-issue comics series published in 2010. Once the premise is accepted, however, Hickman's world produces an exceptionally rich time-travel story—before it folds in upon itself and disappears.

The question of when in the past representatives of the church will be sent is addressed immediately. Hickman offers a transcript in which the "window of opportunity" is considered. Though there are no practical limits on the technology, there are ethical ones. As Pope Pius XIII says,

Returning to anytime before the resurrection [of Christ] is unacceptable. We are servants of Christ not collaborators. I will not entertain some grand fundamentalist scheme of an artificial Kingdom of Heaven. (*PR* 1.13)

This practical limit narrows the field. In the world of 2053, Catholicism has (apparently) lost irrecoverable ground to the spread of Islam. If they are to avoid merely adding to the blood of the Crusades, "It must be a time before Muhammad and after the resurrection," advises one bishop. "Then it must be Rome," adds another. "And if it is Rome, then it must be Constantine," concludes the Pope (all 1.13).

With the invention of time travel, the Catholic Church in *Pax Romana* plans to send back soldiers who are practicing Catholics, armed with modern weaponry including nuclear weapons, to assist Constantine and ensure that the Roman Empire does not fall, and thereby secure the eventual success of the church. This action will change the world and destroy the present timeline, which is judged to have failed.[2] The reader of the series knows that this is in fact what has happened: the story begins in an unrecognizable world, in which a series-7 Gene Pope of the Unified Church, a wrinkled old man wearing an imposing mitre and breathing through tubes, tells a bedtime story to the four-year-old Emperor Constans IV, tenth Emperor of Holy Rome, in the megacity

---

odd-numbered pages appear at the left of the collected edition, and even-numbered on the right, contrary to normal printing practice. Hickman's layout depends on the viewer's seeing the two-page spread, odd and even (De Blieck 2008). My thanks go to the editors of this volume for their helpful comments.

[2] The world of 2053 is presented as a future extrapolated from the (familiar) present of the reader; it is not an alternate future. The effect of time travel will be to erase and "rewrite" this timeline.

Constantinople at a time "Post-aurora, before the synthetic rains . . ." (*PR* 1.4, and see 1.7), and this frame narrative persists throughout the series (1.1–8, 2.1–2, 5–6, 3.22–24, 4.21–30). The church has succeeded; the advance of Islam is stopped, and there are colonies on the Moon and Mars. This success is explicit in terms familiar to readers of SF, too, reckoned in terms of genetically enhanced longevity, memory technologies, and space exploration.[3]

This chapter considers how *Pax Romana* relates to different segments of its readership. Any comic will have multiple audiences, each with different degrees of familiarity with the medium. As with any literary form, comics build on the readership's previous knowledge. Some individuals will approach the work as readers of science fiction (SF), looking particularly for how the series creates associations with a variety of other time-travel narratives. Others, perhaps attracted by the Latin title, will be drawn due to an interest in classical history, and particularly the military history of the late Empire. The previous knowledge brought to the text by the reader proves relevant in both cases and enriches the experience offered. While these approaches are complementary, the way *Pax Romana* relates to these audiences differently does shape how the work is interpreted. By drawing together elements of both readings, the narrative can be seen to offer a particular attitude towards antiquity and the classical past.

The setting for Hickman's rewrite of history, beginning with Constantine, means that most of what we know as classical antiquity persists: Homer, Pericles, Alexander, Plautus, Augustus, Plutarch . . . all make exactly the same contributions they always have. *Pax Romana* invites the reader to consider a world in which everything after antiquity never happened. What is taken away is not classical content, and Hickman's reader is given only antiquity and the imagined future—classics and SF, and nothing in between. The (rewritten) future of the Gene Pope is not presented as a paradise, however, and even given the limited perspective from the room in Constantinople, the reader is alienated in part because of the dogmatic insistence that is explicitly authenticated: the world does not allow relativism or postmodern subjectivity,

[3] Though this newly remade world has had geostationary satellites since the year 312, there is no mention of America in the rewritten timeline nor of any mundane concerns of New World exploration. Nor are there references to extraterrestrial species, so the theological question of their relationship to the church and God's grace is not addressed.

and I imagine even a faithful Catholic reader would not identify with the Byzantine, fractured, visually incomplete world Hickman's art presents. For example, the apparently haphazard splash of color in the background of Figure 14-1 (*PR* 1.7) blends with the black ink to suggest chaos and an uncontrolled world, underneath which exists no material support. The Emperor's legs remain apparently un-inked: they are just pencils, an incomplete comics creation. The Gene Pope's mitre appears to flare with an inner light that reveals even more emptiness on the page.

Hickman's artistic style is severe, but it serves a specific narrative purpose and can be tied to the sources on which he draws. *Pax Romana* offers the same infographics feel he had used in *The Nightly News* (2006–2007). Many elements are familiar, not from comics, but from graphic design and advertising. Hickman uses a limited color palette on any given page,[4] and while panel organization can be straightforward, he regularly employs inset windows and other devices to present additional information, such as a brief biography of a character just introduced. The result can be very text-heavy, as layout, substance and absence, maps, and spattered paint all demand attention and invite interpretation. When Cardinal Pelle is shot, the reader sees the body falling, suddenly drawn in red ink, with blood spatters extending beyond the panel border (*PR* 1.32; see Figure 14-2). Overlapping the panel is a small circle in which four single bullets are visible. They look identical but are numbered one through four, and in the main panel the four points where the bullets enter his body are carefully numbered, evoking a photograph in an official autopsy report, perhaps. There are no sound effects in the panel that would allow a sense of imminence to the event (compare the gunfire at 4.14 and 15). The military emblem in the bottom right just outside the panel border is one of a series of markers that appear regularly in the series, serving as punctuation for the narrative beats.[5] Finally,

---

[4] In an interview with Hickman, De Blieck observes, *PR*'s limited color palette "isn't used to color in the characters, specifically, who often remain black and white set aside or on top of the colors." Hickman responds, "To me, one thing is certain: There needs to be much more risk-taking in the coloring of American comics" (De Blieck 2008).

[5] Compare the appearance of a different marker in Figure 14-1, where the black papal sign is seen in the bottom right corner, and its reverse is found in the black cloud at the Gene Pope's right shoulder. This forms an implied left-to-right diagonal across the page that integrates visually with the mostly vertical arrangement of speech balloons, the complementary left-to-right movement of the white-and-black character biographies, and the right-to-left diagonal of the background ink.

Figure 14-1 The Emperor and the Gene Pope. From Jonathan Hickman, 2009. *Pax Romana*. New York: Image Comics.

And what of our will?

Figure 14-2 The death of Cardinal Pelle. From Jonathan Hickman, 2009. *Pax Romana*. New York: Image Comics.

in black at the bottom, the words of Brigadier General Nicholas Chase appear in a box, separate from any appearance of the character and not in a speech balloon. While the fact is lost as the body twists and falls, at the beginning of the next chapter, an element of Chase's mindset while he shot the Cardinal emerges: the four bullets are said to have entered the body in the sign of the cross, *signum crucis* (2.2)

There can be a clinical feeling with much of this art, allowing the viewer to remain emotionally unattached. Pages regularly do not have enough panels to suggest movement, which means characterization happens in snapshots and in dialogue. While the dialogue can be expressive, much is dedicated to exploring ideas. Sometimes dialogue overtakes the page completely: in each chapter, there is a two-page spread offering a transcript of an extended conversation (*PR* 1.13–14, 2.9–10, 3.7–8, 4.3–4).[6] Text replaces the comics format completely, and

[6] "There's a lot of text on the pages, more so than in most comics. You really have to *read* this comic, both in word balloons and in paragraphs—whether as transcripts of discussions or excerpts of mythical books" (De Blieck 2008).

individuals are identified by a two-letter code, and may not have any visual identity in the series beyond a single small image on that page.[7]

Hickman's style makes the reader work hard to extract coherent narrative motivations for the characters, which again can be alienating. This is where *Pax Romana* separates itself from many time-travel stories, avoiding the straightforward action adventure promised by Romans with assault rifles. The mercenaries' mission is "to save the world, establish a true universal religion, and create a new culture" (Burgas 2011):

> This leads into a two-page discussion (using mostly text) about manufacturing religion, free will, slavery, social engineering, and the right of their group to do any of this. They agree to do it, of course, but Hickman shows us that they're not completely united.

One consequence of this format is that ideas are evaluated on their own merits, independently of the character to whom they are attributed. The movements and choices of individuals would seem to matter less from this perspective, and the characters regularly insist on a perspective of a larger scale.

There remains a continued conflict, however, between the large-scale social engineering being planned and the ordinary concerns of individuals within the fiction. The Gene Pope's embedded tale describes the mission led by Cardinal Pelle into the past to assist Constantine. The military leader chosen is Brigadier General Nicholas Chase, a distinguished American soldier who, it emerges, is nephew to the Pope (*PR* 1.15, 1.20). He selects four individuals as his command group, who in turn will lead the roughly 5,000 soldiers—the Eternal Army—that will be brought into the past (1.19, 1.22). Following the jump to the year 312, Chase hears Pelle's plan ("After that, we consolidate our relationship between the Church and Constantine to position and strengthen our doctrinal dominance through Nicaea, Constantinople, Ephesus, *etc.*," 1.29) and decides that this is an

<hr />

[7] The layout for this approach finds its precedent in the formal experiments of Dave Sim's self-published comic *Cerebus* (1977–2004): see particularly *Reads*, issues 175–186 (written by Sim, illustrated by Sim and Gerhard; collected 1995), where a substantial part of the narrative is presented in a dense column of small-type text alongside a single image. The lack of clear integration between text and image challenges the notion of what a comic is or should be. Furthermore, "reads" are presented as the medium of mass popular literature within the world of *Cerebus*, and so constitute the in-world equivalent of comics.

insufficiently ambitious means to remake the world, and kills him (1.32; see Figure 14-2). The next chapter lays out Gen. Chase's plan: "I mean for us to do our duty and completely change the direction of human history" (2.8); "There will be no *dark ages*—no *long night* before the *dawn of modernity* . . . " (2.11). Battles are won with tanks, helicopters, and sniper teams (2.21–22), and dynastic marriages are made between Constantine's family and the time travelers: his half-sister Constantia marries not Licinius, but one of the command group, Colonel Fabio Rossi (2.23–24), even though Rossi has shown himself to be an atheist (2.9).

A significant feature of Hickman's accomplishment in the series is his ability to identify specific moments that have helped shape our present-day world. Even if one disagrees with the moments he isolates, there is a need for argument: a case needs to be made. This is perhaps most clearly seen in his representation of the First Council of Nicaea, held in the year 325 (*PR* 3.2–5). This was the first time theologians from the whole church came together to discuss matters of doctrine, establishing a Christian orthodoxy. Among the accomplishments of the Council of Nicaea was the clear opposition to the (heretical) doctrine of Arius, on the nature of Christ's relationship with God the Father. The historical debate was divisive against Arian believers, and resulted in the formulation of the Nicene Creed, which is still used regularly in Christian churches.[8] Chase urges Constantine to act clearly, as the historical Constantine did at the original Council of Nicaea, but in a more inclusive direction that can be seen to extend the religious amnesty offered by the Edict of Milan in 313:

From this day forward there will be two accepted doctrines of religious faith in the Holy Empire of Rome: Orthodox Christendom and the Free Religions of the People. Both will be *state supported*—both will be *state protected*. . . . Christendom and the Lesser Path to Heaven—for pious men who choose to make the more difficult journey. (3.5; Constantine speaks)

This is a much more deliberate edict than the gesture of toleration of Christianity known from (our) historical sources. Chase's goal, through

---

[8] The creed (statement of faith) affirms the divinity and consubstantial nature of Christ, and denies that He is a creature ("begotten, not made, being of one substance with the Father"), in direct opposition to Arius. It is employed in Catholic, Protestant, and Orthodox liturgies.

Constantine, is to break the authoritarian power of religion (3.7: "we want to eliminate religion as a method of control"; Colonel Emmanuel Mfede, one of the command group, speaks). By changing Constantine's position at Nicaea, Chase (and Hickman) open up the possibility for a much more radical revisioning of society.

Fans of SF will recognize in this plan to reshape society, with the aim of removing from human history an extended period of stagnation and decay, affinities with the *Foundation* series by Isaac Asimov. This series (an original trilogy published from 1951–1953, collecting stories he wrote beginning in 1942, followed by four more novels in 1982–1993) posited the science of "psychohistory," a complex mathematics that permitted long-term sociological predictions. When a cataclysmic collapse of the long-standing Galactic Empire is predicted, Hari Seldon proposes a means to reduce the period of ensuing barbarism drastically to a mere 1,000 years, through the Encyclopedia Galactica Foundation that he establishes. The series examines the consequences of sociopolitical crises as well as what happens when exceptional individuals interrupt the order that the science of psychohistory has predicted.

In *Pax Romana*, the programmatic quality of psychohistory is articulated by Chase and his senior officers. Col. Mfede outlines their intergenerational ambitions. Using the political and economic virtues of democracy, Communism, and fascism at different times, he argues,

We intend . . . to enact radical socio-political change and then use their inherent weaknesses to directly implement progressively better systems. Every three to five generations we will change the government of Rome until we achieve this. Revolution—Stabilization—Consolidation. (*PR* 3.7)[9]

The plan expects rebellion and insurrection; indeed, it depends on it for the comparatively rapid mobilization of industrialization and enlightenment. Provisions are made early for dealing with those most likely to upset the predicted sequence of events:

[9] This is presented as part of a transcript of events, and the dialogue in the ellipsis is ungrammatical. It is hard not to hear echoes of the social forces that drive human behavior in Asimov's world as well. There is, however, some simplification, and at times Hickman's presentation of social catalysts gets muddled: "Hickman makes a classic blunder here by confusing economic systems—communism—with governmental systems—democracy—but we understand what he means" (Burgas 2011).

Yes, man will evolve quickly, so as soon as possible we need a support struc-ture in place for clearly identifying the most talented and ambitious citi-zens. We must keep them personally satisfied and out of the government and our higher military ranks until our democracy is established. (3.8; Nicholas Chase speaks)

Scientists, on the other hand, are well cared for: Mfede announces, "I introduced the scientific method to a group of scholars last week a full 1300 years early" (3.8; we are told with understatement that it "Went well").

The detached view that contemplates the effects of change over centu-ries can therefore be seen to resonate with the cool and impersonal artistic style Hickman employs. Despite the characters' efforts, however, three obstacles are introduced to the smooth running of the long-term plan. First, when Constantine's death seems imminent, Rossi has dynas-tic ambitions for his children (*PR* 3.16: "When Constantine dies, [his son] Crispus must be eliminated. . . . We should sit one of my children on the throne. It's the only way we can ensure control until we can implement our first uprising"). Second, over twenty-five years, Gen. Chase has formed a personal attachment to Constantine, whose death-bed request in 337 is at odds with Rossi's plan (3.19–21). Chase's own uncertainty about the long-term success of his enterprise (3.20: "Soon . . . *very soon*, we will be rudderless") leads him to place value in an indi-vidual commitment. In case the reader misses the significance of this deviation from the plan, Hickman reverts to the frame narrative and has the Gene Pope spell it out:

Compassion and *loyalty*. . . . These are remarkable qualities in a man, but for the General, they meant a relaxing of standards. . . . *Loyalty* to a man when *loyalty* should have only been permitted to the cause. And *compassion*. . . . *Compassion* where there should have been none. (3.22)

Thirdly, some mercenaries led by a Jamaican gunrunner who were lost in the original time-travel event appear "upstream" in 337 (3.25–30, and cf. 1.17–18).

The shape of the new world becomes clear in the final chapter of the series, which covers the years 337–361: as in Asimov's *Foundation* series, the reader is not provided with the full sweep of changed history, but isolated moments from which an account of events can be constructed. Interpersonal rivalries and Machiavellian schemes among the command team lead to the murder of Crispus and Chase, and the division of the Roman Empire among his command team. Some readers will naturally see in this an analogue to the wars and infighting of the successors following the death of Alexander the Great in 323 B.C.E. (these rival generals are sometimes known as "the Diadochi"). The map of the world in 361 shows a Roman Empire divided into three (*PR* 4.19–20; cf. 3.13–14 which showed a unified Empire in 332):[10] the Holy Roman Empire coincides more or less with continental Europe; the Kingdom of Africa (led by Col. Mfede) coincides roughly with the Islamic world in the seventh century; and the Refuge of Briton is in the British Isles, led by the French logistics expert Colonel Manon Karembeau, who has stolen two nuclear weapons and forced détente (see 4.6–7, 11–12). Indeed, she has been shown to be the member of the command group most dedicated to the long-term cause: "Only a fool would believe that individuals can change the world. Only a perfectly executed plan by a unified group could hope to accomplish our goals" (3.12; see Figure 14-3). It is therefore significant that Briton appears no longer to be a meaningful political entity in the time of the frame narrative (1.8: "At any time, only the King of Africa, myself, and the Holy Roman Emperor—*you*—know the entire story," says the Gene Pope, "Can you keep a *secret*?").[11]

The emphasis on secrecy and specific sources is present throughout the series. The text-only transcripts already discussed offer an excerpt from closed meetings (*PR* 1.13–14), a reconstruction "from the genetic memories of existing participant lines" (2.9–10), private journals and an unauthorized biography (3.7–8), and secret recordings (4.3–4). In addition, two specific sources are cited at length. *The Secret Vatican Archives* refers to documents in the era of the Gene Pope, which are regularly used to provide biographical information about new characters (1.7, 10, 11, 15, 22; 2.18; 3.2, 6; see Figure 14-1). There is also a source in antiquity, *The Hidden Records*, apparently written by Nicholas Chase (1.6, 30–33; 2.3, 12, 14, 21–23, 25; see Figure 14-2, where Chase's words in black are a continuation of an earlier identified excerpt from these records). Two things should draw the reader's notice from this cite-specific referencing.

---

[10] *PR* 4.20: "the civilized world was divided into three parts"; cf. Julius Caesar *De Bello Gallico* 1.1, *Gallia est omnis divisa in partes tres* . . . ("All Gaul is divided into three parts . . .").

[11] The exclusion of Briton here would seem to suggest that it no longer exists as a political power, and is not simply being excluded.

Figure 14-3 Conspiracy within the command group. From Jonathan Hickman, 2009. *Pax Romana*. New York: Image Comics.

The classically informed reader will want to draw similarities with Procopius' *Secret History* (*Anecdota*), the sixth-century palinode in which the historian revised his appraisal of the Emperor Justinian in the years following the publication of the more favorable *Wars of Justinian* (*de Bellis*). Procopius' work is nonexistent in the rewritten world, since it comes so late in Antiquity. The remade world will never know of Justinian nor of his annalist. Chase's account, *The Hidden Records*, therefore serves as a kind of replacement for the *Secret History*, as both works serve to give new accounts of already familiar events. Procopius also provides an account of the military campaigns of Justinian's general Belisarius, whose expansionist ideals and strained relationship with the emperor are also detailed in these works. It is possible to see aspects of each of these individuals in Nicholas Chase: at different moments, he can be seen as puppeteer and true ruler, as the ambitious senior military presence, and as the historian of them both.

Chase is depicted with an eye patch (one eye was lost in a campaign before the series begins), and as a result some readers may make an association with Alexander's general, Antigonus I Monophthalmus (382–301 B.C.E.). The classical association is not primary, but having erased a world where all the alternative possibilities exist, Antigonus exists as the most prominent parallel for Chase from antiquity.[12] After the death of Alexander, Antigonus comes closest of all the Diadochi to holding Alexander's empire together. The connection with the wars of the Successors can therefore serve as a pre-echo of the eventual division of the Holy Roman Empire, and the evocation of Antigonus will deepen the resonance for some readers. The reader who makes this association is then able to see Chase, not as the supreme commander of the mission (the Alexander analogue), but as *primus inter pares* (first among equals)

---

[12] Rather than a winking allusion to the legend of the blind Belisarius begging in his old age, it is likely that the primary association of this image for viewers will be not to an individual from antiquity, but to Horatio Nelson, whose single eye allowed him to disregard orders that went against his military judgement at the Battle of Copenhagen in 1801, or to Rooster Cogburn in the film *True Grit* (dir. Henry Hathaway, 1969), whose mysterious past (as an outlaw for Cogburn, or as an American for Chase) is put aside to make him represent civilizing progress. Of course, there are other possible influences on this design choice, and there is no way for the author to control the associations made: it may be understood to draw on the sly wisdom of the god Odin, or on the dare-anything attitude of Snake Plissken (*Escape from New York*, dir. John Carpenter, 1981), or, for readers after 2010, the version of Rooster Cogburn in the Coen Brothers' remake of *True Grit*.

among the command team. As a result, Chase's eventual defeat is anticipated by the classical model, and with the erasing of antiquity, that
model is one of the few remaining for later interpretation of the events.

The reader of SF coming to Hickman's *Pax Romana* is less likely to
make associations with Procopius and the struggles of Hellenistic king-
doms than s/he will with Frank Herbert's six-volume SF series, *Dune*
(1965–85), and the fourth volume in that series in particular, *God
Emperor of Dune* (1981). As Hickman himself admitted when asked
about his inspirations, "Now that I'm out of the planning/plotting stage
and actually writing, it's Frank Herbert more than anything else."[13] In
God Emperor of Dune, Herbert considers human history in its most
macroscopic terms, as the immortal God Emperor Leto Atreides II,
genetically enhanced to possess racial memories extending back to the
Bronze Age (and the hybrid body of a sandworm), contemplates *la
longue durée*. The Emperor adopts "the Golden Path" to avoid societal
stagnation and ensure human survival. Like *Pax Romana, God Emperor
of Dune* draws together a number of fictional sources in its composition,
allowing the author to present both first- and third-person embedded
narratives, quotations from Leto's speeches and from *The Stolen
Journals*. Hickman has adapted elements of both form and content from
Herbert's novel, and these concerns overlap with the associations with
Asimov's *Foundation* series.

Pax Romana encourages different conclusions, depending on the
background knowledge the reader brings, and while I expect a greater
number of readers will possess the SF repertoire to draw upon, the
classical frame provided by the setting is deeply integrated into the
story. The series asks Hickman's readers to consider the legacy of classical antiquity to the modern day. In that respect, his choice of the
fourth century as the mercenaries' destination can be seen to challenge any deprecating associations readers might have with late

---

[13] De Blieck 2008. I take the book's dedication, "for the Little King and the Old Worm"
as a reference to Herbert. Hickman's enthusiasm for *God Emperor of Dune* predates the
release of *Pax Romana*: on a web board in 2007, he posted, "I've read the original six
Dune novels probably about 7–8 times each. Love them" (post 4); "I loved *God Emperor
of Dune*. | I agree with the sentiment that it is the worst narrative of the six, but the ideas
behind it were easily the most ambitious of the series. | Frank had a big ole' brain." (post
11, [sic]; | indicates paragraph breaks in original post). The author's excitement for ideas
over narrative anticipates the stylistic innovations of *Pax Romana*.

antiquity. While there need not be a causal association, the debt of *Foundation* to the ancient world is also programmatic for *Pax Romana*. Asimov's vision of a collapsing galactic empire was inspired by Edward Gibbon's account, *The History of the Decline and Fall of the Roman Empire* (6 volumes, 1776–1789), and the role of Christianity as a contributor to the decline and a perpetuator of the resulting stability necessarily centers on Constantine. Hickman, seeking to present a scope similar to that of Asimov (albeit, with just four issues, in a much more limited format), reaches to the same historical moment when creating his alternative to the post-classical world. The accuracy of Gibbon's diagnosis is irrelevant: the changes introduced by the state's incorporation of Christianity are established as a plausible "end of antiquity" that provides a point of departure for SF exploration.

Hickman's debt to Gibbon is explicit in his title. Though the phrase *Pax Romana* ("Roman Peace") can be understood with varying degrees of irony to reflect certain aspects of Chase's plan, it originates in Gibbon's history as a description of the comparative political stability that characterized the first two centuries of the Empire (roughly, from Augustus to Marcus Aurelius), a time after Christ but before the state acceptance of Christianity. "Roman Peace" is what the mercenaries seek to preserve in the world of Constantine, incorporating religious tolerance so that the virtues of Empire (as perceived by characters within the story) may be maintained without any Decline or Fall.

Any view of societal continuity and development, whether framed in terms of SF or classical history, is necessarily threatened by the inclusion of time travel. Unlike Asimov's and Herbert's works, Hickman incorporates time travel, which itself comes laden with a series of SF associations that many readers will possess. When Chase and his soldiers are sent back in time, the final panel on the page presents a "BOOM!" and the words, unattributed to any particular speaker, "All of that has to come to an end" (*PR* 1.24). What follows is a two-page spread offering a reverse timeline, and a painted, jagged line on a white background that is broken by a number of events, marked carefully and precisely dated. At the bottom of the page are fifteen events between the years 2053 and 312 (all but two of which coincide with the history we know; two are in the reader's future); the top of the page has unfamiliar events, identified with the same dates in Roman numerals (1.25–26). Time is and is not what the reader knows. Even the choice of 2053 for the world that is lost is perhaps not accidental: the notion of a plastic timeline, easily transformed and shaped by the time traveler, finds its *locus classicus* in Ray Bradbury's short story "A Sound of Thunder." In that story, a time traveler from 2055 goes on a safari for a *Tyrannosaurus rex*, and the inadvertent destruction of a single insect apparently changes the present timeline to which he returns.[14] Hickman's story predates (and therefore retroactively cancels) the story that most clearly provides a model for the philosophical implications of time travel that he accepts. The explicit goal of time travel in *Pax Romana* is to change the past so as to change the future. There is a single timeline, and causality holds: events in past time lead to a different present and a changed future. The ontological problem, well examined in SF, can be resolved if an equilibrium is assumed, whereby the changed future will cause different events to affect the past, repeatedly, until there is no change in the timeline (this is sometimes called "Niven's Law," since it derives from an essay by SF writer Larry Niven [1971], "The Theory and Practice of Time Travel"). One alternative, that there is a single timeline and history is fixed, permits a time traveler to act but guarantees that his acts will not contradict established facts (this approach to time travel is taken to its most extreme articulation in two of Robert A. Heinlein's short stories, "By His Bootstraps" and "—All You Zombies—").[15]

Hickman avoids the inevitable time-travel paradoxes by accepting that when the Eternal Army appears in the new timeline (the past, Constantine's Rome in 312) they are fully part of that world. There is no going back, the characters are assured, and the implication is that whatever happens is the new world.[16] There is an intrinsic faith being expressed by the time travelers in *Pax Romana*, not only that God's

[14] Bradbury's story, first published in *Collier's*, June 28, 1952, and reprinted in *The Golden Apples of the Sun* (1953) and many places since, possesses an affinity with the so-called butterfly effect in chaos theory. The story's prominence as a cultural touchstone outside of SF is demonstrated by its use in "Time and Punishment," a short story in "Treehouse of Horror V," a 1994 episode of the Fox television series *The Simpsons* (episode 109, 2F03; first broadcast October 30, 1994).

[15] See also his 1957 novel *The Door into Summer*. This is close to the situation presented in another Hickman time travel story, *The Red Wing* (written by Hickman, illustrated by Nick Pitarra; 4 issues, Image Comics, 2011; collected 2011). Compare also the multiple historical analogues served by Nicholas Chase in *Pax Romana*.

[16] The perennial problem is glossed over quickly by a scientist in 2053: "It's pretty amazing and, oh, we disproved paradox as well" (*PR* 1.9).

creation is such that events can be rewritten (hence the concern about arriving before the Resurrection, which would therefore frustrate and possibly cancel the purpose of God's Incarnation), but also that the Eternal Army will not lose memories or existence because their birth-timeline no longer exists—as happens in the film *Back to the Future*, for instance (directed by Robert Zemeckis, 1985). The mercenaries become part of the new world, with superior knowledge and technology from a place that does not exist (nor can it ever exist, now). From a position of faith, such a view is possible since it already accepts that events can happen that do not conform to the laws of physics and causality (miracles, for instance). Indeed, the Eternal Army arrives at a time when Constantine himself is thought to have received divine aid in the form of a celestial sign: *in hoc signo vinces* ("In this sign, you will conquer") is the usual Latin rendering (adopted by the Jesuits, for instance) for the Greek of Eusebius, *Life of Constantine* 1.28, τούτῳ νίκα (imperative, "Conquer with this"), that accompanied the sign that inspired Constantine in his battle against the Emperor Maxentius at Milvian Bridge, which led to Constantine asserting sole rule of the Empire.[17] While Hickman does not spell this out, the Catholic time machine affirms within the story a theocentric universe.[18]

It all comes back to Milvian Bridge in 312, where Constantine would secure his control of the Western Empire and prepare for the adoption of Christianity as the official religion of the Empire. The battle creates its own historical echoes, since the crucial meeting at

[17] Constantine's vision is the subject of his initial conversation with Nicholas Chase. Chase asks, "I tell you Constantine—*I gotta know . . . Is this, your sign*, purely political or did you really have a vision?" (*PR* 2.14). After a pause, the Emperor stops calling for his guards and asks, "Exactly how would you know *the difference*?" This, in turn, makes Chase pause, before he says to himself and the audience as much as to Constantine, "And here I thought you were going to be *simple*." The previous page (2.13) has shown Constantine staring at a giant chi-rho symbol, the sign of Christ (ΧΡιστός) that appears on silver coins issued by Constantine c. 317 and was part of his *labarum* (Constantine's military standard).

[18] There is no discussion of timelines splitting, or any assumption that the world left back in 2053 in any way continues: all believe that the present that is left simply disappears. This can be seen to articulate a kind of heroism that resides in the faith of the Pius XIII: he sacrifices himself and his world to ensure the possibility of success of the Catholic Church. That success, however, is tempered by the fact that it is measured purely in earthly terms, measurable from the position of an individual within creation. The pope's choice may equally be understood to reflect a doubt that God is in fact in control of His world.

Milvian Bridge on the river Tiber resonates with the central importance of Caesar's crossing the river Rubicon in 49 B.C.E., when he
famously uttered the words *iacta alea est*, according to Suetonius
(*Divus Julius* 32, "the die is cast," an adaptation of Menander fragment 64.4 ἀνερρίφθω κύβος ["let the die be cast"]; cf. Athenaeus
559d). According to *The Hidden Records*, the events at Milvian Bridge
are the first thing that needs to be stopped: "the battle had to be
avoided at all cost" (*PR* 2.3). By denying Constantine what has come
to be his defining moment, Chase and the Catholic soldiers have
denied him his (metaphorical) Rubicon. The four-year-old Emperor,
like many readers perhaps, "would like to have seen *a fight! CRASH!*
Hit! Hit!" (2.5), but Chase's plan, being enacted at the same time in
Cisalpine Gaul where the time travelers have arrived, "North of the
Rubicon" (1.27, 2.7), requires only the assassination of Cardinal Pelle
(see Figure 14-2). That decision—stranded in time, isolated from the
Catholic Church, and elevating oneself to supreme commander of the
Eternal Army—becomes the fateful choice from which there is no
return. Moments of individual exemplary accomplishment are put
aside so that ordinary social forces may shape the future of Rome.
Hickman's alternate history is framed in terms of an engine of regular
ongoing change, and as a result, Chase's mission needs to downplay
the accomplishments of individuals. Rather than Milvian Bridge, *Pax
Romana* forges another Rubicon.

"The future is not set": travel in time to the past to change the future,
to prevent certain events from happening. The promise of *The Terminator*
(directed by James Cameron, 1984), as it has spilled out into more general cultural awareness, inevitably shapes any reading of *Pax Romana*
and its repeated injunction to "destroy the past, create the future." In
The Terminator, Judgement Day (when machines become self-aware)
has to be stopped, since it is assumed that any pre-Singularity human
existence will be a better alternative. *Pax Romana* understands humans
better than that. In Hickman's world, the Catholic Church acts to
rebuild creation from the moment where it can have the greatest effect
on the course of human events. It lacks the mathematics of psychohistory and the Golden Path, but trusts in divine will. The world is remade,
and the end of antiquity inaugurates a new future that will never be. But
it remains a human world, where human passions and the concerns of

individuals can outweigh the larger effects of sociological pressures.[19] Factionalism, strife, envy, ambition, pride, mercy, doubt, lust, and faith all still exist and are shown to shape events at the level of the individual. It is not the world that Pelle and Pope Pius XIII hope for, but it is one that for all its strangeness is still recognizable as true.

[19] This is not specifically to invoke a nineteenth-century "Great Man" theory of historiography in which history is seen specifically in the eyes of influential individuals, though Hickman does seem to be aware of the problematic aspects of such an approach. Despite their shared etymology, "history" only becomes "story" when it is shaped, and a natural tendency is to shape it around the accomplishments of individuals, since that offers helpful constraints for determining what is relevant. This is no less true of ancient history, when the lives of individual leaders are such crucial sources, and it is natural to gravitate towards Alexander, Caesar, and Constantine (among others) when working to delimit an individual story. The use of time travel in *Pax Romana* helps secure the place of a Great Man, since the Church decides to affirm Constantine's accomplishment and make him even more important, more determinative of the future course of events, even as the mission works to devolve responsibility for future events into engineered cyclical processes.

Suggestions for Further Reading and Viewing

Robert W. Cape, Jr.

Between the publication of Mary Shelley's *Frankenstein; or, The Modern Prometheus* (1818) and Ridley Scott's motion picture *Prometheus* (2012), there have appeared several hundred SF stories, movies, and television shows that have made serious use of classical elements and themes. It would be impossible to mention all that deserve attention, and they would not indicate the range of treatment authors have given this material. It seems more useful, therefore, to assemble a sample of the variety of stories and treatments across time, genre, and media, from pulp shorts to epic trilogies. All of the following stories (save one) include characters, motifs, events, myths, etc., drawn explicitly from the classical worlds of Greece and/or Rome. The list is roughly chronological and is limited primarily to American and British science fiction (SF).

STORIES AND NOVELS

Mary Shelley, *Frankenstein; or, The Modern Prometheus* (1818/1831)

A reconception of the Prometheus story, transforming elements of defying God, creating life, and bringing "fire" from heaven to earth into a paradigmatic act defining the advent of the age of technology. Victor Frankenstein also suffers pain and loneliness for his creation. Plutarch's *Lives* introduces the monster to humanity, specifically to "higher thoughts," and teaches him "to admire and love the heroes of past ages." See Weiner (this volume, chapter two).

Edgar Allan Poe, "Mellonta Tauta" (1849)

Poe translates a manuscript found "in a jug floating in the Mare Tenebrarum," purporting to be the account of a hot-air balloon holiday excursion over the

Atlantic, one thousand years in the future. The satire is revealed by the date, April 1, 2848; absurd translations from Greek, Latin, and Etruscan; and references to an ancient Turkish or Hindu philosopher, "Aries Tottle." An early example of SF emphasizing the ubiquity of advanced machines in the future and fantastic voyages.

Jules Verne, *Twenty Thousand Leagues Under the Sea* (1870)

A classic example of SF in the genre of the fantastic voyage, utilizing futuristic technology, Verne's tale alludes to Homer's *Odyssey* in the name, character, and wanderings of Captain Nemo. In his wanderings, Nemo discover Plato's Atlantis a full decade before Ignatius Donnelly's work spurred popular interest in that "lost continent." On Verne's *Journey to the Center of the Earth* see Stevens (this volume, chapter three).

H. G. Wells, *The Time Machine* (1895)

The classical elements used in the story suggest the decay of civilization and the loss of historical understanding. The time traveler's machine stops near a great white sphinx, alluding to the riddle Oedipus solved about the ages of mankind, and the broken statue of the faun symbolizes the shattered classical past. On Wells's *The First Men in the Moon* see Keen (this volume, chapter four).

John Lewis Burtt, "The Lemurian Documents" (1932): "No 1—Pygmalion," "No 2—The Gorgons," "No 3—Daedalus and Icarus," "No 4—Phaeton," "No 5—The Sacred Cloak of Feathers," "No 6—Prometheus" (*Amazing Stories* 1932)

A series of stories offering euhemerist accounts of Greek gods by recording their deeds in the lost city of Mu, a precursor of Lemuria/Atlantis. Representative of stories in the pulp magazines of the (Hugo) Gernsbackian era, "The Lemurian Documents" focuses on the consequences of contemporary technological advances by describing their first appearance millennia ago and their contributions to the fall of Atlantis.

Stanley G. Weinbaum, "A Martian Odyssey" (*Wonder Stories* 1934)

Named by the Science Fiction Writers of America as one of the best SF stories of the early years, "Odyssey" recalls the wanderings of Homer's Odysseus, as one of the first humans to explore Mars relates his travels on the planet after his auxiliary rocket ship crashed. Many classical elements appear as features on the

Martian landscape. Weinbaum also used classical elements creatively in other stories, such as "The Lotus Eaters" (*Astounding Stories* 1935). On the *Odyssey* in SF, see Rogers (this volume, chapter ten).

Murray Leinster, "Sideways in Time" (*Astounding Stories* 1934)

An early story about multiple timelines and parallel universes that helped spawn the genre. A mathematician predicts a cataclysmic event that will reveal alternate timelines, and plans to gain wealth and power from it. The first evidence that he is correct is the appearance of a Roman legion from a time when the Roman Empire never fell. Other historical epochs are represented, including another Roman era.

Lester Del Rey, "Helen O'Loy" (*Amazing Science Fiction* 1938)

Another story classified as one of the best of the early years. The first female robot is named after Helen of Troy. The story does not significantly develop the ancient tales about Helen, but serves as a meditation on the nature of the ideal woman, ancient and future.

L. Sprague de Camp, *Lest Darkness Fall* (1939/1941), "A Gun for Aristotle" (*Astounding Science Fiction* 1956)

Lest Darkness Fall is one of the classic alternate-history SF stories, where an archaeologist is transported to sixth-century C.E. Rome and realizes that, through technological innovations, Europe can avoid the Dark Ages. It draws elements from Mark Twain's *A Connecticut Yankee in King Arthur's Court* (1889) but emphasizes technology and has less social satire. It was reprinted in 1996, together with a novella by David Drake, "To Bring the Light," in which an ancient Roman woman is transported back to the time of the founding Rome. "A Gun for Aristotle" is another influential time-travel tale, this time featuring a scientist who wants scientific thinking to develop sooner in history and travels back to Aristotle to teach him the scientific method.

Isaac Asimov, *Foundation Trilogy* (*Foundation* [1951], *Foundation and Earth* [1952], *Second Foundation* [1953])

Although the *Foundation* novels do not engage classical peoples, places, or gods, the trilogy was famously modeled on Gibbon's *Decline and Fall of the*

Roman Empire (1776–1789), assuming that human history repeats itself in predictable cycles. The attempt to bypass the European Dark Ages shows affinities with L. Sprague de Camp's *Lest Darkness Fall* (1941). On the influence of the *Foundation* trilogy, see Marshall (this volume, chapter fourteen).

Ray Bradbury, "The Golden Apples of the Sun" (1953)

A space ship named Prometheus, or Icarus, travels to the sun to bring its energy to earth. Elements of the Prometheus myth take on a new significance, especially the *hubris* of technological advancement. There are many references to classical literature and to Verne.

Frederik Pohl, "The Midas Plague" (*Galaxy* 1954)

Reverses the meaning of the "Midas touch" and serves it up as social commentary on contemporary consumerism and technology. The only classical element is the title, but the reader is expected to know the Midas saga in order to understand the meaning of the story.

Robert Silverberg, "Gorgon Planet" (*Nebula* 1954), *Hawksbill Station* (1968), *The Man in the Maze* (1969), *Roma Eterna* (2003)

From his first published story, "Gorgon Planet," to his recent *The Last Song of Orpheus* (2010), Silverberg has drawn upon classical elements in many of his stories. The title "Gorgon Planet" suggests that initial reports about a newly discovered planet having no life may be in error. *Hawksbill Station* and *Man in the Maze* rework the issues of disability, social inclusion, honor, and pragmatism vs. loss of innocence found in Sophocles' *Philoctetes*. *Roma Eterna* offers an alternate history, sans the success of Christianity, where Romans discover and conquer the New World and develop space travel.

Walter M. Miller, Jr., *A Canticle for Leibowitz* (1959)

In three stories set approximately 600 years apart, beginning with a post-apocalyptic Earth of the twenty-sixth century, monks at the abbey of St. Leibowitz struggle to balance a need to preserve all ancient information that has miraculously survived, with an imperative to maintain their religious teaching. This future scenario is reminiscent of the European Middle Ages and Renaissance, and Latin is again the international language. The story questions whether human ethics and morality advance in tandem with technology. See Grayson (this volume, chapter six).

Mack Reynolds, *Time Gladiator* (1966)

A twenty-first-century Etruscologist studying ancient weaponry becomes a hero of the gladiatorial games in a totalitarian United States. Detailed references to gladiatorial combat and historical facts abound in this Cold War tale of international political intrigue that pits the protagonist against a Russian counterpart.

Samuel R. Delany, *The Einstein Intersection* (1969)

A new Orpheus travels a very different path to rescue his Eurydice, not to Hades but to a planet humans destroyed at least 30,000 years ago, where new life forms inhabit old bodies, adopt old customs, and relive old myths in new ways. The Minotaur, Phaedra, and Helen of Troy figure prominently in new guises as the new version of humanity struggles to embrace sexual, biological, and mythical difference.

C. J. Cherryh, "Cassandra" (*The Magazine of Fantasy and Science Fiction* 1978) and, with Janet Morris, "Basileus" (1986)

The protagonist in "Cassandra" lives a tortured life with the same gift and curses as her ancient Greek namesake in a pre-apocalyptic modern city. In "Basileus," one of the first in the popular *Heroes in Hell* series, Julius Caesar intrigues in the underworld with Alexander the Great, Machiavelli, and other historical rulers. Death has not changed their natures, and their political and military machinations seem similar to those of rulers at the end of the Cold War.

Gene Wolfe, "The Woman Who Loved the Centaur Pholus," (*Isaac Asimov's Science Fiction Magazine* 1979), "The Woman the Unicorn Loved," (*Isaac Asimov's Science Fiction Magazine* 1981)

Stories featuring denizens of the classical bestiary are often labeled "fantasy," but these two clearly employ SF to account for mythical beasts, while also raising issues of bioethics, civic activism, and even college campus interdisciplinarity. Wolfe often poses his stories at the intersection of genres and frequently includes Greek and Latin terms and classical characters, as in the alternate Greek history series *Latro in the Mist* (*Soldier of the Mist* [1986] and *Soldier of Arete* [1989]).

David Drake, *Ranks of Bronze* (1986), *Legions of Fire* (2010), *Out of the Waters* (2011), *Monsters of the Earth* (2013)

In *Ranks of Bronze*, the army Crassus is thought to have lost in 54 B.C.E. is purchased by aliens for low-tech mercenary purposes. The Romans are exceptionally skilled fighters, perhaps more skilled than their highly advanced new masters realize. *Ranks of Bronze* is now a classic in the subclass of military SF and well suited to a Roman theme. Drake's recent novels, the first of four in a series, *The Books of the Elements*, are fantasy SF steeped in the history (including less commonly read historians) and literature of the early Roman Empire. Drake's frequent disclaimers, such as "It is not a novel about Rome and the Roman Empire in 30 CE, under the emperor Tiberius," suggest the difficulties some readers have in distinguishing historical fiction from fantasy/SF.

Harry Turtledove: *The Videssos Cycle* (*The Misplaced Legion* [1987], *An Emperor for the Legion* [1987], *The Legion of Videssos* [1987], *The Swords of the Legion* [1987]); The *Atlantis* series (*Opening Atlantis* [2007], *The United States of Atlantis* [2008], *Liberating Atlantis* [2009])

Combining alternate-universe SF and military SF, Turtledove's Videssos Cycle finds a Roman legion transported to another universe and empire (Videssos) in turmoil—similar to the fighting between the eastern and western halves of the Roman Empire in late antiquity. The stoic Roman tribune defeats the crazed, evil magician who planned to overthrow the leaders, and restores order to the empire. The Atlantis series applies the idea of Atlantis to an island separated from the eastern coast of North America that develops an alternate timeline. In an unrelated Atlantis story, "The Daimon" (2010), Alcibiades does not return to Athens after being recalled from Syracuse, threatening to end ancient democracy prematurely.

Turtledove is also known for writing well-researched and accurate historical novels, such as *Justinian* (1998) and the Hellenic Traders series (*Over the Wine Dark Sea* [2001], *The Gryphon's Skull* [2002], *The Sacred Land* [2003], *Owls to Athens* [2004]), about two cousins who are seafaring traders after the death of Alexander the Great.

Janet Morris, *Tempus* (1987), and, with Chris Morris, *Tempus Unbound* (1989), *The Sacred Band* (2010)

A fantasy series about the Sacred Band of Stepsons, an elite army modeled on the fourth-century B.C.E. Sacred Band of Thebes. The stories explore the fraught personal relationships of mixed hetero- and homosexual troops, only sometimes paired, as they fight for their commander, the immortal Tempus. Morris includes archaeological and historical details, from physical items to social practices, religion, and philosophy, to create a fantasy world that is, in many ways, more historically accurate than many popular accounts of antiquity.

Walter Jon Williams, *Aristoi* (1992)

The *Aristoi* are the elite of the galaxy (they must pass strenuous examinations and master the many *daemones* in their heads), but their whole order is threatened. They create their own worlds and are treated like gods (they are called *Aristoi kai Athanatoi*, although they can die) by the *Demos*, whom they and their *Therapontes* serve. Rich with Greek terms put to new use, with quotes from Greek authors, and allusions to classical Greece, Williams extrapolates how ancient marginalized geniuses (*à la* Socrates) might become both benevolent rulers and dissatisfied with a utopia of their own creation.

Dan Simmons, *Ilium* (2003) and *Olympos* (2005)

The Trojan War is repeated exactly as before, for the entertainment of the gods, but this time it is on Mars (which has been terraformed), the gods are nanotech-infused post-humans, and twentieth- and twenty-first-century Classics professors (recreated from their DNA) report to the Muse daily to ensure that everything conforms to the *Iliad*. Simmons weaves this reenactment of the Trojan War with two other narrative threads (and extensive Shakespeare and Proust) to explore issues such as ancient and modern concepts of fate, the role women might have played in the ancient world, and the importance of historical memory and personal initiative to humanity. Issues in current Homeric scholarship are creatively and humorously addressed, and Odysseus becomes more than a mere psychological archetype. On *Ilium* see Grobéty (this volume, chapter twelve).

Margaret Atwood, *Penelopiad* (2005)

Penelope returns from the underworld to tell her version of her life before, with, and after Odysseus. Her narrative challenges the reception of her character since antiquity and her relationship to Helen's reception, and introduces her guilt at her complicity in the execution of the maids. The dead maids provide a contrapuntal chorus to Penelope's song and reveal an unexpectedly discordant world of women in ancient Greece. Atwood adapted the story for the theater, and it has been produced in Canada and England.

Sophia McDougall, *Romanitas* (2005), *Rome Is Burning* (2007), *Savage City* (2010)

An alternate-history trilogy in which the Roman Empire never falls. Western history develops in the standard way, except that slavery is not abolished and forms the economic basis of Rome's rule over most of the earth. All power is in the hands of the emperor, and the political intrigues at court over policies and imperial succession rival those in the time of Tiberius.

Ursula K. LeGuin, *Lavinia* (2008)

The story of Lavinia in her own words, revealing insight from her conversations with a dying poet from the future who never knew her well and never gave her voice. She retells key elements from the latter half of the *Aeneid* from her point of view and extends her story through the ascendency of Silvius Aeneas. She emerges transformed at the end, and immortal, for "he did not sing me enough life to die." See Provini (2014).

John C. Wright, "The Far End of History" (2009), *The Golden Age* trilogy (*The Golden Age* [2002], *The Phoenix Exultant* [2003], and *The Golden Transcendence* [2003])

In "The Far End of History" the tale of Penelope and Odysseus assumes cosmic proportions when they interact as sentient planets in a far-away galaxy at the end of the future as we know it. Seen as part of the new space opera genre, Wright's grand, ambitious stories, such as those in *The Golden Age* trilogy, are thoroughly infused with a multitude of meaningful classical references, characters, and institutions.

Tansy Rayner Roberts, *Love and Romanpunk* (2011)

The Julio-Claudians were more than merely politically astute and exceptionally devious: through their veins coursed the blood of lamias, werewolves, vampires, and at least one dragon. Blending SF, fantasy, and a soupçon of steampunk, members of the family reappear throughout history as monsters and as monster-slayers, in familiar locales as well as in an Ostia-theme park in Australia and a flying Roman toga-bar dirigible.

JUVENILE/YOUNG ADULT LITERATURE

Rick Riordan, *Olympian Demigod* series: Series One: *Percy Jackson and the Olympians* (5 titles, 2005–2009), Series Two: *The Heroes of Olympus* (5 books, 2010–2014)

Percy, a twelve-year old boy with dyslexia and ADHD, encounters strange beings in school and learns that his best friend is a faun and his Latin teacher is Chiron the centaur, and that they have been protecting him from a variety of Greek mythological creatures. He is taken to Camp Half-Blood, where he learns he is the son of Poseidon, and meets several young demigods like himself. He and his teenage peers have several adventures to help the gods on Olympus (now in

New York) restore order in the wake of attacks by the Titans. The second series features Roman gods. Two movies have been made based on the first series.

Kelly McCullough, *WebMage* Series: *WebMage* (2006), *Cybermancy* (2007), *Codespell* (2008), *MythOS* (2009), *Spell Crash* (2010)

In the twenty-first century, the three Fates control the destiny of the multiverse with a computer program, but when Atropos wants to code out free will, her great-grandson many times over, Ravirin (a college-age computer hacker of extraordinary power) refuses to help her. The series features several Greek gods and demigods who continue their ancient alliances and schemes and run the multiverse with sentient computers but can be hampered by their own progeny, who are now amazingly gifted computer geeks.

Suzanne Collins, *The Hunger Games* trilogy: *The Hunger Games* (2008), *Catching Fire* (2009), *Mockingjay* (2010)

In a post-apocalyptic country, Panem, the Capitol institutes technologically enhanced gladiatorial games, and subject cities send pairs of children as tribute to fight in them, as Athens sent children to fight the Minotaur. Greek and Roman names pervade the Capitol, and the notion of *panem et circenses* is taken to its logical conclusion in a futuristic totalitarian state. Two of the three books have been made into movies, where the classical elements are reduced. See Makins (this volume, chapter thirteen).

BROADCAST TELEVISION AND CABLE SERIES AND EPISODES

Star Trek: *The Original Series*, "Who Mourns for Adonais?" (1967), "Bread and Circuses" (1968), "Plato's Stepchildren" (1968); and Star Trek: *The Next Generation*, "Darmok" (1991)

In *Star Trek: The Original Series*, the crew of *Enterprise* explores space and finds other planets where aspects of Earth's past still survive. Many classical elements and names appear throughout the shows, but three episodes relate to the Greek and Roman past. "Who Mourns for Adonais?" contrasts ancient belief in the gods with modern logic and science, as the crew meets the god Apollo. "Bread and Circuses" blends SF and alternate history to ask what Rome would look like in the twentieth century if Christianity had not taken root. "Plato's Stepchildren" posits a future society built on Plato's *Republic*, until access to exceptional power derails the utopian plan. The epic of Gilgamesh and the importance of a shared cultural heritage play a central role in the *Star Trek: The Next Generation* episode, "Darmok." See Kovacs (this volume, chapter nine).

Battlestar Galactica (1978–1980), (2003–2009)

At the end of our galaxy, twelve colonies of humans are attacked by Cylons, a cybernetic/cyborg race, and a ragtag fleet of survivors flees to a legendary thirteenth colony, Earth. Including elements from many world religions, classical Greek and Roman characters assume principal roles and complicate the storyline, suggesting either rediscovery or creation of human life on Earth. The franchise has many television and other media offshoots. See Tomasso (this volume, chapter eleven).

Stargate Atlantis (2004–2009)

Egyptian history and religion play an important role in the pilot episode of *Stargate*, as in the film that inspired the series (1994; dir. R. Emmerich), and many episodes use classical names and motifs. The lost city of Atlantis (on another world) is found to be the site of a new Star Gate and spawns a new series of its own.

Doctor Who, *"The Fires of Pompeii"* (2008), "The Pandorica Opens" (2010)

"The Fires of Pompeii" finds the Doctor in Pompeii just as Vesuvius is about to erupt (caused by aliens), and puts him in a historical dilemma about saving citizens of the city. There are important consequences for the family of Caecilius, whom Latin students familiar with the *Cambridge Latin Course* will recognize. "The Pandorica Opens" introduces a Roman centurion who travels through time and meets the Doctor in other episodes.

MOVIES

Hercules and the Captive Women (also *The Conquest of Atlantis*) (1961), *Hercules Against the Moon Men* (1964)

These are two of the many low-budget, Italian sword-and-sandal movies featuring some SF elements. In *Hercules and the Captive Women*, Hercules saves his friends from the Amazon queen who uses the "stone from Uranus" (uranium) to mutate children into blond supermen or cripples. Atomic energy destroys Atlantis. In *Hercules Against the Moon Men*, Hercules/Maciste destroys the alien invaders who are plotting with a nearby queen to take over the world.

Clash of the Titans (1981), (2010)

A fantasy film about the adventures of Perseus, who kills Medusa and rescues Andromeda. The mechanical owl, Bubo, introduces a slight science fictional element, though it seems quite similar to Hephaestus' automata in Homer. Bubo and the mythological creatures were created by Ray Harryhausen, whose Talos in *Jason and the Argonauts* (1963) is another automaton. *Clash* was remade in 2010, with a sequel, *Wrath of the Titans* (2012); these films are also predominantly fantasy, although Hephaestus' hut and lock to Hades are lightly science fictional.

Bill and Ted's Excellent Adventure (1989)

A SF comedy in which two slacker teens use a time machine to collect historical figures for their history paper. They capture Socrates as their representative ancient Greek. Some connections are made between classical philosophy and lyrics to Kansas' prog-rock song "Dust in the Wind" in the service of comedy.

Star Wars I: The Phantom Menace (1999), Star Wars II: Attack of the Clones (2002), Star Wars III: Revenge of the Sith (2005)

The "prequels" to George Lucas's original three *Star Wars* films (which were released in 1977–1983). These films provide backstory to the change from Republic to Galactic Empire, modeling it on the transition from Roman Republic to Roman Empire. Visual elements such as pod races, arena executions of prisoners fed to beasts, and a lightsaber duel in an amphitheater-like setting recall circus racing and executions/*venationes*/gladiatorial combat specifically in famous films about ancient Rome.

Prometheus (2012)

In Ridley Scott's return to the *Alien* franchise, two archaeologists discover multiple ancient cave paintings suggesting our creators came from, and wish us to travel to, the stars. A billionaire interested in immortality funds an expedition in a spaceship, dubbed *Prometheus*, which finds the Titanesque aliens, resembling Greek statues of the gods. The thrill of discovery is diminished when the explorers find that the creators, the Engineers, want to destroy their creation, humanity, *à la* Mary Shelley's *Frankenstein*, and unleash alien horrors that pre-figure those in Ridley Scott's movie *Alien* (1979). See Rogers and Stevens (2012b); on the *Aliens* series, see Rogers (this volume, chapter ten).

Elysium (2013)

An Island of the Blessed floats in the upper atmosphere of Earth, but rather than the ancient Greek abode of the blessed dead, this Elysium is the paradise for the rich, who live in complete luxury and have technology that can cure all disease. On Earth, millions of the working poor inhabit ruined cities and struggle for basic survival and dignity, until a hero can travel to Elysium and change things for everyone. The reworking of the classical concept of Elysium is extreme.

Works Cited

Agel, Jerome. 1970. *The Making of Kubrick's 2001*. New York: Signet.

Ahl, Frederick. 1976. *Lucan: An Introduction*. Ithaca, NY: Cornell University Press.

Ahl, Frederick, trans. 2007. *Virgil: The Aeneid*. Oxford: Oxford University Press.

Alden, Maureen. "Paradigms." In *The Homeric Encyclopedia*. Ed. M. Finkelberg. Malden, MA: Wiley-Blackwell. 624–626.

Aldiss, Brian W. 1976. *Billion Year Spree: The True History of Science Fiction*. New York: Schocken Books.

Aldiss, Brian W. 1995. *The Detached Retina: Aspects of SF and Fantasy*. Syracuse, NY: Syracuse University Press.

Aldiss, Brian W., and David Wingrove. 2001. *Trillion-Year Spree*. London: House of Stratus Ltd.

Aldiss, Brian, et al. 2006. "Roundtable on SF Criticism," *Science Fiction Studies* 33.3.389–404.

Aldrete, Greg S., and David J. Mattingly. 2010. "Feeding the City: The Organization, Operation, and Scale of the Supply System for Rome." In *Life, Death, and Entertainment in the Roman Empire*. Eds. D. S. Potter and D. J. Mattingly. Second edition. Ann Arbor: University of Michigan Press. 195–228.

Allen, Richard H. 1899. *Star-Names and Their Meanings*. New York: Stechert & Co.

Amis, K. 1974 [1960]. *New Maps of Hell: A Survey of Science Fiction*. New York: Arno Press.

Angenot, Marc. 1979. "The Absent Paradigm: An Introduction to the Semiotics of Science Fiction." *Science Fiction Studies* 6.1.9–19.

Angenot, Marc, and Darko Suvin. 1979. "Not Only but Also: Reflections on Cognition and Ideology in Science Fiction and SF Criticism." *Science Fiction Studies* 6.168–179.

Asa, Robert. 1999. "Classic *Star Trek* and the Death of God." In *Star Trek and Sacred Ground: Explorations of Star Trek, Religion and American Culture*. Eds. J. Porter and D. McLaren. Albany: SUNY Press. 33–59.

Ashley, Mike. 1997. "Lucian." In *The Encyclopedia of Fantasy*. Eds. J. Clute and J. Grant. London: Orbit. 597–598. Available at http://sf-encyclopedia. co.uk/fe.php?nm=lucian. Accessed March 2, 2013.

Ashley, Mike. 2011. *Out of the World: Science Fiction but Not as You Know It*. London: British Library.

Asma, Stephen. 2009. *On Monsters: An Unnatural History of Our Worst Fears.* Oxford, UK: Oxford University Press.

Attlee, James. 2011. *Nocturne: A Journey in Search of Moonlight.* Chicago: University of Chicago Press.

Atwood, Margaret. 2005. *The Penelopiad.* Edinburgh, New York, Melbourne: Canongate.

Austin, R. G., ed. 1986. *P. Virgili Maronis Aeneidos Liber Sextus.* Oxford, UK: Clarendon Press.

Baccolini, Raffaella, and Tom Moylan. 2003. "Dystopia and Histories." In *Dark Horizons: Science Fiction and the Dystopian Imagination.* Eds. R. Baccolini and T. Moylan. New York: Routledge. 1–12.

Baccolini, Raffaella. 2003. "'A Useful Knowledge of the Present Is Rooted in the Past': Memory and Historical Reconciliation in Ursula K. Le Guin's *The Telling.*" In *Dark Horizons: Science Fiction and the Dystopian Imagination.* Eds. R. Baccolini and T. Moylan. New York: Routledge. 113–134.

Bailey, Cyril. 1947. *Titi Lucreti Cari De Rerum Natura Libri Sex.* Oxford, UK: Clarendon.

Baker, Djoymi. 2001. "'Every Old Trick Is New Again': Myth in Quotations and the *Star Trek* Franchise." *Popular Culture Review* 12.67–77. Reprinted in Kapell (2010; q.v.).

Bakhtin, Mikhail M. 1986. *Speech Genres and Other Late Essays.* Trans. V. W. McGee. Austin: University of Texas Press.

Bakker, Egbert J. 2005. *Pointing at the Past: From Formula to Poetics.* Washington, D.C.: Center for Hellenic Studies.

Bakker, Egbert J. 2011. "Time." In *The Homeric Encyclopedia.* Ed. M. Finkelberg. Malden, MA: Wiley-Blackwell. 877–879.

Baldick, Chris. 1987. *Myth, Monstrosity, and Nineteenth-Century Writing.* Oxford, UK: Clarendon Press.

Bare, Richard L., dir. 1962. "To Serve Man." *The Twilight Zone.* Written by Rod Serling. March 2, 1962.

Baricco, Alessandro. 2006. *An Iliad.* Trans. A. Goldstein. New York: Alfred A. Knopf.

Barker, Elton T. E. 2008. "Momos Advises Zeus: Changing Representations of 'Cypria' Fragment 1." In *Quaderni del Dipartimento di Scienze dell'Antichità e del Vicino Oriente dell'Università Ca' Foscari*, 4. Eds. E. Cingano and L. Milano. Padova: S.A.R.G.O.N. Editrice e Libreria. 33–73.

Barker, Elton T. E., and Joel P. Christensen. 2011. "On Not Remembering Tydeus: Agamemnon, Diomedes and the Contest for Thebes." *Materiali e discussioni per l'analisi dei testi classici* 66.1.9–44.

Barrett, Michèlle, and Duncan Barrett. 2001. *Star Trek: The Human Frontier.* New York and London: Routledge.

Barthes, Roland. 1957. "Nautilus et bateau ivre." In *Mythologies.* Paris: Seuil, Collection "Points." 80–82.

Barthes, Roland. 1989. *The Rustle of Language*. Trans. R. Howard. Berkeley, Los Angeles: UCLA Press.

Bataille, Sylvaine. 2014. "*Battlestar Galactica* et l'héritage gréco-latin." In *L'Antiquité dans l'imaginaire contemporain: Fantasy, science-fiction, fantastique*. Eds. Mélanie Bost-Fiévet and Sandra Provini. Paris: Classiques Garnier. 465–482.

Batchelor, John. 1985. *H. G. Wells*. Cambridge, UK: Cambridge University Press.

Baudrillard, Jean. 1994. *Simulacra and Simulation*. Trans. S. F. Glaser. Ann Arbor: Michigan University Press.

Baudrillard, Jean. 1996. *The System of Objects*. Trans. J. Benedict. New York: Verso.

Baxter, John. 1970. *Science Fiction in the Cinema*. New York: A. S. Barnes & Co.

Baxter, Stephen. 2006. *Emperor. Time's Tapestry: Book One*. London: Gollancz.

Beal, Timothy K. 2001. *Religion and Its Monsters*. London: Routledge.

Beck, William. 2011. "Kleos." In *The Homeric Encyclopedia*. Ed. M. Finkelberg. Malden, MA: Wiley-Blackwell. 442–443.

Beja, Morris. 1971. *Epiphany in the Modern Novel*. Seattle: University of Washington Press.

Bennett, Betty T. 1980. *The Letters of Mary Wollstonecraft Shelley*. Vol. 1. Baltimore, MD: Johns Hopkins University Press.

Berman, Jeffrey. 1976. "Forster's Other Cave: The Platonic Structure of 'The Machine Stops'." *Extrapolation* 17.2.172–181.

Berryman, Sylvia. 2003. "Ancient Automata and Mechanical Explanation." *Phronesis* 48.4.344–369.

Biskind, Peter. 1983. *Seeing Is Believing: How Hollywood Taught Us to Stop Worrying and Love the Fifties*. New York: Henry Holt.

Blasingame, James. 2009. "An Interview with Suzanne Collins." *Journal of Adolescent and Adult Literacy* 52.8.726–727.

Bleiler, Everett F. 1990. *Science-Fiction: The Early Years*. Kent, OH: Kent State.

Bloch, Ernst. 1968. *Das Prinzip Hoffnung*. Frankfurt: Suhrkamp.

Bloch, Ernst. 1976. *Experimentum Mundi*. Frankfurt: Suhrkamp.

Bloom, Harold, ed. 1991. *Odysseus/Ulysses*. New York: Chelsea House Publishers.

Bloom, Harold. 2011. *The Anatomy of Influence*. New Haven, CT: Yale University Press.

Boitani, Pierre. 1994. *The Shadows of Ulysses: Figures of a Myth*. Trans. A. Weston. Oxford, UK: Oxford University Press.

Bondanella, Peter. 1987. *The Eternal City: Roman Images in the Modern World*. Chapel Hill, NC: University of North Carolina Press.

Booker, M. Keith. 2006. *Alternate Americas: Science Fiction Film and American Culture*. Westport, CT: Praeger.

Boss, Pete. 1990. "Altair IV Revisited: *Forbidden Planet*." *Movie* 34/35.59–64.

342 *Works Cited*

Bost-Fiévet, Mélanie and Sandra Provini, eds. 2014. *L'Antiquité dans l'imaginaire contemporain: Fantasy, science-fiction, fantastique.* Paris: Classiques Garnier.

Bourne, Frank C. 1977. "Caesar the Epicurean." *Classical World* 70.417–432.

Bozzetto, Roger. 1992. *L'obscur objet d'un savoir.* Aix en Provence, France: Publications de l'Université de Provence.

Bozzetto, Roger. 2000. "Kepler et *le Songe*: Naissance de la visée spéculative fondée sur la science au sens moderne du terme." *Quarante-Deux.* Available at http://www.quarante-deux.org/archives/bozzetto/ecrits/jalons/kepler. html. Accessed Nov. 26, 2011.

Brake, Mark L., and Neil Hook. 2008. *Different Engines: How Science Drives Fiction and Fiction Drives Science.* New York: Palgrave Macmillan.

Brantlinger, Patrick. 1980. "The Gothic Origins of Science Fiction." *Novel: A Forum on Fiction* 14.30–43.

Braund, Susanna Morton. 1997. "Virgil and the Cosmos: Religious and Philosophical Ideas." In *The Cambridge Companion to Virgil.* Ed. C. Martindale. Cambridge, UK: Cambridge University Press. 204–221.

Braund, Susanna Morton, and Wendy Raschke. 2002. "Satiric Grotesques in Public and Private: Juvenal, Dr. Frankenstein, Raymond Chandler, and 'Absolutely Fabulous'." *Greece & Rome* 49.62–84.

Broderick, Damien. 2003. "New Wave and Backwash: 1960–1980." In *The Cambridge Companion to Science Fiction.* Eds. E. James and F. Mendlesohn. Cambridge, UK: Cambridge University Press. 48–63.

Brosnan, J. 1978. *Future Tense. The Cinema of Science Fiction.* New York: St. Martin's Press.

Brown, Lesley, ed. 1993. *The New Shorter Oxford English Dictionary on Historical Principles: Volume I, A–M.* Oxford, UK: Clarendon Press.

Brown, Sarah Annes. 2008. "'Plato's Stepchildren': SF and the Classics." In *A Companion to Classical Reception.* Eds. L. Hardwick and C. Stray. Oxford, UK: Blackwell Publishing. 415–427.

Brown, Sarah. A. 2012. "Science Fiction and Classical Reception in Contemporary Women's Writing." *Classical Receptions Journal* 4.2.209–223.

Buchan, Mark. 2004. *The Limits of Heroism: Homer and the Ethics of Reading.* Ann Arbor: University of Michigan Press.

Buchanan, J. 2001. "*Forbidden Planet* and the Retrospective Attribution of Intentions." In *Retrovisions: Reinventing the Past in Film and Fiction.* Eds. D. Cartmell, I. Hunter, and I. Whelan. London: Pluto Press. 148–162.

Bukatman, Scott. 1993. *Terminal Identity.* Durham, NC; and London: Duke University Press.

Bukatman, Scott. 1997. *Blade Runner.* London: BFI Publishing.

Burgas, Greg. 2011. "Comics You Should Own: *Pax Romana.*" *Comic Book Resources.* Available at http://goodcomics.comicbookresources. com/2011/12/10/comics-you-should-own-pax-romana/. Accessed May 10, 2012.

Burkert, Walter. 1992. *The Orientalizing Revolution: Near Eastern Influence on Greek Culture in the Early Archaic Age*. Trans. M. E. Pinder and W. Burkert. Cambridge, MA: Harvard University Press.

Burriss, Eli Edward. 1926. "The Classical Culture of Percy Bysshe Shelley." *Classical Journal* 21.344–354.

Bushman, Brad J., and Craig A. Anderson. 2009. "Comfortably Numb: Desensitizing Effects of Violent Media on Helping Others." *Psychological Science* 20.3.273–277.

Butcher, William. 1991. *Verne's Journey to the Center of the Self: Space and Time in the* Voyages Extraordinaires. New York: St. Martin's Press.

Butcher, William. 2006. *Jules Verne: The Definitive Biography*. New York: Thunder's Mouth Press.

Butcher, William, ed. and trans. 2008. *Journey to the Center of the Earth*. Oxford, UK: Oxford University Press.

Butler, Andrew M. 2003. "Postmodernism and Science Fiction." In *The Cambridge Companion to Science Fiction*. Eds. E. James and F. Mendlesohn. Cambridge, UK: Cambridge University Press. 137–148.

Butour, M. 1949. "Le Point suprême et l'age d'or à travers quelques oeuvres de Jules Verne." *Arts et lettres* 15.3–31.

Caeners, Torsten. 2008. "Humanity's Scarred Children: The Cylons' Oedipal Dilemma in *Battlestar Galactica*." *Extrapolation* 49.3.368–384.

Calame, Claude. 2005. "From the Civilisation of Prometheus to Genetic Engineering: The Role of Technology and the Uses of Metaphor." *Arion* 13.2.25–57.

Calvert, Clay. 2004. *Voyeur Nation: Media, Privacy, and Peering in Modern Culture*. Boulder, CO: Westview.

Calvino, Italo. 1986. *The Uses of Literature*. Trans. P. Creagh. San Diego, CA: Harcourt Brace Jovanovich.

Calvino, Italo. 1997. "Two Interviews on Science and Literature." In *The Literature Machine: Essays*. Trans. P. Creagh. London: Vintage. 28–38.

Cameron, James, dir. 1984. *The Terminator*. Orion Pictures.

Cameron, James, dir. 1986. *Aliens*. Screenplay by James Cameron. Twentieth Century Fox Home Entertainment.

Campbell, Joseph. 1949. *The Hero with a Thousand Faces*. New York: Pantheon.

Campbell, Mary Baine. 2002. "Alternative Planet: Kepler's *Somnium* (1634) and the New World." In *The Arts of 17th Century Science: Representations of the Natural World in European and North American Culture*. Eds. C. Jowitt and D. Watt. Aldershot, UK: Ashgate. 232–249.

Campos, Miguel A. G. 1998. "Shakespeare in Outer Space: *Forbidden Planet* as Adaptation of *The Tempest*." *Sederi* 9.285–291.

Canary, Robert H. 1974. "Science Fiction as Fictive History." *Extrapolation* 16.1.81–95.

Caroti, S. 2004. "Science Fiction, *Forbidden Planet*, and Shakespeare's the *Tempest*." *Comparative Literature and Culture* 6.1. Special thematic issue,

Shakespeare on Film in Asia and Hollywood. Ed. C. Ross. Available at http://clcwebjournal.lib.purdue.edu/clcweb04-1/caroti04.html/. Accessed September 20, 2014.

Carpenter, John, dir. 1981. *Escape from New York*. AVCO Embassy Pictures / Barber International.

Carroll, Larry. 2009. "Will Ripley Rise Again? Sigourney Weaver on 'Alien' Saga: 'I Just Don't Feel That It's Quite Finished.'" *MTV Movies Blog*. February 20, 2009. Available at http://moviesblog.mtv.com/2009/02/20/will-ripley-rise-again-sigourney-weaver-on-alien-saga-i-just-dont-feel-that-its-quite-finished/. Accessed September 20, 2014.

Carter, Michael. 2008. "(Un)Dressed to Kill: Viewing the *Retiarius*." In *Roman Dress and the Fabrics of Roman Culture*. Eds. J. Edmondson and A. Keith. Toronto, Canada: University of Toronto Press. 113–135.

Caspar, Max. 1993. *Kepler*. Trans. C. Doris Hellman. New York: Dover.

Cavender, Gray. 2004. "In Search of Community on Reality TV: *America's Most Wanted* and *Survivor*." In *Understanding Reality Television*. Eds. S. Holmes and D. Jermyn. London: Routledge. 154–172.

Chelebourg, Christian. 1988. "Le Paradis des fossiles." In *Modernités de Jules Verne*. Ed. J. Bassière. Paris: Presses Universitaires de France. 213–227.

Chen-Morris, Raz. 2005. "Shadows of Instruction: Optics and Classical Authorities in Kepler's 'Somnium.'" *Journal of the History of Ideas* 66.2.223–243.

Cherniss, Harold, and William C. Helmbold, trans. 1957. *Plutarch: Moralia*. Vol. 12. New York: Loeb Classical Library.

Christianson, Gale E. 1976. "Kepler's *Somnium*: Science Fiction and the Renaissance Scientist." *Science Fiction Studies* 3.1.79–90.

Chwast, Seymour, adapt. 2012. *Homer: The Odyssey*. New York: Bloomsbury.

Cifuentes, D. 1998. "'Blade Runner,' or Theseus' Struggle with the Minotaur." *Pensamiento* 54.449–456.

Cirasa, Robert. 1984. "An Epic Impression: Suspense and Prophetic Conventions in the Classical Epics and Frank Herbert's *Dune*." *Classical and Modern Literature* 4.195–213.

Clare, R. J. 1998. "Representing Monstrosity: Polyphemus in the Odyssey." *Monsters and Monstrosity in Greek and Roman Culture*. Ed. C. Atherton. Bari, Italy: Levante Editori. 1–17.

Clarke, Arthur C. 1968. "Clarke's Third Law on UFOs." *Science Magazine*. January 19, 1968.

Clarke, Arthur C. 1993. "Introduction." In H. G. Wells. *The First Men in the Moon*. London: Everyman. xxix–xxxiv.

Clarke, Arthur C. 1999. *Profiles of the Future: An Inquiry into the Limits of the Possible, Millennium Edition*. London: Gollancz.

Clarke, Frederick S., and Steve Rubin. 1979. "Making *Forbidden Planet*." *Cinefantastique* 8.2/3.4–67.

Clausen, Wendell, ed. 1995. *Virgil: Eclogues*. Oxford, UK: Clarendon Press.

Clay, Jenny S. 1999. "The Whip and the Will of Zeus." *Literary Imagination* 1.1.40–60.

Clay, Jenny S. 2011. *Homer's Trojan Theater: Space, Vision and Memory in the Iliad*. Cambridge, UK: Cambridge University Press.

Clayton, Jay. 1996. "Concealed Circuits: Frankenstein's Monster, the Medusa, and the Cyborg." *Raritan* 15.4.53–69.

Clayton, Jay. 2006. "*Frankenstein*'s Futurity." In *The Cambridge Companion to Mary Shelley*. Ed. E. Schor. Cambridge, UK: Cambridge University Press. 84–99.

Clute, John, and Peter Nicholls. 1993. *The Encyclopedia of Science Fiction*. Second edition. New York: St. Martin's Press.

Clute, John. 2011. *Pardon This Intrusion: Fantastika in the World Storm*. Harold Wood, UK: Beccon.

Clute, John. 2012. "Lucian." In *The Encyclopedia of Science Fiction*. Third edition. Eds. J. Clute, D. Langford, G. Sleight, and P. Nicholls. Available at http://sf-encyclopedia.com/entry/lucian. Accessed January 24, 2012.

Coen, Joel and Ethan Coen, dir. 2010. *True Grit*. Paramount Pictures.

Cohen, Jeffrey. 1997. *Monster Theory: Reading Culture*. Minneapolis: University of Minnesota Press.

Collins, Suzanne. 2008. *The Hunger Games*. New York: Scholastic.

Collins, Suzanne. 2009. *Catching Fire*. New York: Scholastic.

Collins, Suzanne. 2010. *Mockingjay*. New York: Scholastic.

Compère, Daniel. 1977. *Un Voyage imaginaire de Jules Verne: Voyage au centre de la Terre*. Paris: Minard, Archives Jules Verne.

Condos, Theony, trans. and comm. 1997. *Star Myths of the Greeks and Romans: A Sourcebook*. Grand Rapids, MI: Phanes Press.

Connor, James A. 2005. *Kepler's Witch: An Astronomer's Discovery of Cosmic Order Amid Religious War, Political Intrigue, and the Heresy Trial of His Mother*. New York: Harper Collins.

Conte, Gian Biagio. 1994. *Latin Literature: A History*. Trans. J. Solodow. Baltimore, MD: Johns Hopkins University Press.

Conte, Gian Biagio. 1996. *The Rhetoric of Imitation: Genre and Poetic Memory in Other Latin Poets*. Ed. C. Segal. Ithaca, NY: Cornell University Press.

Costa, Charles D. N., trans. 2005. *Lucian: Selected Dialogues*. Oxford, UK: Oxford University Press.

Cox, Fiona. 2011. *Sibylline Sisters: Virgil's Presence in Contemporary Women's Writing*. Oxford, UK: Oxford University Press.

Crossley, Robert. 2005. "The Grandeur of H. G. Wells." In *A Companion to Science Fiction*. Ed. D. Seed. Oxford, UK: Blackwell Publishing. 353–363.

Cuomo, Serafina. 2007. *Technology and Culture in Greek and Roman Antiquity*. Cambridge, UK: Cambridge University Press.

Cyrino, Monica. 2005. *Big Screen Rome*. Malden, MA: Blackwell.

Cyrino, Monica. 2014. "Ancient Sexuality on Screen." In *A Companion to Greek and Roman Sexualities*. Ed. T. K. Hubbard. Chichester, UK: John Wiley & Sons. 613–628.

d'Aulaire, Ingri and Edgar Parin. 1962. *D'Aulaires' Book of Greek Myths*. New York: Delacorte.

David, Lennard J. 2010. *The Disability Studies Reader*. Third edition. London: Routledge.

Davis, Gregson. 2008. "Reframing the Homeric: Images of the Odyssey in the Art of Derek Walcott and Romare Bearden." In *A Companion to Classical Receptions*. Eds. L. Hardwick and C. Stray. Malden, MA: Blackwell. 401–414.

Dawson, Gowan. 2003. "Intrinsic Earthliness: Science, Materialism, and the Fleshly School of Poetry." *Victorian Poetry* 41.113–130.

Day, Kirsten. 2008. "Introduction." In *Celluloid Classics: New Perspectives on Classical Antiquity in Modern Cinema*. Ed. K. Day. *Arethusa* 41.1.1–9.

De Blieck, Jr., Augie. 2008. "The Commentary Track: 'Pax Romana' #1 w/ Jonathan Hickman." *Comic Book Resources*. Available at http://www.comicbookresources.com/?page=article&id=12260. Accessed May 10, 2012.

de Jong, Irene J. F. 1987. *Narrators and Focalizers: The Presentations of the Story in the* Iliad. London: Duckworth.

Delany, Samuel R., Sinda Gregory, and Larry McCaffery. 1987. "The Semiology of Silence." *Science Fiction Studies* 14.2.134–164.

Deleuze, Gilles. 1995. *Difference and Repetition*. New York: Columbia University Press.

Denis, Lara. 1999. "Kant on the Wrongness of 'Unnatural' Sex." *History of Philosophy Quarterly* 16.225–248.

Derleth, August, ed. 1950. *Beyond Time and Space*. New York: Pellegrini and Cudahy.

Desser, David. 1985. "*Blade Runner*: Science Fiction and Transcendence." *Literature/Film Quarterly* 13.3.172–179.

Desser, David. 1991. "The New Eve: The Influence of *Paradise Lost* and *Frankenstein* on *Blade Runner*." In *Retrofitting "Blade Runner": Issues in Ridley Scott's "Blade Runner" and Philip K. Dick's "Do Androids Dream of Electric Sheep?"* Ed. J. B. Kerman. Bowling Green, OH: Bowling Green State University Popular Press. 53–65.

Dick, Philip K. 1968. *Do Androids Dream of Electric Sheep?* New York: Ballantine.

DiTommaso, Lorenzo. 1992. "History and Historical Effect in Frank Herbert's *Dune*." *Science Fiction Studies* 19.311–325.

DiTommaso, Lorenzo. 2007. "The Articulation of Imperial Decadence and Decline in Epic Science Fiction." *Extrapolation* 48.2.267–291.

Dodds, E. R. 1951. *The Greeks and the Irrational*. Berkeley: University of California Press.

Dodds, E. R. 1983 [1966]. "On Misunderstanding the *Oedipus Rex.*" In *Oxford Readings in Greek Tragedy*. Ed. E. Segal. Oxford, UK: Oxford University Press. 177–188.

Doležel, Lubomír. 1998. *Heterocosmica*. Baltimore, MD: Johns Hopkins University Press.

Donahue, W. H., trans. and ed. 2000. *Optics: Paralipomena to Witelo and Optical Part of Astronomy*. Santa Fe, NM: Green Lion Press.

Douthwaite, Julia. 2012. *The Frankenstein of the French Revolution*. Chicago: The University of Chicago Press.

Dover, Gary. 2001. "Thieves, Boxers, Sodomites, Poets: Being Flash to Byron's Don Juan." *Proceedings of the Modern Language Association* 116.562–578.

DuBois, Page. 1991. *Centaurs and Amazons: Women and the Pre-History of the Great Chain of Being*. Ann Arbor: Michigan University Press.

Dunn, Thomas. 1988. "The Deep Caves of Thought: Plato, Heinlein, and Le Guin." *Spectrum of the Fantastic: Selected Essays from the Sixth International Conference on the Fantastic in the Arts*. Ed. D. Palumbo. New York: Greenwood Press. 105–112.

Dutta, M. B. 1995. "'Very Bad Poetry, Captain': Shakespeare in *Star Trek.*" *Extrapolation* 36.1.38–45.

Eco, Umberto. 1978. *A Theory of Semiotics*. Bloomington: Indiana University Press.

Edgeworth, Robert J. 1990. "The Poverty of Invention; or, Mining the Classics with Janet Morris and Harry Turtledove." *Extrapolation* 31.1.15–23.

Edmunds, Lowell. 1997. "Myth in Homer." *A New Companion to Homer*. Eds. I. Morris and B. Powell. Leiden, Netherlands: Brill. 415–441.

Edmunds, Lowell. 2003. *Intertextuality and the Reading of Roman Poetry*. Baltimore, MD: Johns Hopkins University Press.

Edwards, Walter Manoel, Robert Browning, and Graham Anderson. 2003 [1996]. "Lucian." In *The Oxford Classical Dictionary*. Revised third edition. Eds. S. Hornblower and A. Spawforth. Oxford, UK: Oxford University Press. 886–887.

Eizykman, Boris. 1985. "Temporality in Science-Fiction Narrative (La temporalité dans la narration de SF)." *Science Fiction Studies* 12.66–87.

Eliot, Thomas Stearns. 1945. *What is a Classic?* London: Faber & Faber.

Emlyn-Jones, Chris. 2008 [2000]. "Power and Identity in Greek culture—The Second Sophistic." In *AA309 Culture, Identity and Power in the Roman Empire. Block 3: Roman Greece and Asia Minor*. Third edition. Ed. L. Nevett. Milton Keynes, UK: Open University. 30–57.

Esposito, Paulo. 1996. "Lucrezio Come Intertesto Lucaneo." *Bollettino di studi latini* 26.517–544.

Eurich, Nell. 1967. *Science in Utopia: A Mighty Design*. Cambridge, MA: Harvard University Press.

Evans, Arthur B. 1988. *Jules Verne Rediscovered: Didacticism and the Scientific Novel.* New York, Westport, CT, and London: Greenwood Press.

Evans, Arthur B. 1996. "Literary Intertexts in Jules Verne's *Voyages Extraordinaires.*" *Science Fiction Studies* 23.2.171–187.

Everest, Kelvin, and Geoffrey Matthews. 1989, 2000. *The Poems of Shelley.* Two volumes. New York: Longman.

Evslin, Bernard. 1966. *Heroes, Gods, and Monsters of the Greek Myths.* New York: Random House.

Fagan, Garrett G. 2011. *The Lure of the Arena: Social Psychology and the Crowd at the Roman Games.* Cambridge, UK: Cambridge University Press.

Fagles, Robert, trans. 1998. *Homer: The Iliad.* New York: Penguin.

Farrell, Joseph, and Michael C. J. Putnam, eds. 2010. *A Companion to Virgil's* Aeneid *and its Tradition.* Malden, MA: Blackwell.

Farrell, Joseph. 1997. "The Virgilian Intertext." In *The Cambridge Companion to Virgil.* Ed. C. Martindale. Cambridge, UK: Cambridge University Press. 222–236.

Farrell, Joseph. 2001. *Latin Language and Latin Culture.* Cambridge, UK: Cambridge University Press.

Feeney, Denis C. 1991. *The Gods in Epic: Poets and Critics of the Classical Tradition.* Oxford, UK: Oxford University Press.

Feldherr, Andrew. 2010. *Playing Gods: Ovid's* Metamorphoses *and the Politics of Fiction.* Princeton, NJ: Princeton University Press.

Felton, Debbie. 2012. "Rejecting and Embracing the Monstrous in Ancient Greece and Rome." *The Ashgate Research Companion to Monsters and the Monstrous.* Eds. A. S. Mittman and P. J. Dendle. Surrey, UK: Ashgate Publishing. 103–131.

Feyerabend, Paul. 2010 [1975]. *Against Method.* Fourth edition. London and New York: Verso.

Fincher, David, dir. 1992. *Alien*³. Screenplay by David Giler, Walter Hill, and Larry Ferguson. Twentieth Century Fox Home Entertainment.

Finocchiaro, M. A., trans. and ed. 1997. *Galileo on the World Systems: A New Abridged Translation and Guide.* Berkeley: University of California Press.

Fischer, N. 2003. "Hubris." *Oxford Classical Dictionary,* Revised third edition. Eds. S. Hornblower and A. Spawforth. Oxford, UK: Oxford University Press. 732–733.

Foley, John Miles. 1991. *Immanent Art: From Structure to Meaning in Traditional Oral Epic.* Bloomington: Indiana University Press.

Foley, John Miles. 1999. *Homer's Traditional Art.* University Park, PA: Pennsylvania State University Press.

Ford, Andrew. 1992. *Homer: The Poetry of the Past.* Ithaca, NY: Cornell University Press.

Foucault, Michel. 1967. *Madness and Civilization: A History of Insanity in the Age of Reason.* Trans. R. Howard. London: Tavistock.

Franklin, H. Bruce. 1978. *Future Perfect: American Science Fiction of the Nineteenth Century.* Oxford, UK: Oxford University Press.

Fredericks, Sigmund C. 1976. "Lucian's *True History* as SF." *Science Fiction Studies* 3.1.8.49–60.

Fredericks, Sigmund C. 1980. "Greek Mythology in Modern Science Fiction: Vision and Cognition." Classical Mythology in Twentieth Century Thought and Literature. Proceedings, Comparative Literature Symposium, Texas Tech University, Vol. XI. Eds. W. M. Aycock and T. M Klein. Lubbock: Texas Tech Press. 89–105.

Freedman, Carl. 2000. *Critical Theory and Science Fiction.* Hanover, NH: Wesleyan University Press.

Freud, Sigmund. 2003 [1919]. *The Uncanny.* Trans. D. McLintock. New York and London: Penguin Classics.

Fried, Lewis. 2001. "*A Canticle for Leibowitz*: A Song for Benjamin." *Extrapolation* 42.4.362–373.

Friedländer, P. 2007. "Pattern of Sound and Atomistic Theory in Lucretius." In *Oxford Readings in Lucretius.* Ed. M. R. Gale. Oxford, UK: Oxford University Press. 351–370.

Futrell, Alison. 1997. *Blood in the Arena: The Spectacle of Roman Power.* Austin: University of Texas Press.

Gallardo C., Ximena. and C. Jason Smith. 2004. *Alien Woman: The Making of Lt. Ellen Ripley.* New York: Continuum.

Gantz, Timothy. 1996. *Early Greek Myth.* 2 vols. Baltimore, MD: Johns Hopkins University Press.

Garland-Thomson, Rosemarie. 1996. "Introduction: From Wonder to Error—A Genealogy of Freak Discourse in Modernity." In *Freakery: Cultural Spectacles of the Extraordinary Body.* Ed. R. Garland-Thomson. New York: New York University Press. 1–19.

Garland-Thomson, Rosemarie. 1997. *Extraordinary Bodies: Figuring Physical Disability in American Culture and Literature.* New York: Columbia.

Garland, Robert. 1995. *The Eye of the Beholder: Deformity and Disability in the Graeco-Roman World.* Ithaca, NY: Cornell University Press.

Garvey, Tom. 2014. "'*All this has happened before. All this will happen again.*' Les léçons d'Hésiode dans la série *Battlestar Galactica.*" In *L'Antiquité dans l'imaginaire contemporain: Fantasy, science-fiction, fantastique.* Eds. Mélanie Bost-Fiévet and Sandra Provini. Paris: Classiques Garnier. 215–228.

Gaskin, Richard.1990. "Do Homeric Heroes Make Real Decisions?" *Classical Quarterly* 40.1–15.

Geary, Patrick J. 1994. *Phantoms of Remembrance: Memory and Oblivion at the End of the First Millennium.* Princeton, NJ: Princeton University Press.

Gemmell, David. 2006. *Troy: Lord of the Silver Bow.* London: Corgi Books.

Gemmell, David. 2007. *Troy: Shield of Thunder.* London: Corgi Books.

Gemmell, David, and Stella Gemmell. 2008. *Troy: Fall of Kings*. London: Corgi Books.

Georgiadou, Aristoula, and David H. J. Larmour. 1998. *Lucian's Science Fiction Novel* True Histories: *Interpretation and Commentary*. Leiden, Netherlands: Brill.

Germain, David. 2009. "Sith Invites Bush Comparisons." CBS News. Available at http://www.cbsnews.com/2102-890_162-695449.html. Accessed June 14, 2011.

Gilder, Joshua, and Anne-Lee Gilder. 2004. *Heavenly Intrigue: Johannes Kepler, Tycho Brahe, and the Murder Behind One of History's Greatest Scientific Discoveries*. New York: Doubleday.

Gillespie, Stuart, and Philip Hardie, eds. 2007. *The Cambridge Companion to Lucretius*. Cambridge, UK: Cambridge University Press.

Gilmore, David. 2003. *Monsters: Evil Beings, Mythical Beasts, and All Manner of Imaginary Terrors*. Philadelphia: University of Pennsylvania Press.

Gleason, Maude W. 1999. "Truth Contests and Talking Corpses." In *Constructions of the Classical Body*. Ed. J. Porter. Ann Arbor: University of Michigan Press. 287–313.

Gomme, Arnold W. 1921. *Mr. Wells as Historian*. Glasgow, UK: MacLehose, Jackson & Co.

González, Antonio B., and Ana M. Calvo. 1997. "Monsters on the Island: Caliban's and Prospero's Hideous Progeny." *Atlantis* 19.15–20.

Gowers, Emily. 1995. "The Anatomy of Rome from Capitol to Cloaca." *Journal of Roman Studies* 85.23–32.

Graf, Fritz. 2011. "Myth." In *The Homeric Encyclopedia*. Ed. Margalit Finkelberg. Malden, MA: Wiley-Blackwell. 545–548.

Grafton, Anthony, Glenn W. Most, and Salvatore Settis, eds. 2010. *The Classical Tradition*. Cambridge, MA: Harvard University Press.

Graziosi, Barbara. 2002. *Inventing Homer: the Early Reception of Epic*. Cambridge, UK: Cambridge University Press.

Graziosi, Barbara. 2008. "The Ancient Reception of Homer." *A Companion to Classical Receptions*. Eds. L. Hardwick and C. Stray. Malden, MA: Blackwell. 26–37.

Graziosi, Barbara, and Johannes Haubold. 2005. *Homer: The Resonance of Epic*. London: Duckworth.

Graziosi, Barbara, and Emily Greenwood, eds. 2007. *Homer in the Twentieth Century*. Oxford, UK: Oxford University Press.

Greenberg, Raz. 2012. "*Alien Resurrection*: The Script that Shaped Joss Whedon's Career." In *Joss Whedon: The Complete Companion*. Ed. M. A. Money. London: Titan Books. 431–440.

Greenblatt, Stephen. 2011. *The Swerve: How the World Became Modern*. New York: W. W. Norton & Company.

Greenwood, Emily. 2010. *Afro-Greeks: Dialogues Between Anglophone Caribbean Literature and Classics in the Twentieth Century.* Oxford, UK: Oxford University Press.

Griffin, Russell M. 1973. "Medievalism in *A Canticle for Leibowitz.*" *Extrapolation* 14.112–125.

Gunn, James. 2006. *Inside Science Fiction.* Second edition. Lanham, MD: Scarecrow Press.

Habicot, Nicolas. 1613. *Gigantostéologie, ou Discours des os d'un géant.* Paris: J. Houzé.

Hainsworth, J. B. 1991. *The Idea of Epic.* Berkeley: University of California Press.

Hall, Edith. 2008. *The Return of Ulysses: A Cultural History of Homer's Odyssey.* Baltimore, MD: Johns Hopkins University Press.

Halliwell, Stephen. 1998 [1986]. *Aristotle's Poetics.* Second impression. Chicago: University of Chicago Press.

Hallyn, Fernand. 1993. *The Poetic Structure of the World: Copernicus and Kepler.* Trans. D. M. Leslie. New York: Zone Books.

Hamilton, Edith. 1942. *Mythology.* Boston: Little, Brown, and Company.

Hankey, Robin. 1990. "'Evil' in the Odyssey." In *"Owls to Athens": Essays on Classical Subjects Presented to Sir Kenneth Dover.* Ed. E. M. Craik. Oxford, UK: Clarendon Press. 87–95.

Hansen, William F. 1990. "Odysseus and the Oar: A Folkloric Approach." In *Approaches to Greek Myth.* Ed. L. Edmunds. Baltimore, MD: Johns Hopkins University Press. 239–272.

Haraway, Donna. 1991. *Simians, Cyborgs and Women: The Reinvention of Nature.* New York: Routledge.

Haraway, Donna. 2004. *The Haraway Reader.* London: Routledge.

Hardie, Philip. 1993. *The Epic Successors of Virgil: A Study in the Dynamics of a Tradition.* Cambridge, UK: Cambridge University Press.

Hardie, Philip. 2007. "Lucretius and Later Latin Literature in Antiquity." In *The Cambridge Companion to Lucretius.* Eds. S. Gillespie and P. Hardie. Cambridge, UK: Cambridge University Press. 111–127.

Hardie, Philip. 2009. *Lucretian Receptions: History, the Sublime, Knowledge.* Cambridge, UK: Cambridge University Press.

Hardwick, Lorna. 1992. "Convergence and Divergence in Reading Homer." In *Homer: Readings and Images.* Eds. C. Emlyn-Jones, L. Hardwick, and J. Purkis. London: Duckworth. 227–248.

Hardwick, Lorna. 2003. *Reception Studies.* Oxford, UK: Oxford University Press.

Hardwick, Lorna, and Christopher Stray, eds. 2008. *A Companion to Classical Receptions.* Malden, MA: Wiley-Blackwell.

Hark, Ina Rae. 2008. *Star Trek. BFI TV Classics.* Basingstoke and New York: Palgrave Macmillan.

Harley, James. 1999. "The Scenic Ideals of Roman Blood Spectacles and Their Role in the Development of Amphitheatrical Space." In *Theatre and Violence*. Ed. J. W. Frick. Tuscaloosa: University of Alabama Press. 41–48.

Harpold, Terry. 2005. "Verne's Cartographies." *Science Fiction Studies* 32.1.95. 18–42.

Harris, S. 2001/2002. "The Return of the Krell Machine: Nanotechnology, the Singularity, and the Empty Planet Syndrome." Available at http://www.grg.org/charter/Krell2.htm. Accessed June 10, 2011.

Harris, Trevor. 2000. "Measurement and Mystery in Verne." In *Jules Verne: Narratives of Modernity*. Ed. E. J. Smyth. Liverpool, UK: Liverpool University Press. 109–121.

Harrison, Niall. 2008. "*Alice in Sunderland*." Torque Control. Available at http://vectoreditors.wordpress.com/2008/02/20/alice-in-sunderland/. Accessed August 4, 2011.

Harrisson, Juliette. 2014. "Les combats de gladiateurs dans la fiction speculative." In *L'Antiquité dans l'imaginaire contemporain: Fantasy, science-fiction, fantastique*. Eds. Mélanie Bost-Fiévet and Sandra Provini. Paris: Classiques Garnier. 321–338.

Hartley, L. P. 1953. *The Go-Between*. New York: Stein and Day.

Hathaway, Henry, dir. 1969. *True Grit*. Paramount Pictures.

Heath, John. 2005. *The Talking Greeks*. Cambridge, UK: Cambridge University Press.

Heiden, Bruce. 1996. "The Three Movements of the *Iliad*." *Greek, Roman, and Byzantine Studies* 37.5–22.

Herbert, Frank. 2005 [1965]. *Dune*. 40th Anniversary Edition. New York: Ace Books.

Herbert, Gary. 1990. "The Hegelian 'Bad Infinite' in Walter Miller's *A Canticle for Leibowitz*." *Extrapolation* 31.160–169.

Hersey, George L. 2009. *Falling in Love with Statues: Artificial Humans from Pygmalion to the Present*. Chicago: University of Chicago Press.

Heubeck, Alfred, and Arie Hoekstra. 1989. *A Commentary on Homer's Odyssey. Volume II: Books IX–XVI*. Oxford, UK: Clarendon Press.

Hickes, Francis, trans. 1634. *Certaine Select Dialogues of Lucian Together with His True Historie*. Oxford, UK: William Turner.

Hickes, Francis, trans. 1894 [1634]. *Lucian's True History*. London: privately printed.

Hickman, Jonathan. 2007. "Frank Herbert's *Dune* and Beyond." *Jinxworld Forums* (web board thread, posting as "JHickman"). Available at http://www.606studios.com/bendisboard/showthread.php?104787-Frank-Herbert-s-Dune-and-beyond. Accessed May 10, 2012.

Hickman, Jonathan. 2009. *Pax Romana*. New York: Image Comics.

Highet, Gilbert. 1949. *The Classical Tradition: Greek and Roman Influences on Western Literature*. Oxford, UK: Oxford University Press.

Hill, D. E., ed. and trans. 1999. *Ovid. Metamorphoses IX–XII*. Warminster, England: Aris & Phillips, Ltd.

Hillier, Russell. 2004. "SF Intertextuality: Hebrew Runes Among the Ruins in *A Canticle for Leibowitz.*" *Science Fiction Studies* 31.1.169–173.

Hinds, Stephen. 1998. *Allusion and Intertext: Dynamics of Appropriation in Roman Poetry.* Cambridge, UK: Cambridge University Press.

Hine, Daryl, trans. 2005. *Hesiod: Works of Hesiod and the Homeric Hymns.* Chicago: University of Chicago.

Hine, Harry M., trans. 2010. *Lucius Annaeus Seneca: Natural Questions.* Chicago: University of Chicago Press.

Hingley, Richard. 2005. *Globalizing Roman Culture: Unity, Diversity, and Empire.* London: Routledge.

Hintz, Carrie, and Elaine Ostry. 2003. "Introduction." In *Utopian and Dystopian Writing for Children and Young Adults.* Eds. C. Hintz and E. Ostry. New York: Routledge. 1–20.

Hofstadter, Dan. 2009. *The Earth Moves: Galileo and the Roman Inquisition.* New York: W. W. Norton.

Hollinger, Veronica. 1999. "Contemporary Trends in Science Fiction Criticism." *Science Fiction Studies* 26.2.232–262.

Holt, Philip. 1992. "H. G. Wells and the Ring of Gyges." *Science Fiction Studies* 19.2.236–247.

Holtsmark, Erling B. 1991. "The *Katabasis* Theme in Modern Cinema." In *Classics and Cinema. (Bucknell Review* Vol. 35, No. 1.) Ed. M. M. Winkler. Lewisburg, PA: Bucknell University Press. 60–80.

Hopkins, David. 2010. *Conversing with Antiquity.* Oxford, UK: Oxford University Press.

Housman, A. E. 1927. *M. Annaei Lucani Belli Civilis Libri Decem.* Oxford, UK: Blackwell.

Humphrey, John W., John P. Oleson, and Andrew N. Sherwood. 1998. *Greek and Roman Technology: A Sourcebook.* London: Routledge.

Humphries, Rolfe, trans. 1983. *Ovid: Metamorphoses.* Bloomington: Indiana University Press.

Huntingdon, John. 1982. *The Logic of Fantasy: H. G. Wells and Science Fiction.* New York: Columbia.

Hurst, Isobel, ed. 2006. *Victorian Women Writers and the Classics: The Feminine of Homer.* Oxford, UK: Oxford University Press.

Ingpen, Roger, ed. 1909. *The Letters of Percy Bysshe Shelley.* London.

Jacoff, Rachel. 2010. "Virgil in Dante." In Farrell and Putnam (2010; q.v.), 147–157.

James, Edward. 2003. "Utopias and Anti-Utopias." In *The Cambridge Companion to Science Fiction*, Eds. E. James and F. Mendlesohn. Cambridge, UK: Cambridge University Press. 219–229.

James, Louis. 1994. "Frankenstein's Monster in Two Traditions." In *Frankenstein, Creation, and Monstrosity.* Ed. Stephen Bann. London: Reaktion Books. 77–94.

James, Paula. 2009. "Crossing Classical Thresholds: Gods, Monsters, and Hell Dimensions in the Whedon Universe." *Classics for All: Reworking*

Antiquity in Mass Culture. Eds. D. Lowe and K. Shahabudin. Cambridge, UK: Cambridge Scholars Publishing. 237–260.

Jameson, Frederic. 1990. *Postmodernism: The Cultural Logic of Late Capitalism.* Durham, NC: Duke University Press.

Janney, A. W. 2000. "Oedipus E-mails His Mom: Computer-Mediated Romance Develops as a Science Fiction Sub-Genre." *Extrapolation* 41.2.160–174.

Jentsch, Ernst. 1997 [1906]. "On the Psychology of the Uncanny." *Angelaki* 2.1.7–16.

Jeunet, Jean-Pierre, and Marc Caro, dir. 1991. *Delicatessen.* UGC and Miramax.

Jeunet, Jean-Pierre, and Marc Caro, dir. 1995. *The City of Lost Children.* Sony Picture Classics.

Jeunet, Jean-Pierre, dir. 1997. *Alien Resurrection.* Screenplay by Joss Whedon. Twentieth Century Fox Home Entertainment.

Jeunet, Jean-Pierre, dir. 2001. *Amélie.* UGC, Miramax.

Johnson, W. R. 2000. *Lucretius and the Modern World.* London: Duckworth.

Johnson, Monte, and Catherine Wison. 2007. "Lucretius and the History of Science." In *The Cambridge Companion to Lucretius.* Eds. S. Gillespie and P. Hardie. Cambridge, UK: Cambridge University Press. 131–148.

Johnston, E. I. 1933. "How the Greeks and Romans Regarded History." *Greece & Rome* 3.7.38–43.

Jolly, John. 1986. "The Bellerophon Myth and *Forbidden Planet.*" *Extrapolation* 27.1.84–89.

Jones, Frederick L., ed. 1947. *Mary Shelley's Journal.* Norman: University of Oklahoma Press.

Jones, Gweneth. 2003. "The Icons of Science Fiction." In *The Cambridge Companion to Science Fiction.* Eds. E. James and F. Mendlesohn. Cambridge, UK: Cambridge University Press: 230–240.

Jones, John. 1962. *On Aristotle and Greek Tragedy.* London: Chatto and Windus. Reprinted 1982. Palo Alto, CA: Stanford University Press.

Joshel, Sandra R., Margaret Malamud, and Maria Wyke. 2001. "Introduction." In *Imperial Projections: Ancient Rome in Modern Popular Culture.* Eds. S. R. Joshel, M. Malamud, and D. T. McGuire, Jr. Baltimore, MD: and London: Johns Hopkins University Press. 1–22.

Jowett, Benjamin, trans. 2009. *Plato: Timaeus.* Rockville, MD: Serenity Publishers.

Jowett, Lorna. 2008. "Mad, Bad, and Dangerous to Know? Negotiating Stereotypes of Science." In *Cylons in America: Critical Studies in Battlestar Galactica.* Eds. T. Potter and C. W. Marshall. New York, London: Continuum International Publishing Group. 64–75.

Joyce, James. 1963. *Stephen Hero.* Ed. T. Spencer, rev. J. J. Slocum and H. Cahoon. Norfolk, VA: New Directions.

Jung, Carl. 1959. *Flying Saucers: A Modern Myth of Things Seen in the Skies.* New York: Harcourt, Brace.

Kafka, Janet. 1975. "Why Science Fiction?" *The English Journal* 64.5.46–53.

Käkelä, Jari. 2008. "Asimov's *Foundation* Trilogy: From the Fall of Rome to the Rise of Cowboy Heroes." *Extrapolation* 49.3.432–449.

Kallendorf, Craig, ed. 2007. *A Companion to the Classical Tradition*. Malden, MA: Blackwell.

Kapell, Matthew W., ed. 2010. *Star Trek as Myth: Essays on Symbol and Archetype at the Final Frontier*. Jefferson, NC: McFarland & Company.

Kaveney, Roz. 2005. *From Alien to the Matrix: Reading Science Fiction Film*. London and New York: I. B. Tauris.

Kaveney, Roz, and Jennifer Stoy, eds. 2010. Battlestar Galactica: *Investigating Flesh, Spirit, and Steel*. New York: I. B. Tauris.

Kawin, Bruce F. 1995. "Children of the Light." Revised version. In *Film Genre Reader II*. Ed. B. Grant. Austin: University of Texas, Austin Press. 308–329.

Kay, Richard. 2002. "Vitruvius and Dante's Giants." *Dante Studies* 120.17–34.

Kearns, Emily. 2004. "The Gods in the Homeric Epics." In *The Cambridge Companion to Homer*. Ed. R. Fowler. Cambridge, UK: Cambridge University Press. 59–73.

Keen, Tony. 2006. "The 'T' Stands for Tiberius: Models and Methodologies of Classical Reception in Science Fiction." Available at http://tonykeen. blogspot.ca/2006/04/t-stands-for-tiberius-models-and.html. Accessed September 20, 2014.

Keen, Antony. 2008. Comment on Niall Harrison. "*Alice in Sunderland*." Torque Control. Available at http://vectoreditors.wordpress.com/2008/02/20/ alice-in-sunderland/#comment-33326. Accessed August 4, 2011.

Keen, Antony. Forthcoming. *Martial's Martians and Other Stories: Studies in Greece and Rome and Science Fiction and Fantasy*. Harold Wood, UK: Beccon.

Kennedy, Duncan. 1997. "Virgilian Epic." In *The Cambridge Companion to Virgil*. Ed. C. Martindale. Cambridge, UK: Cambridge University Press. 145–154.

Kerman, Judith B. 1991. *Retrofitting Blade Runner: Issues in Ridley Scott's Blade Runner and Philip K. Dick's "Do Androids Dream of Electric Sheep?"* Bowling Green, KY: Bowling Green State University Press.

Kidd, Douglas. 1997. *Aratus: Phaenomena*. Cambridge, UK: Cambridge University Press.

Knerr, Anthony. 1984. *Shelley's Adonais: A Critical Edition*. New York: Columbia University Press.

Knight, Damon, ed. 1962. *A Century of Science Fiction*. New York: Simon & Schuster.

Knight, Damon. 1996 [1956]. *In Search of Wonder: Essays on Modern Science Fiction*. Third edition. Chicago: Advent.

Knighten, Merrell. 1994. "The Triple Paternity of *Forbidden Planet*." *Shakespeare Bulletin* 12.3.36–37.

Koestler, Arthur. 1959. *The Sleepwalkers: A History of Man's Changing Vision of the Universe*. New York: Macmillan.

Kovacs, George. 2011. "Comics and Classics: Establishing a Critical Frame." In *Classics and Comics*. Eds. G. Kovacs and C. W. Marshall. Oxford, UK: Oxford University Press. 3–24.

Kreitzer, Larry. 2004. "The Cultural Veneer of *Star Trek*." *Journal of Popular Culture* 30.1–28.

Kuhn, Thomas S. 1996. *The Structure of Scientific Revolutions*. Chicago: University of Chicago Press.

Kyle, Donald G. 1998. *Spectacles of Death in Ancient Rome*. London: Routledge.

Lada-Richards, Ismene. 1998. "'Foul Monster or Good Saviour?' Reflections on Ritual Monsters." *Monsters and Monstrosity in Greek and Roman Culture*. Ed. C. Atherton. Bari, Italy: Levante Editori. 41–82.

Laimé, Arnaud. 2014. "De la marge à la trame. Figures du scholiast dans *Ilium* et *Olympos* de Dan Simmons." In *L'Antiquité dans l'imaginaire contemporain: Fantasy, science-fiction, fantastique*. Eds. Mélanie Bost-Fiévet and Sandra Provini. Paris: Classiques Garnier. 117–134.

L'Allier, Louis. 2014. "*L'Anabase* de Xénophon et l'imaginaire contemporain: L'exemple de la série *Battlestar Galactica*." In *L'Antiquité dans l'imaginaire contemporain: Fantasy, science-fiction, fantastique*. Eds. Mélanie Bost-Fiévet and Sandra Provini. Paris: Classiques Garnier. 285–297.

Lambert, Ladina. 2002. *Imagining the Unimaginable: The Poetics of Early Modern Astronomy*. Amsterdam: Rodopi.

Lanier, Doris. 1995. *Absinthe—The Cocaine of the Nineteenth Century: A History of the Hallucinogenic Drug and Its Effect on Artists and Writers in Europe and the United States*. Jefferson, NC: McFarland.

Larmour, David H. J. 2007. "Holes in the Body: Sites of Abjection in Juvenal's Rome." In *The Sites of Rome: Time, Space, Memory*. Eds. D. H. J. Larmour and D. Spencer. Oxford, UK: Oxford University Press. 168–210.

Lattimore, Richmond, trans. 1961. *Homer: The Iliad*. Chicago: University of Chicago Press.

Laurence, Ray. 1997. "Writing the Roman Metropolis." In *Roman Urbanism: Beyond the Consumer City*. Ed. H. M. Parkins. London: Routledge. 1–20.

Lear, John. 1965. *Kepler's Dream: With Full Text and Notes of the Somnium Sive Astronomia Lunaris, Joannis Kepleri*. Trans. P. Frueh Kirkwood. Berkeley: University of California Press.

Lecercle, Jean-Jaques. 1988. *Frankenstein: Mythe et Philosophie*. Paris: Presses Universitaires de France.

Lendon, J. E. 2000. "Gladiators." *Classical Journal* 95.4.399–406.

Lerer, S. 2000. "*Forbidden Planet* and the Terrors of Philology." *Raritan* 19.3.73–86.

Lesky, Albin. 2004. "Divine and Human Causation in Homeric Epic." Trans. L. Holford-Strevens. In *Oxford Readings in Homer's* Iliad. Ed. D. L. Cairns. Oxford, UK: Oxford University Press. 170–202.

Leterrier, Louis, dir. 2010. *Clash of the Titans*. Warner Bros. Pictures.

Lévi-Strauss, Claude. 1963. *Structural Anthropology.* Trans. C. Jacobson. New York: Basic Books.

Levine, George. 1979. "The Ambiguous Heritage of *Frankenstein.*" In *The Endurance of Frankenstein.* Eds. G. Levine and U. C. Knoepflmacher. Berkeley: University of California Press. 3–30.

Lewis, C. T., and C. Short. 1879. *A Latin Dictionary.* Available at http://www.perseus.tufts.edu/hopper. Accessed December 14, 2011.

Lexicon Iconographicum Mythologiae Classicae. 1981–2009. Zurich: Artemis.

Leydon, R. 2004. "*Forbidden Planet*: Effects and Affects in the Electro Avant Garde." In *Off the Planet: Music, Sound, and Science Fiction Cinema.* Ed. P. Hayward. Eastleigh, UK: John Libbey Publishing. 61–76.

Liebesman, Jonathan, dir. 2012. *Wrath of the Titans.* Warner Bros. Pictures.

List, M. and W. Gerlach, eds. 1969. *Joannis Keppleri: Somnium seu Opus Posthumum de Astronomia Lunari.* Osnabrück, Germany: Otto Zeller.

Lively, Genevieve. 2006. "Science Fiction and Cyber Myths: or, Do Cyborgs Dream of Dolly the Sheep?" In *Laughing with Medusa: Classical Myth and Feminist Thought.* Eds. V. Zajko and M. Leonard. Oxford, UK: Oxford University Press. 275–294.

Loraux, Nicole. 1982. "Ce que vit Tirésias." In *L'Écrit du temps 2: Langues familières, langues étrangères.* Paris: Editions de Minuit. 99–116.

Lowenthal, David. 1999. *The Past Is a Foreign Country.* Cambridge, UK: Cambridge University Press.

Luciano, P. 1987. *Them or Us: Archetypal Interpretations of Fifties Alien Invasion Films.* Bloomington: Indiana University Press.

Lundquist, Lynne. 1996. "Myth and Illiteracy: Bill and Ted's Explicated Adventures." *Extrapolation* 37.3.212–223.

Lynn-George, Michael. 1988. *Epos: Word, Narrative, and the* Iliad. Atlantic Highlands, NJ: Humanities Press International.

MacCary, W. Thomas. 1982. *Childlike Achilles. Ontogeny and Phylogeny in the* Iliad. New York: Columbia University Press.

MacDonald, D. L. 1986. "Orientalism and Eroticism in Byron and Merrill." *Pacific Coast Philology* 21.60–64.

MacDonald, Dennis R. 1994. *Christianizing Homer: The* Odyssey, *Plato, and the* Acts of Andrew. Oxford, UK: Oxford University Press.

Macherey, Pierre. 1966. *Pour une théorie de la production littéraire.* Paris: Maspero.

Macleod, Ken. 2003. "Politics and Science Fiction." In *The Cambridge Companion to Science Fiction.* Eds. E. James and F. Mendlesohn. Cambridge, UK: Cambridge University Press. 230–240.

Makins, Marian. 2014. ""Written in a language called Latin about a place called Rome": Réception de l'Antiquité et résistance dans la trilogie *Hunger Games.*" In *L'Antiquité dans l'imaginaire contemporain: Fantasy, science-fiction, fantastique.* Eds. Mélanie Bost-Fiévet and Sandra Provini. Paris: Classiques Garnier. 339-357.

Manganiello, Dominic. 1986. "History as Judgment and Promise in *A Canticle for Leibowitz*." *Science Fiction Studies* 13.2.159–169.

Manguel, Alberto. 2007. *Homer's* the Iliad *and the* Odyssey: *A Biography*. New York: Grove Press.

Margolis, Rick. 2008. "A Killer Story." *School Library Journal* 54.9. Available at http://www.schoollibraryjournal.com/article/CA6590063.html. Accessed March 1, 2013.

Margolis, Rick. 2010. "The Last Battle." *School Library Journal* 56.8. Available at http://www.schoollibraryjournal.com/slj/home/885800312/the_last_battle_with_mockingjay.html.csp. Accessed March 1, 2013.

Marshall, C. W. Forthcoming. "Odysseus and the *Infinite Horizon*." In *Son of Classics and Comics*, Eds. G. Kovacs and C. W. Marshall. Oxford, UK: Oxford University Press.

Marshall, C. W., and Tiffany Potter. 2014. "Remapping Terrorism Stereotypes in *Battlestar Galactica*." In *Muslims and American Popular Culture*. Eds. I. Omidvar and A. R. Richards. Santa Barbara, CA: Praeger. 61–72.

Marshall, Tim. 1995. *Murdering to Dissect: Grave-Robbing,* Frankenstein, *and the Anatomy Literature*. Manchester, UK: Manchester University Press.

Martin, Andrew. 1985. *The Knowledge of Ignorance: From Genesis to Jules Verne*. Cambridge, UK: Cambridge University Press.

Martin, Charles, trans. 2010. *Ovid:* Metamorphoses. New York: Norton.

Martin, Richard P. 1993. "Telemachus and the Last Hero Song." *Colby Quarterly* 29.3.222–240.

Martindale, Charles, and Michelle Martindale. 1990. *Shakespeare and the Uses of Antiquity*. London: Routledge.

Martindale, Charles. 1997. "Green Politics: The *Eclogues*." In *The Cambridge Companion to Virgil*. Ed. C. Martindale. Cambridge, UK: Cambridge University Press. 107–124.

Martindale, Charles, and Richard F. Thomas, eds. 2006. *Classics and the Uses of Reception*. Malden, MA: Wiley-Blackwell.

Mastronarde, Donald, ed. 2002. *Euripides:* Medea. Cambridge, UK: Cambridge University Press.

Mathieson, Kenneth. 1985. "The Influence of Science Fiction in the Contemporary American Novel." *Science Fiction Studies* 12.1.22–32.

McClellan, A. 2010. "Creating the Grotesque: Zombification in Lucan's *Bellum Civile*, Shelley's *Frankenstein*, and Romero's *Day of the Dead*." Presented at conference on "All Roads Lead From Rome: The Classical (non)Tradition in Popular Culture," Rutgers NJ, April 9, 2010.

McConnell, Frank. 1981. *The Science Fiction of H. G. Wells*. Oxford, UK: Oxford University Press.

McGiveron, Rafeeq. O. 1997. "'Do You Know the Legend of Hercules and Antaeus?' The Wilderness in Ray Bradbury's *Fahrenheit 451*." *Extrapolation* 38.2.102–109.

McIntee, David. 2005. *Beautiful Monsters: The Unofficial and Unauthorised Guide to the Alien and Predator Films*. Surrey: Telos Publishing Ltd.

Meckler, Michael, ed. 2006. *Classical Antiquity and the Politics of America*. Waco, TX: Baylor University Press.

Mellor, Anne K. 1987. "*Frankenstein*: A Feminist Critique of Science." In *One Culture: Essays on Literature and Science*. Ed. George Levine. Madison: University of Wisconsin Press. 287–312.

Mellor, Anne K. 1988. *Mary Shelley: Her Life, Her Fiction, Her Monsters*. New York: Methuen.

Mellor, Anne K. 2003. "Making a 'Monster': An Introduction to *Frankenstein*." In *The Cambridge Companion to Mary Shelley*. Ed. E. Schor. Cambridge, UK: Cambridge University Press. 1–25.

Mendlesohn, Farah. 2003a. "Introduction: Reading Science Fiction." In *The Cambridge Companion to Science Fiction*. Ed. Edward James and Farah Mendlesohn. Cambridge, UK: Cambridge University Press. 1–12.

Mendlesohn, Farah. 2003b. "Religion and Science Fiction." In *The Cambridge Companion to Science Fiction*. Ed. Edward James and Farah Mendlesohn. Cambridge, UK: Cambridge University Press. 263–275.

Mendlesohn, Farah, and Edward James. 2009. *A Short History of Fantasy*. London: Middlesex University Press.

Menzel, Donald H. 1975. "Kepler's Place in Science Fiction." *Vistas in Astronomy* 18.896–904.

Merril, Judith, ed. 1967. *The Year's Best Science Fiction*. New York: Dell.

Miéville, China. 2005. "Introduction." In H. G. Wells. *The First Men in the Moon*. London: Penguin Classics. xiii–xxviii.

Miller, Christopher M. 2005. "Shelley's Uncertain Heaven." *English Literary History* 72.577–603.

Miller, Rand. 1989. "The Being and Becoming of 'Frankenstein'." *SubStance*, Special Issue: *Writing the Real*. 18.60.60–74.

Miller, Robert J. 1994. *The Complete Gospels. Annotated Scholars Version*. Sonoma, CA: Polebridge Press.

Miller, Jr., Walter M. 2006. *A Canticle for Leibowitz*. New York: Eos.

Mitchell, David, and Sharon Snyder. 2000. *Narrative Prosthesis: Disability and the Dependencies of Discourse*. Ann Arbor: University of Michigan Press.

Monro, D. B., and T. W. Allen. 1902. *Homeri Opera. Vol. II: Iliad XIII–XXIV*. Oxford, UK: Oxford University Press.

Montiglio, Silvia. 2011. *From Villain to Hero: Odysseus in Ancient Thought*. Ann Arbor: University of Michigan.

Morris, Sarah P. 1992. *Daidalos and the Origins of Greek Art*. Princeton, NJ: Princeton University Press.

Morrison, Lucy, and Staci L. Stone. 2003. *A Mary Shelley Encyclopedia*. London: Greenwood Press.

Morsberger, R. 1961. "Shakespeare and Science Fiction." *Shakespeare Quarterly* 12.2.161.

Most, Glenn. 1992a. "*Disiecti Membra Poetae*: The Rhetoric of Dismemberment in Neronian Poetry." In *Innovations of Antiquity*. Ralph Hexter and Daniel Seldon, eds. New York: Routledge. 391–419.

Most, Glenn. 1992b. "Il poeta nell'Ade: Catabasi epica e teoria dell'epos tra Omero e Virgilio." *Studi Italiani di Filologia Classica* Series 3. 10.2.1014–026.

Mulhall, Stephen. 2008 [2002]. *On Film*. Hoboken, NJ: Taylor & Francis.

Muller, Vivienne. 2012. "Virtually Real: Suzanne Collins's *The Hunger Games* Trilogy." *International Research in Children's Literature* 5.1.51–63.

Mumford, Lewis. 1961. *The City in History: Its Origins, Its Transformations, and Its Prospects*. New York: Harcourt, Brace and World.

Murdock, Andrew, and Rachel Aberly. 1997. *The Making of* Alien Resurrection. New York: HarperPrism.

Murray, Oswyn. 1993. *Early Greece*. Second edition. Cambridge, UK: Harvard University Press.

Myrsiades, Kostas, ed. 2009. *Reading Homer: Film and Text*. Madison, WI and Teaneck, NJ: Fairleigh Dickinson University Press.

Nagy, Gregory. 1979. *The Best of the Achaeans: Concepts of the Hero in Archaic Greek Poetry*. Baltimore, MD: Johns Hopkins University Press.

Nagy, Gregory. 1996. *Poetry as Performance: Homer and Beyond*. Cambridge, UK: Cambridge University Press.

Nelkin, Dorothy. 1996. "The Gene as a Cultural Icon: Visual Images of DNA." *Art Journal* 55.56–61.

Nicolson, Marjorie Hope. 1948. *Voyages to the Moon*. London and New York: Macmillan.

Nisbet, Gideon. 2008. *Ancient Greece in Film and Popular Culture*. Second Edition. Exeter, UK: Bristol Phoenix.

Niven, Larry. 1971. "The Theory and Practice of Time Travel." In *All the Myriad Ways*. New York: Ballantine. 110–123.

Obertino, James. 1993. "Moria and Hades: Underworld Journeys in Tolkien and Virgil." *Comparative Literature Studies* 30.2.153–169.

O'Higgins, Dolores. 1988. "Lucan as 'Vates'." *Classical Antiquity* 7.208–226.

Ott, Brian, and Cameron Walter. 2000. "Intertextuality: Interpretive Practice and Textual Strategy." *Critical Studies in Media Communication* 17.429–446.

Ouellette, Laurie, and James Hay. 2008. *Better Living Through Reality TV: Television and Post-Welfare Citizenship*. Malden, MA: Blackwell.

Ower, John. 1979. "'Aesop' and the Ambiguity of Clifford Simak's 'City'." *Science Fiction Studies* 6.2.164–167.

Pache, Corinne O. 2010. "'So Say We All': Reimagining Empire and the *Aeneid*." *The Classical Outlook* 87.4.132–136.

Palumbo, Donald. 1998. "The Monomyth as Fractal Pattern in Frank Herbert's *Dune*." *Science Fiction Studies* 25.433–458.

Parrett, Aaron. 2004. *The Translunar Narrative in the Western Tradition.* Aldershot, UK: Ashgate.

Parrinder, Patrick. 1980. "Science Fiction as Truncated Epic." *Bridges to Science Fiction.* Eds. G. E. Slusser, G. R. Guffey, and M. Rose. Carbondale: University of Southern Illinois Press. 91–106.

Parrinder, Patrick. 1996. *Shadows of the Future: H. G. Wells, Science Fiction and Prophecy.* Liverpool, UK: Liverpool University Press.

Parrinder, Patrick, ed. 2001. *Learning from Other Worlds: Estrangement, Cognition, and the Politics of Science Fiction and Utopia.* Durham, NC: Duke University Press.

Parrinder, Patrick. 2005. "Note on the Text." In H. G. Wells, *The First Men in the Moon.* London: Penguin Classics. xxx–xxxvii.

Pascoe, Judith. 2006. "*Proserpine* and *Midas*." In *The Cambridge Companion to Mary Shelley.* Ed. E. Schor. Cambridge, UK: Cambridge University Press. 180–190.

Paul, Joanna. 2010. "Cinematic Receptions of Antiquity: the Current State of Play." *Classical Receptions Journal* 2.1.136–155.

Paxson, James J. 1999. "Kepler's Allegory of Containment, the Making of Modern Astronomy, and the Semiotics of Mathematical Thought." *Intertexts* 3.2.105–123.

Paxson, James J. 2001. "Revisiting the Deconstruction of Narratology: Master Tropes of Narrative Embedding and Symmetry." *Style* 35.1.126–150.

Pearse, Roger, trans. 2002. "Codices 166-185 [Extracts]." The Tertullian Project. Available at http://www.tertullian.org/fathers/photius_copyright/photius_04bibliotheca.htm. Accessed August 5, 2011.

Pearson, Anna M. 1999. "From Thwarted Gods to Reclaimed Mystery?" In Porter and McLaren (1999a; q.v.), 13–32.

Petersen, Wolfgang, dir. 2004. *Troy.* Warner Bros..

Pollin, Burton R. 1965. "Philosophical and Literary Sources of Frankenstein." *Comparative Literature* 17.2.97–108.

Poole, William. 2010. "Kepler's *Somnium* and Francis Godwin's *The Man in the Moone*: Births of Science-Fiction 1593-1638." In *New Worlds Reflected: Travel and Utopia in the Early Modern Period.* Ed. C. Houston. Aldershot, UK: Ashgate. 57–70.

Porter, Jennifer E., and Darcee L. McLaren, eds. 1999a. *Star Trek and Sacred Ground.* Albany: State University of New York Press.

Porter, Jennifer E., and Darcee L. McLaren. 1999b. "Introduction." In Porter and McLaren (1999a; q.v.), 1–9.

Priestman, Martin. 1999. *Romantic Atheism: Poetry and Freethought, 1780–1830.* Cambridge, UK: Cambridge University Press.

Priestman, Martin. 2007. "Lucretius in Romantic and Victorian Britain." In *The Cambridge Companion to Lucretius.* Eds. S. Gillespie and P. Hardie. Cambridge, UK: Cambridge University Press. 289–305.

Provini, Sandra. 2014. "L'épopée au féminin. De l'*Énéide* de Virgile à *Lavinia* de Ursula Le Guin." In *L'Antiquité dans l'imaginaire contemporain: Fantasy, science-fiction, fantastique*. Eds. Mélanie Bost-Fiévet and Sandra Provini. Paris: Classiques Garnier. 81–100.

Prucher, Jeff, ed. 2007. *Brave New Worlds: The Oxford Dictionary of Science Fiction*. Oxford, UK: Oxford University Press.

Pucci, Pietro. 1998. *The Song of the Sirens: Essays on Homer*. Oxford, UK: Rowman & Littlefield Publishers.

Quint, David. 1993. *Epic and Empire: Politics and Generic Convention from Virgil to Milton*. Princeton, NJ: Princeton University Press.

Rabkin, Eric S. 1976. *The Fantastic in Literature*. Princeton, NJ: Princeton University Press.

Rauch, Alan. 1995. "The Monstrous Body of Knowledge in Mary Shelley's *Frankenstein*." *Studies in Romanticism* 34.2.227–253.

Raymond, François, and Daniel Compère. 1976. *Le développement des études sur Jules Verne*. Paris: Minard, Archive des Lettres Modernes.

Reed, J. D. 1997. *Bion of Smyrna: The Fragments and the* Adonis. Cambridge, UK: Cambridge University Press.

Reichart, Jasia. 1994. "Artificial Life and the Myth of Frankenstein." In *Frankenstein, Creation and Monstrosity*. Ed. S. Bann. London: Reaktion. 136–157.

Rieu, E. V., trans. 1959. *Apollonius: The Voyage of the Argo*. New York: Penguin.

Roberts, Adam. 2006a. *The History of Science Fiction*. Basingstoke, UK: Palgrave Macmillan.

Roberts, Adam. 2006b. "Hard Fantasy (1996: *Fairyland*—Paul McAuley)." In *The Arthur C. Clarke Award: A Critical Anthology*. Ed. P. Kincaid, with A. M. Butler. Daventry, UK: Serendip Foundation. 119–130.

Roberts, Ian F. 2000. "Oppenheimer's Heir: Morbius and Atomic Technology in *Forbidden Planet*." *Journal of Popular Film and Television* 38.4.170–175.

Robinson, Charles E., ed. 1996. *The Frankenstein Notebooks: A Facsimile Edition of Mary Shelley's Manuscript Novel, 1816–17*. New York: Garland.

Robinson, Charles E., ed. 2009. *The Original Frankenstein*. New York: Vintage.

Robinson, Christopher. 1979. *Lucian and His Influence in Europe*. London: Duckworth.

Rogers, Brett M., and Walter Scheidel. 2004. "Driving Stakes, Driving Cars: California Car Culture, Sex, and Identity in *Buffy the Vampire Slayer*." *Slayage: The Online International Journal of Buffy Studies* 4.1–2 [13–14]. Available at http://www.slayageonline.com/Numbers/slayage13_14.htm. Accessed September 14, 2014.

Rogers, Brett M., and Benjamin Eldon Stevens. 2012a. "Review Essay: Classical Receptions in Science Fiction." *Classical Receptions Journal* 4.1.127–147.

Rogers, Brett M., and Benjamin Eldon Stevens. 2012b. "A New 'Modern Prometheus'?" *OUPblog*. Available at http://blog.oup.com/2012/07/

modern-prometheus-classical-reception-sci-fi/. Accessed September 14, 2014.

Roisman, H. 2008. "The *Odyssey* from Homer to NBC: The Cyclops and the Gods." *A Companion to Classical Receptions*. Eds. L. Hardwick and C. Stray. Malden, MA: Blackwell. 315–325.

Rose, Peter W. 1997. "Ideology in the *Iliad*: Polis, Basileus, Theoi." *Arethusa* 30.151–199.

Rosen. Edward, trans. and ed. 1965. *Kepler's Conversation with Galileo's Sidereal Messenger*. New York: Johnson Reprint Corporation.

Rosen, Edward, trans. and ed. 1967. *Kepler's Somnium: The Dream, or Posthumous Work on Lunar Astronomy*. Madison: University of Wisconsin Press.

Rubens, Beattie, and Oliver Taplin. 1989. *An Odyssey Round Odysseus*. BBC Books.

Russo, Joseph, Manuel Fernández-Galiano, and Alfred Heubeck. 1992. *A Commentary on Homer's* Odyssey. *Volume III: Books XVII–XXIV*. Oxford, UK: Clarendon Press.

Rütten, Ulrich. 1997. *Phantasie und Lachkultur: Lukians "Wahre Geschichten."* Tübingen, Germany: Gunter Narr Verlag.

Ryman, Geoff. 2010. "Adam and (Mitochondrial) Eve: A Foundation Myth for White Folks." In Kaveney and Stoy (2010; q.v.), 36–58.

Sammon, Paul M. 1996. *Future Noir: The Making of* Blade Runner. London: Gollancz.

Sanford, Eva Matthews. 1931. "Lucan and His Roman Critics." *Classical Philology* 26.233–257.

Sawyer, Andy. 2008. "The Overlap Between Science Fiction and Other Genres." Gresham College. Available at http://www.gresham.ac.uk/lectures-and-events/science-fiction-as-a-literary-genre. Accessed August 5, 2011.

Scafella, Frank. 1981. "The White Sphinx and *The Time Machine*." *Science Fiction Studies* 8.3.255–265.

Scheidel, Walter. 2007. "Marriage, Families, and Survival: Demographic Aspects." In *A Companion to the Roman Army*. Ed. Paul Erdkamp. Chichester, UK: John Wiley & Sons. 417–434.

Schein, Seth L. 1984. *The Mortal Hero: An Introduction to Homer's* Iliad. Berkeley: University of California Press.

Schein, Seth. 2008. "'Our Debt to Greece and Rome': Canons, Class and Ideology." In *A Companion to Classical Receptions*. Ed. L. Hardwick. Malden, MA: Blackwell. 75–85.

Scholes, Robert, and Eric Rabkin. 1977. *Science Fiction: History, Science, Vision*. Oxford, UK: Oxford University Press.

Schor, Esther, ed. 2003. *The Cambridge Companion to Mary Shelley*. Cambridge, UK: Cambridge University Press.

Schwartz, Emmanuel. 2004. *The Legacy of Homer*. New York: Dahesh Museum of Art/Princeton University Art Museum/Yale University Press.

Scott, Ridley, dir. 1979. *Alien*. Screenplay by Dan O'Bannon. Twentieth Century Fox Home Entertainment.

Scott, Ridley, dir. 2007 [1982]. *Blade Runner. Four-Disc Collector's Edition*. Warner Brothers.

Seaton, R. C., ed. and trans. 2003. *Apollonius of Rhodes: The Argonautica*. Cambridge, UK: Harvard.

Seed, David. 1996. "Recycling the Texts of the Culture: Walter M. Miller's *A Canticle for Leibowitz*." *Extrapolation* 37.3.257–271.

Seed, David. 2011. *Science Fiction: A Very Short Introduction*. Oxford, UK: Oxford University Press.

Segal, Charles. 1992. "Divine Justice in the *Odyssey*: Poseidon, Cyclops, and Helios." *American Journal of Philology* 113.4.489–518.

Shanower, Eric. 2001. *Age of Bronze, Volume 1: A Thousand Ships*. Berkeley: Image Comics.

Shanower, Eric. 2004. *Age of Bronze, Volume 2: Sacrifice*. Berkeley: Image Comics.

Shanower, Eric. 2007. *Age of Bronze, Volume 3: Betrayal, Part One*. Berkeley: Image Comics.

Shelley, Mary. 1818. *Frankenstein; or, The Modern Prometheus*. London: Lackington, Hughes, Harding, Mavor & Jones.

Shelley, Mary. 2007. *Frankenstein; or, The Modern Prometheus*. Ed. M. Hindle. London: Penguin.

Shelley, Percy Bysshe. 1880. "On *Frankenstein*." In *The Words of Percy Bysshe Shelley in Verse and Prose*. Ed. H. B. Forman. London: Reeves and Turner. 11–15.

Sheppard, David. 2012. *The Eternal Return*: Oedipus, The Tempest, Forbidden Planet. *Tales of the Mythic World*. Vol. 2. Smashwords Edition.

Sherwin, Paul. 1981. "*Frankenstein*: Creation as Catastrophe." *Publications of the Modern Language Association* 96.883–903.

Shilleto, Arthur R., trans. 1886. *Pausanias' Description of Greece*. London: George Bell and Sons.

Sidwell, Keith, trans. 2004. *Lucian: Chattering Courtesans and Other Sardonic Sketches*. London: Penguin.

Simmons, Dan. 1985. *Song of Kali*. London: Gollancz.

Simmons, Dan. 1989. *Hyperion*. London: Gollancz.

Simmons, Dan. 1990. *The Fall of Hyperion*. London: Gollancz.

Simmons, Dan. 1991. *Summer of Night*. New York: Warner Books.

Simmons, Dan. 1994. *Fires of Eden*. London: Headline Book Publishing.

Simmons, Dan. 1995. *Endymion*. New York: Bantam Books.

Simmons, Dan. 1997. *The Rise of Endymion*. New York: Bantam Books.

Simmons, Dan. 1999. *The Crook Factory*. New York: Harper-Collins.

Simmons, Dan. 2002. *A Winter Haunting*. New York: Harper-Collins.

Simmons, Dan. 2003. *Ilium*. London: Gollancz.

Simmons, Dan. 2005. *Olympos*. London: Gollancz.

Simmons, Dan. 2007. *The Terror*. London: Bantam Books.

Simmons, Dan. 2009. *Drood*. Boston: Little, Brown, and Company.

Simmons, Dan. 2010. *Black Hills*. London: Quercus.

Simonis, Annette. 2014. "Voyages mythiques et passages aux Enfers dans la littérature fantastique contemporaine: *Le Seigneur des Anneaux* et *À la croisée des mondes*." In *L'Antiquité dans l'imaginaire contemporain: Fantasy, science-fiction, fantastique*. Eds. Mélanie Bost-Fiévet and Sandra Provini. Paris: Classiques Garnier. 241–252.

Singh, Tarsem, dir. 2011. *Immortals*. Relativity Media / Universal Pictures.

Singleton, Charles S. 1970. *The Divine Comedy*. Princeton, NJ: Princeton University Press.

Slatkin, Laura M. 2011. "Gods." In *The Homer Encyclopedia: Vol. I*. Ed. M. Finkelberg. Malden, Oxford, Chichester: Blackwell. 317–321.

Slonczewski, Joan, and Michael Levy. 2003. "Science Fiction and the Life Sciences." In *The Cambridge Companion to Science Fiction*. Eds. E. James and F. Mendlesohn. Cambridge, UK: Cambridge University Press. 174–185.

Smith, R. Scott, and Stephen M. Trzaskoma, trans. 2007. *Apollodorus' Library and Hyginus' Fabulae*. Indianapolis, IN: Hackett.

Snell, Bruno. 1953. *The Discovery of the Mind in Early Greek Philosophy and Literature*. Trans. T. G. Rosenmeyer. Cambridge, UK: Harvard University Press.

Snyder, Jane McIntosh. 1980. *Puns and Poetry in Lucretius' De Rerum Natura*. Amsterdam: B. R. Grüner.

Snyder, Sharon L., ed. 2002. *Enabling the Humanities*. New York: Modern Language Association.

Sontag, Susan. 1966. *Against Interpretation: and other essays*. New York: Farrar, Straus and Giroux.

Stableford, Brian, and David R. Langford. 2013. "Moon." In *The Encyclopedia of Science Fiction*. Third edition. Eds. J. Clute, D. Langford, G. Sleight, and P. Nicholls. Available at http://sf-encyclopedia.com/entry/moon. Accessed March 2, 2013.

Stableford, Brian. 1999a [1993]. "Moon." In *The Encyclopedia of Science Fiction*. Corrected paperback second edition. Eds. J. Clute and P. Nicholls. London: Orbit. 820–821.

Stableford, Brian. 2005. *The A to Z of Science Fiction Literature*. Lanham, MD: Scarecrow.

Stableford, Brian. 2012a. "Fantastic Voyages." In *The Encyclopedia of Science Fiction*[3]. Eds. J. Clute, D. Langford, G. Sleight, and P. Nicholls. Available at http://sf-encyclopedia.com/entry/fantastic_voyages. Accessed March 2, 2013.

Stableford, Brian. 2012b. "Proto SF." In *The Encyclopedia of Science Fiction*³. Eds. J. Clute, D. Langford, G. Sleight and P. Nicholls. Available at http://sf-encyclopedia.com/entry/proto_sf. Accessed March 2, 2013.

Standish, David. 2004. *Hollow Earth: The Long and Curious History of Imagining Strange Lands, Fantastical Creatures, Advanced Civilizations, and Marvelous Machines below the Earth's Surface*. Cambridge, MA: Da Capo Press.

Stanford, William B. 1962. *Homer: Odyssey XIII–XXIV*. London: Macmillan.

Stanford, William B. 1964. *The Ulysses Theme*. Barnes and Noble.

Stein, Herbert H. 2010. "*Forbidden Planet*." *Psychoanalytic Association of New York Bulletin* 48.1.16–22.

Steinbrunner, Chris, and Burt Goldblatt. 1972. *Cinema of the Fantastic*. New York: Saturday Review Press.

Stevens, Benjamin Eldon. 2013. "Virgil in A. S. Byatt's *The Children's Book*." Paper presented at the annual Conference of the International Association for the Fantastic in the Arts. Orlando, FL, March 2013.

Stoler, John A. 1984. "Christian Lore and Characters' Names in *A Canticle for Leibowitz*." *Literary Onomastics Studies* 11.1.77–91.

Stoppard, Tom. 1997. *The Invention of Love*. New York: Grove Press.

Stover, Leon E. 1998. "Editor's Introduction." In H. G. Wells. *The First Men in the Moon: A Critical Text of the 1901 London First Edition, with an Introduction and Appendices*. Ed. L. E. Stover. Jefferson, NC: McFarland. 1–32.

Stoy, Jennifer. 2010. "Of Great Zeitgeist and Bad Faith: An Introduction to *Battlestar Galactica*." In Kaveney and Stoy (2010; q.v.), 1–36.

Strick, P. 1982. "Space Invaders." In *Movies of the Fifties*. Ed. A. Lloyd, consultant editor D. Robinson. London: Orbis. 31–34.

Strong, James. 1890. "Arkos." In *Strong's Exhaustive Concordance*. Available at http://concordances.org/greek/715.htm. Accessed December 14, 2011.

Sugar, Gabrielle. 2009. "Medieval Universes and Early Modern Worlds: Conceptions of the Cosmos in Johannes Kepler's *Somnium*." In *Renaissance Medievalisms*. Ed. Konrad Eisenbichler. Toronto: Center for Reformation and Renaissance Studies. 303–319.

Sullivan, C. W. 2001. "Folklore and Fantastic Literature." *Western Folklore* 60.279–296.

Sunstein, Emily W. 1989. *Mary Shelley: Romance and Reality*. Baltimore, MD: Johns Hopkins University Press.

Sutton, Thomas C., and Marilyn Sutton. 1969. "Science Fiction as Mythology." *Western Folklore* 28.230–237.

Suvin, Darko. 1972. "On the Poetics of the Science Fiction Genre." *College English* 34.3.372–382.

Suvin, Darko. 1979. *Metamorphoses of Science Fiction: On the Poetics and History of a Literary Genre*. New Haven: Yale University Press.

Swain, Simon. 1996. *Hellenism and Empire: Language, Classicism and Power in the Greek World, a.d. 50–250.* Oxford, UK: Oxford University Press.

Swanson, Roy A. 1976. "The True, the False, and the Truly False: Lucian's Philosophical Science Fiction." *Science Fiction Studies* 3.3.10.228–239.

Swinford, Dean. 2006. *Through the Daemon's Gate: Kepler's* Somnium, *Medieval Dream Narratives, and the Polysemy of Allegorical Motifs.* New York: Routledge.

Taplin, Oliver. 1999. "Spreading the Word Through Performance." In *Performance Culture and Athenian Democracy.* Eds. S. Goldhill and R. Osborne. Cambridge, UK: Cambridge University Press. 33–57.

Tarratt, M. 1970. "Monsters from the Id." In *Films and Filming.* 17.3.38–42 and 17.4. 40–42. Cited here from the reprinted version in 1995, *Film Genre Reader II.* Ed. B. Grant. Austin: University of Texas, Austin Press. 330–349.

Tasker, Yvonne. 1998. *Working Girls: Gender and Sexuality in Popular Culture.* London and New York: Routledge.

Tavormina, M. Teresa. 1988. "A Gate of Horn and Ivory: Dreaming True and False in *Earthsea.*" *Extrapolation* 29.4.338–348.

Telotte, J. P. 1995. *Replications: A Robotic History of the Science Fiction Film.* Urbana: University of Illinois Press.

Thalmann, William G. 1988 "Thersites: Comedy, Scapegoats and Heroic Ideology in the *Iliad.*" *Transactions of the American Philological Association* 118.1–28.

Theall, D. F. 1980. "On Science Fiction as Symbolic Communication." *Science Fiction Studies.* 7.247–262.

Thornburg, Mary K. Patterson. 1987. *The Monster in the Mirror: Gender and the Sentimental/Gothic Myth in* Frankenstein. Ann Arbor, MI: UMI Research Press.

Tiffany, Daniel. 2009. *Infidel Poetics: Riddles, Nightlife, Substance.* Chicago: University of Chicago Press.

Todorov, Tzvetan. 1975. *The Fantastic: A Structural Approach to a Literary Genre.* Ithaca, NY: Cornell University.

Tolkien, J. R. R. 1966. "Tree and Leaf: On Fairy Stories." In *The Tolkien Reader.* New York. 33–99.

Tomcho, Thomas J., John C. Norcross, and Christopher J. Correia. 1994. "Great Books Curricula: What Is Being Read?" *The Journal of General Education* 43.2.90–101.

Trushell, J. 1995. "Return of *Forbidden Planet?*" *Foundation* 64.82–89.

Tsagarakis, Odysseus. 1977. *Nature and Background of Major Concepts of Divine Power in Homer.* Amsterdam: B. R. Grüner Publishing Co.

Tucker, Robert A. 1971. "Lucan and the French Revolution: The *Bellum Civile* as a Political Mirror." *Classical Philology* 66.6–16.

Turner, Paul. 1959. "Shelley and Lucretius." *The Review of English Studies.* 10.269–282. University Press.

Turner, Paul, trans. 1961. *Lucian: Satirical Sketches. A New Translation.* Harmondsworth, UK: Penguin. Reprinted edition 1990, Bloomington: Indiana University Press.

Unwin, Timothy. 2000. "The Fiction of Science, or the Science of Fiction." In *Jules Verne: Narratives of Modernity.* Ed. E. J. Smyth. Liverpool, UK: Liverpool University Press. 46–59.

van Wees, Hans 1992. *Status Warriors: War, Violence, and Society in Homer and History.* Amsterdam: J. C. Gieben.

Vernant, Jean-Pierre. 1982. *The Origins of Greek Thought.* Ithaca, NY: Cornell University Press.

Verne, Jules. 1864a. *Voyage au centre de la terre.* Paris: Pierre-Jules Hetzel.

Verne, Jules. 1864b. "Edgar Poe et ses oeuvres." *Musée des familles.* 31.7.193–208.

Verne, Jules. 1866. *Voyages et aventures du capitaine Hatteras.* Paris: Pierre-Jules Hetzel.

Vidal-Naquet, Pierre. 1996. "Land and Sacrifice in the *Odyssey.*" Trans. A. Szegedy-Maszak. In *Reading the Odyssey.* Ed. S. Schein. Princeton, NJ: Princeton University Press. 33–53.

von Möllendorff, Peter. 2000. *Auf der Suche nach der verlogenen Wahrheit: Lukians Wahre Geschichten.* Tübingen: Gunter Narr Verlag.

von Staden, Heinrich. 1975. "Greek Art and Literature in Marx's Aesthetics." *Arethusa* 8.1.119–144.

Wachhorst, Wyn. 1996. "Kepler's Children: The Dream of Spaceflight." *Yale Review* 84.112–131.

Wachowski, Andrew, and Laurence Wachowski, dir. 1999. *The Matrix.* Warner Bros..

Wagar, W. Warren. 1983. "Round Trips to Doomsday." In *The End of the World.* Eds. E. S. Rabkin, M. H. Greenberg, and J. D. Olander. Carbondale: Southern Illinois University Press. 73–96.

Walde, Christina. 2006. "Caesar, Lucan's *Bellum Civile,* and Their Reception." In *Julius Caesar in Western Culture.* Ed. M. Wyke. Malden, MA: Blackwell. 45–61.

Walter, Jochen. 2014. "'That is not dead which can eternal lie': L'Antiquité dans l'oeuvre de H. P. Lovecraft." In *L'Antiquité dans l'imaginaire contemporain: Fantasy, science-fiction, fantastique.* Eds. Mélanie Bost-Fiévet and Sandra Provini. Paris: Classiques Garnier. 451–463.

Waquet, Françoise. 2001. *Latin: or, The Empire of a Sign.* Trans. J. Howe. London: Verso.

Warner, Marina. 2005. "Introduction." In H. G. Wells. *The Time Machine.* London: Penguin Classics. xiii–xxviii.

Warren, B. 2010. *Keep Watching the Skies! American Movies of the Fifties (The 21st Century Edition).* Jefferson, NC: McFarland.

Wasserman, Earl. 1959. *The Subtler Language: Critical Readings of Neoclassic and Romantic Poems.* Baltimore, MD: Johns Hopkins University Press.

Weiner, Jesse. 2011. "Mutable Monuments and Atomistic Poetry in Lucan's *Bellum Civile.*" Dissertation: University of California, Irvine.

Wells, H. G. 1888. "The Chronic Argonauts." *The Science Schools Journal.*

Wells, H. G. 1893. "The Man of the Year Million." *Pall Mall Budget.* November 16, 1893. 1796–1797.

Wells, H. G. 1895. "The visibility of change in the Moon." *Knowledge* 18.230–231. Reprinted in H. G. Wells, 1975. *Early Writings in Science and Science Fiction by H. G. Wells.* Eds. R. Philmus and D. Y. Hughes. Berkeley: University of California Press. 114–118.

Wells, H. G. 1901. *The First Men in the Moon.* London: George Newnes.

Wells, H. G. 1926. *The First Men in the Moon.* From the Bookshelf.

Wells, H. G. 1931. *The Outline of History.* London: George Newnes.

Wells, H. G. 1933. *Scientific Romances.* London: Gollancz.

Wells, H. G. 1934. *Experiment in Autobiography: Discoveries and Conclusions of a Very Ordinary Brain (Since 1866).* London: Faber and Faber.

Wells, H. G. 1956. *The First Men in the Moon.* London: Collins.

Wells, H. G. 1993. *The First Men in the Moon.* London: Everyman.

Wells, H. G. 1998. *The First Men in the Moon: A Critical Text of the 1901 London First Edition, with an Introduction and Appendices.* Ed. L. Stover. Jefferson, NC: McFarland.

Wells, H. G. 2001. *The First Men in the Moon.* London: Gollancz.

Wells, H. G. 2003. *The First Men in the Moon.* New York: Modern Library.

Wells, H. G. 2005. *The First Men in the Moon.* Ed. P. Parrinder. Notes by S. McLean. London: Penguin Classics.

Wells, H. G. 2007. *The First Men in the Moon.* Charleston: BiblioBazaar.

Welsh, Jarrett T. 2006. "Cato, Plautus, and the Metaphorical Use of *Anulus.*" *Phoenix* 60.133–139.

West, D. A. 1990. "The Bough and the Gate." In *Oxford Readings in Vergil's Aeneid.* Ed. S. J. Harrison. Oxford, UK: Oxford University Press. 224–238.

Westfahl, Gary. 1999. "The Popular Tradition of Science Fiction Criticism, 1926–1980." *Science Fiction Studies* 26.2.187–212.

Westfahl, Gary. 2009. "Introduction: Science Fiction at the Crossroads of Two Cultures." In *Science Fiction and the Two Cultures.* Eds. G. Westfahl and G. Slusser. Jefferson, NC: McFarland & Co. 1–9.

Westfahl, Gary, Arthur B. Evans, Donald M. Hassler, and Veronica Hollinger. 1999. "Introduction: Towards a History of Science Fiction Criticism." *Science Fiction Studies* 26.2.161–162.

Westfahl, Gary, Arthur B. Evans, Donald M. Hassler, and Veronica Hollinger. 1999. "A History of Science Fiction Criticism: Collective Works Cited and Chronological Bibliography." *Science Fiction Studies* 26.2.263–283.

Westman, R. S. 1975. "Michael Maestlin's Adoption of the Copernican Theory." *Studia Copernicana* 14.53–63.

Whalley, G., trans. and comm. 1997. *Aristotle's Poetics, Translated and with a Commentary by George Whalley*. Eds. J. Baxter and P. Atherton. Montréal: McGill-Queen's University Press.

Whitmarsh, Tim. 2005. *The Second Sophistic*. Cambridge, UK: Cambridge University Press.

Whitmarsh, Tim. 2006. "True Histories: Lucian, Bakhtin, and the Pragmatics of Reception." In *Classics and the Uses of Reception*. Eds. C. Martindale and R. F. Thomas. Oxford, UK: Blackwell Publishing. 103–115.

Wiedemann, Thomas. 1992. *Emperors and Gladiators*. London: Routledge.

Wierzbicki, James. 2005. *Louis and Bebe Barron's* Forbidden Planet. *A Film Score Guide*. Scarecrow Film Score Guides, No. 4. Lanham, MD: The Scarecrow Press.

Willcock, Malcolm M. 1964. "Mythological Paradeigmata in the *Iliad*." *Classical Quarterly* 14.141–151.

Wills, Christopher. 2010. *The Darwinian Tourist*. Oxford, UK: Oxford University Press.

Willson, Jr., Robert F. 2000. *Shakespeare in Hollywood, 1929–1956*. Madison and Teaneck, NJ: Fairleigh Dickinson University Press.

Wilson, Donna F. 2002. *Ransom, Revenge, and Heroic Identity in the* Iliad. Cambridge, UK: Cambridge University Press.

Winkler, Martin M. 2001. "The Roman Empire in American Cinema After 1945." In *Imperial Projections: Ancient Rome in Modern Popular Culture*. Eds. S. R. Joshel, M. Malamud, and D. T. McGuire, Jr. Baltimore, MD: Johns Hopkins University Press. 50–76.

Winkler, Martin. 2009. *Cinema and Classical Texts: Apollo's New Light*. Cambridge, UK: Cambridge University Press.

Winterer, Caroline. 2002. *The Culture of Classicism*. Baltimore, MD: Johns Hopkins University Press.

Worland, Rick, and David Slayden. 2000. "From Apocalypse to Appliances: Postwar Anxiety and Modern Convenience in *Forbidden Planet*." In *Hollywood Goes Shopping*. Eds. D. Desser and G. Jowett. Minneapolis: University of Minnesota Press. 139–156.

Wright, M. R. 1981. *Empedocles: The Extant Fragments*. New Haven, CT: Yale University Press.

Wyke, Maria. 1997. *Projecting the Past: Ancient Rome, Cinema and History*. New York and London: Routledge.

Zajko, Vanda. 2008. "'What Difference Was Made?': Feminist Models of Reception." *A Companion to Classical Receptions*. eds. L. Hardwick and C. Stray. Malden, MA: Blackwell. 195–206.

Zemeckis, Robert, dir. 1985. *Back to the Future*. Universal Pictures.

Ziolkowski, Jan, and Michael C. J. Putnam, eds. 2008. *The Virgilian Tradition: The First Fifteen Hundred Years*. New Haven, CT: Yale University Press.

Index